"This book is important reading for scholars [illegible] aptures the contours of an emerging new era [illegible] power increasingly is based on knowledge [illegible] des detailed empirical mappings of [illegible] pri-marily located in the US and [illegible] knowledge from universities and open sour[illegible] ble assets. It shows how intellectual monopoly [illegible] global inequality. The book raises important issues in [illegible] views on intellectual property, anti-trust policy and develop[illegible] gies."

— *Beng[illegible] Lundvall*, Emeritus Professor, Aalborg University and Lund University.

"*Capitalism, Power and Innovation* is a must read for scholars, policy makers, and activists who would like to understand the developing forms of intellectual monopoly capitalism. The volume brings together theoretical analyses, empirical research, and case studies and presents the reader with new insights on the rise of intellectual monopolies in sectors such as technology and pharmaceuticals; the interplays of the US and China through their intellectual monopolies; and the impact of intellectual monopoly capitalism on developing economies. As such, it not only provides an elaboration of the emergence and the rise of the intellectual monopolies but also untangles the effects of intellectual monopoly capitalism at various levels. The contributions in this volume are also an excellent starting point for researchers delving into the question of how science and technology is being transformed by powerful interests in modern capitalism."

— *Prof. Özgür Orhangazi*, Kadir Has University.

"Knowledge and innovation can be the basis of development. Much of today's innovation occurs in transnational innovation networks. This book asserts that these networks are organized through power relations and are increasingly dominated by intellectual monopolies. Unfortunately, the developing countries participating in these networks are not approaching the borders or advancing on the path of development. Cecilia Rikap contributes new evidence and looks through different lenses at the relationship between knowledge, innovation networks and power. She analyses how intellectual income is captured, what are the channels for that and who captures it. On this basis, she proposes specific policies to allow developing countries to benefit more from the knowledge created even in these countries, and to avoid an extractivism of pure knowledge from the periphery to the centre. Thank you for this effort, which nurtures the discussion to have a better and less unequal world."

— *Gabriela Dutrénit*, Distinguished Professor at the Autonomous Metropolitan University and coordinator of the Latin American Network on Learning, Innovation and Competence building (LALICS).

"In a time when intangible assets have become a critical factor of value creation and economic growth, our understanding of capitalism and its implications needs ground-breaking thinking. Cecilia Rikap's book on *Capitalism, Power and Innovation* presents frontier research on the nature and formation of intellectual monopoly capitalism and its impact of the peripheries. It is a must read for scholars and policy makers."

— *Prof. Xiaolan Fu*, Technology and Management Centre for Development, Department of International Development, University of Oxford

"*Capitalism, Power and Innovation* gives us the right tools to understand how a digitalisation driven by an interplay between the US GAFA (Google, Apple, Facebook and Amazon) and the likes from China can deeply constrain countries development and the fate of workers around the world. This roadmap is thus very welcome."

— *Prof. Pascal Petit*, Emeritus Research Director at the CNRS.

CAPITALISM, POWER AND INNOVATION

In contemporary global capitalism, the most powerful corporations are innovation or intellectual monopolies. The book's unique perspective focuses on how private ownership and control of knowledge and data have become a major source of rent and power. The author explains how at the one pole, these corporations concentrate income, property and power in the United States, China, and in a handful of intellectual monopolies, particularly from digital and pharmaceutical industries, while at the other pole developing countries are left further behind.

The book includes detailed empirical mappings of how intellectual monopolies develop and transform knowledge from universities and open-source collaborations into intangible assets. The result is a strategy that combines undermining the commons through privatization with harvesting from the same commons. The book ends with provoking reflections to *tilt the scale against intellectual monopoly capitalism* and arguing that desired changes require democratic mobilization of workers and citizens at large.

This book represents one of the first attempts to capture the contours of an emerging new era where old perspectives lead us astray, and the old policy toolbox is hopelessly inadequate. This is true for the idea that the best, or only, way to promote innovation is to transform knowledge into private property. It is also true for anti-trust policies focusing exclusively on consumer prices. The formation of global infrastructures that lead to *natural monopolies* calls for public rather than private ownership.

Scholars and professionals from the social sciences and humanities (in particular economics, sociology, political science, geography, educational science and science and technology studies) will enjoy a clear and all-embracing depiction of innovation dynamics in contemporary capitalism, with a particular focus on asymmetries between actors, regions and topics. In fact, its topical issue broadens the book's scope to those curious about how innovation networks shape our world.

Cecilia Rikap is a tenure researcher at the Consejo Nacional de Investigaciones Científicas y Técnicas (CONICET) and associate researcher at the Centre de Population et Développement (CEPED), IRD/Université de Paris and COSTECH, Université de Technologie de Compiègne. She is also an undergraduate lecturer at the Universidad de Buenos Aires and postgraduate lecturer at the Universidad Nacional de Quilmes in Argentina.

ROUTLEDGE STUDIES IN THE ECONOMICS OF INNOVATION

The Routledge Studies in the Economics of Innovation series is our home for comprehensive yet accessible texts on the current thinking in the field. These cutting-edge, upper-level scholarly studies and edited collections bring together robust theories from a wide range of individual disciplines and provide in-depth studies of existing and emerging approaches to innovation, and the implications of such for the global economy.

THE IMPACT OF THE SHARING ECONOMY ON BUSINESS AND SOCIETY
Digital Transformation and the Rise of Platform Businesses
Edited by Abbas Strømmen-Bakhtiar and Evgueni Vinogradov

AUTOMATION, INNOVATION AND WORK
The Impact of Technological, Economic, and Social Singularity
Jon-Arild Johannessen and Helene Sætersdal

THE POLITICAL ECONOMY OF DIGITAL AUTOMATION
Measuring its Impact on Productivity, Economic Growth and Consumption
Sreenath Majumder and Anuradha SenGupta

ARTIFICIAL INTELLIGENCE, AUTOMATION AND THE FUTURE OF COMPETENCE AT WORK
Jon-Arild Johannessen

CAPITALISM, POWER AND INNOVATION
Intellectual Monopoly Capitalism Uncovered
Cecilia Rikap

For more information about this series, please visit: www.routledge.com/Routledge-Studies-in-the-Economics-of-Innovation/book-series/ECONINN

CAPITALISM, POWER AND INNOVATION

Intellectual Monopoly Capitalism Uncovered

Cecilia Rikap

Routledge
Taylor & Francis Group
LONDON AND NEW YORK

First published 2021
by Routledge
2 Park Square, Milton Park, Abingdon, Oxon OX14 4RN

and by Routledge
52 Vanderbilt Avenue, New York, NY 10017

Routledge is an imprint of the Taylor & Francis Group, an informa business

British Library Cataloguing-in-Publication Data
A catalogue record for this book is available from the British Library

Library of Congress Cataloging-in-Publication Data
Names: Rikap, Cecilia, author.
Title: Capitalism, power and innovation : intellectual monopoly capitalism uncovered / Cecilia Rikap.
Description: Abingdon, Oxon ; New York, NY : Routledge, 2021. | Series: Routledge studies in the economics of innovation | Includes bibliographical references and index.
Identifiers: LCCN 2020046362 (print) | LCCN 2020046363 (ebook) | ISBN 9780367357634 (hardback) | ISBN 9780429341489 (ebook)
Subjects: LCSH: Intellectual capital. | Monopolies. | Information technology—Economic aspects. | Technological innovations—Economic aspects. | Capitalism—Political aspects. | Power (Social sciences)—Economic aspects.
Classification: LCC HD35 .R55 2021 (print) | LCC HD35 (ebook) | DDC 338.8/2—dc23
LC record available at https://lccn.loc.gov/2020046362
LC ebook record available at https://lccn.loc.gov/2020046363

ISBN: 978-0-367-35763-4 (hbk)
ISBN: 978-0-367-75029-9 (pbk)
ISBN: 978-0-429-34148-9 (ebk)

Typeset in Times New Roman
by codeMantra

TO IRENE, WHO MADE ME BETTER

CONTENTS

FIGURES

TABLES

ACKNOWLEDGEMENTS

I would like to start by thanking David Flacher, Hugo Harari-Kermadec and Ariel Slipak, my co-authors in three chapters of this book. Next, I must thank Joel Rabinovich, who encouraged me to write the book proposal that, after several mutations, resulted in the manuscript on your hands or screen. Joel and other colleagues provided insights and suggestions to the overall proposal as well as to different chapters and have inspired and walked with me along this path. In particular, I would like to thank Bengt-Åke Lundvall for our countless email exchanges with the most fruitful discussions and for providing me challenging and stimulating suggestions. A special thanks to Cédric Durand, not only for writing the foreword but also for his trust in my conditions as a researcher and for our work together, which has of course inspired this whole book.

I am extremely grateful to my friends and colleagues Nicolás Águila and Juan Martín Graña. I lost track of the times we have shared our thoughts about the topics of this book as well as on many more enriching discussions. Other colleagues have also inspired my research, in particular scholars and friends from the Centre d'Économie de Paris Nord, from the Instituto de Investigaciones Económicas of the Universidad de Buenos Aires, from the Centre de Population et Développement of the IRD/Université de Paris, in particular its director Rigas Arvanitis, from the IDHES of the Université Paris Saclay, and from the Young Scholars Initiative of the Institute for New Economic Thinking (YSI/INET). Another special recognition goes to all my friends and colleagues, from the most diverse disciplines, with whom I often engage in interdisciplinary debates; you expand my sight.

Going several years back in time, I would also like to acknowledge my PhD director, Pablo Levín, for his past lessons on what a researcher should be and do. Without him there would be no book, not only because in different parts I build on his theoretical contributions, but also because I grew up as a researcher working at his side.

This book would not have been possible without the support of the Institut Francilien Recherche Innovation Société (IFRIS). Furthermore, I am very grateful to all the scholars I interviewed and whose insights are at the core of Chapters 12 and 13, as well as to key informants working in the digital economy, including a special thanks to my friend Felipe Lerena. I would also like to thank Michael Kwet for his comments and proofreading.

Finally, I would like to emphasize that knowledge production is a social activity. The capacity to recognize in others complementing ideas expands our individual and social understandings. Even though I take full responsibility of the flaws of this book, it is a result of collective efforts even in those chapters where I am the single author. Collective efforts in the sense that research questions spring from collective discussions with colleagues from different disciplines inside and outside academia, in conferences, at seminars, interviews, public demonstrations and more. All my debt to all of them. The book also draws inspiration from multiple readings of past and present authors from diverse disciplines, although my background is in political economy. As these authors inspired me, I aim this research outcome would inspire in colleagues, students, and the public in general a desire to criticize, analyse and understand contemporary capitalism as a necessary step in its active transformation.

FOREWORD

(Author: Cédric Durand)
September 30, 2020

Capitalism, Power and Innovation is a tremendously important book for academics, policy-makers and activists interested in the *devenir* of the capitalist mode of production and its accelerating mutations. Based on sound theoretical ground and nourished with solid empirical inquiry, Cecilia Rikap proposes an impressive account of the massive movement of knowledge appropriation characteristic of our time. This research digs critically into the depth of innovation theory and navigates the world economy. It goes from the West Coast corporations to Chinese commanding heights, via Big Pharma and world class public universities to address three fundamental questions: What are the roots of the rising concentration of economic power at the world scale? What are the distinctive qualities of digital operations vis-à-vis industrial production processes? What are the implications of intellectual monopolization for socioeconomic development prospects? These issues, along with the ecological crisis, are the most urgent that our generation must confront and the author's vivid engagement with them offers new venues in many directions.

The great achievement of the book is its ability to grasp the whole network of intellectual monopolization and articulate its logic. Predation of publicly funded research through private-public partnerships, centralization of individual private data on digital platforms, merger and acquisition backed by the assetization of knowledge, data extraction up to the last reckon of the world are the main channels of a dense network of innovation-by-capture. This process is not restricted to the digital giants but concerns electricity, engineering and automotive companies alike. It is thus not a dynamic limited to a single sector, but a general-purpose economic rationality of 21st-century capitalism.

In very inspiring developments, the author also manages to articulate business strategies and state power. She points out a polarization between, on the one hand, state-like ambition of the biggest digital corporations and, on the other hand, the imperialist agenda pursued through the intertwining of intellectual monopolies and states apparatuses in the United States and China.

Rikap's argument is backed by carefully built stylized facts and compelling network analyses of scientific publications and patents. Attentive to business leaders' explicit reasons, she is not shy to convoke spicy quotes to illustrate the demonstration, which provokes a healthy sensation of concreteness to the tragic unfolding of intellectual monopolization that she documents. Indeed, the implications of her analysis for income inequalities, ongoing labour exploitation and thwarted development in the periphery are clearly delineated.

One outstanding quality of Rikap's research is that it doesn't hide its own motivations and responsibility as a scholar. In the last part of the book, she pushes her thesis to ultimate conclusions in terms of policymaking. Some immediate measures to counterbalance intellectual monopolization are outlined without losing sight of greater ambitious emancipatory goals. Among these, her proposal to raise a progressive tax depending on the size of the databases, her invitation to regulate industry-university collaboration and her subtle discussion of the specific challenges for peripheral countries in these matters deserve to be seriously considered.

With *Capitalism, Power and Innovation* the reader will not only learn a lot. This refreshing contribution re-engages with a tradition of political economy that dares to combine rigorous analysis with a communicative sense of the urgency to shift the world economy trajectory. In our turbulent times, Rikap's book is a much needed contribution that brings economics' critical researches closer to real changes.

1

INTRODUCTION

1 Introduction

What is new with contemporary (global) leading corporations? If gigantic monopolies are a repeated phenomenon in capitalism's history, why all the fuz we see everyday regarding high concentration? It is not concentration in itself, but why and how it happened, as well as the socio-economic and political consequences of capital concentration what should be answered to identify where the novelty arises.

Leading corporations of the 21st century are intellectual monopolies. Eight of the top ten companies in market capitalization can be considered as such (PWC, 2019, 2020). They rely on a permanent and expanding monopoly over portions of society's knowledge. The private appropriation of knowledge results in intangible assets,[1] triggering what has been dubbed intellectual, knowledge or technoscientific rents (Birch, 2019; Durand & Milberg, 2019; Foley, 2013; Pagano, 2014; Rikap, 2018; Teixeira & Rotta, 2012), and concentration of intangible assets has become the main driver of capital concentration.

What is missing in other analyses on the rise of intangibles is the concept of predation, briefly defined as a direct relation of spoliation. Predation is at the basis of the higher concentration of intangible assets by intellectual monopolies. Intellectual monopolies, as we will show throughout this book, predate knowledge from other organizations. Intellectual monopolies may not monopolize the markets they operate, which can even be competitive markets like Amazon's marketplace, where Amazon sells its products with millions of other sellers. Their monopolistic condition relies on their capacity to significantly and systematically monopolize knowledge, which generally – but not always – contributes to market concentration.

Therefore, this is a stage within capitalism where we see a continuous reinforcement of knowledge monopolies. The result is a broken tie between innovation[2] and growth explained – at least in part – by the perpetuation of intellectual rentierism and predation.

Figures 1.1 and 1.2 show the evolution of GDP growth and GDP per capita growth (imperfect but the best available indicators with long-term data for economic growth).[3] Besides their cyclical behaviour, the downward trend that starts in the 1970s but further expands since the 1980s is self-evident. There is a prevailing idea of secular stagnation, as popularized by Larry Summers from the IMF in 2013, led by low private (tangible) investment in a context of low interest rates (Haskel & Westlake, 2018; Summers, 2016). Figure 1.3 presents the evolution of applied and issued patents of the United States Patent and Trademark Office (USPTO). Patenting is not a sufficient proxy for innovation since it only covers disclosed inventions, and it is subject to patent thickets and includes patents providing zero royalties. Nevertheless, Figure 1.3 provides evidence of expanding inventions and, more importantly, of an expanding knowledge monopoly, since the 1990s and accelerating more than ever in the past decade, in line with the spread of digital capitalism. In this century, it was not only – and not mainly – patents that present an impressive rise. Figure 1.4 presents data for the top 20 world intellectual property rights offices on patents, trademark and industrial designs' applications for the period 2004–18. The rise in trademarks stands out.

As the link between innovation and growth weakened, different authors have shown that the share of corporate profits is growing (Haskel & Westlake, 2018; Rotta, 2018) and that the concentration of intangible assets is

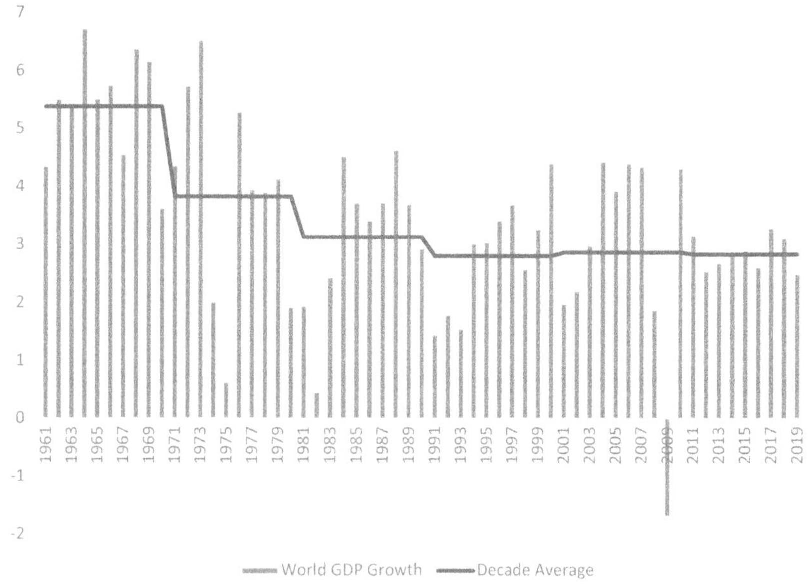

Figure 1.1 World GDP annual growth.
Source: World Bank.

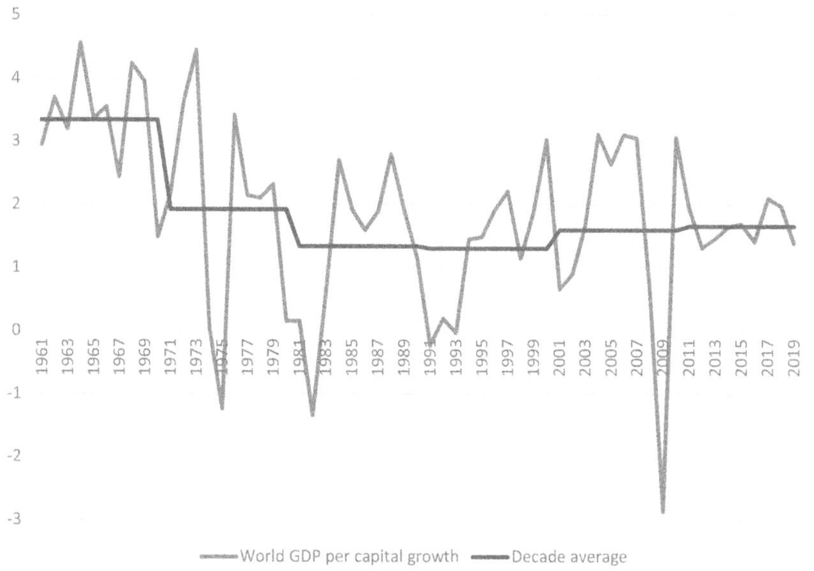

Figure 1.2 World GDP per capita annual growth.
Source: World Bank.

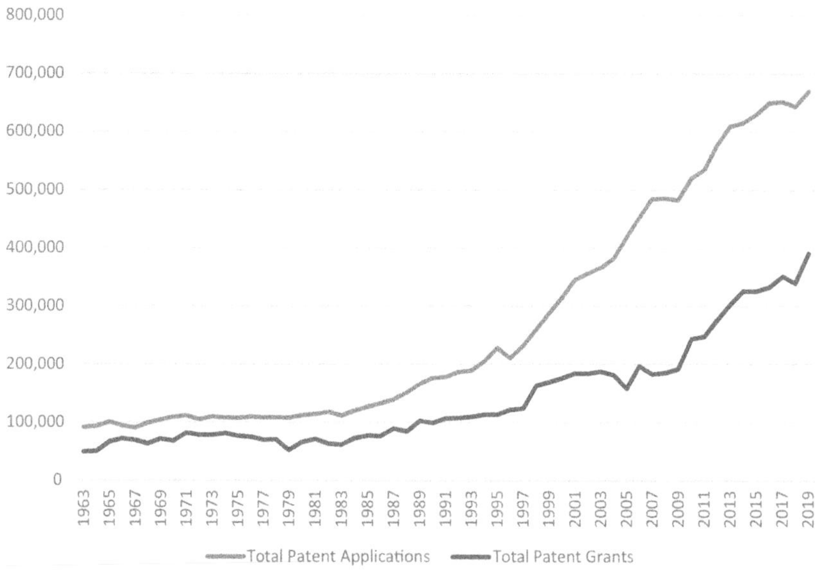

Figure 1.3 Applied and granted patents per year.
Source: USPTO.

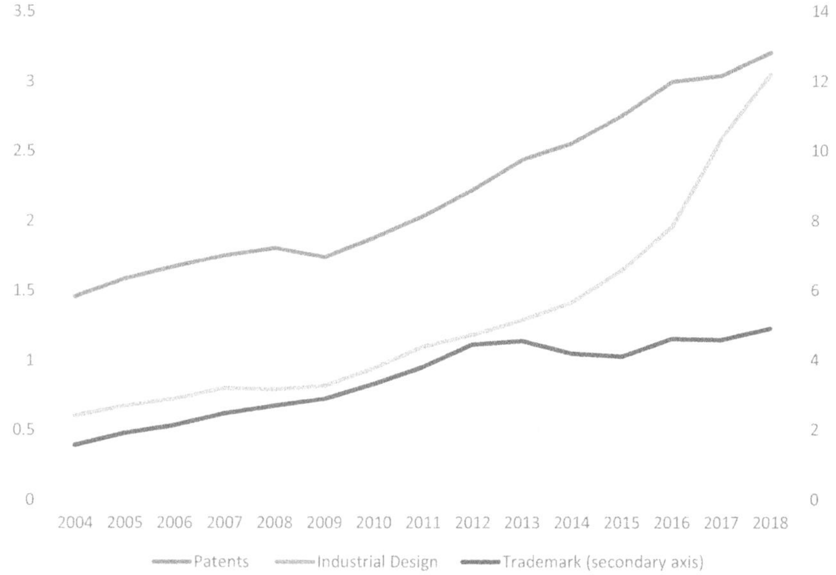

Figure 1.4 Patents, industrial designs and trademark. Application class counts for the top 20 offices (in millions).

Source: WIPO.

driving the concentration of profits. Overall, the 0.001% of global largest corporations earn around one-third of all corporate profits (Wier & Reynolds, 2018). Intangible intensive corporations enjoy the highest profit rates (Covarrubias et al., 2020; Orhangazi, 2018). A recent OECD report analysed firms' mark-ups across 26 countries (the United States and a sample of European and Asian economies) between 2001 and 2014 and found that increases in mark-ups were concentrated at the top of the mark-up distribution. Mark-ups remained flat for companies at the bottom half. Moreover, mark-ups were higher in digital-intensive sectors, and the spread in mark-ups between digitally intensive and less digitally intensive sectors has significantly augmented (Calligaris et al., 2018).

The concentration of intangible assets is a general phenomenon. Clarivate Analytics (2019) defines the top 100 innovators by considering their total number of granted patents together with indicators of success, globalization and influence.[4] Since 2011, when the ranking was created, only 204 organizations made it at least once to the top 100 innovators, 35 of which appeared every year. This strong core of organizations profiting from intellectual rents is dominated by multinationals (97 of the 100 organizations in 2018–19). Moreover, in 2018–19, this data shows that the top 100 innovators' patent portfolios are becoming more successful, global and influential compared with the rest of the patenting organizations, which showed little growth or even fell for these indicators. Figures are particularly shocking for US listed corporations. In 1975, only 17% of S&P 500 assets were intangibles, by 2018 that figure was 84%. Intangibles already represented 80% of S&P 500 assets in 2005 but the total assets value was half of the 2018 figure. Overall, in the 21st century, intangible assets accumulate at an increasing pace and lay in the hands of leading global corporations from core countries.[5]

What we are witnessing is the climax of a process that began almost half a century ago with the formation of Global Value Chains (GVC) led by multinational corporations that retained the exclusive knowledge on how to integrate the supply chain. It was also in the 1970s that the big pharma blockbuster drug model emerged signalling a turning point in terms of intellectual property and rents. And, as Chapter 4 explains in detail, the initial policy transformations that paved the way for intellectual monopoly capitalism date from the 1980s. Hence, even if we focus on a 21st century phenomenon, intellectual monopoly capitalism has a history that we also address in this book.

In our epoch, intangibles assets' rise cannot be understood detached from the digital economy. As shown by UNCTAD (2019), Global Internet Protocol (IP) traffic, which is a proxy for data flows, grew between 2002 and 2017 from about 100 gigabytes (GB) to more than 45,000 GB per second. And it keeps growing at an exponential speed, with estimations at 150,700 GB per second by 2022, a forecast made before the Covid-19 pandemic that has resulted in an unprecedented acceleration of the digital economy. As Microsoft's CEO claimed by late April 2020, "We've seen two years' worth of digital transformation in two months".[6]

The digital economy is highly asymmetric. By the time this is being written, its five leading corporations represent over 25% of the S&P 500. The combined market capitalization of Google, Apple, Facebook, Amazon and Microsoft (GAFAM) (5.587 trillion USD)[7] is even above Japan's 2019 GDP (5.01 trillion USD).[8] As well as their counterparts in China (Baidu, Alibaba, Tencent and Huawei, hereon BATH), GAFAM concentrate profits and (tangible and intangible) capital based on monetizing knowledge and data. Their continuous innovations rely on their exclusive access to big data sources, thus predating from society by curtailing access to an input that was socially constructed. Furthermore, they analyse data with artificial intelligence algorithms that, more often than not, were developed by a myriad of (other) organizations. They use that data to orient their business and innovate based on customized models that are capable of predicting and shaping each individual's behaviours with the greatest existing accuracy. Besides high-tech, data-driven intellectual rents are being harvested in healthcare industries, with the pioneering example of Myriad and 23andMe (primarily owned by Google since 2010) mapping the human genome (Pistor, 2019; Rose & Rose, 2014).

Beyond GAFAM and BATH, by 2019, the United States (US) and China concentrated 90% of the market capitalization value of the 70 largest digital platforms of the world (UNCTAD, 2019). These two countries are absolute leaders in artificial intelligence (Castro et al., 2019). Moreover, three giant US corporations (Amazon, Microsoft and Google) and a Chinese one (Alibaba) concentrate around 75% of the public cloud computing market. Amazon Web Services (AWS) alone has around 40% of the market, followed by Microsoft, with almost 20% (Synergy Research Group, 2019).

Although at the forefront of this new stage in capitalism, intellectual monopoly capitalism goes beyond digital industries. It was also in this century, in particular in the last ten years, that the exhaustion of the blockbuster drug model forced big pharmaceuticals to reinvent themselves. Under this latter model, large pharmaceuticals invested in drugs to treat pathologies affecting as many people as possible. The aim was to achieve sales of over 1 billion USD. At least since the 2000s, new blockbuster drugs became more the exception than the rule, while old blockbusters' patents expired (Collier, 2011; Lazonick et al., 2017). To retain their intellectual monopolies, thus keep granting extraordinary profits, two main knowledge management strategies became a too frequent practice: the organization of global innovation networks where big pharmaceuticals subordinate research institutions and start-ups and the latter's acquisitions (in particular in the sub-field of biotechnology) (Baranes, 2016; Montalban & Sakinç, 2013; Rikap, 2019). Legal monopoly based on patents is still the primary source of intellectual rents for big pharmaceuticals. However, they also became predators that monetize inventions produced and funded elsewhere, thus not only relying – as it had been the case in the past – on basic knowledge produced in academic research institutions and public research organizations but actually outsourcing almost every step of their innovation processes while keeping the economic profits.

All in all, two industries drive the concentration of intangible assets. Together, ICT and health industries concentrate almost 60% of the world's top 2,500 corporations' business expenditure in R&D (BERD) (European Commission, 2019). Intellectual monopolies are also emerging in other industries, such as the automobile industry. Led by Tesla, the whole industry is becoming intangible driven. For instance, Toyota and Mitsubishi are among the top 20 artificial intelligence patent applicants worldwide. Siemens is the world leader in artificial intelligence patents applied to life and medical sciences, in particular related to medical images (World Intellectual Property Organization, 2019). Even the State Grid Corporation of China (SGCC), a utility company, has become an intellectual monopoly (see Chapter 9). Overall, the XXI century exhibits a shift in the strategies of global leader corporations towards the concentration of intangibles. Within this trend, this book will show that intellectual monopolies are expanding their multiple sources of intellectual rents through predatory practices.

The next section reflects on Marx's and Schumpeter's conceptualizations as starting points of our investigation. Section 3 elaborates on the specificities of intellectual monopoly capitalism, and Section 4 reflects on innovation as a power relationship. Finally, Section 5 briefly introduces the different sections and chapters of this book.

2 *Back to the future*: Marx and Schumpeter legacy as a starting point

It is always a source of inspiration to have great authors as starting points to rethink contemporary inquiries, especially in the midst of turbulent times. This book draws this kind of inspiration from Marx and Schumpeter's conceptualizations of what today we call innovation and its link with economic growth. It also goes back to Veblen's ideas on predation, but we leave this discussion for later, and we start from what was supposed to be the normal flow of capitalism.

According to Marx (1867, 1894), labour productivity continuously increases in capitalism as a result of advances in the techniques used; technical change is fuelled by individual capitals' competition in the market. The firm that introduces a new technique enjoys the privilege of the innovator, which, for the author, was a temporary windfall. The firm that develops or is a first adopter of the new technique may sell its commodity above the individual production price and obtain an above-normal profit, given that the rest of the commodities of that class continue to be produced with the old technique of higher unit cost. As the social production price remains above the innovative enterprise's individual price, the extraordinary profit for the innovating firm holds.

For Marx (1867, 1894), the development of productive forces is accidental, random. No single firm is more likely to innovate than another. Its consequence in the market (a price above the individual price of production of the innovating firm) is transitory. At the system level, the successive instances of an individual capital innovating followed by adaption and adoption by others generates a permanent development of the productive forces (what today might be reframed as an increase in productivity at the system level) that results in economic growth.

Schumpeter (1934), in line with Marx's idea of productive forces development, conceives the introduction of new products, techniques and the creation of new markets (later on called innovations) as the driving force or explanation of the economic cycle. Schumpeter (1934) is also in line with Marx's (1894) idea that the competition between individual capitals is resolved through the introduction (or not) of the new techniques available. In this process, the creation of new firms is at the expense of the destruction of those lagging behind, what Schumpeter (1934) calls the creative destruction. Its net effect is economic growth. As soon as all the (surviving) firms of the branch adopted the innovation, the entrepreneur loses its innovative character together with the associated extraordinary profits.

However, in his late work, when analysing monopolistic practices, Schumpeter (1942) argues that, in some cases, the creative side of the creative destruction remains in the hands of the same (big) corporations. It is the case of big laboratories with huge R&D investments needed to sustain the creative destruction process. For the author, the monopoly power of the innovator – usually expressed in higher prices – is more than compensated by the "long-run process of expansion which they protect rather than impede. There is no more of paradox in this than there is in saying that motorcars are traveling faster than they otherwise would *because* they are provided with brakes" (Schumpeter, 1942, pp. 88–89). From this evolutionary perspective, it is implicitly assumed that this monopoly is necessary for the evolution of the system – i.e. for overall economic growth.

> The best way of getting a vivid and realistic idea of industrial strategy is indeed to visualize the behavior of new concerns or industries that introduce new commodities or processes (such as the aluminum industry) or else reorganize a part or the whole of an industry (such as, for instance, the old Standard Oil Company).
>
> As we have seen, such concerns are aggressors by nature and wield the really effective weapon of competition. Their intrusion can only in the rarest of cases fail to improve total output in quantity or quality, both through the new method itself—even if at no time used to full advantage— and through the pressure it exerts on the preexisting firms.
>
> (Schumpeter, 1942, p. 89)

Big corporations concentrating innovation are supposed to be "good concentration" – as understood today by Covarrubias et al. (2020) and Philippon (2019) – because their advantage is based on innovation, thus on increasing productivity, therefore contributing to a drop in prices, thus an increase in consumers' surplus.

Summing up, in Marx and Schumpeter's ideas – even in the latter's late work where he recognizes the central place of monopolies for innovation – there is an underlying link between innovation and economic growth. What these authors did not anticipate, and others fail to identify (see for example Covarrubias et al., 2020; Philippon, 2019) when studying contemporary capitalism, is that once the overall innovation process is monopolized, not every laggard will be *destroyed*. Intellectual monopolies may find it more effective to subordinate a portion of less productive firms, in particular, those that are fast adopters of the new techniques introduced by the intellectual monopoly. These firms remain active but without technical autonomy. They will be planned by those big corporations that organize global capital accumulation, predating a portion of the surplus value of resulting subordinate companies. Predation and rentiership are at the basis of intellectual monopolies' exponential accumulation while curtailing the overall growth at the system level. This is the main thesis we will try to unfold in this book.

Greater inequalities emerge as the link between innovation and economic growth weakens. Under intellectual monopoly capitalism, intellectual rents perpetuate in time and are concentrated in fewer hands. This value appropriation brings more polarization, inequalities and marginalization at every possible level. As we mentioned, the share of corporate profits increases, albeit inequality also rises within the working class (see Chapter 10), within and between industries, regions and countries. According to the Credit Suisse Global Wealth Report, the wealthiest 1% owns 44% of the world's wealth, while 56.6% of the world's population holds less than 2%. Figures evidencing the obscenity of wealth concentration have become so common, but the solutions so rare, that we risk assuming this as a stylized structural fact of human life.

Why and how what was supposed to be a temporary advantage – that could contribute to overall economic growth – became permanent? Moreover, how did this advantage result in the subordination of firms, universities and even states?

3 Intellectual monopoly capitalism as a new stage of global capitalism

Intellectual rents enjoyed by the innovator were supposed to disappear once the rest of the industry adopts the new technique. They disappeared if the secret was broken, the patent expired or when another firm innovated, overcoming the innovating firm's advantage. The fundamental change of our epoch is the continuous reinforcement of knowledge monopolies leading to a perpetuation of the core, maximizing rentiership over time.

Intellectual monopoly is not only – nor mainly – a result of giant corporations' in-house R&D. Their knowledge monopoly is based on appropriating and monetizing knowledge results from their multiple innovation networks. Intellectual monopolies strategically decide which steps of their production and innovation networks belong to their core business and what should be outsourced. Intellectual monopolies also outsource innovation steps by actively engaging in open access or open science initiatives, monetizing knowledge commons. By organizing global corporate innovation networks of continuous innovation, a reduced group of corporations systematically renews and expands intellectual monopoly (thus, rents). The result is increasing intellectual rents in fewer hands, which are not even partially given back to the public through corporate taxes since tax avoidance is easier for companies that are intensive in intangible capital (Bryan et al., 2017; Pozsar, 2018).

Besides outsourcing knowledge (cum innovation) production, their capacity to manage knowledge production opens multiple alternatives that they use at their discretion. Acquiring technology through mergers and acquisitions (M&As) stands out, with big pharma and high-tech giants as prominent examples. In this case, the full innovation process – thus associated risks – is outsourced to other firms. Finally, in the digital age, harvesting big data is another prominent source of intangible assets.

Depending on the diversity of knowledge management techniques and on the multiplicity of monopolized technologies, intellectual monopolies differ in scope. Some are focused on narrow niches – such as Siemens' dominance of artificial intelligence (AI) for life and medical sciences inventions or SGCC's lead in AI-related inventions for energy management (World Intellectual Property Organization, 2019). Meanwhile, others expand their power, dominating multiple – sometimes even general-purpose – technologies. GAFAM and BATH are examples of the latter.

All in all, intellectual monopoly capitalism can be conceived as the stage in capitalism where capital accumulation (and distribution) is led by a core of intellectual monopolies that base their accumulation (and power) on their permanent and expanding monopoly (and assetization) of predated knowledge. In the rest of this section, we further elaborate on some of this epoch's main features.

3.1 Intellectual monopoly capitalism is a global phenomenon

Concentration driven by monopolizing intangible assets is not just a US phenomenon. Unlike different authors from mainstream and heterodox economic perspectives who have restricted their study of recent concentration and intangibles to the United States (Covarrubias et al., 2020; Lambert, 2019; Orhangazi, 2018; Schwartz, 2016, 2019; Zingales, 2017), here we think of capital accumulation at a global level and explain national differences always in relation to the global trend.[9] Such a general understanding is necessary to analyse the overall implications and depth of the current transformation. This book is an attempt to study *capitalism*, *power* and *innovation*, integrating three levels of analysis: global, national and network. At the national level, it distinguishes between core and peripheral countries.[10] At the network level, it focuses on how intellectual monopolies plan, organize and predate from their innovation networks, thus also including a broad set of subordinate firms and other institutions.

In more concrete terms, intellectual monopoly capitalism is a global phenomenon with different expressions around the world. The persistently uneven distribution of innovation in the world is a structural truth that intellectual monopoly capitalism is worsening. Intellectual monopolies originate in core countries, in particular in the United States, but their effects are spread all over the world. By 2019, the top ten companies accumulated 13.5% (and the top 100, 47%) of the world's Business Expenditure in R&D (BERD). This top ten included six US (all GAFAM excepting Facebook plus Intel and Johnson & Johnson), one South-Korean (Samsung), one German (Volkswagen), one Chinese (Huawei) and one Swiss (Roche) corporation (European Commission, 2019). In the case of patents, 72 out of Clarivate Analytics (2019) top 100 innovators originally came from the United States and Japan.

3.2 Intellectual monopolies are capitalist planners

Intellectual monopoly power extends beyond the market and takes the form of capitalist planning of production and innovation. We define planning as the capacity of certain firms to organize long-term capital accumulation beyond their legally owned capital. Intellectual monopolies plan the production and innovation processes of subordinated firms and other organizations (such as universities and public research organizations) by directly controlling management's critical parameters. They also define R&D agendas, clauses of exclusivity, commercial credit conditions, quality standards and other regulatory matters.

GVC leaders provide early examples of the planning capacity enabled by monopolizing access to knowledge. These leading corporations monopolize knowledge on how to reintegrate the chain and on who can do what to make the GVC work (Durand & Milberg, 2020). Furthermore, this book argues that intellectual monopolies (whether or not they lead GVC) command R&D, modularized in steps. They keep the exclusive knowledge over the whole process, including who is best suited for each knowledge module and how to integrate those modules if successful results are achieved. Hence, the intellectual monopoly may not be so "innovative" in-house, but still collects intellectual rents from its exclusive knowledge over the organization of the innovation process. Its rents are further extended by predation since intellectual monopolies monetize R&D results achieved by other actors participating in their innovation networks. Additionally, intellectual monopolies are increasingly becoming data driven. Their advantage lies in planning a vicious circle where they keep the exclusive access to new sources of centralized data that are processed and analysed – at least in part – with knowledge that was produced as a commons, but that these corporations privately monetize.

Overall, we are now living in a system where capital accumulation itself is driven and sustained by a global structure of sabotage based on intangibles' predation and assetization. This process is controlled and planned by a few giant corporations that have become intellectual monopolies. As different chapters in this book show, they even monetize knowledge that is still being produced as a commons in universities, public research organizations and open access or open source communities. This further limits knowledge spillovers while evidencing that those giant corporations' accumulation is based on rentiership and predation. Indeed, knowledge still triggers spillovers but only for a few organizations that keep a circumscribed monetization capacity. Thus, the effects on economic growth are also circumscribed to intellectual monopolies.

4 Innovation as a power relationship

Innovation in capitalism has thus grown as a power relationship. "Inventors" (those working on intellectual monopolies' innovations) will at most receive a one-time payment if their contribution was indispensable for accomplishing the final steps of the innovation process. Rents will be kept in the hands of the intellectual monopoly that surveilled the whole process. As a result of this division of intellectual labour, the industrial landscape is split between corporations that control production, distribution and consumption by controlling innovation processes and a myriad of organizations whose best alternative is to subordinate.

Among the consequences, industries are being disrupted and reconfigured, and even the nature of the innovation process is changing since, within artificial intelligence, deep learning and neural networks are also impacting on how R&D is performed (Cockburn et al., 2018). Overall, intellectual monopoly capitalism is the most accomplished version of science and technology (S&T) reduced to productive engines (Godin, 2006). In this context, innovation needs to be understood as a contextualized process. As Schumpeter concludes (1942, p. 110), the capitalist enterprise is the propelling force of technological progress. Hence, we argue, S&T will be set in a concrete direction aimed at contributing the most to the expansion of capital accumulation, which is not a smooth, nor an equally beneficial process. Innovation in capitalism is not only about technical transformations. Its direction, what is prioritized, and even the limits of what is (and what is not) considered an innovation is politically (thus contextually) determined. Furthermore, as in general in capitalism, political decisions are at least partially explained by economic interests. The Manhattan project, fracking techniques and digital surveillance are only some of the multiple instructive examples.

Intellectual monopoly capitalism made apparent that S&T, as any process based on human labour, should be studied not only from its implications but also as a social relation of production. In other words, innovating always has a twofold meaning. One looks forward and starts when the innovation was achieved, thus studying the effects of innovation as an accomplished result. The subordination of complementors in digital platforms (such as third-party sellers in e-commerce platforms) as well as of outsourced firms in GVC exemplify how innovations (or more broadly intangibles), once monopolized, are used to subordinate other organizations. The other approach looks backward and delves into the social relations of production that take place in order to innovate. This is innovation as a process: what in contemporary capitalism we conceptualized as innovation networks increasingly organized and planned by intellectual monopolies.

Our attempt in this book is to analyse both aspects together, conceiving innovation in capitalism as a process and product, as a power relationship of (creative) production.

In the next section, we further develop the core of the intellectual monopoly capitalism framework by briefly presenting the rest of this book.

5 Summarizing the content of this book

This introduction is followed by a section that presents our general understanding of intellectual monopoly capitalism. Chapter 2 conceptualizes intellectual monopolies and their effects on the production and innovation networks they plan, thus control. Within their innovation networks, special attention is paid in Chapter 3 to how they profit from the knowledge commons, including open access initiatives. This chapter also initiates a series of reflections on the historical conditions that enabled the emergence of intellectual monopoly capitalism, here focusing on the advances of knowledge privatization since the 1980s. Big pharmaceuticals and tech giants are the paradigmatic examples of how intellectual monopolies benefit not only from knowledge privatization but also from knowledge commons and open access. Their engagement provides them with access to knowledge that they integrate into innovation processes. Furthermore, they can use the work of highly skilled scientists and developers that voluntarily participate in these initiatives, while they enjoy a privileged position to promote their complementary products.

Chapter 4, co-authored with Ariel Slipak, delves into the geopolitics of intellectual monopoly capitalism by analysing policies pursued by the US and China that contributed to this global transformation. The chapter also elaborates on the dialectic relationship between the US and Chinese states and their corresponding intellectual monopolies. The close relationship between the Chinese state and intellectual monopolies that originated in China is an expected result of this chapter, given the role of the former as a central planner. However, the same can be said of the United States and its (hidden) industrial policy. In the case of the US, the chapter identifies the growing political influence of US intellectual monopolies. They go from the role played by IBM, Pfizer and Microsoft drafting what ended up being the TRIPS agreement (Drahos, 1995), to Google's former chief executive Eric Schmidt and Bill Gates being in charge of *re-imagining* New York after the Covid-19 pandemic.[11] The chapter also refers to the internal clashes of power between each state and its respective intellectual monopolies.

This first part of the book concludes with a chapter on the interplay between the emergence of intellectual monopolies and the transformations experienced by research universities, written with Hugo Harari-Kermadec. We distinguish between research universities that subordinate to intellectual monopolies and academic intellectual monopolies. The latter refers to the small group of research universities (as well as public research organization from certain core countries) that collaborates with intellectual monopolies on a relatively more equal basis – at least in comparison with subordinate research universities. However, this greater bargaining power comes at the expense of losing traditional university features and subordinating researchers' agendas to what university managers consider as a potentially more profitable business.

This part is followed by studies of selected global intellectual monopolies from the United States (Apple, Amazon and Pfizer), China (SGCC) and Europe (Novartis and Roche) in the second part of the book. Each chapter adds new layers to our understanding of intellectual monopoly capitalism.

Chapter 6 explores how large pharmaceuticals collaborate and cooperate for technology. As intellectual monopolies, they not only plan innovation networks subordinating leading research universities and start-ups accumulating intellectual rents but also subordinate and influence the agenda of the National Institutes of Health and the US Food and Drug Administration.

From the high-tech industry, we explore the cases of Apple (Chapter 7) and Amazon (Chapter 8). Besides other historical forms of intellectual rentiership such as legal rents driven from intellectual property rights and the exclusive knowledge to organize, plan and integrate production and innovation networks, intellectual monopolies centralize constant streams of new data. Big data is used to improve their machine-learning algorithms, thus transforming the innovation process. Algorithms learn by themselves by processing big data with deep learning and neural network approaches. Data-driven intellectual monopolies can thus be defined as intellectual monopolies that innovate from processing privatized constant streams of (new) data.

Beyond pharma and high-tech, intellectual monopoly capitalism is expanding and reconfiguring global accumulation. In China, not only BATH companies are intellectual monopolies. Chapter 9 studies the inception of new intellectual monopolies. It shows how the SGCC's intellectual monopoly sprang from China's national innovation system, particularly, predating from public universities and relying on state funding. Moreover, this company is another example of a data-driven intellectual monopoly, this time relying on data collected from its smart grid.

By synthesizing the common traits of these cases, Chapter 10 argues that intellectual monopoly capitalism is an era within capitalism where capital accumulation is increasingly driven (and hampered) by rent-seeking and predation. Regardless of their specificities, intellectual monopolies share one main trait: they derive part of their profits from intellectual rents extracted from their global innovation networks. They sabotage society by privately monetizing intangible goods. The more their rents grow, the more the rest of the world will be deprived of access to knowledge and of a greater portion of the total value produced. Intellectual monopolies are also the corporations leading the rankings of offshored retained earnings and declare profits in tax havens, further favouring their shareholders by minimizing paid taxes. This points to the entangled connection between an accumulation strategy based on rentiership and predation that results in levels of earnings and financial strength that allow to further expand rents, this time by participating in financial markets (see Chapters 7 and 10). The consequences for different types of workers are also preliminary explored in Chapter 10.

Intellectual monopolies outsource innovation steps in academic research institutions, public research organizations and start-up firms, which are typically organizations from core countries. Therefore, what are the effects of intellectual monopoly capitalism on the peripheries? Part 3 contributes to answering this question.

The global scope of intellectual monopoly challenges states' power. States could be reconceived as some of the multiple powerful actors within contemporary capitalism. As states hierarchical order remains, the implications of intellectual monopoly capitalism at the national (or regional) level will differ according to the rank of each state in that order. Intellectual monopolies act as ruling bodies, with the extreme case of tech giants' capacity to govern the digital economy. Microsoft's announcement of the opening of a representation to the United Nations is an example of these companies' ruling power. Other examples include Alibaba's proposal of a "Digital Free Trade Zone,"[12] and Facebook's creation of a "supreme court" to decide over the moderation of controversial content. The latter was relabelled "oversight board" after being criticized as well as its (not so successful) digital currency, Libra.[13]

In the peripheries, intellectual monopolies systematically pass over – less powerful – states. Part 3 begins with an assessment of innovation and upgrading policies for development under intellectual monopoly capitalism (Chapter 11). We argue that, in this context, innovation studies (including the idea of an entrepreneurial state), as well as GVC and catching-up approaches, have shortcomings in providing viable policy recommendations. In this new global order, peripheral countries' specific traits result in a greater technological gap with (intellectual monopolies and their innovation networks from) core countries and reinforce underdevelopment. However, the relatively more developed countries within the peripheries exhibit an unbalanced knowledge and innovation structure with their leading research institutions integrated into global knowledge networks, thus risking being subordinated to intellectual monopolies, while local firms generally lag behind.

We introduce the concepts of knowledge and data extractivism to account for the effects of intellectual monopoly capitalism on the peripheries. Knowledge extractivism is at the centre of the study cases presented in Chapters 12 and 13. Chapter 12 analyses Singapore's innovation hub. Together with

David Flacher, we show how global intellectual monopolies are profiting not only from their corporate R&D settled in Singapore but also from the innovation capabilities of Singapore's research universities and start-ups (all of which rely on public funds). Chapter 13 provides evidence of pharmaceutical knowledge extractivism from the University of Buenos Aires, in Argentina, by distinguishing between how its R&D outcomes are integrated into global innovation networks and the (almost inexistent) economic benefits associated with those outcomes. Finally, and to wrap up, Chapter 14 elaborates on alternatives to tilt the scale against intellectual monopolies. It includes a set of policy recommendations to prevent knowledge and data extractivism while contributing to structural changes. It is also a call for action, addressed to social movements, workers' unions and scholars. We should all be responsible for counterbalancing intellectual monopoly capitalism, particularly given states' recognized limitations and lack of determination.

Summing up, this book not only elaborates on the emergence of intellectual monopolies but also focuses on the effects of intellectual monopoly capitalism at different levels of analysis. Among other questions, we ask: What is the fate of the rest of the firms – which are the overwhelming majority of the industrial landscape – and how do they manage to remain profitable while subordinating to intellectual monopolies? How are science and technology transformed in this context? What are the implications for research universities and for other public research organizations? What is the place of the peripheries as profits concentrate in a handful of corporations from core countries? What is the role played by those core countries' states in the emergence and spread of intellectual monopoly? These are only some of the questions that run through this book.

Notes

1 Defined by the OECD (2011) as: "computerized information (such as software and databases); innovative property (such as scientific and nonscientific R&D, copyrights, designs, trademarks); and economic competencies (including brand equity, firm-specific human capital, networks joining people and institutions, organisational know-how that increases enterprise efficiency, and aspects of advertising and marketing)".

2 Chapter 2 will further elaborate on the innovation concept. For the moment, it suffices to say that we refer to innovation in a broad sense, thus not restricting it to innovations based on science and technology.

3 Among other limitations of GDP measures, they include the price of intangible assets when they are traded (such as licenses or copyrights), thus overstates the value created in the world for a given period. This overestimation leads us to think that the actual trend is worse than what Figures 1.1 and 1.2 show given the rise in intangible assets that even led Haskel and Westlake (2018) to title their book "Capitalism without capital".

4 Success is defined as the ratio of patent applications to granted patents in the last five years. Global patents are defined as quadrilateral patents meaning that the same invention is patented in the four major patent offices: the Chinese Patent

Office, the European Patent Office, the Japanese Patent Office and the United States Patent & Trademark Office. Finally, the influence of a patent portfolio results from counting citations by other companies' in the last five years.

5 https://www.zerohedge.com/markets/staggering-84-all-sp500-assets-are-now-intangible.

6 https://www.microsoft.com/en-us/microsoft-365/blog/2020/04/30/2-years-digital-transformation-2-months/.

7 Data corresponds to May 26, 2020.

8 Data results from multiplying World Bank 2018 data by Japan's declared GDP growth for 2019.

9 Phillippon (2019) considers both the US and Europe. However, since his focus is on market concentration and not intellectual monopoly, his conclusion is that market concentration has strengthened, mainly in the United States.

10 The book refers to core and peripheral countries instead of other conceptualizations because we include China in the core. Beyond this particularity, the persistence of divergence between countries – which we argue deepens under intellectual monopoly capitalism – put into question the idea of "developing countries."

11 https://www.washingtonpost.com/education/2020/05/06/cuomo-questions-why-school-buildings-still-exist-says-new-york-will-work-with-bill-gates-reimagine-education/

12 https://www.cnbc.com/2018/02/12/concerns-over-alibaba-led-digital-free-trade-zone-in-malaysia.html.

13 https://www.ft.com/content/b5540c88–9914-11e9-8cfb-30c211dcd229.

References

Baranes, A. I. (2016). *An original institutionalist approach to the structure, conduct, and performance of the pharmaceutical industry: The importance of intangible assets* [PhD Thesis]. University of Missouri-Kansas City.

Birch, K. (2019). Technoscience rent: Toward a theory of rentiership for technoscientific capitalism. *Science, Technology, & Human Values.* doi:10.1177/0162243919829567.

Bryan, D., Rafferty, M., & Wigan, D. (2017). Capital unchained: Finance, intangible assets and the double life of capital in the offshore world. *Review of International Political Economy, 24*(1), 56–86.

Calligaris, S., Criscuolo, C., & Marcolin, L. (2018). *Mark-ups in the digital era* (OECD Science, Technology and Industry Working Papers). OECD.

Castro, D., McLaughlin, M., & Chivot, E. (2019). *Who is winning the AI race: China, the EU or the United States?* Center for Data Innovation.

Clarivate Analytics. (2019). *Top 100 global innovators 2018–2019.* Clarivate Analytics

Cockburn, I. M., Henderson, R., & Stern, S. (2018). *The impact of artificial intelligence on innovation.* National Bureau of Economic Research.

Collier, R. (2011). Bye, bye blockbusters, hello niche busters. *Canadian Medical Association. 183*(11), E697–E698; doi:10.1503/cmaj.109-3874

Covarrubias, M., Gutiérrez, G., & Philippon, T. (2020). From good to bad concentration? US industries over the past 30 years. *NBER Macroeconomics Annual, 34*(1), 1–46.

Drahos, P. (1995). Global property rights in information: The story of TRIPS at the GATT. *Prometheus, 13*(1), 6–19.

Durand, C., & Milberg, W. (2020). Intellectual monopoly in global value chains. *Review of International Political Economy*, *27*(2), 404–29. doi:10.1080/09692290.2 019.1660703
European Commission. (2019). *EU R&D scoreboard*. European Commission.
Foley, D. K. (2013). Rethinking financial capitalism and the ""information" "economy. *Review of Radical Political Economics*, *45*(3), 257–68.
Godin, B. (2006). The linear model of innovation: The historical construction of an analytical framework. *Science, Technology, & Human Values*, *31*(6), 639–67.
Haskel, J., & Westlake, S. (2018). *Capitalism without capital: The rise of the intangible economy*. Princeton University Press.
Lambert, T. E. (2019). Monopoly capital and innovation: An exploratory assessment of R&D effectiveness. *International Review of Applied Economics*, 1–14. doi: 10.1080/02692171.2019.1620703
Lazonick, W., Hopkins, M., Jacobson, K., Sakinç, M. E., & Tulum, Ö. (2017). *US Pharma's financialized business model*. Institute for New Economic Thinking.
Marx, K. (1867). *El capital. Crítica de la economía política (Tomo I)*. Fondo de Cultura Economica.
Marx, K. (1894). *El Capital. Crítica de la economía política (Tomo III)*. Fondo de Cultura Economica.
Milanovic, B. (2016). *Global inequality: A new approach for the age of globalization*. Harvard University Press.
Montalban, M., & Sakinç, M. E. (2013). Financialization and productive models in the pharmaceutical industry. *Industrial and Corporate Change*, *22*(4), 981–1030.
OECD. (2011). *New sources of growth: Intangible assets*. OECD Publishing.
Orhangazi, Ö. (2018). The role of intangible assets in explaining the investment–profit puzzle. *Cambridge Journal of Economics, 43*(5), 1251–86.
Pagano, U. (2014). The crisis of intellectual monopoly capitalism. *Cambridge Journal of Economics*, *38*(6), 1409–29.
Philippon, T. (2019). *The great reversal: How America gave up on free markets*. Harvard University Press.
Piketty, T. (2014). *Capital in the 21st century*. Harvard University Press.
Pistor, K. (2019). *The code of capital: How the law creates wealth and inequality*. Princeton University Press.
Pozsar, Z. (2018). Repatriation, the echo-taper and the €/$ basis. *Global Money Notes*, 11.
PWC. (2019). *Global top 100 companies by market capitalisation*. PWC.
PWC. (2020). *Global top 100 companies by market capitalisation*. PWC.
Rikap, C. (2018). Innovation as economic power in global value chains. *Revue d'Économie Industrielle*, *163*, 35–75.
Rikap, C. (2019). Asymmetric power of the core: Technological cooperation and technological competition in the transnational innovation networks of big pharma. *Review of International Political Economy*, *26*(5), 987–1021. doi:10.1080/09692290.2019.1620309
Rose, H., & Rose, S. P. R. (2014). *Genes, cells, and brains: The promethean promises of the new biology*. Verso Trade.
Rotta, T. N. (2018). Unproductive accumulation in the USA: A new analytical framework. *Cambridge Journal of Economics*, *42*(5), 1367–92.

Schumpeter, J. A. (1934). *The theory of economic development: An inquiry into profits, capital, credit, interest, and the business cycle.* Transaction Publishers.
Schumpeter, J. A. (1942). *Capitalism, socialism and democracy.* Routledge.
Schwartz, H. M. (2016). Wealth and secular stagnation: The role of industrial organization and intellectual property rights. *The Russell Sage Foundation Journal of the Social Sciences, 2*(6), 226–49.
Schwartz, H. M. (2019). American hegemony: Intellectual property rights, dollar centrality, and infrastructural power. *Review of International Political Economy, 26*(3), 490–519. doi:10.1080/09692290.2019.1597754
Summers, L. H. (2016). The age of secular stagnation: What it is and what to do about it. *Foreign Affairs, 95*(2), 2–9.
Synergy Research Group. (2019). *Amazon, Microsoft, Google and Alibaba strengthen their grip on the public cloud market.* https://www.srgresearch.com/articles/amazon-microsoft-google-and-alibaba-strengthen-their-grip-public-cloud-market
Teixeira, R. A., & Rotta, T. N. (2012). Valueless knowledge-commodities and financialization: Productive and financial dimensions of capital autonomization. *Review of Radical Political Economics, 44*(4), 448–67.
UNCTAD. (2019). *Digital Economy Report 2019: Value creation and capture–Implications for developing countries.* United Nations.
Wier, L., & Reynolds, H. (2018). *Big and "unprofitable": How 10% of multinational firms do 98% of profit shifting.* WIDER Working Paper.
World Intellectual Property Organization. (2019). *WIPO Technology Trends 2019. Artificial Intelligence.* WIPO.
Zingales, L. (2017). Towards a political theory of the firm. *Journal of Economic Perspectives, 31*(3), 113–30.

Part 1

INTELLECTUAL MONOPOLY CAPITALISM

2

THE EMERGENCE OF INTELLECTUAL MONOPOLY CAPITALISM

1 Introduction

Intellectual monopolies are corporations that base their accumulation on continuously monopolizing access to knowledge. They collect intellectual rents from their in-house innovations but also appropriate data, knowledge and value from other actors participating in their innovation and production networks and platforms. Some intellectual monopolies are data-driven. These are companies that innovate on the basis of processing havested data from individuals and other organizations with machine learning. These algorithms transform data into digital intelligence that is used to keep innovating.

The monopolistic condition of intellectual monopolies does not refer to their market positions, despite some of them may operate in highly concentrated markets. Their monopoly lies in increasingly transforming knowledge into intangible assets, which allows them to capture greater rents. These corporations build on their knowledge monopoly to outsource steps of their production processes, keeping most of the generated value. Although intellectual monopolies working on the same or close industries are rivals and compete for technology, they also engage in technological cooperation for steps of their innovation processes.

As was introduced in Chapter 1, empirical evidence for the United States (US) shows that R&D is being used to expand concentration. R&D efforts were shown to be positively and significantly correlated with corporate net profits and with performance in Standard & Poor's stock market index (Lambert, 2019). Likewise, based on the distribution of cash holdings by US corporations, Schwartz (2016) suggests that an uneven distribution of intellectual property rights (IPRs) explains profits differentials. In the same vein, Orhangazi (2018) revealed that intangible-intensive industries' rate of profit grew faster than their total assets. Beyond the United States, in every major economy the mark-ups of firms at the top of the mark-up distribution have grown and are higher in digital-intensive sectors (Calligaris et al., 2018).

This chapter starts by delving into the emergence of intellectual monopolies. Then, Section 3 analyses the effects of innovation as an accomplished result monopolized by a few intellectual monopolies. This section explores the subordination of complementors in digital platforms as well as of outsourced firms in global value chains (GVC) (Gereffi, 2014; Gereffi et al., 2005; Sturgeon, 2009). These are examples of how corporations monopolizing knowledge subordinate others. Section 4 elaborates on how intellectual monopolies plan and control innovation processes beyond their capital legal ownership by organizing multiple global innovation networks from which they predate and assetize knowledge results. Section 5 offers a typology of subordinate firms. Finally, Section 6 concludes by reflecting on intellectual monopolies' sources of profits.

2 Intangible assets, rents and the emergence of intellectual monopoly capitalism

2.1 Intangible assets and intellectual rents

The OECD (2011, p. 1) defines intangible assets as: "computerized information (such as software and databases), innovative property (such as scientific and non-scientific R&D, copyrights, designs, trademarks) and economic competencies (including brand equity, firm-specific human capital, networks joining people and institutions, organisational know-how that increases enterprise efficiency, and aspects of advertising and marketing)". Thus, intangible assets comprise knowledge that has been introduced to the economic sphere.

Historically, this integration of knowledge into the economic sphere was conceived as an innovation.[1] In Chapter 1, we recalled Schumpeter's (1934) innovation definition. It refers to the creation of a new production techniques or product. This definition includes the creation of a new market. For instance, the development of a brand could lead consumers to conceive a product as different from all the other equal ones in terms of their material properties. Therefore, if society values a Nike shoe as unique, then this shoe will be sold in a separate market of its own, and the creation of this market can be considered an innovation. Products are useful as far as they satisfy a twofold condition: they are useful due to their technical specificities and be socially recognized as useful.[2] When a new market is created without a technical change, we draw on Marx's (1867, Chapter 1) use-value concept to say that the innovation transformed the social dimension even if, in its materiality, the product serves for the same use as previously existing ones.

Innovations can be science-based or non-science based (Ernst, 2009). The latter generally refers to the use of existing capacities in a different (new) way. They are early technical adaptations. Moreover, technical changes are not only the result of engineering transformations but also new designs.[3]

Once knowledge is assetized, its owner can garner intellectual rents, also dubbed knowledge, or technoscientific rents (Birch, 2019; Durand & Milberg, 2020; Foley, 2013; Pagano, 2014; Rikap, 2018; Teixeira & Rotta, 2012). Given that intangible assets spring from the private appropriation of knowledge, they exclude others from accessing and mobilizing that knowledge for their and others' benefit. In Baranes's (2016) terms, they give the privilege to access, thus to use certain ideas while locking-out others. Copyright, trademarks or patents are legal locking-out mechanisms. The strengthening of IPRs is a key precondition of the emergence of intellectual monopoly capitalism (see Chapters 3 and 4). Knowledge is also monopolized when it is kept as industrial secrets or tacit knowledge.[4] Beyond legal monopoly rents, Durand and Milberg (2020) suggest three other types of intellectual rents: vertical natural monopoly, intangibles-differential rents and data-driven innovation rents. Chapter 7 analyses this taxonomy more in detail showing that Apple enjoys the four mentioned types of intangibles-driven rents.

Vertical natural monopoly rents refer to GVC leaders' exclusive knowledge covering the whole chain and, thus, the capacity to integrate it assuring network complementarities. The different scale economies between intangible and tangible assets result, according to Durand and Milberg (2020), in intangibles-differential rents. In addition, under intellectual monopoly capitalism, (big) data are a source of knowledge. Since big data remain under the exclusive access of a certain firm, analysed data become intangible assets. As a result, Durand and Milberg (2020, p. 421) defined data-driven innovation rents as "benefits accruing from the enhancement of innovation capabilities derived from data centralization".

Data rentiership is of utmost importance for expanding a companies' degree of intellectual monopoly. Big data are processed with machine-learning algorithms producing digital intelligence (UNCTAD, 2019). Within machine-learning techniques, deep learning and neural networks are characterized by algorithms that learn and improve themselves as they process more data. This has led Cockburn et al. (2018) to consider this technology a general-purpose method of invention. Therefore, monopolizing big data results in monopolizing a source of potentially unlimited inventions. This innovation *cum* economic potential of analysed data is beneath data rentiers' quest for owning and controlling new sources of big data. As more sources of data are monopolized by the same intellectual monopoly, more accurate the predictions of their algorithms will be, and they will be able to shape behaviours even more. Therefore, their business and innovations will blossom at the expense of society at large.

Summing up, intangible assets are monetized knowledge, from the assetization of the most basic forms of knowledge (centralized and processed data) to revolutionary science-based innovations. This appropriation of knowledge grants its owner monopoly power that enables it to garner intellectual rents.

2.2 The emergence of intellectual monopolies

Intellectual monopolies spring from the continuous monopolization (*cum* assetization) of knowledge. It is possible to conceive a scenario where some haphazardly successful firms reinvest at least part of their intellectual rents in further monopolizing different forms of knowledge, thus expanding their accumulation of intangible assets when successful. The systematic expansion of knowledge monopoly grants a continuous advantage to these firms, and potentially an endless source of power that can lead to globally expanded unequal or asymmetrical market-exchanges.

The result is a monopolized process of cumulative causation. Creative successes are self-reinforced or lead to a virtuous circle for firms monopolizing knowledge at the expense of the rest of the system. Since knowledge is a cumulative process with economies of scale, it demands minimum knowledge thresholds to allow copies, leaving big companies in a better position to appropriate their own and others' intellectual rents (Antonelli, 1999; Dosi, 1988). Pagano recently pointed out to knowledge cumulativeness (2014, p. 1423) to explain how firms that have more "intellectual endowments will continue to do (possibly increasingly) better than those lacking this monopoly power."

These conditions contribute to explain how, once a firm continuously wins the innovation race, the resulting gap with the rest of the firms producing the same or similar products widens, blocking these other firms. It is the capacity to continually renew its intellectual monopoly that we state constitutes a source of lasting power. In other words, systematically winning the monopolistic competition for knowledge entails a cumulative causation effect that lies in the hands of few (leading) corporations. In this respect, we expand Pagano's (2014, p. 1413) definition of an intellectual monopoly because the author restricted it to the "legal monopoly over some items of knowledge, which extends well beyond national boundaries". Knowledge monopoly can be extended in time, regardless of legal ownership, if a company manages to innovate anew before others adopt its previous innovation.

Our conceptualization of (intellectual) rentiership differs in two core aspects when compared with the historical rent concept. Since the pioneering work of Ricardo (1817), there has been a tendency to think of rents as a disruption of capitalism's normal unfolding. "Rents are often framed as distortions of markets (e.g., Tullock, 1993), or as unearned income (e.g., Sayer, 2015), or as a burden on the 'real economy' (e.g., Mazzucato, 2018)" (Birch, 2019, p. 16). In this book, we put forward and elaborate on the idea that rents are not a distortion of the normal functioning of capitalism. Rents are intrinsic to capitalism, not a collateral effect but an inherent feature of capital accumulation.

Moreover, contrary to historical approaches (Marx, 1894; Ricardo, 1817) and more recent conceptualizations (Pagano, 2014), we argue that intellectual monopolies are not passive rentiers. The extension of intellectual rents throughout time is the result of proactive innovation behaviour, even if those innovating may end up not being the intellectual monopolies themselves, but subordinate organizations planned by the former – as we explain later in this chapter. As explained by Teixeira and Rotta (2012, p. 464), "knowledge-commodity producers do more than only passively receive rents. They actively use the revenues from patents and monopoly rights to pursue aggressive strategies in R&D investments, marketing, mergers, and acquisitions". Hence, rent-seeking enhances intellectual monopolies' capital accumulation and, as a result of the increased market capitalization of intellectual monopolies, also enriches their shareholders.

Rentiership also demands active behaviours towards property rights, not only in terms of the management of private assets but also to enforce and reinforce property rights themselves (Birch, 2017). A particular patenting strategy has been to create patent thickets, which increases enforcement transaction costs and chances to threaten others trying to copy their products (Ernst, 2016; Noel & Schankerman, 2013). Hence, large-scale patenting – often the case of intellectual monopolies – demands skills to face claims in courts and a deterrence capacity. These conditions contribute to set a high entry barrier for newcomers and benefits big players (Pagano, 2014). Furthermore, those corporations failing to sustain (by expanding or constantly reinventing) their intellectual monopolies, do become parasitic rentiers. The latter's advantage risks being quickly overcome by active intellectual monopolies. Overall, the emergence of intellectual monopolies is a dual process because the enhancement of the leaders simultaneously reduces the remaining firms' possibilities to catch-up vis-à-vis a high speed moving target (Levín, 1997; Pagano, 2014; Rikap, 2018).[5]

Intellectual monopolies also underpin their innovation leadership by exercising political power. From lobbying to bribing, big corporations bargain with political representatives all around the world (Zingales, 2017). As it was the case of former big corporations, intellectual monopolies are lobbying experts with big pharma as historic masters and tech giants as record-breaking examples (Gagnon, 2015).[6] Moreover, intellectual monopolies use their power and global scale to offshore intellectual property and earnings to tax havens. In general, big corporations use globalization to profit from loopholes and minimize paid taxes. Chapter 10 delves into these dynamics, while Chapters 7 and 8 also look at them although focused on Apple and Amazon, respectively.

All in all, intellectual monopolies are far from the parasitic rentier picture. As we further elaborate in the rest of this chapter, they are proactive planners of portions of global capitalism beyond their legally owned capital, including the organization of innovation processes.

3 Using innovation to subordinate others

Intellectual monopolies organize and plan production (including logistics and commercialization) beyond their capital's legal ownership. This possibility to plan and profit from outsourcing requires the know-how and know-who to reintegrate production. This exclusive knowledge kept by leader corporations in global production networks or value chains constitutes a source of intellectual monopoly. In Durand and Milberg's (2020) taxonomy, this is what they understand as vertical natural monopoly rents. Based on their innovation supremacy, intellectual monopolies organize and plan production processes, appropriating part of the value produced at subordinate companies (Rikap, 2018).

Capital outsourcing is not a new phenomenon (see Contractor et al., 2010; Milberg & Winkler, 2013; Smith, 2016; Sturgeon, 2009, among many others). Nonetheless, intellectual monopoly imprints specific characteristics. The 2008 great recession is a turning point in GVC-trade understood as tangible commodities' exchanges (World Bank, 2020, p. 19). In the aftermath of the crisis, GVC-trade recovered but never reached its pre-crisis levels. Furthermore, it shows a downward trend since 2011 (Shin, 2019), which was reinforced by the US–China trade war since 2018.[7] While the trade of manufactured goods stagnated, the trade of digital services has accelerated (WTO, 2019) (see Figure 2.1).

Within the GVC literature, the degree of power asymmetry between the leader and the rest of the chain influences outsourcing decisions. Outsourcing also depends on the degree of codifiability of the information needed to guarantee successful results from outsourcing (Strange & Humphrey, 2018). Furthermore, outsourcing – as well as offshoring – depends on what each intellectual monopoly considers as a core activity, which cannot be universally defined. In abstract terms, the core is integrated by the activities kept in-house to preserve and expand a corporation's intellectual monopoly.

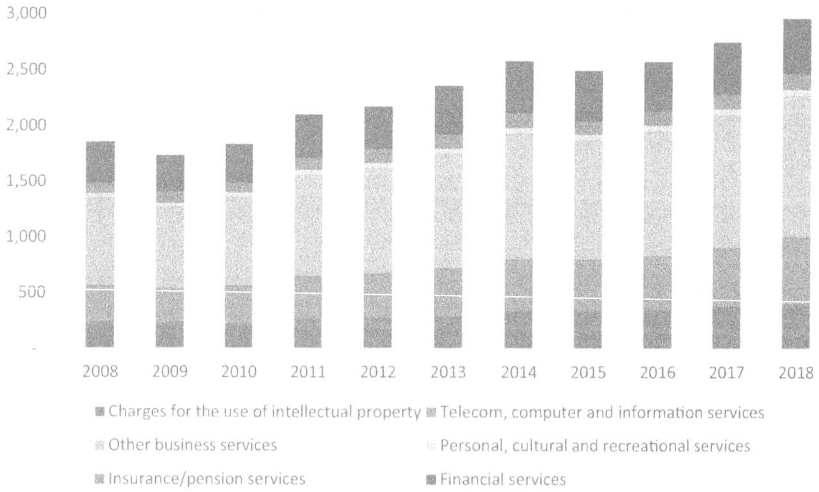

Figure 2.1 World trade of ICT-enabled services (USD billion).
Source: Author's calculation based on World Trade Organization data.

Some intellectual monopolies include in their core business activities that require in-house large (tangible) capital expenditures. This is the case of Amazon, Microsoft, Google and Facebook in the form of data centres and undersea bandwidth, indispensable to store and process data, thus to assure their data-driven rents. For Amazon and Inditex,[8] the core includes the distribution chain (storage included) because part of their innovations concerns logistics and storage (on Amazon, see Chapter 8). Likewise, State Grid Corporation of China finds distribution – in this case of electricity – at its core. This state-owned enterprise bases its intellectual monopoly on smart grid innovations using artificial intelligence (see Chapter 9). In turn, other intellectual monopolies follow a more traditional GVC strategy, such as Apple (see Chapter 7). Large pharmaceuticals even outsource most of the innovation steps because they can still garner the associated intellectual rents (see Chapter 6).

Therefore, industrial structures are more diverse and put into question the idea that research, development, design, technology and business intelligence are the strategic activities for leader corporations (Serfati, 2008). Even steps from all the latter processes are outsourced, while some intellectual monopolies keep in-house steps of the production process that had been considered as perfect candidates for outsourcing.

When outsourcing, the reduction of capital commitment diminishes associated risks, including losses due to demand fluctuations, discontinuities in capital turnover, costs associated with technical changes, to the fulfilment of labour legislation, future workers' demands, among others. Reducing capital commitment also lessens exit barriers (Rikap, 2018). At the same time, in line with Munkirs's (1983) private sector planning theory, where a small number of corporations (the core) plan the whole industry, intellectual monopolies plan outsourced capital's turnover. We may even say that the production unit is split from the legal ownership of capital. In other words, the unit of capital accumulation is not defined by ownership because the intellectual monopoly plans the whole network even if it is not legally bound to a portion of its planned social capital.

Planning does not necessarily require direct control by commanding subordinate enterprises what to do and how to do it. When codifiability is high, intellectual monopolies plan production networks by defining key productive parameters in legal contracts. Intellectual monopolies define clauses of exclusivity, commercial credit conditions, quality standards and other regulations (Rikap, 2018). It has been explained that leaders set performance requirements and standards, conditioning entry and mobility within GVCs (Gereffi, 2014, p. 28). This idea can be extended to every intellectual monopoly. Having an active role in setting international standards is a sign of intellectual leadership.

Setting international standards reduces outsourcing costs because augmenting codifiability diminishes the product specifications that the leader needs to share with other actors of the chain. When information cannot be so easily codified to be defined in advance in legal contracts or official standards, Strange and Humphrey (2018) point out that leaders exercise direct coordination or control of the rest of their chain, personally supervising suppliers.

Intellectual monopolies that control platforms, as Dolata (2020) argues, are market creators. As such, they are rule-setters. Inside their controlled platforms, they decide the norms and standards of what can and cannot be done and how. High-tech intellectual monopolies subordinate suppliers and companies that offer in their marketplaces. Subordinate firms range from app developers for Google or Apple to third-party sellers offering in Amazon and Alibaba e-commerce platforms. They all accept fees and sales and payment conditions, receiving payments at some time after the transaction (Bergvall-Kareborn & Howcroft, 2011; Norfield, 2017; Rikap, 2020). Tech giants even replace and complement states' surveillance role, which also contributes to a process of – technically mediated – curation and shaping of human behaviours and social relationships (Dolata, 2020; Morozov, 2019; Rouvroy & Berns, 2013; Srnicek, 2017; Zuboff, 2019). These companies are an extreme case of intellectual monopoly not only because of the size and scope of their predatory and rentier behaviours (see Chapters 7 and 8), but also due to their ability to control and organize the (digital) economy. Big tech intellectual monopolies were even dubbed new republics.[9]

Overall, intellectual monopolies directly or indirectly control and plan portions of global capitalism. Their planning capacity ranges from defining the concrete dimensions of each production step taking place in subordinate companies to the setting of norms, standards and behavioural patterns. They set the rules that govern markets and production and, as we argue next, they also govern innovation networks or systems. In the rest of this book, we refer to production and innovation networks or systems, including, in each case, production and innovation platforms.

4 Innovation as a process under intellectual monopoly capitalism: knowledge predation

Innovation as a process under intellectual monopoly capitalism refers to how the innovation process is organized. A corporation that became an intellectual monopoly must have had a systemic internal capacity to innovate in order to differentiate itself from the rest of the industry. Nonetheless, once it becomes an intellectual monopoly, innovations are not compelled to be produced (at least not entirely) in-house.

Knowledge modularity was enabled by advancements in scientific disciplines together with specific innovations in computational capabilities and the instruments used to perform experiments, analyse and record results (Arora & Gambardella, 1994). As a result, Antonelli (1999, p. 243) draws attention to the "deverticalisation of knowledge production activities from the boundaries of the corporation".

The modularization of the innovation process has been conceptualized as the formation of innovation circuits (Levín, 1977) and global innovation networks (Ernst, 2009; Liu et al., 2013; Parrilli et al., 2013). Innovation circuits were initially defined by Levín (1977) as the interlocking of all the actors and institutions that participate in the creation of an innovation, including from the basic research discovery (if it is a science-based innovation) to the required industrial adaptations to adopt the innovation. In accordance, global innovation networks focus on how "innovation is being sliced and diced into modular building blocks of specialized tasks for geographically dispersed R&D teams" (Ernst, 2009, p. 3).

In both cases, innovation steps take place in different places and organizations, but the overall process is organized and controlled by a leading corporation.[10] The concepts of innovation circuit and global innovation network complement each other. The former is conceived to describe the uniqueness of each innovation as a creative process organized by a leading corporation through power relations. Meanwhile, the latter highlights the institutionalization of those relationships. It shows how certain actors have become systematic participants of an intellectual monopoly's innovation circuits, thus evolving into an innovation network. Recently, Rikap and Lundvall (2020) argued that intellectual monopolies organize multiple innovation circuits and networks simultaneously, all of them belonging to their global corporate innovation system, a concept initially introduced by Granstrand (2000).

These approaches are entirely in line with the claim of a new division of innovative labour. The growing modularity of knowledge is feasible due to the greater use of general or abstract knowledge for innovating (in particular in the case of science-based innovations) (Arora & Gambardella, 1994; Arora et al., 1997). Innovations can be conceived as a twofold process integrating the production of modules and their combination. The former "is the production of basic knowledge components of 'general-purpose' technologies or of basic product designs", which are then combined to achieve tailored applications (Arora et al., 1997, p. 125).

Once knowledge is modularized, it can be produced anywhere. Innovation circuits can have a global, transnational, regional, national or local scale. The choices between (1) outsourcing or contributing to collaborative R&D environments and (2) in-house investment in intangibles' production depends – among others – on the nature of the intangibles. Decisions are driven by the aim of the intellectual monopoly to maximize intangible assets accumulation, thus augmenting intellectual rents. Intellectual monopolies foster other organizations to take the riskiest endeavours as far as they can still profit from successful results. The organization of R&D in the pharmaceutical field is, perhaps, the most extreme example (see Chapter 6).

Intellectual monopolies also share the production and planning of certain innovation stages or modules. For instance, infrastructural innovations that are not specific to one intellectual monopoly will be more prone to outsourcing but could also be potentially planned (and conducted) together with other intellectual monopolies. This could be the case of innovations that require industry standards' transformation or that demand national or international regulatory agencies' approvals.

We conceive technological cooperation as the intersection of multiple innovation circuits conducted and planned by different intellectual monopolies, thus interconnecting phases of different innovation circuits (Rikap, 2019). In this respect, we add another dimension to Munkirs and Sturgeon's (1985) structural intra-dependence based on shared administrative control, stock control and ownership of the means of production. We add that cooperation between leaders can also rely on the joint production of knowledge modules.

At the same time, intellectual monopolies engage in fierce technological competition. Technological competition is unfolded by intellectual monopolies by organizing multiple innovation circuits and modules or stages of innovation circuits planned by each of them independently, intending to achieve innovations to remain ahead and profit from intellectual rents. Chapter 6 further elaborates on the interplay between technological cooperation and competition between intellectual monopolies.

4.1 Predation within the innovation process

Companies that produce at least one stage of an innovation circuit but cannot garner significant intellectual rents – which are collected by intellectual monopolies – were initially called by Levín (1997) technological capital enterprises. We have renamed them innovating companies to stress the fact that their role is to produce (steps of) innovations. The archetypical example of an innovating firm is the start-up. More generally, these are firms specialized in the production of knowledge and technology that emerged together with the de-verticalization of knowledge production.

Innovating firms participate in intangible goods' production processes but are unable to assetize at least part of the resulting knowledge, which is monopolized by intellectual monopolies. The latter predate knowledge from their innovation circuits (thus also from their innovation networks). As first introduced in Rikap (2020), we draw here on Veblen's (1899) understanding of predation as a direct manifestation of superior force. Intellectual monopolies establish a direct production relation of spoliation exercising their superiority by planning the activities of other firms and institutions. As a result, all the participating organizations produce knowledge that is mainly transformed into intangible assets by the intellectual monopoly, expanding its intellectual rents. Hence, the result is the appropriation of value through monopolizing knowledge produced outside that corporations' legally owned capital. Concerning this predatory capacity, from a Marxian tradition, Foley (2013, p. 259) insists on the difference between "value creation, surplus value generation, and surplus value appropriation". The specificity of the so-called information economy, for the author, does not lay on how value is created but on the introduction of new modes of surplus-value appropriation such as informational rents.[11]

To preserve their power, intellectual monopolies simultaneously organize multiple innovation circuits. They define the general orientations and desired results, of course, without being able to anticipate every step to be followed in order to achieve those results and leaving degrees of autonomy to subordinate actors. Inside innovation circuits, results remain uncertain, but the associated economic risk is diverted by the intellectual monopoly to other participants, eliminating – as when they outsource production steps – a source of exit barriers (Rikap, 2018).

In this context, the aspiration of whoever achieves a serendipitous or haphazard innovation (if it is not an intellectual monopoly) will be to sell it to an intellectual monopoly. Otherwise, it will have slimmer chances to profit from that success. Start-ups aim to develop their innovations to the point where it is more profitable for an intellectual monopoly to acquire them. However, as Chapter 12 explores for the case of Singapore, most start-ups fail, which is even true for Silicon Valley start-ups.[12] Being acquired is the destiny of a slim minority. The acquisition of that successful minority of innovating companies results in higher levels of intangible assets concentration by intellectual monopolies. Pharma and high-tech intellectual monopolies are prominent examples (Bourreau & de Streel, 2020; Lazonick et al., 2017; Lopez Giron & Vialle, 2017; Montalban & Sakinç, 2013; Rikap, 2019; World Intellectual Property Organization, 2019). In line with Harvey (2002), a twofold process reinforces their monopoly power: capital centralization (mergers and acquisitions) and the reinforcement of intangibles' assetization.

Private firms are not the only organizations participating in innovation circuits and networks. Research universities and public research organizations also integrate them, generally occupying subordinated positions (see Chapter 5). Furthermore, states are often risk-takers. In particular, core states have been significant R&D investors, especially of radical and path-breaking innovations, only marginally enjoying their associated profits (Barringer & Slaughter, 2016; Mazzucato, 2015, Chapter 3) (see Chapter 4).

Intellectual monopolies are also in an advantageous position to steer public or academic research agendas. Intellectual monopolies influence global academic research agendas by integrating into their innovation networks leading research institutions within a field, besides profiting from their research capacity. Leading academic institutions start a locomotive effect in their field. The reorientation of their research agenda towards intellectual monopolies' priorities influences other institutions. Leading academic institutions publish in the most prestigious academic journals (managed by a few big publishers also intellectual monopolies themselves) defining dominant scientific agendas. By reading these publications, the mainstream circuit of knowledge even reaches those that are very far from the intellectual monopolies' innovation networks, but that still may refocus their research priorities to assimilate their investigations into what they perceive as the new global prevailing agenda.

Intellectual monopolies may also assetize intangibles entirely produced elsewhere, enlarging their intellectual rents. This process has been described as a blind technology transfer (Codner et al., 2012), and we expand the concept and rename it blind knowledge transfer since not only technological achievements but all forms of knowledge are being turned into intangible assets (see Chapter 13). Blind knowledge transfer is a form of accumulation by dispossession where no predatory action took place. No direct manifestation of superior force took place to the point that intangible producers ignore that the product of their work contributed to a privatized innovation.

All in all, intellectual monopolies' control over production and innovation processes involves a wide network of organizations – acting as suppliers, clients, complementors or producers of steps of innovation processes. In the next section, we introduce a taxonomy of subordinate firms.

5 A taxonomy of subordinate firms

Drawing on Levín's taxonomy (1997), we propose four types of companies under intellectual monopoly capitalism (see Table 2.1). Besides intellectual monopolies, we distinguish three types of (subordinate) firms. Firms' hierarchical order inside production and innovation systems results in profit rate differentials. We conceive this hierarchy as a specific form of the power relation described by Dockès (2000). For the latter, an agent subordinates to its superior not only because it occupies an inferior position but also because, by integrating a hierarchical order, it will subordinate those below. In our proposed taxonomy, firms also differ in terms of (degrees of) technical autonomy, profit sources and working conditions (for the latter, see Chapter 10).

Complier companies participate in intellectual monopolies' planned production processes or systems in a subordinated way. They are typically tangible capital-intensive suppliers or complementors that lack technical autonomy. Some of them even become giant production units such as electronics contract manufacturers like Foxconn or global automobile suppliers (Frigant & Jullien, 2014; Starosta, 2010). They systematically invest in (tangible) capital to be at the forefront of the technical frontier required by

Table 2.1 Types of enterprises' main characteristics

Type of enterprise	*Intellectual Monopoly*	*Complier*	*Laggard*	*Innovating*
Participates in production networks?	Yes	Yes	Yes	No
Technical autonomy?	Yes	No	No	-
Participates in Innovation systems/ networks?	Yes	No	No	Yes
Position in Power (Planning) relation	Dominant	Subordinated	Extremely subordinated	Subordinated
Profit Rate	Highest	Consistently above interest rate	Lowest, around interest rate	Consistently above interest rate

intellectual monopolies, which results in shortening product cycles. They rely on intellectual monopolies' new technologies, which they adopt fast to keep their businesses going. Early adoption of intellectual monopolies' requirements (in terms of quality, standards, delivery times) allows them to be privileged among other subordinated companies. All this process results in innovations at the firm level and can even produce "new-to-the-world" (Furman et al., 2002) process innovations. However, their overall production process is structured by and responds to the intellectual monopoly. In this overarching sense, they lost their technical autonomy.

Since intellectual monopolies exercise a predatory relationship with them, profits are usually below that corresponding to their advanced capital. Intellectual rents, if they exist, will be slim. As we mentioned, as early adopters of new techniques, they may accomplish process innovations. Complier companies' profit-seeking poses limits to intellectual monopolies' predatory activity. For instance, they cannot buy at a price so low that it leaves complier companies with a rate of profit persistently below the interest rate. If this were the case, then complier firms would be liquidated, and the remains reinvested in the financial system or another business. In fact, in order to systematically adopt the techniques demanded by intellectual monopolies and sustain product quality, their rate of profit must be persistently above the interest rate. Intellectual monopolies' predation is partly offset by the worsening of labour conditions and salaries (see Chapter 10).

These companies are typically located in countries with the lowest salaries within those with the required productive capacities, also taking into account transportation costs (which are specific to each industry). Recent relocalization of manufacturing firms from China to other Asian countries like Vietnam provides evidence not only of the effects of the US–China war but also of the changing nature of China, from a mainly complier companies' country to hosting intellectual monopolies (see Chapters 4 and 9). In the case of firms operating through a tech-giants' platform, those with the highest sales levels will have greater chances to bargain with that intellectual monopoly. They will also have the necessary funds to, for instance, comply with all the required fees to be better showcased on Amazon.com or win keywords auctions, thus getting top positions in Google searches. Other examples of complier companies are UPS and FedEx in their relationship with Amazon, giving the latter privileged treatment while charging higher fees to smaller clients to compensate (Rikap, 2020).

Unlike compliers, laggard companies fail to adopt intellectual monopolies' demands. When they participate in their production systems, they use outdated techniques, thus perform simple and labour-intensive tasks. Usually, they are not direct suppliers of intellectual monopolies but integrate their production networks by supplying complier firms. In order to be hired, laggard companies offer at the lowest price, paying even lower salaries than compliers and worsening labour conditions, which are typically precarious and flexible (Graña, 2014). In the bottom of the hierarchy, self-employed workers that formally sell the product of their work instead of their labour power can be considered as laggard companies.

Although laggard companies survive with a profit rate around the level of the interest rate, in extreme cases, the owner's salary becomes the minimum condition for survival when they face exit barriers (Iñigo Carrera, 2016). Therefore, they are extremely subordinated to other links, losing most (or even all) of their profits when exchanging with other enterprises. An illustrative example of the tactics or responses followed by laggard firms to survive is given by Parker and Cox (2013) for the visual effects' service firms. These enterprises have low (or even sometimes no) margins and face power asymmetries in film's production networks, dominated by Hollywood intellectual monopolies (which we may add that are now being challenged by Netflix and Amazon). Some visual effects' service firms provide cheaper low-technology services, avoiding over-engineering solutions. Another safer bet is to remain small enough to avoid idle capacity.

In this context, the remaining bargaining power of subordinated firms directly depends on the distance they take from their competitors. Indeed, if only one company is capable of fulfilling an intellectual monopoly's requirement, this company will enjoy more bargaining power than if its competitors are on its heels. While there are generally multiple laggard companies performing the same tasks, such as small firms fixing iPhones around the world (Rikap, 2018), it is more likely to find complier companies that outperform or even temporarily monopolize a production stage. In this case, this company will retain higher profits as long as that advantage lasts. Complier firms compete among them both for prices and techniques to ensure their place in intellectual monopolies' production networks.

The third type of subordinated firm is the innovating company. As we explained in Section 4, these are the firms that participate in intellectual monopolies' innovation circuits. They produce innovation steps or modules but fail to garner at least part of the associated intellectual rents which are appropriated by the intellectual monopoly. Rents are innovating companies' main form of profits. Even if intellectual monopolies garner most of the intellectual rents derived from successful innovation, innovating companies survive by profiting from a portion of those rents and due to seed-money and venture capital that bets on their future intangible assets. However, being acquired is usually their main aim. As we mentioned, these are generally start-up companies. Another example are apps and games developers. Innovating companies have the highest rate of failure within all the above-mentioned types of subordinate firms because they take the innovation risks. Likewise, they enjoy greater profit rates when successful precisely because they garner a portion of their innovations' associated rents.

In the next section, we close this chapter referring to the sources of profit enjoyed by intellectual monopolies.

6 Intellectual monopolies sources of profit

Following Bettelheim's (1975, p. 57) distinction between possession and property, subordinate companies have "the ability to put the means of production into operation" (possession), but they partially lack "the power to dispose of the products obtained with the help of these means of production" (property). The latter lays in the hands of the intellectual monopoly. Resulting concentration of higher profits facilitates intellectual monopolies' perpetuation. In comparison, lower profits – in particular for laggard firms – diminish their capacity to catch up or leapfrog.

In its most abstract form, the intellectual monopoly profits are the sum of (1) profits derived from its own capital accumulation (including production and innovation processes) which include accumulation by dispossession in the case of monopolized knowledge produced in-house (Harvey, 2007), (2) earnings from its predatory activities and (3) the extraction of financial rents (Chapter 7 further elaborates on the latter and Chapter 10 delves into the interplay between capital accumulation, rentiership and predation).

Concerning its (own) capital accumulation (1), collected profits result from surplus value and intellectual rents. Rents are always an appropriation of total social surplus value. Intellectual rents are payments made by others to gain access to monopolized intangibles, either to directly gain access them (for instance, by paying royalties) or to consume resulting products whose price includes an extraordinary profit. In both cases, rents reflect the capacity – now concentrated by intellectual monopolies – to appropriate surplus value. Intellectual rents are always a form of accumulation by dispossession because the assetization of intangible goods deprives others of mobilizing that knowledge for production and other purposes, including further advancing knowledge.[13]

Regarding predation (2), intellectual monopolies plan and organize production (including commercialization and distribution) and innovation networks or systems, capturing the biggest share of resulting profits. Predation is a particular form of dispossession. It may take place both when exchanging commodities (as in the case of transactions within a GVC or platform) and within an intellectual monopoly's overall innovation networks conforming its corporate innovation system. Predation is a zero-sum game, whatever the intellectual monopoly appropriates through predation, is what subordinated firms and other organizations lose. Intellectual monopolies seize value produced in complier and laggard firms, and garner intellectual rents from the private appropriation of intangibles produced in their innovation networks.

All in all, intellectual monopoly capitalism can be conceived as an era where capital accumulation is driven by corporations that have systematically monopolized knowledge (and data) in multiple and complementary ways, transforming it into intangible assets, including but not limiting the concept of intellectual monopoly to the concentration of IPRs. Their knowledge monopoly enables them to subordinate other firms controlling and planning production systems. Yet, intellectual monopolies' intangible assets spring from monopolizing knowledge that was not mainly produced in-house but in multiple innovation networks integrated by multiple organizations. Intellectual monopolies' knowledge predation from these networks contributes to enlarging their garnered intellectual rents, thus expanding its profits. Considering also that they predate value from their production networks, it may be said that intellectual monopolies extract knowledge and value from diverse industrial structures (GVC, platforms, innovation circuits and networks). The overall effects for global capitalism are a slowdown in the pace of economic growth and more inequality.

The next chapter is dedicated to further elaborate on intellectual monopolies' capacity to subordinate spheres of capitalism, analysing how they profit from the knowledge commons and open access initiatives, which were born to counterbalance knowledge privatization. Chapter 3 is followed by an analysis of the historical conditions that enabled the emergence of intellectual monopoly capitalism, focusing on legal and policy transformations in the United States and China, in Chapter 4.

Notes

1 We should note here that within the set of intangible assets some authors have included such things as clientele or trade connections. Our intangible goods concept excludes them and it is based not only on Veblen (1908b, pp. 111–12) but also on the OECD (2011) definition.

2 Only looking at their materiality could lead us, for instance, to sell Walkmans in the XXI century.

3 In fact, the United States Patent and Trademark Office has a single database that includes designs.

4 Tacit knowledge and industrial secrets can be considered as included in Veblen's concept of goodwill, defined as every intangible asset that is not protected by law (Gagnon, 2007). Contemporary classifications of intangible assets sometimes include goodwill, like the International Financial Reporting Standards (*IFRS 3 — Business Combinations*, n.d.), and sometimes exclude it, such as the OECD (2011, p. 1). Goodwill is still ambiguously defined and dubiously measured. It has become a black box where firms include unmeasured intangibles. It is defined as the difference between a company's book and market value and is a communicating vessel between intangible and financial rentierism (see Chapter 10).

5 Just investing in R&D, marketing and advertising as much as leader enterprises would not be enough to reach them. Anyway, it is certainly a necessary condition.

6 https://www.washingtonpost.com/technology/2020/01/22/amazon-facebook-google-lobbying-2019/ and https://edition.cnn.com/2019/01/23/health/phrma-lobbying-costs-bn/index.html.

7 The reduction of GVC-trade could also be related to the adoption of new technologies such as 3D printers and robotics that may lead to reshore or resource certain stages of production processes.

8 On Inditex, see for instance https://www.ft.com/content/c2b8e86d-d580-47f6-8f2d-13357b528dde?segmentId=b0d7e653-3467-12ab-c0f0-77e4424cdb4c.

9 https://www.ft.com/content/36f838c0-53c5-11ea-a1ef-da1721a0541e.

10 We elaborate here on Ernst's (2008, 2009) concept of global innovation networks as hierarchically organized by leader firms since other authors conceived global innovation networks as structures that are not necessarily subjected to hierarchical relations (Chaminade et al., 2016; Liu et al., 2013).

11 After providing evidence of knowledge predation in Chapters 6–9, Chapter 10 provides a more elaborated discussion on predation.

12 https://www.startups.com/community/questions/396/for-every-success-story-in-silicon-valley-how-many-are-there-that-fail.

13 We conceive knowledge as a continuous good, not as an aggregate of independent units but one single corpus or network where every concept is relevant (makes sense) only contextualized and related to other concepts, a common stock in the words of Veblen (1908a).

References

Antonelli, C. (1999). The evolution of the industrial organisation of the production of knowledge. *Cambridge Journal of Economics*, *23*(2), 243–60.

Arora, A., & Gambardella, A. (1994). The changing technology of technological change: General and abstract knowledge and the division of innovative labour. *Research Policy*, *23*(5), 523–32.

Arora, A., Gambardella, A., & Rullani, E. (1997). Division of labour and the locus of inventive activity. *Journal of Management & Governance*, *1*(1), 123–40.

Baranes, A. I. (2016). *An original institutionalist approach to the structure, conduct, and performance of the pharmaceutical industry: The importance of intangible assets* [PhD Thesis]. University of Missouri-Kansas City.

Barringer, S. N., & Slaughter, S. (2016). University trustees and the entrepreneurial university: Inner circles, interlocks, and exchanges. In Slaughter, S. and Taylor, B. (Eds.) *Higher education, stratification, and workforce development* (pp. 151–71). Springer. http://link.springer.com/chapter/10.1007/978-3-319-21512-9_8

Bergvall-Kareborn, B., & Howcroft, D. (2011). Mobile applications development on Apple and Google platforms. *Communications of the Association for Information Systems*, *29*(1), 565–80.

Bettelheim, C. (1975). *Economic calculation and forms of property: An essay on the transition between capitalism and socialism* (Translated by John Taylor). Monthly Review Press.

Birch, K. (2017). Rethinking value in the bio-economy: Finance, assetization, and the management of value. *Science, Technology, & Human Values*, *42*(3), 460–90.

Birch, K. (2019). Technoscience rent: Toward a theory of rentiership for technoscientific capitalism. *Science, Technology, & Human Values*, *45*(1), 3–33.

Bourreau, M., & de Streel, A. (2020). *Big tech acquisitions.* Brussels, Centre on Regulation in Europe.

Calligaris, S., Criscuolo, C., & Marcolin, L. (2018). *Mark-ups in the digital era* (OECD Science, Technology and Industry Working Papers). OECD.

Chaminade, C., De Fuentes, C., Harirchi, G., & Plechero, M. (2016). The geography and structure of global innovation networks: Global scope and regional embeddedness. In Shearmur, R., Carrincazeaux, C., and Doloreux, D. (Eds.) *Handbook on the geographies of innovation.* Edward Elgar Publishing.

Cockburn, I. M., Henderson, R., & Stern, S. (2018). *The impact of artificial intelligence on innovation.* National Bureau of Economic Research.

Codner, D. G., Becerra, P., & Díaz, A. (2012). Blind technology transfer or technological knowledge leakage: A case study from the South. *Journal of Technology Management & Innovation*, *7*(2), 184–95.

Contractor, F. J., Kumar, V., Kundu, S. K., & Pedersen, T. (2010). *Global outsourcing and offshoring: An integrated approach to theory and corporate strategy.* Cambridge University Press.

Dockès, P. (2000). Pouvoir, autorité et convention d'obéissance. *Journal of World-Systems Research*, *6*(3), 920–45.

Dolata, U. (2020). *Platform-regulation. Coordination of markets and curation of sociality on the Internet* [SOI Discussion Paper]. Stuttgarter Beiträge zur Organisations-und Innovationsforschung.

Dosi, G. (1988). Sources, procedures, and microeconomic effects of innovation. *Journal of Economic Literature*, *26*(3), 1120–71.
Durand, C., & Milberg, W. (2020). Intellectual monopoly in global value chains. *Review of International Political Economy*, *27*(2), 404–29. doi:10.1080/09692290.2019.1660703
Ernst, D. (2008). *Can Chinese IT firms develop innovative capabilities within global knowledge networks?* https://papers.ssrn.com/sol3/papers.cfm?abstract_id=2742950
Ernst, D. (2009). *A new geography of knowledge in the electronics industry? Asia's role in global innovation networks.* https://papers.ssrn.com/sol3/papers.cfm?abstract_id=2742923
Ernst, D. (2016). *Global strategic patenting and innovation–policy and research implications.* East-West Center Working Papers.
Foley, D. K. (2013). Rethinking financial capitalism and the "information" economy. *Review of Radical Political Economics*, *45*(3), 257–68.
Frigant, V., & Jullien, B. (2014). Comment la production modulaire transforme l'industrie automobile. *Revue d'économie Industrielle*, *145*, 11–44.
Furman, J. L., Porter, M. E., & Stern, S. (2002). The determinants of national innovative capacity. *Research Policy*, *31*(6), 899–933.
Gagnon, M.-A. (2015). Shaping the social determinants of value through economic ghostmanagement: An institutionalist approach to capital accumulation. In Jo, T and Lee, F. S. (Eds), *Marx, Veblen and the Foundation of Heterodox Economics.* (pp. 228–51) Routledge.
Gereffi, G. (2014). Global value chains in a post-Washington consensus world. *Review of International Political Economy*, *21*(1), 9–37.
Gereffi, G., Humphrey, J., & Sturgeon, T. (2005). The governance of global value chains. *Review of International Political Economy*, *12*(1), 78–104.
Graña, J. M. (2014). El proceso de heterogeneización y segmentación laboral como resultado del rezago productivo. *Razón y Revolución*, *26*. http://www.revistaryr.org.ar/index.php/RyR/article/view/127
Granstrand, O. (2000). *Corporate innovation systems: A comparative study of multi-technology corporations in Japan, Sweden and the USA.* Chalmers University.
Harvey, D. (2002). *Spaces of capital: Towards a critical geography.* Routledge.
Harvey, D. (2007). *A brief history of neoliberalism.* Oxford University Press.
IFRS 3—Business Combinations. (n.d.). https://www.iasplus.com/en/standards/ifrs/ifrs3 (23 November 2017)
Iñigo Carrera, J. (2016). The general rate of profit and its realisation in the differentiation of industrial capitals. In G. Charnock & G. Starosta (Eds.), *The new international division of labour* (pp. 25–53). Springer. http://link.springer.com/chapter/10.1057/978-1-137-53872-7_2
Lambert, T. E. (2019). Monopoly capital and innovation: An exploratory assessment of R&D effectiveness. *International Review of Applied Economics*, 1–14. doi:10.1080/02692171.2019.1620703
Lazonick, W., Hopkins, M., Jacobson, K., Sakinç, M. E., & Tulum, Ö. (2017). *US Pharma's financialized business model.* Institute for New Economic Thinking.
Levín, P. (1977). Circuitos de innovación. *Revista Interamericana de Planificación*, *XX*(44). http://www. revistaespacios. com/a81v01n01/81010120. html

Levín, P. (1997). *El capital tecnológico*. Catálogos. http://www.econ.uba.ar/www/institutos/economia/Ceplad/elcaptec.htm

Liu, J., Chaminade, C., & Asheim, B. (2013). The geography and structure of global innovation networks: A knowledge base perspective. *European Planning Studies*, *21*(9), 1456–73.

Lopez Giron, A. J., & Vialle, P. (2017). A preliminary analysis of mergers and acquisitions by Microsoft from 1992 to 2016: A resource and competence perspective. *28th European Regional Conference of the International Telecommunications Society (ITS): "Competition and Regulation in the Information Age."* 28th European Regional Conference of the International Telecommunications Society (ITS): "Competition and Regulation in the Information Age," Passau, Germany.

Rikap, C. & Lundvall, B (forthcoming) Big Tech, knowledge predation and the implications for development. *Innovation and Development*. doi: 10.1080/2157930X.2020.1855825

Marx, K. (1867). *El capital. Crítica de la economía política (Tomo I)*. Fondo de Cultura Economica.

Marx, K. (1894). *El Capital. Crítica de la economía política (Tomo III)*. Fondo de Cultura Economica.

Mazzucato, M. (2015). *The entrepreneurial state: Debunking public vs. private sector myths* (Vol. 1). Anthem Press.

Milberg, W., & Winkler, D. (2013). *Outsourcing economics: Global value chains in capitalist development*. Cambridge University Press.

Montalban, M., & Sakinç, M. E. (2013). Financialization and productive models in the pharmaceutical industry. *Industrial and Corporate Change*, *22*(4), 981–1030.

Morozov, E. (2019, February 4). Capitalism's new clothes. *The Baffler*. https://thebaffler.com/latest/capitalisms-new-clothes-morozov

Munkirs, J. R. (1983). Centralized private sector planning: An institutionalist's perspective on the contemporary US economy. *Journal of Economic Issues*, *17*(4), 931–67.

Munkirs, J. R., & Sturgeon, J. I. (1985). Oligopolistic cooperation: Conceptual and empirical evidence of market structure evolution. *Journal of Economic Issues*, *19*(4), 899–921.

Noel, M., & Schankerman, M. (2013). Strategic patenting and software innovation. *The Journal of Industrial Economics*, *61*(3), 481–520.

Norfield, T. (2017, July 27). Amazon: Becoming the market. *Economics of Imperialism*. https://economicsofimperialism.blogspot.com/2017/07/amazon-becoming-market.html

OECD. (2011). *New sources of growth: Intangible assets*. OECD Publishing.

Orhangazi, Ö. (2018). The role of intangible assets in explaining the investment–profit puzzle. *Cambridge Journal of Economics, 43*(5), 1251–86.

Pagano, U. (2014). The crisis of intellectual monopoly capitalism. *Cambridge Journal of Economics*, *38*(6), 1409–29.

Parker, R., & Cox, S. (2013). Power relations and small and medium-sized enterprise strategies for capturing value in global production networks: Visual Effects (VFX) service firms in the Hollywood film industry. *Regional Studies*, *47*(7), 1095–110.

Parrilli, M. D., Nadvi, K., & Yeung, H. W. (2013). Local and regional development in global value chains, production networks and innovation networks: A

comparative review and the challenges for future research. *European Planning Studies*, *21*(7), 967–88.
Ricardo, D. (1817). *Principios de Economía Política y Tributación*. Fondo de Cultura Economica.
Rikap, C. (2018). Innovation as economic power in global value chains. *Revue d'Économie Industrielle*, *163*, 35–75.
Rikap, C. (2019). Asymmetric power of the core: technological cooperation and technological competition in the transnational innovation networks of big pharma. *Review of International Political Economy*, *26*(5), 987–1021. doi:10.1080/09692290.2019.1620309
Rikap, C. (2020). Amazon: A story of accumulation through intellectual rentiership and predation. *Competition & Change*. doi:10.1177/1024529420932418
Rouvroy, A., & Berns, T. (2013). Gouvernementalité algorithmique et perspectives d'émancipation. Le disparate comme condition d'individuation par la relation? *Réseaux*, *177*(1), 163–96. Cairn.info. doi:10.3917/res.177.0163
Schumpeter, J. A. (1934). *The theory of economic development: An inquiry into profits, capital, credit, interest, and the business cycle*. Transaction publishers.
Schwartz, H. M. (2016). Wealth and secular stagnation: The role of industrial organization and intellectual property rights. *The Russell Sage Foundation Journal of the Social Sciences*, *2*(6), 226–49.
Serfati, C. (2008). Financial dimensions of transnational corporations, global value chain and technological innovation. *Journal of Innovation Economics & Management*, *2*, 35–61.
Shin, H. S. (2019). *What is behind the recent slowdown?* BIS.
Smith, J. (2016). *Imperialism in the twenty-first century: Globalization, super-exploitation, and capitalism's final crisis*. New York University Press.
Srnicek, N. (2017). *Platform capitalism*. Polity.
Starosta, G. (2010). The outsourcing of manufacturing and the rise of giant global contractors: A Marxian approach to some recent transformations of global value chains. *New Political Economy*, *15*(4), 543–63.
Strange, R., & Humphrey, J. (2018). What lies between market and hierarchy? Insights from internalization theory and global value chain theory. *Journal of International Business Studies*, *50*, 1401–13.
Sturgeon, T. J. (2009). From commodity chains to value chains: Interdisciplinary theory building in an age of globalization. In J. Bair (Ed.), *Frontiers of commodity chain research* (pp. 110–15). Stanford University Press. http://isapapers.pitt.edu/84/
Teixeira, R. A., & Rotta, T. N. (2012). Valueless knowledge-commodities and financialization: Productive and financial dimensions of capital autonomization. *Review of Radical Political Economics*, *44*(4), 448–67.
UNCTAD. (2019). *Digital Economy Report 2019: Value creation and capture–Implications for developing countries*. United Nations.
Veblen, T. (1899). *The theory of the leisure class: An economic theory of institutions*. Macmillen.
Veblen, T. (1908a). On the nature of capital. *The Quarterly Journal of Economics*, *22*(4), 517–42.
Veblen, T. (1908b). On the nature of capital: Investment, intangible assets, and the pecuniary magnate. *The Quarterly Journal of Economics*, *23*(1), 104–36.

World Bank. (2020). *World Development Report 2020: Trading for development in the age of global value chains*. World Bank Publications.
World Intellectual Property Organization. (2019). *WIPO Technology Trends 2019. Artificial Intelligence*. WIPO.
WTO. (2019). *World Trade Statistical Review 2019*. World Trade Organization.
Zingales, L. (2017). Towards a political theory of the firm. *Journal of Economic Perspectives*, *31*(3), 113–30.
Zuboff, S. (2019). *The age of surveillance capitalism: The fight for the future at the new frontier of power*. Profile Books.

3

KNOWLEDGE PRIVATIZATION AND POWER RELATIONS IN THE KNOWLEDGE COMMONS

1 Introduction

The progressive use of open-source software (OSS) by high-tech giants as well as big pharmaceuticals' incursion into knowledge commons in health and biomedical research revives ideas on how capitalist relations *engraft* elements of other social relations in its own favour. This idea comes from Mariátegui (1979) who explains that when the Spaniards conquered Latin America, elements of the slave economy were *engrafted* in capitalist relations by building on Inca's pre-existent exploitation relations. This led the author to conclude that capital –as a social relation of exploitation – can profit from other social relations. As far as it can do so, it does not need to reconvert those production relations into typical capitalist ones. The survival of slavery also evidences this sort of colonizing arm of capital over pre-existent social relations that exist as a clandestine and illegal – nonetheless frequent – practice in certain parts of the world (Miers, 2000).

OSS and the knowledge commons were born seeking to produce knowledge collaboratively and voluntarily and to benefit communities at large, counterbalancing or subverting knowledge privatization and assetization (Coriat, 2012, 2013, 2015; Orsi, 2015; Orsi & Zimmermann, 2011; Schrape, 2018; Williams, 2010). However, we will argue that intellectual monopolies have engrafted elements of these collaborative relationships in their innovation systems. Therefore, we elaborate on how capital accumulation can also be based on knowledge commons and open access despite their subversive origin.

As we developed in-depth in Chapter 2, 21st-century global leader corporations are intellectual monopolies accumulating a significant share of their profits from a higher concentration of intangible assets, triggering intellectual rents. In this chapter, we start by acknowledging key stepping-stones in the legal and political transformation that fostered intellectual monopoly capitalism. We argue that knowledge commons and open access emerged as a reaction to knowledge privatization. However, we show that this reaction is also being used by intellectual monopolies to strengthen their lead.

In Chapter 2 we explained that intellectual monopolies garner rents from knowledge produced beyond their in-house innovation efforts since they plan and organize innovation networks from which they appropriate and assetize resulting knowledge. Building on the latter, this chapter argues that intellectual monopolies develop specific innovation networks as open access or knowledge commons initiatives. In other words, the main contribution of this chapter is to conceptualize how – and under which circumstances – open access and knowledge commons are strategies followed by intellectual monopolies to achieve knowledge modules or steps later integrated into broader innovation and production processes from which they privately profit.

To empirically illustrate these dynamics, we explore multiple cases of open access or knowledge commons where intellectual monopolies have been involved and trace their (potential) benefits. We have selected cases from pharmaceutical and high-tech industries, which are paradigmatic fields in a twofold way. First, they are at the forefront in terms of intellectual monopoly capitalism showing the highest concentrations of intangible assets and profits, as shown by Orhangazi (2018) for the United States. Second, and at least partially to counterattack the effects of knowledge privatization, there is a vast and vibrant community working on open access and knowledge commons in these fields (see, for instance, Stallman, 2002; Williams, 2010). Overall, we show that by engaging in these apparently non-market initiatives, intellectual monopolies find new businesses, favour their innovation flow, reduce capital commitments (including R&D investments) and innovation risks and increase profits by monetizing free work.

The rest of this chapter is organized as follows. Section 2 refers to the main features of intellectual monopoly capitalism, focusing on legal and political transformations that favoured knowledge privatization. Section 3 conceptually analyses open access and knowledge commons. These theoretical sections are followed by illustrative examples of the interrelations between intellectual monopolies and forms of open access or knowledge commons for pharmaceutical and high-tech fields in Section 4. Section 5 concludes.

2 Intellectual monopoly capitalism and the privatization of knowledge

The year 1980 represents an inflection point for public knowledge privatization in the United States and even beyond considering its global hegemony. That year the Bayh-Dole Act authorized academic institutions to patent public-funded research results and to transfer this knowledge to private firms by providing exclusive licenses or creating joint ventures (Berman,

2011; Bok, 2003; Mowery, 2005; Orsi & Coriat, 2006). It meant that universities became entitled to economically profit from their research and eventually led to the creation of technology transfer offices (TTOs) in every US university (Merrill et at, 2004). According to Angell (2004), the Bayh-Dole Act not only favoured spin-off biotechnology companies, but also (and primarily) big pharmaceuticals working with universities. In 1965, research areas connected with the pharmacy industry had 15% of total university patents in the USPTO, rising to 35% by 1988 (Mowery, 2005).

The Bayh-Dole Act was one of a series of critical elements of a general US policy aimed at strengthening intellectual property rights (IPRs) globally (Mowery, 2005; Pestre, 2003). It was coupled with many court decisions that further strengthened the IPRs system in the following years (Berman, 2011; Mowery, 2005). The time span of IPRs was extended; more severe sanctions for infringements were introduced, and the definition of what IPR could protect was expanded widely to include living beings, software and architectural work. As Orsi and Coriat (2006) explain, the Bayh-Dole Act contributed to transforming US knowledge advantage in pharmaceutical and computing science into a market advantage, while the right to patent generic knowledge excluded rivals. Altogether, these transformations reinforced US supremacy on top of which they paved the way for intellectual monopoly capitalism (see Chapter 4 for a deeper analysis of US policies contributing to the emergence of intellectual monopoly capitalism).

The concentration of legal intellectual rents was benefited by the international strengthening of IPRs, which formally began in 1995 with the Trade Related Aspects of Intellectual Property Rights (TRIPS) agreement. For Dreyfuss and Frankel (2014, p. 459), TRIPS not only meant a step towards international law-making for intellectual property. It was also a shift in how intellectual property was conceived, from barrier to trade – as it was considered in the General Agreement on Tariffs and Trade – to become "a tradable commodity in the name of facilitating trade". The US government played a crucial role in conditioning trade agreements to the strengthening of IPRs in developing countries, thus pushing for new World Trade Organization (WTO) rules regarding IPRs. As we mentioned in Chapter 1, behind this global expansion of IPRs lies the pressure of multinational US-based intellectual monopolies, such as IBM, Microsoft and Pfizer, that were concerned about the rise of piracy and generic drugs in developing countries (Drahos, 1995).

After TRIPS, an international regime of IPRs was incepted. A set of free trade agreements, bilateral investment treaties and regional pacts followed. They transformed IPRs into an investment asset, emphasizing the "property" rhetoric (Orsi & Coriat, 2006). Among other changes, this allowed patent holders to demand arbitrations at the international level, which until then was a states' dispute that took place at the WTO (Dreyfuss & Frankel, 2014).

Wade (2019) argues that these transformations reproduced core-periphery dynamics, reinforced in a twofold way: by leading companies and by core states because the latter actively seek to protect their global corporations. Global stricter agreements on IPRs benefit countries at the forefront of new technologies, limiting *learning by copying*, thus reducing chances to economically profit from successful reverse engineering in the peripheries. More in general, in line with Teixeira and Rotta (2012), knowledge privatization is a new form of enclosure that deprives labour of knowledge as a means of production. As Figures 1.3 and 1.4 in Chapter 1 show, IPRs increase in the 21st century stands out. Between 2009 and 2019, USPTO applied patents per year grew 40% and granted patents more than doubled.[1]

Overall, these legal and political transformations fostered the rise of intangible over tangible assets (Chen et al., 2017; Crouzet & Eberly, 2018; Haskel & Westlake, 2018). Intangibles' supremacy was further encouraged by a 1984 US regulation that authorized market entry and listing of companies with a deficit as long as they had sufficient intangible capital (Orsi & Coriat, 2006).

According to Harvey (2002), TRIPS strengthened monopoly power by reinforcing intangibles' assetization. As we discussed in more detail in Chapter 2, intellectual monopolies have been associated with the concentration of IPRs (Boldrin & Levine, 2008; Pagano, 2014; Schwartz, 2016) and more broadly with the assetization of intangible goods thus to exclusive access to knowledge (Durand & Milberg, 2020; Orhangazi, 2018). Knowledge can be transformed into an asset by law, using copyright, trademarks, industrial designs or patents, depending on its nature. It can also be assetized when it is kept as industrial secrets or tacit knowledge. By turning knowledge into assets, intellectual monopolies appropriate the alternatively called intellectual rents, also called technoscientific and knowledge rents (Birch, 2019; Durand & Milberg, 2020; Foley, 2013; Kaplinsky, 1998; Pagano, 2014; Teixeira & Rotta, 2012). As Harvey (2007) explains, intellectual rents are accumulation by dispossession because knowledge's form of property changed from public or common to private.

As it was also further developed in Chapter 2, intellectual monopolies renew their leadership by introducing continuous innovations. Systematic innovations reinforce entry barriers that depend on their sustained and colossal investments in R&D, as evidenced by Nuccio and Guerzoni (2019), but also rely on their capacity to capture and predate knowledge from other organizations. Rikap (2019) explained that intellectual monopolies simultaneously control and orient R&D by organizing multiple innovation networks integrated by different organizations (typically research institutions and start-ups). This outsourcing innovation strategy contributes to preserve and enlarge intellectual monopolies' position of power by predating knowledge results from those networks. Knowledge is turned into assets, triggering greater intellectual rents.

In this chapter, we broaden the scope of intellectual monopolies' corporate innovation systems, understood as all the innovation networks planned by the intellectual monopoly together with its in-house R&D. Here we add that innovation networks can also be integrated by actors participating in open access or knowledge commons. In fact, innovation networks themselves can be organized as an open-access or knowledge commons initiative still led by the intellectual monopoly. Closed innovation strategies could be complemented with these alternative forms of knowledge production as far as intellectual monopolies can still garner private benefits. If they extract value and intellectual rents that they would not get otherwise, complementary forms of innovation will actually maximize intellectual monopolies' gains while strengthening their economic power. The next section further explores the emergence and conceptualization of open access and knowledge commons followed by an exploratory analysis of how pharmaceutical and high-tech intellectual monopolies take advantage of them.

3 Knowledge commons and open access to knowledge

Alternative forms of knowledge (*cum* innovation) production have been explicitly developed to counterbalance or offer an alternative to knowledge privatization. This is the case of open science or open access – the latter particularly related to OSS – (Scheufen, 2014; Schrape, 2018) and the knowledge commons (Coriat, 2012, 2013, 2015; Orsi, 2015; Orsi & Zimmermann, 2011).

OSS has its origins in free software with the pioneering work of Richard Stallman, founder of the Free Software Foundation. Copyleft – in opposition to copyrights – states that every software using and adapting free software must also be free (Stallman, 2002; Williams, 2010). But *free* means two things in English, that the price is zero and freedom. It was the latter meaning what the free software movement embraced when they voted for "open source" as their new name in a free software summit in Mozilla's launch party; Stallman was not invited. This paved the way for different licencing alternatives to copyrights all considered as open source. The most popular one is Apache, which is more business friendly because it does not require to make the software using OSS free, as copyleft does. The former became widely used and, by 2010, a popular version of Apache web server software was being distributed by IBM, which was a proprietary modified version of the original free software (Williams, 2010).

The Open Source Initiative defines OSS after a series of conditions that include but are not limited to open-source code. It must be freely distributed software, include at least part of the source code, allow distribution of the source code as well as of its compiled form. The licence must allow modifications and derived work and must not discriminate against persons, groups or fields.[2] Overall, the Open Source Initiative promotes open access to intangible goods that are produced in a shared or collaborative way. It is worth noting that most big US companies increasingly use OSS influenced by cheaper costs and network effects (Spinellis & Giannikas, 2012).

The coexistence of these two forms of software has led Casadesus-Masanell and Ghemawat (2006) to argue that there is a duopoly between open source and proprietary software. Moving a step further, and recognizing that intellectual monopolies nowadays dominate proprietary software, Boldrin and Levine (2008) claimed that these two forms of property are incompatible. They added that only open access to or competition for innovation – unlike intellectual monopolies – trigger real, transformative innovations. Using the example of Microsoft, the authors argued that this intellectual monopoly only reacted against piracy and looked after its IPRs once it lagged in innovation, but not during its "early creative days" (Boldrin & Levine, 2008, p. 17). They interpret Microsoft's reaction as a way to protect itself after its shortfall of new ideas and growing competition. Simultaneously, the authors highlighted the emergence of OSS as a successful initiative of continuous new developments based on free and open competition.

Overall, and as shown by Spinellis and Giannikas's (2012) literature review, there are multiple scientific analyses focused on the reasons beneath private companies' adoption of OSS as well as on the software market understood as divided between these two supposedly incompatible forms of property. Less attention has been paid to private companies' involvement not only in adopting or using but in developing and boosting OSS projects. Here we argue that the latter has become a regular practice of high-tech intellectual monopolies' innovation strategy.

We share with Boldrin and Levin (2008) that IPRs are not a precondition for innovation. Nevertheless, our analysis nuances the dichotomy between both systems and shows how intellectual monopoly goes beyond IPRs and other forms of closed knowledge like secrecy, profiting from open access as in the case of high-tech giants profiting from OSS.

In some respects, OSS initiatives intersect with the knowledge (or, more precisely, digital) commons. However, the latter always have explicit managing rules (concerning access, use, production, among others), which is not always the case with OSS initiatives. Knowledge commons were defined by some authors following a resource-based definition, focusing on the internet (David, 2000; Hess & Ostrom, 2007). Other authors consider that the commons is a different innovation regime. In Coriat and Orsi's framework, the resource is a needed condition of a commons – in the case of knowledge commons these are intangible resources – but two other conditions must be met to speak of a commons: a bundle of rights attributed to different stakeholders and a governing structure that, in the case of knowledge commons, assures shared resources' enrichment and growth (Coriat, 2011, 2012, 2013, 2015; Orsi, 2015; Orsi & Zimmermann, 2011).

Another group of authors considers commons as an alternative social relation to commodities, each of them characterized by its own logics and practices. Contributions to this conception come both from activists (Bauwens, 2015; Bollier & Helfrich, 2015; Helfrich, 2015) and academics (Dardot & Laval, 2014). From a Marxian framework, according to Dardot and Laval (2014), commodities and commons are not just different kinds of products but also different ways of producing; thus, different social relations of production. They differ in *how* something is produced, focusing on the bonds established during that process, instead of the produced goods. Considering commons as a social relationship means that everything could be produced as commons. Likewise, and it has been the case, everything can be produced as a commodity, even knowledge.

The commodity-producer is a worker detached from the product of her work, whose goal is to sell resulting products, thus guaranteeing her social reproduction. Even if under capitalism humans are in contact with more human beings than ever before, individuality is at the basis of commodity producers' logic. On the contrary, the commons social relationship is explicitly based on coproduction logics and practices, solidarity and sharing (Dardot & Laval, 2014). It is a self-governing process, while market laws govern commodity production. Among the logics that construct the commons' social relationship, Bollier and Helfrich (2015) and Helfrich (2015) suggest three factors as indispensable: sustainability, equality and freedom.

All these approaches recognize the commons as separate from – or even in contradiction with and counterbalancing – capitalist accumulation. Without neglecting this potential, the following section shows how intellectual monopolies have engrafted knowledge commons as well as open access under their accumulation strategy.

4 How intellectual monopolies profit from open access and knowledge commons. Illustrative experiences

There are multiple examples of intellectual monopolies engaging in developing open access or joining knowledge commons. What is the rationale for this behaviour? Reputational gains could be an underlying reason. According to Orsi (2012), big pharmaceuticals get involved in commons as a strategy to regain governments and public opinion's sympathy. We suggest a complementary –and possibly more compelling – explanation. IPRs (and other forms of closed knowledge) may not always be the best alternative for triggering greater economic profits from successful innovations. We will elaborate on this statement by analysing big pharmaceuticals' participation in knowledge commons and high-tech intellectual monopolies engagement in OSS.

4.1 Knowledge commons in the pharmaceutical innovation system

The literature agrees that big pharmaceuticals changed their R&D strategy when existing blockbuster patents were expiring while they failed to discover new blockbuster drugs. Their new R&D strategy combines mergers and acquisitions with the outsourcing of most of their R&D (Collier, 2011; Lazonick et al., 2017; Montalban & Sakinç, 2013; Tralau-Stewart et al., 2009). As identified by Tralau-Stewart et al. (2009), this new strategy meant a new division of intellectual labour. Universities deliver new therapeutic entities, and companies remain in charge of pre-clinical and clinical development. The result of this process, however, has been an unequal distribution of intellectual rents. As shown in depth in Chapter 6, while big pharmaceuticals have dense R&D networks that include all major universities in the world, they do not share with these institutions the resulting IPRs.

This turn in big pharmaceuticals' R&D strategies towards relying more on outsourced innovation systems is in line with Gagnon's (2015) findings, which put into question the relevance of big pharma's R&D investments. The author has shown that in 2011 US pharmaceuticals spent more on promotional activities directed to healthcare professionals (US$54 billion) than on R&D (US$50 billion). In the same year, they paid US$8.4 billion to physicians, US$4 billion were paid in direct-to-consumer advertising and US$228 million in lobbying. Anyway, big pharmaceuticals remain among top companies in the world in terms of business expenditure in R&D, with five big pharmaceuticals in the top 20 (European Commission, 2019).

Big pharmaceuticals' new R&D strategy includes participating in commons-based initiatives. Using different forms of property over knowledge for their own benefit is not new for these intellectual monopolies. According to Rai (2007), in the late 1990s, big pharmaceuticals attempted to put all the single nucleotide polymorphism (SNPs) information into the public domain to prevent small biotechnology companies from owning a large number of SNP patents. The SNPs are used to identify genes useful for finding cures for complex diseases and for predicting responses to therapies. The same happened with the Genetic Association Information Network (GAIN) created in 2007. The outcome of this project (information about the haplotypes associated with particular diseases) was also put into the public domain following action by big pharmaceuticals (Rai, 2007). Pharma intellectual monopolies are interested in these initiatives because they reinforce their dominant position.

Besides limiting rivals and potential reputational gains, big pharmaceuticals profit from knowledge commons to find new promising businesses. Sheridan (2011) studies knowledge commons involving universities and big pharmaceuticals. The author analyses experiences where the latter socialize their R&D resources and facilities with academic researchers so they can develop their research with state-of-the-art technology. If they arrive at a successful result, the big pharma hosting them has the privilege of being the first one to negotiate the exclusive license or, in some cases, it can share the IPRs. This strategy has almost zero cost for the intellectual monopoly since researchers use their already installed equipment and facilities. Sheridan (2011) also points out the example of Eli Lilly's "Open Innovation Drug Discovery", where academics and researchers can submit new structures that are tested against known diseases' targets in Eli Lilly's laboratories. The big pharma keeps the right of first negotiating IPR agreements over the results. Even if results are not patented, the enterprise will learn from top researchers working for free in its laboratories. Thus, both alternatives represent a source of greater profits for the pharmaceutical company.

Other examples of knowledge commons deal with finding new cures or treatments for malaria. A specific malaria project was driven by the Drugs for Neglected Diseases Initiative and resulted in the improvement of an existing drug based on a molecule patented by Sanofi. The project relied on the free work of public laboratories in France and different affected countries. As part of the deal, whenever this improved drug is bought for public provision in affected countries, the price is meagre, while Sanofi can freely decide the price when selling it to privates (Branciard, 2012). It is crystal clear that peripheral countries would have never been able to buy a new malaria drug unless it was affordable. Therefore, Sanofi has cross-subsidized the price of this drug. Without compromising further R&D investments, Sanofi got an improved drug that it sells globally but at differentiated prices according to states' payment capacities. Furthermore, even if it sells at low but profitable prices to peripheral countries, selling millions of drugs to affected countries' public sector[3] still assures greater revenues without additional costs.

Sanofi does not have the exclusive licence of this resulting drug, leaving the door open for generics production. However, intellectual monopolies like Sanofi do not necessarily depend on owning patents in order to profit from innovations. Their lobby, advertising and direct payment to physicians contribute to place their products as the preferred ones over generic versions. Moreover, scale and planning capacity allows intellectual monopolies to overcome potential competition, in this case, from generic producers. This is why they can accept not having the exclusive license of a result that was anyway produced elsewhere.

Moreover, generic producers do not necessarily sell at prices that would compromise big pharmaceuticals' profits. In the case of HIV/AIDS drugs, Sagaon-Teyssier et al. (2016, p. 8) showed that "formal or informal agreements between generic firms may *de facto* slow down or even reverse long-term trends towards price decreases" and that the expiration of a patent is not enough to boost generic companies.

Another example is the WIPO Re:Search[4] project, born in 2011. It is based on the royalty-free licence of thousands of molecules whose patents are owned by big pharmaceuticals (such as Alnylam Pharmaceuticals, AstraZeneca, GlaxoSmithKline, Merck, Novartis, Pfizer and Sanofi), universities and public and not-for-profit organizations. The aim is to promote research for neglected tropical diseases, malaria and tuberculosis. This project represents a source of additional profits without capital expenditures for big pharmaceuticals; they only have to release their IPRs, patents that low-income countries would not have been in the position to license anyway. Without engaging in additional R&D, they still get extra profits when selling successful results. Hence, big pharmaceuticals' production costs will only include the reproduction value, which is negligible compared to the R&D investment done by universities or public research organizations in order to find vaccines or treatments from molecules.

Summing up, allowing universities to access patented molecules or equipment and facilities freely allows big pharmaceuticals to organize R&D within their innovation networks that may eventually open up commercial opportunities. Earnings from renting facilities or from royalties from their patented molecules are lower than potential intellectual rents in case successful discoveries are achieved without likewise investments, thus at low (or even zero) risks. Hence, these initiatives not only contribute to clean big pharma's reputation but also to expand their profits.

4.2 Open source and the digital commons

Big tech companies have not always embraced OSS and the digital commons. Microsoft's intellectual monopoly had strongly relied on the tightening of IPRs, in particular TRIPS, and the authorization to patent or claim copyrights for software (Arthur, 2012). Its former CEO had even claimed that OSS was *a cancer.*[5] However, since the beginning of the 21st century, with IBM as a pioneer, US big ICT corporations got involved in OSS projects. This strategy became quite popular since these intellectual monopolies have found multiple ways to profit and specially to garner rents for sponsoring and hosting OSS projects, profiting from ideas and knowledge produced in the open-source environment. Over time, OSS became an indispensable part of the innovation strategy of all sorts of information and technology companies (Schrape, 2018).

In this chapter, we are interested in the inequalities between intellectual monopolies and the rest of the system. While it is quite clear that most OSS developers also work for private organizations, therefore these two realms were never really detached, the capacity of intellectual monopolies to profit from OSS development is a relatively new and undertheorized phenomenon. It is not only IBM or later Samsung aiming to counterbalance the power of Microsoft or Google, which are promoting OSS as rivals to the latter.[6] Google and Microsoft themselves, as well as Facebook and to a lesser extent Amazon, profit by organizing corporate innovation systems that combine private/proprietary and open-source projects. For their private business, they organize innovation networks with universities and start-up companies that secretly contribute to their R&D objectives (becoming public only if and once IPRs protect results). Meanwhile, besides potential reputational gains, they profit in the following complementary ways from OSS.

1 By integrating OSS initiatives, intellectual monopolies get access to code that they can reuse for their own private innovations. As Lan et al. (2019) show, OSS attracts large numbers of developers and complementors worldwide, expanding the amount of code that can be privately reused.
2 OSS projects also provide information on the type of recurrent problems faced by smaller companies, which are valuable inputs for new services to be offered by tech giants in their cloud services. In more general terms, OSS is a business for companies offering adjacent or complementary services. It is what Red Hat (Linux's provider) profits from, but it is also what US tech giants do when they foster OSS projects that are complementary to their cloud services, which is a billion-dollar market.[7]
3 Intellectual monopolies get potential users' feedback in advance because open-source developers are usually employees of companies that will buy code or features – for instance through cloud servicing – that may result from the OSS project.
4 By placing modules of their in-house innovation in open-source platforms, intellectual monopolies profit from developers' free work. Intellectual monopolies profit from the work of OSS developers without hiring them, thus without associated capital commitments. Eventually, developers not working for tech giants who often include in their duties collaborating with OSS (Schrape, 2018) may end up having a double (unpaid) shift. They work for the company paying their salary and for OSS projects that more often than not end up reinforcing the power and profits of high-tech intellectual monopolies. This can be considered as a paradox since OSS sprang from a resistance to software privatization. When needed, intellectual monopolies grant funds to developers working on projects of their particular interest as a means to foster or reorient her coding. However, even this payment is cheaper than hiring the developer in-house with a stable position. Moreover, it grants a wider set of opportunities regarding whom to encourage. Intellectual monopolies can choose from millions of OSS developers, and funding one at some point is a decision that can easily be reconsidered if they find someone else with potentially more path-breaking ideas.

GitHub is a development platform for developers. It had more than 31 million registered developers as of September 30, 2018, soaring to more than 50 million, as stated in its introductory page, by 2020.[8] Reports for 2018 show that public and open-source activity across this platform is mostly concentrated after 5 pm, further increasing as the night arrives. Moreover, even if overall activity lowers during weekends, it is OSS and public projects (as compared to private projects hosted by GitHub for which companies pay fees and have closed access) those with the highest weekend workloads.[9]

5 A potentially fifth rationale for intellectual monopolies' engagement in OSS could be the short innovation cycle that characterizes the international software industry (Schrape, 2018). Coupled with the high investments needed to develop such standards for platforms, if the timespan to profit from that investment is short, it may make more sense to leave basic infrastructures as OSS developed beyond high-tech intellectual monopolies. Meanwhile, intellectual monopolies focus on innovations that can be greatly monetized, expanding their intellectual rents.

Considering these ways of profiting from OSS, in what follows, we focus on Microsoft's and Google's incursions into OSS. Among US digital giants, they have been the most active in the digital commons' ecosystem.

Microsoft diversified its innovation strategy since 2014, both in terms of technologies and ways to organize innovation networks. From an intellectual monopoly mostly based on legal monopoly rents, it became a data-driven intellectual monopoly. As stated in its most recent annual report, its ability to convert data processed with machine learning algorithms into digital intelligence is driving its competitive advantage (Microsoft, 2019).

A key point in Microsoft's recent astonishing evolution is how it changed from a copyright paradigm rivalling with Linux and other OSS, to partner with them (and by doing so significantly profit from them). Microsoft included a Linux kernel in Windows 10 to profit from Linux developments. This includes profiting from features developed by freelancers working on the Linux platform because they can be integrated into Microsoft business at no cost and potentially offering future direct or indirect gains.[10]

To complement or even to feed this Linux Kernel, Microsoft bought Github for $7.5bn in 2018. The acquisition was announced amid subscriptions' explosion, with 8 million new developers that joined between October 2017 and September 2018. Github provided Microsoft professional data of millions of developers and data on more than 140 million repositories (almost a third of which were created between October 2018 and September 2019).[11] Overall, it is used as a platform to profit in all the ways mentioned earlier.

In the case of Google, its innovation system combines closed in-house and secretly kept innovations – which typically support major or path-breaking innovations – with different forms of open innovation (Steiber & Alänge, 2013, p. 259). In the latter, this intellectual monopoly either outsources knowledge steps or uses open access to extract more value, this time from the work of independent developers while opening other data collection fronts.

A frequently used outsourcing strategy concerns apps development. Every handset in the world but iPhone (and other Apple products) runs on Android, an open-source platform for mobile phone applications launched in 2008. By offering Android as OSS for free, Google bundles other products by default, such as Chrome, and encapsulates handset users to buy or download for free but with Ads applications through Google Play. Applications are innovative products of an army of external developers. This scheme has a zero cost for Google, and the same goes for Apple's iOS but the latter is mostly a closed source. In both platforms, individuals or small innovating companies incur in all the production costs, while Google and Apple decide which apps will be sold and when, without paying any direct remuneration to developers and keeping a fee from the app's price or associated Ads (Bergvall-Kareborn & Howcroft, 2013).[12] As we pointed out in Chapter 2, innovating companies subordinated to intellectual monopolies only enjoy a portion of their innovations' triggered rents. They assume all the risks and, if successful, enjoy only a share of the revenues.

Profiting from the free work of highly trained developers was also at the basis of Google's decision to move Kubernetes to open source in 2014. Kubernetes is a container system for running multiple programs on demand and simultaneously, in a more efficient way than virtual servers. In its website, it says, "Kubernetes builds upon a decade and a half of experience that Google has with running production workloads at scale, combined with best-of-breed ideas and practices from the community" (https://kubernetes.io/docs/concepts/overview/what-is-kubernetes/), thus explicitly recognizing the unpaid contribution of external developers. Kubernetes is also an open window for offering cloud services that are complementary to the former. Google can particularly target companies that suddenly increased traffic in Kubernetes, which implicitly shows a growing and healthy business.

High-tech intellectual monopolies, in particular Microsoft and Google, not only own OSS platforms but are also among top organizations running OSS projects. By October 2018, Github's top three open-source projects in terms of the number of participating developers belonged to high-tech intellectual monopolies: Microsoft/vscode with 19,000 developers, facebook/react-native with 10,000 developers and tensorflow/tensorflow (9,300 developers). The latter is a huge machine-learning library that Google put in open source in 2015.[13] Other intellectual monopolies' projects in the top ten were MicrosoftDocs/azure-docs (7,800 developers) and Google's kubernetes/kubernetes (6,500 developers).

If we couple this information with figures on intellectual monopolies' employees that have a profile in GitHub, we can provide evidence of intellectual monopolies profiting from unpaid work. Microsoft had, by October

2018, 7,700 registered developers, Google had 5,500 and Facebook had 1,700[14], thus way less than the number of developers that collaborated with their top OSS projects. Albeit developers' voluntary decision to participate, GitHub becomes close to an informal labour market.

Comparing these projects with the case of Android point to two modes of profiting from OSS. In the case of Android, developers do not contribute to the core infrastructure of the platform but create complementary products and keep the property of the result, thus partially profiting from it. In the case of GitHub OSS projects led by Google, Microsoft and Facebook, the result is OSS, thus potentially useful for anyone. However, it is monetized only once it is integrated into more complex systems. We may expect that other parts of those more complex systems are kept as private software by tech giants.

Overall, it may be argued that when innovations rely on codified knowledge that can be modularized, relying on others' building blocks can become a preferred strategy. Intellectual monopolies build the foundations of their innovations from the creative work of OSS developers as well as academic researchers (see Chapters 7 and 8 on Apple and Amazon), avoiding risks and reducing R&D investments. These foundational steps or building blocks will not be what differentiates each intellectual monopoly. Still, these innovations could be structural (and indispensable) steps in order to achieve new hits. If open-source developers build the foundations, then the tech giant only needs to "encourage" (typically by funding) those working in line with its priorities.

By modularizing intangibles, as tech giants further engage in OSS, what differentiates each of them will remain a secret to keep rivals at bay. For instance, it was made clear in a document for its workers that Microsoft "cautions employees not to use the cloud version of GitHub 'for Highly Confidential types of information, specs or code.' The on-premises version of GitHub does not appear on the list."[15] This restriction makes it clear that open source is used for developments that are not at intellectual monopolies' core and that they are far from genuinely supporting these initiatives. Their strategy seems to be twofold: profit from IPRs and secrecy while, at the same time, they exploit OSS.

5 Final remarks

Our results are in line with Dolata's (2017) claims for high-tech giants; intellectual monopolies have a closed core and open peripheries when it comes to innovation. Both analysed cases show that intellectual monopolies establish a balance between secrecy for what is considered as most sensitive, and openness when they can still garner intellectual rents. Openness not only leads to outsourcing knowledge modules in universities, public research institutions or innovating companies (see Chapters 2 and 5). It also involves participating in open access and knowledge commons' initiatives from which they privately profit.

High-tech giants keep in secret the most path-breaking algorithms. The basic infrastructure is kept in-house, but the apps and software that run on top are significantly outsourced or retrieved from OSS projects. In the case of big pharmaceuticals' strategy towards knowledge commons, there is a clear split between core and peripheral countries' diseases that often guides their decisions. When incentives are not enough to privately invest or support university research on certain diseases, different forms of knowledge commons tend to be preferred.

Therefore, we may argue that in order to define the mode in which each innovation module will be produced, intellectual monopoly considers different factors. Who are the most suitable actors for succeeding in producing that knowledge module? Could rents be maximized if it outsources the module, thus the risk? Would the latter question's answer hold if it shares the result with others instead of individually compromising the needed investments and keeping risks in-house but also keeping all the potential intellectual rents? At the basis of each innovation circuit (defined in Chapter 2 as all the organizations participating in a single innovation project controlled by an intellectual monopoly), the intellectual monopoly calculates an economic and risk equation. It can either de-compromise intangible capital investment and profit from part of the resulting intellectual rents when successful, or compromise intangible capital and solely face risks but keep all the potential rents. The intellectual monopoly is capable of decoupling that circuit in multiple innovation modules, and, for each of them, it recalculates the equation.

Hence, the innovation strategy of an intellectual monopoly can be summed up as a set of meticulously coordinated interplays. It combines multiple modes of producing intangibles and actors (individual workers, public research organizations, innovating companies) according to what it considers most suitable for each innovation circuit within its corporate innovation system. In terms of the specific strategies analysed in this chapter, as far as the intellectual monopoly keeps expanding its knowledge monopoly (and thus capture more rents), it will encourage open science and knowledge commons' initiatives.

This chapter analysed cases where intellectual monopolies garner rents even when knowledge formally remains public. These cases highlight the need to conceptualize further Pagano's (2014) understanding of intellectual monopolies as limited to the concentration of IPRs. In this respect, Durand and Milberg's (2020) taxonomy is more comprehensive and provides further insights for understanding intellectual monopoly capitalism, as we develop in Chapter 7. The types of intangible rents they recognize should be analysed in an integrated manner if we aim to fully grasp the scope of contemporary intellectual monopoly capitalism, in particular of high-tech intellectual monopolies.

To conclude, we still consider that there is room for contesting IPRs (and intellectual monopolies in particular) by further nurturing the knowledge commons and OSS. Regardless of pessimistic views that claim that these initiatives have lost their subversive potential (Schrape, 2018), not every commons or open-source platform has been opened to intellectual monopolies' participation and private profit. Wikipedia is an example of a digital commons that has, so far, remained detached from them. Further developing and supporting these commons, at least to assure their survival in the context of expanding intellectual monopolies, should be out of the question. Still, it is clear that they are not enough to limit private profiting from knowledge, which requires stronger policies at the global level tackling multiple dimensions of intellectual monopoly capitalism. For instance, in the case of OSS, concrete policies could contribute to mitigating the private appropriation of intellectual rents. In terms of licences, Copyleft could be preferred over Apache Licence 2.0 because the former is stricter in terms of how users of the code can profit from it. Chapter 14 offers complementary policy recommendations.

In any case, this chapter has highlighted that our understanding of intellectual monopoly capitalism requires delving into the place of national states, in particular the United States, as guarantors of IPRs. Chapter 4 addresses this claim and elaborates on the interrelations between the US and Chinese states and their respective intellectual monopolies.

Notes

1 https://www.uspto.gov/web/offices/ac/ido/oeip/taf/us_stat.htm.
2 The full definition is available at https://opensource.org/osd.
3 According to the WHO, malaria-infected population surpasses the 200 million. http://www.who.int/features/factfiles/malaria/es/.
4 The official WIPO Re:Search web page hosts a complete description of the project and its members (http://www.wipo.int/pressroom/en/articles/2011/article_0026.html).
5 See for instance https://www.economist.com/leaders/2019/07/25/what-microsofts-revival-can-teach-other-tech-companies?cid1=cust/ednew/n/bl/n/2019/07/25n/owned/n/n/nwl/n/n/la/283453/n.
6 Scharpe (2018) claims that in the past IBM tried to offset Microsoft by investing hundreds of USD millions in Linux. IBM also offered services connected to OSS, thus reinforcing the latter was a way to boost its own business.
7 CBInsights (2018) estimated that cloud computing will be a USD 513 billion market and cloud storage USD 90 billion, by 2022 (a forecast made before the digital boom triggered by the Covid-19 pandemic).
8 Even if real figures are certainly lower because they are based on accounts and not on real contributions of distinct people, it is for sure a community of millions of developers.
9 https://octoverse.github.com/2018/.
10 https://www.theverge.com/2019/5/6/18534687/microsoft-windows-10-linux-kernel-feature.
11 https://octoverse.github.com/.
12 Apple was accused of having a gatekeeper role in the US Congress big tech hearing of 2020. Surprisingly, this was not a major complaint against Google.
13 More information at https://www.tensorflow.org/.

14 https://octoverse.github.com/2018/.
15 https://www.geekwire.com/2019/no-slack-microsoft-puts-rival-app-internal-list-prohibited-discouraged-software/.

References

Arthur, C. (2012). *Digital wars: Apple, Google, Microsoft and the battle for the Internet.* Kogan Page Publishers.

Bauwens, M. (2015). The political economy of peer production. *CTheory.*

Bergvall-Kareborn, B., & Howcroft, D. (2013). The Apple business model: Crowdsourcing mobile applications. *Accounting Forum, 37,* 280–89.

Berman, E. P. (2011). *Creating the market university: How academic science became an economic engine.* Princeton University Press.

Birch, K. (2019). Technoscience rent: Toward a theory of rentiership for technoscientific capitalism. *Science, Technology, & Human Values, 45*(1), 3–33.

Bok, D. (2003). *Universities in the marketplace.* Princeton University Press. http://www.jstor.org/stable/pdf/3699915.pdf

Boldrin, M., & Levine, D. K. (2008). *Against intellectual monopoly.* Cambridge University Press.

Bollier, D., & Helfrich, S. (2015). Overture. In D. Bollier & S. Helfrich (Eds.), *Patterns of commoning* (pp. 1–12). The Commons Strategy Group.

Branciard, A. (2012). *Des modèles de recherche-développement ouverts et collaboratifs dans le domaine pharmaceutique: Vers des "communs"?* ANR Propice, Working Paper 2012/17.

Casadesus-Masanell, R., & Ghemawat, P. (2006). Dynamic mixed duopoly: A model motivated by Linux vs. Windows. *Management Science, 52*(7), 1072–84.

CBInsights. (2018). *Amazon strategy teardown.* CBInsights.

Chen, W., Gouma, R., Los, B., & Timmer, M. P. (2017). *Measuring the income to intangibles in goods production: A global value chain approach.* World Intellectual Property Organization-Economics and Statistics Division.

Collier, R. (2011). *Bye, bye blockbusters, hello niche busters.* Canadian Medical Association.

Coriat, B. (2011). Communs "fonciers", communs "informationnels". Traits communs et différences. *Communication Au Séminaire Rencontre Des Acteurs et Des Chercheurs de l'Économie Sociale et Solidaire, Avec Elinor OSTROM (Prix Nobel d'Economie 2009), Paris, ANR Propice, WP, 4.* http://anr-propice.mshparisnord.fr/25-26_avril/coriat_communs-fonciers-informationnels.pdf

Coriat, B. (2012). La construction de communs comme alternative à la privatisation des connaissances Promesses et difficultés. *MS. Médecine Sciences, 28.* http://cat.inist.fr/?aModele=afficheN&cpsidt=26141404

Coriat, B. (2013). Le retour des communs. Sources et origines d'un programme de recherche. *Revue de La Régulation. Capitalisme, Institutions, Pouvoirs, 14.* https://regulation.revues.org/10463?lang=en

Coriat, B. (2015). Communs 'fonciers', communs 'informationnels'. Comment définir un commun. In B. Coriat (Ed.), *Le retour des Communs. La crise de l'idéologie propiétaire* (pp. 31–55). Les liens qui libèrent.

Crouzet, N., & Eberly, J. (2018). Intangibles, investment, and efficiency. *AEA Papers and Proceedings, 108,* 426–31.

Dardot, P., & Laval, C. (2014). *Commun: Essai sur la révolution au XXIe siècle*. la Découverte.

David, P. A. (2000). A tragedy of the public knowledge "commons." *Global science, intellectual property and the digital technology Boomerang. MERIT, Maastricht*. http://core.ac.uk/download/pdf/9309380.pdf

Dolata, U. (2017). *Apple, Amazon, Google, Facebook, Microsoft: Market concentration-competition-innovation strategies* [SOI Discussion Paper]. Stuttgarter Beiträge zur Organisations-und Innovationsforschung.

Drahos, P. (1995). Global property rights in information: The story of TRIPS at the GATT. *Prometheus*, *13*(1), 6–19.

Dreyfuss, R., & Frankel, S. (2014). From incentive to commodity to asset: How international law is reconceptualizing intellectual property. *Michigan Journal of International Law*, *36*(4), 557–602.

Durand, C., & Milberg, W. (2020). Intellectual monopoly in global value chains. *Review of International Political Economy*, *27*(2) 404–429. doi:10.1080/09692290.2019.1660703

European Commission. (2019). *EU R&D scoreboard*. European Commission.

Foley, D. K. (2013). Rethinking financial capitalism and the "information" economy. *Review of Radical Political Economics*, *45*(3), 257–68.

Gagnon, M. A. (2015). *Shaping the social determinants of value through economic ghostmanagement: An institutionalist approach to capital accumulation*. In Jo, T and Lee F. S. (Eds), *Marx, Veblen and the Foundation of Heterodox Economics*. Routledge. 228–51.

Harvey, D. (2002). *Spaces of capital: Towards a critical geography*. Routledge.

Harvey, D. (2007). *A brief history of neoliberalism*. Oxford University Press.

Haskel, J., & Westlake, S. (2018). *Capitalism without capital: The rise of the intangible economy*. Princeton University Press.

Helfrich, S. (2015). Patterns of commoning. In D. Bollier & S. Helfrich (Eds.), *Patterns of commoning* (pp. 26–46). The Commons Strategy Group.

Hess, C., & Ostrom, E. (2007). Introduction: An overview of the knowledge commons. In C. Hess & E. Ostrom (Eds.), *Understanding knowledge as a commons. From theory to practice* (pp. 3–26). MIT Press.

Kaplinsky, R. (1998). *Globalisation, industrialisation and sustainable growth: The pursuit of the nth rent*. Institute of Development Studies, University of Sussex.

Lan, S., Liu, K., & Dong, Y. (2019). Dancing with wolves: How value creation and value capture dynamics affect complementor participation in industry platforms. *Industry and Innovation*, *26*, 943–63. doi:10.1080/13662716.2019.1598339

Lazonick, W., Hopkins, M., Jacobson, K., Sakinç, M. E., & Tulum, Ö. (2017). *US pharma's financialized business model*. Institute for New Economic Thinking.

Mariátegui, J. C. (1979). Siete ensayos sobre la realidad peruana. *Editorial Amauta, Lima*.

Microsoft. (2019). *Annual Report 2019*. Microsoft.

Miers, S. (2000). Contemporary forms of slavery. *Canadian Journal of African Studies/La Revue Canadienne Des Études Africaines*, *34*(3), 714–47.

Montalban, M., & Sakinç, M. E. (2013). Financialization and productive models in the pharmaceutical industry. *Industrial and Corporate Change*, *22*(4), 981–1030.

Mowery, D. (2005). The Bayh-Dole Act and high-technology entrepreneurship in US universities: Chicken, egg, or something else? In G. Libecap (Ed.), *University entrepreneurship and technology transfer: Process, design, and intellectual property* (pp. 39–68). Elsevier. http://s1.downloadmienphi.net/file/downloadfile4/206/1391153.pdf#page=62

Nuccio, M., & Guerzoni, M. (2019). Big data: Hell or heaven? Digital platforms and market power in the data-driven economy. *Competition & Change*, *23*(3), 312–28. doi:10.1177/1024529418816525

Orhangazi, Ö. (2018). The role of intangible assets in explaining the investment–profit puzzle. *Cambridge Journal of Economics*, *43*(5), 1251–86.

Orsi, F. (2012). Session 1. Is biotechnologies a laboratory for academic capitalism. *Médecine Sciences: M/S*, *28*, 9.

Orsi, F. (2015). Revisiter la propriété pour construire les communs. In B. Coriat (Ed.), *Le retour des Communs. La crise de l'idéologie propiétaire* (pp. 59–79). Les liens qui libèrent.

Orsi, F., & Coriat, B. (2006). The new role and status of intellectual property rights in contemporary capitalism. *Competition & Change*, *10*(2), 162–79.

Orsi, F., & Zimmermann, J.-B. (2011). *Propriété intellectuelle et globalisation: Des TRIPS au modèle open-source. Les exemples des médicaments et du logiciel.* http://hal.ird.fr/halshs-00561477/

Pagano, U. (2014). The crisis of intellectual monopoly capitalism. *Cambridge Journal of Economics*, *38*(6), 1409–29.

Pestre, D. (2003). *Science, argent et politique: Un essai d'interprétation: une conférence-débat orgnanisée par la groupe Sciences en questions, Paris, INRA, 22 novembre 2001.* Editions Quae.

Rai, A. K. (2007). Knowledge commons: The case of the biopharmaceutical industry. *First Monday*, *12*(6). http://firstmonday.org/ojs/index.php/fm/article/viewArticle/1909/1791

Rikap, C. (2019). Asymmetric power of the core: Technological cooperation and technological competition in the transnational innovation networks of big pharma. *Review of International Political Economy*, *26*(5), 987–1021. doi:10.1080/09692290.2019.1620309

Sagaon-Teyssier, L., Singh, S., Dongmo-Nguimfack, B., & Moatti, J. P. (2016). Affordability of adult HIV/AIDS treatment in developing countries: Modelling price determinants for a better insight of the market functioning. *Journal of the International AIDS Society*, *19*(1). https://www.ncbi.nlm.nih.gov/pmc/articles/PMC5073219/

Scheufen, M. (2014). *Copyright versus open access: On the organisation and international political economy of access to scientific knowledge.* Springer.

Schrape, J. F. (2018). Open source communities: The sociotechnical institutionalization of collective invention. In Dolata, U. and Schrape, J. F. (Eds) *Collectivity and power on the Internet* (pp. 57–83). Springer.

Schwartz, H. M. (2016). Wealth and secular stagnation: The role of industrial organization and intellectual property rights. *The Russell Sage Foundation Journal of the Social Sciences*, *2*(6), 226–49.

Sheridan, C. (2011). Industry continues dabbling with open innovation models. *Nature Biotechnology*, *29*(12), 1063–65.

Spinellis, D., & Giannikas, V. (2012). Organizational adoption of open source software. *Journal of Systems and Software*, *85*(3), 666–82.

Stallman, R. (2002). *Free software, free society: Selected essays of Richard M. Stallman*. Lulu. com.

Steiber, A., & Alänge, S. (2013). A corporate system for continuous innovation: The case of Google Inc. *European Journal of Innovation Management*, *16*(2), 243–64.

Teixeira, R. A., & Rotta, T. N. (2012). Valueless knowledge-commodities and financialization: Productive and financial dimensions of capital autonomization. *Review of Radical Political Economics*, *44*(4), 448–67.

Tralau-Stewart, C. J., Wyatt, C. A., Kleyn, D. E., & Ayad, A. (2009). Drug discovery: New models for industry–academic partnerships. *Drug Discovery Today*, *14*(1), 95–101.

Wade, R. H. (2019). Catch-up and constraints in the twentieth and twenty-first centuries. *How Nations Learn: Technological Learning, Industrial Policy, and Catch-Up*, 15. In Oqubay, Arkebe and Ohno, Kenichi, (Eds.) How Nations Learn: Technological Learning, Industrial Policy, and Catch-up. Oxford University Press, Oxford, UK. ISBN 9780198841760

Williams, S. (2010). *Free as in freedom (2.0): Richard Stallman and the free software revolution*. Free Software Foundation.

4

THE INTERPLAYS OF THE UNITED STATES, CHINA AND THEIR INTELLECTUAL MONOPOLIES*

1 Introduction

In the 21st century, the most profitable corporations base their power on intellectual rentiership and predation. By accumulating intangible assets, they have become intellectual monopolies that limit access to different types and forms of knowledge. Chapters 2 and 3 elaborate on how intellectual monopolies subordinate other organizations. These corporations organize global corporate innovation systems integrated by multiple innovation networks from which they garner intellectual rents establishing predatory relationships with other network participants. They also organize production processes by using global value chains and platforms extracting value produced by workers in subordinate firms. Intellectual monopolies coordinate and plan the lion's share of global capitalism.

Nevertheless, intellectual monopoly capitalism, as much as it is a global transformation, is also highly territorialized. Core states build and reinforce their geopolitical power based on the promotion and success of their intellectual monopolies, which further expand these companies' concentration of intangibles. Core states also often limit or regulate intellectual monopolies from foreign states. While this book focuses on intellectual monopolies as global planners of production and innovation, this chapter elaborates on how core states remain central players of global capitalism in juxtaposition with global leader corporations acting as intellectual monopolies.

We address the interplay between two core states – the United States (US) and the People's Republic of China, hereon China – and their respective intellectual monopolies. Altogether, these are the most powerful actors of intellectual monopoly capitalism whose intertwined rivalries are at the heart of global geopolitics. In the spirit of Babic et al. (2017), who elaborated on Strange (1993), our starting point is the juxtaposition of powerful actors in capitalism, and we will work on a preliminary unfolding of this premise. Our conceptualization will not attempt to produce a hierarchy of powerful

* This chapter is co-authored with Prof. Ariel Slipak (Universidad de Buenos Aires and Universidad Nacional de Moreno).

actors. We will neither conclude that core states subordinate intellectual monopolies nor that the latter dominates the former. Both types of powerful actors retain spheres of influence, even if they sometimes overlap, resulting in conflicts whose outcomes cannot always be anticipated.

To some extent, intellectual monopoly capitalism relies on the US and Chinese states' policies. Simultaneously, these countries' hegemony has been reinforced by their respective intellectual monopolies. However, on top of what seems like a mutually beneficial relationship, it should be noted that intellectual monopolies do not recognize nationality when it comes to maximizing profit rates. Their planning scope and accumulation strategy are global as well as their assets' allocation, minimizing corporate taxes, capital expenditures and overall risks. This may result, as we also present in this chapter, in clashes of power with their respective home states. Moreover, this chapter also briefly reflects on how intellectual monopolies have replaced state functions as policymakers.

All in all, we unpack the complex and multifaceted relationship between core states and (global) intellectual monopolies. The following section examines the US and China's industrial, innovation, and other policies, highlighting their contribution to the emergence of intellectual monopoly capitalism. Next, Section 3 elaborates on the flip side of this relation: how intellectual monopolies contribute to strengthening their respective state's hegemony. Section 4 deals with intellectual monopolies' own agenda, including their policymaking skills. While that agenda is often aligned to their home states' priorities, they are sometimes in conflict resulting in a tangled turf war. Section 5 concludes.

2 Contribution of the US and Chinese states to the emergence of intellectual monopolies

In this section, we focus on how core states fostered their global intellectual monopoly. To elaborate on this claim, we have chosen two states that, at first sight, could be considered as polar cases: liberal and pro-free-market in the US and led by state planning in China. Regardless of this polar appearance, we show that the same underlying strategy prevailed: strengthening the state's hegemony through spurring the formation of global intellectual monopolies.

It must be noted that the interpenetrations of state and civil society (later dubbed "the economy" or more narrowly "the market") go beyond the effects of policy. There are concrete aspects of the interplay between states and big corporations that will not be centrally addressed in this chapter, such as lobbying, which anyway played a part in orienting the policies discussed next (Wade, 2017; Zingales, 2017). General conceptualizations of the interplay between the state and civil society also identify a multiplicity of states (Cox, 1981). A particular distinction concerns centre/periphery studies, which will be addressed in the last section of this book.

2.1 A marriage of convenience: the United States and big corporations since the Second World War

It is not possible to understand intellectual monopoly capitalism without considering the turns of the US policy since the aftermaths of the Second World War. Perhaps the most evident tie is related to the tightening and spread of intellectual property rights (IPRs) both for the US and from the US to the world (see Chapter 3). On top of this policy, the role of military research as a mission-oriented policy was crucial in the emergence of big pharma and tech giants like Apple (Mazzucato, 2015; Ruttan, 2006). Fostering technology transfer from universities and public research organizations to private companies further contributed to set the ground for intellectual predation (see Chapter 5). Overall, a disguised industrial policy in the US was indispensable for enabling and spurring the monetization of public science by private firms. Additionally, these firms grew under the shelter of a favourable antitrust policy and (known) loopholes in the taxing system (Clausing, 2020; Glick, 2019; Glick & Ruetschlin, 2019).

Given the US global hegemon position, its bundle of policies spread -sometimes with no delay- around the world, either by imitator states or by the US influence in international organizations. Intellectual monopoly capitalism was born not as a local or national but as a global transformation.

2.1.1 US industrial cum science and technology policy since the Second World War

Disguised by dominant pro-free-market ideology, the US technological supremacy lays on its industrial policy, crucial for stimulating innovation in the private sector (Block, 2008; Wade, 2017). Its science and technology (S&T) strategy fulfilled multiple aims. It was vital to guarantee military superiority, defend and increase the power of US multinational corporations and limit other countries' catching-up (from the USSR during the Cold War to Japan in the 70s and China nowadays); thus to sustain the US geopolitical hegemony (Weiss, 2014).

Between the 1920s and the 1960s, the linear model of innovation was established as a transmission belt going from science to growth (Godin, 2006). Public policies shifted in line with science's integration into the economic realm. As illustrated in Vannevar Bush's *Science: The Endless Frontier* report for President Roosevelt after the Second World War, a new imaginary prevailed where basic science needed to be mostly funded by the public sector, assuming that private firms would not have sufficient incentives to invest in science (Bush, 1945).

Since then, the US federal government took a development network state (DNS) commitment (Block, 2008; Wade, 2017). Block (2008, p. 172) explains that US firms already had strong innovation incentives. Therefore, policies aimed at incentivizing them would not spur innovation further. Thus, the US state assumed a "hands on" role; it worked "closely with firms to identify and support the most promising avenues for innovation". Given that a strong and developed higher education and S&T domains were also fulfilled preconditions, the industrial policy was focused on targeted resourcing, opening windows, brokering and facilitation.

During the Cold War, a specific office of the Pentagon, the Advanced Research Projects Agency created in 1958, dubbed DARPA (by adding the word Defense at the beginning of the acronym), worked with relative autonomy and in close connection with the NASA and the US Atomic Energy Commission. DARPA set a research agenda beyond basic science by granting targeted funds for moonshot projects in computer S&T, including the provision of funds to create computer science departments in leading US universities. The rest of this story is quite known. DARPA also pioneered as an institution connecting researchers from different public and private organizations, building an S&T network for computing science, including the origin of the internet.

DARPA and other agencies (such as the National Institutes of Health and the CIA), conformed a cluster of federal agencies collaborating closely with the private sector as a national technology enterprise with the leadership of the US president and supported by the Office of Science and Technology Policy of the Oval Office (Weiss, 2014). Its initial aim was to innovate for the assurance of the US military supremacy. Nevertheless, mainly since the 1980s, technology commercialization became an equally relevant goal. The Stevenson-Wydler Technology Innovation Act of 1980 mandated federal research laboratories to establish technology transfer offices. Since then, innovation policies included patenting and licensing, technology transfer agreements between federal laboratories and the private sector, public procurement, collaborative innovation projects and the creation of new venture capital schemes. Public venture capital, a practice started by the CIA in 1999 through its venture capital arm In-Q-Tel, expanded during the 2000s to the US Army, the Department of Energy, the NASA and the Department of Defense. They all run their venture capitals, taking equity positions in chosen innovating companies (Wade, 2017; Weiss, 2014).[1]

Besides policies implemented by federal laboratories and agencies, S&T policies also targeted academic research. Technological applications and university-industry collaborations were encouraged since the 1970s (Berman, 2011; Block, 2008; Dasgupta & David, 1994; Marginson, 2014; Muscio et al., 2013; Pestre, 2003). Chapter 5 will refer to specific policies that further contributed to intellectual monopoly capitalism. They included the Bayh Dole Act that authorized universities to patent public-funded research and to transfer it to private firms by providing exclusive licences or creating joint ventures (also mentioned in Chapter 3). Biotechnology industry was born in this period as a group of university spin-offs that eventually failed or were acquired by big pharmaceuticals (Berman, 2011; Rose & Rose, 2014). Yet, although the relationship between selected universities, the federal government and the private sector in the United States had been institutionalized at the beginning of the Cold War (Bethell et al., 2009), it was only in the 1990s that university technology transfer became an expanded activity (Noh & Lee, 2019).

To contribute to US corporations' profitable businesses abroad, thus strengthening the US global hegemony, the state pushed for a stringent international IPRs regime. As was explained in Chapter 3, this formally began in 1995 with the "Trade Related Aspects of Intellectual Property Rights" (TRIPS) agreement. TRIPS is the result of US multinationals lobbying and complaining that Third World countries were copying their innovations. The active role of corporations like IBM, Pfizer and Microsoft drafting first versions of this agreement is just one among many examples of how the big US corporations were directly involved in policymaking (Drahos, 1995).

By extending national regulations beyond its territory, the United States exercised a form of infrastructural power on the rest of the world (Schwartz, 2019). In a transnational innovation context, dominant countries' regulations have international implications and eventually become the global benchmark, such as the United States Food and Drug Administration (USFDA) (Lane, 2007). In line with Farrell and Newman's (2010) analysis, the US managed to use a domestic institution to externalize its national rules on a global scale. Furthermore, the USFDA works in close technological cooperation with big pharmaceuticals providing another apparent example of the interpenetrations between core states and intellectual monopolies (see Chapter 6).

2.1.2 Friendly antitrust policy and taxing system

Changes in the antitrust policy further facilitated the inception of intellectual monopolies. A new antitrust regime was born from the "Antitrust Project" of the Chicago School. It opposed the more stringent policies of the New Deal period, even questioning the capacity of any single firm to exercise monopoly power. The Chicago School's overall recommendation was to reduce antitrust policy to a minimum, only aimed at guaranteeing "consumer welfare", which meant to prevent price increases due to excessive market power. The US courts adopted this antitrust program after the crisis of the 1970s (Glick, 2019).

Since the 1980s, the different versions of the Horizontal Merger Guidelines of the US Department of Justice and the Federal Trade Commission require increasingly higher proofs of an anticompetitive scenario to stop mergers and acquisitions (M&A). Furthermore, even if an anticompetitive M&A is proven, the deal could still be authorized if it lacks significant entry barriers to the corresponding market, or if the M&A can lead to efficiency gains (Glick, 2019).

Permissive antitrust policy arrived at a climax during Trump's presidency, with fewer criminal antitrust cases brought to courts than any administration since the 1970s (Shubber, 2019). Such record low levels fuelled the appalling evidence of increasing concentration and mark-ups in the United States since the 1990s. M&A have contributed to expanding knowledge monopolies, especially in pharmaceutical and big tech sectors (Glick & Ruetschlin, 2019; Lopez Giron & Vialle, 2017; Montalban & Sakinç, 2013). As we pointed out in Chapter 2, intellectual monopolies use M&A to acquire proven technology, avoiding S&T risks. Thus, changes in antitrust policy contributed to the emergence of global intellectual monopolies, which became a pillar of the US global hegemonic power (Schwartz, 2019).

Changes in antitrust policies were part of a broader system favouring big business in the United States. By facilitating their artificial deferral of taxes, the US corporate tax system played a central role in the recovery of US multinationals' profit rates and accumulation pace since the 1970s. Since then, given that corporate taxes in the US are supposed to be paid at the place of incorporation, US multinationals have incorporated subsidiaries in tax havens. These subsidiaries operate and are managed in the US but do not pay US corporate taxes.

The US Controlled Foreign Corporation (CFC) regime introduced in 1968 was supposed to prevent profit shifting to subsidiaries. However, two loopholes reduced its effectiveness. The manufacturing exception was meant to encourage multinationals to create significant value in their subsidiaries. Since 2008, criteria for qualifying for such exception were relaxed, and almost any activity performed in the subsidiary could fulfil the new requirements. The other loophole is the check-the-box regime established in 1997. By stating that a subsidiary is only a path-through company or hybrid-entity, intragroup transactions became non-existent (Ting, 2014). Hage and Baines (2020) show that since the mid-1980s there is a regressive corporate tax structure where the top 10% of US listed corporations (defined as those with the highest ratio of net profit to sales) pay a lower worldwide effective income tax rate than the rest of the US listed corporations. And this result holds when distinguishing between jurisdictions (US and foreign).

It was argued by Ting (2014) that the US Government is aware of profit shifting mechanisms but looks away as indirect support to improve the competitiveness of US businesses. Indeed, both this mechanism and the more complex "Double Irish with a Dutch Sandwich"[2] are too popular to go unnoticed. IPRs are used in the latter to move earnings to tax havens. As we explain in Chapters 7 and 10, since it is easier to allocate intangible (rather than tangible) assets in tax havens, intellectual monopolies find it easier to avoid taxes. The 2017 tax and jobs act (Public Law 115–97) pretended to reduce incentives for profit shifting. However, as noted by Clausing (2020), as of 2019 third quarter, there was no evidence of such a reduction. In fact, this act has also been considered an act that benefited M&As.

All things considered, it seems that antitrust policy and corporate taxing are aimed at sustaining US global hegemony by fostering US intellectual monopolies. Still, Chinese firms' successful R&D results in ICT and digital as well as biological and clean energy technologies are a major threat to the US. We explore next how the Chinese state policies fostered the emergence of Chinese intellectual monopolies.

2.2 China's innovation and industrial policies

In 1978, when China started its "reform and opening-up" process led by Deng Xiaoping, S&T was defined as one of its four (to be accomplished) modernizations. Until the end of the 20th century, policies consisted of gradually making economic planning schemes more flexible in favour of market mechanisms and firms' autonomy. The reforms gave greater weight to provincial authorities in economic planning. However, it was always the national state that decided on the country's overall economic orientation (Bustelo Gómez & Fernández Lommen, 1996; Girado, 2017), and this general perspective remains today.

Among its early reforms, the World Bank recognizes that China's creation of Special Economic Zones (SEZ) was strategic. They became poles of attraction for Foreign Direct Investment (FDI) and outsourcing (Zeng, 2010). China's government used foreign multinational firms' desire to gain access to its domestic market and low real wages[3] as the basis for negotiating access to their knowledge. Overall, innovation policy until the end of the 20th century was based on imitation and adaptation through technology transfer and reverse engineering (Delgado-Ramos, 2007). This often took the form of joint ventures where the foreign firms were required to partner with Chinese ones. This enhanced the technological capabilities of domestic (state-owned and private) corporations (Durand & Milberg, 2020).

A flexible implementation of TRIPS agreements and other protectionist policies underpinned the Chinese state in its confrontations with existing intellectual monopolies from core countries, in particular from the ICT industry. A special chapter refers to China's protectionist measures limiting the penetration of US data-driven intellectual monopolies. China's "Great Fire Wall", introduced in 1997, limits access for foreign companies to internet-based businesses (including cloud services), favouring local companies in particular Baidu, Alibaba and Tencent (BAT) (Mueller, 2011; Wu & Gereffi, 2018).

Summing up, during this first period of transformation, China's place in the New International Division of Labour as simultaneously a huge market, and a cheap and under-regulated labour factory attracted outsourcing and offshoring, triggering skyrocketing economic growth (Milberg & Winkler, 2013). This provided an unprecedented economic and geopolitical strength that was used to spur China's innovation system, which included industrial policies focused on chosen sectors and corporate leaders.

Since the 2000s, China's transformation went even further. Lower wages are no longer its main advantage, but high labour productivity. Firms operating in China are increasingly involved in more complex production processes. China's share of high R&D intensive industries grew from 6% in 2003 to 21% by 2020, second after the US, whose share fell from 38% to 32% (National Science Foundation, 2020). Moreover, for decades the state has been massively investing in research and higher education, which, according to Arocena (2018), has been determinant for the success of China's national innovation system. As it is the case of the US, research institutions and state dependencies directly contributed to transforming private and state-owned enterprises into global intellectual monopolies, such as State Grid Corporation of China (see Chapter 9).

SEZ evolved and became high-tech industrial clusters with special tax exemptions. Shenzhen's SEZ has been particularly relevant for the emergence of China's intellectual monopolies. Among others, it is the home of Huawei, Tencent, the drone leader DJI and BYD, a firm specialized in rechargeable batteries and electric vehicles (Chen & Ogan, 2017).

It was also at the beginning of the 21st century that China launched its "go out policy" to increase its global presence. According to World Bank data, China ranked 33rd in net FDI outflows by 2000. By 2019, it ranked fourth. The global expansion of China's intellectual monopolies is significantly dependent on the Chinese state active policy of financing development and infrastructure through new financial institutions mainly driven by China, such as the Asian Infrastructure Investment Bank (AIIB), the New Development Bank (NDB) and the Silk Road Fund.

FDI outflows are oriented towards sectors defined as strategic by China's economic planning authorities. They included the acquisition of firms that own patents or have highly trained personnel or a significant market share in some high-tech manufacturing (Svampa & Slipak, 2018). BAT are globalizing and sourcing knowledge from abroad through acquisitions[4] and collaborations with academic research institutions from other countries. Additionally, Huawei has R&D centres in Germany, Sweden, the United States, France, Italy, Russia and India with institutionalized collaborations in those countries and 40% of its profits correspond to its foreign operations.

A special chapter of the "go out policy" is China's Belt and Road Initiative (BRI), launched in 2013. The BRI illustrates how China positions itself as a geopolitical power. It leverages on its economic capacities while it strengthens partnership with global leader corporations for technological catching-up (such as Siemens partnership with Sinomach), aiming to become itself the world's laboratory (Slipak & Ghiotto, 2019). Becoming an innovation-driven country was one of China's 13th Five-Year-Plan (2016–20) key goals. In the same vein, in 2015 it announced its Made in China (MIC) 2025 programme, an example of state-led industrial policy in advanced technology.

Chinese firms are moving beyond an imitation-driven and towards an innovation-driven stage (Gu et al., 2016), catching-up in patents and trademarks (Godinho & Ferreira, 2012). Hitherto, there has been an explosive rise in Chinese patents (15.3% average annual growth of its published patent applications). After decades of foreign companies leading patent applications, in the last decade, Chinese companies reversed this trend. From 2013 onwards, more than 80% of patent applications at the Chinese Patent Office corresponded to Chinese enterprises reaching almost 90% in 2017. Nevertheless, Chinese organizations remain less successful than foreign ones in granted to applied patents' ratio and still mostly apply for patents only inside China (China Clarivate Analytics, 2018).

China had initially developed a combination of protectionism with fostering inward FDI but compelling foreign firms to transfer technology. Its aim was to build a strong innovation system as the state explicitly sought to develop global innovation leaders (Lee et al., 2016; Nolan, 2012; Wen, 2017). A sign of the accomplishment of this goal has been its move towards a more open strategy supporting negotiations on the liberalization of trade precisely in sectors where it had caught up (Girado, 2017; Weinhardt & ten Brink, 2020). China joined the WTO in 2001 and gradually signed various international conventions related to intellectual property protection.

All in all, in the words of Arocena (2018), China's national innovation system is globalization's main winner. It is led by the state in close partnership with China's global intellectual monopolies.

3 How intellectual monopolies contribute to reinforce core states hegemony

Not only the US and Chinese states have contributed to the emergence of intellectual monopoly capitalism, but their intellectual monopolies became a pillar of each of these countries' global dominance and embodiments of their home countries' S&T supremacy. As Babic et al. (2017, p. 3) argued, states and corporations "use each other to increase their respective power positions".

Intellectual monopoly capitalism leads to a new form of imperialism characterized by the extraction of knowledge and data from around the world, monetized by a few companies mainly from the US, but also from other core countries. Another novelty is that China has joined the core of imperial countries. Under intellectual monopoly capitalism, technological frontiers expand from the results of these corporations' planned innovation networks. At the same time, as argued by Schwartz (2019), setting the technological frontier explains part of core economies' dominance, as it is particularly the case of the US.

Starrs (2013) argued that, under globalization, a country's economic power is based on global corporations' positions and profits. Through the lenses of its global corporations, the US still dominates by afar most economic sectors, including all those associated with new technologies (ICT hardware and software and biotechnology and pharma) (Schwartz, 2019; Starrs, 2013). By December 31, 2019, most of the global top 100 companies in market capitalization came for the US (55 companies representing 60% of the accumulated market capitalization). In 2009, the US had 42 companies representing 45% of the top 100 corporations' market value (PWC, 2020). US corporations are also absolute leaders in Business Expenditure in R&D (BERD). The US accumulated 38% of the top 2,500 corporations' BERD in 2018/19 (European Commission, 2019).[5]

Schwartz (2019) shows that US productive power lays in the hands of those US firms that lead commodity chains capturing a disproportionate share of global profits given the US share of the global economy. This is all the more true, continues the author, for those corporations holding the largest IPRs portfolios. Similarly, Starrs (2013) had found that US corporate dominance is greater in sectors characterized by advanced technology and knowledge. For instance, the US concentrates more than two-thirds of the market capitalization value of the world's 70 largest digital platforms (UNCTAD, 2019). Furthermore, on top of contributing, like other US intellectual monopolies, to sustain and expand the US S&T supremacy and geopolitical power, Google, Apple, Facebook and other US internet companies have provided data access to the US National Security Agency (NSA) for global surveillance.[6]

Even if US global leader corporations offshore retained earnings, they still represent a transfer of resources to the US, in particular to their shareholders and asset managers (Braun, 2020; Schwartz, 2019). US investors are also predominant owners of top European corporations (Starrs, 2013). In particular, the dubbed Big Three or "New Permanent Universal Owners" (BlackRock, Vanguard and State Street) are not only the largest owners of over 90% of S&P 500 companies but also "the largest shareholders in 60 percent of British FTSE 100, 40 percent of the German DAX, 25 percent of the Dutch AEX and 20 percent of the French CAC 40. In the Japanese Topix 100 they are the largest owner for 30 percent of the firms" (Fichtner & Heemskerk, 2018, p. 24). The Big Three close the cycle by assuring that not only a significant share of the distributed corporate profits from US leader corporations are channelled back to the US but also part of the distributed profits of major corporations from other core countries.

Authors highlighting that the US geopolitical power has not declined – and that it has even increased – with globalization driven by its leader corporations recognize only a minor place to China as a still not severe threat to the US global hegemony (Babic et al., 2017; Schwartz, 2019; Starrs, 2013). It is here where we disagree with them. Using their same methodology (each country's share of profits at Forbes Global 2000), 2020 profit data shows that while the US accumulates 38.4% of "Forbes Global 2000" profits, China follows with 16.6%. The third country is Japan, with a meagre 6.7%. Indeed, leading US corporations accumulate most of the profits, but the US had 46% of the top 500 corporations of this ranking in 2012 and, by 2020, it had 33% (167 corporations). In 2012, Japan followed the US in terms of the number of firms in the top 500. China was third with 5.9% of the top 500 firms. By 2020, China was second with 11.2% of the firms. Overall, 266 Chinese corporations in Forbes Global 2000 (56 of which are in the top 500) should not be downplayed. Underestimating China's corporate and state power as the US's main foreign contestant is a risk as serious as neglecting the still global hegemony of the US.

Most business and S&T indicators show that the US is followed – even if sometimes from afar – by China. China became a global centre of economic and geopolitical power in part at the expense of the US (and also Europe and Japan) world power. For instance, since 2012, the US (and also Europe and Japan) has been losing positions to China at the top 1% of BERD corporations (Veugelers, 2018).

In the specific case of digital platforms, China follows the US, with 22% of the value of the world's 70 largest companies (UNCTAD, 2019). China is also the world leader in artificial intelligence adoption and data. In contrast, the US arrives first in terms of talent, research, development and hardware, metrics defined by a recent report of the Center for Data Innovation (Castro et al., 2019). China also seconds the US in unicorns by value. While the US had half of the companies and value on the list, China's 26 unicorns in the top 100 represented 35% of the top 100 unicorns' value by March 2020 (PWC, 2020).

China's corporate profit share in the digital economy is higher than what Forbes Global 2000 shows because it excludes Huawei, which remains a private entity. Huawei's technological leadership in 5G technologies is the most obvious example of how a firm's technological leadership contributes to strengthening its home country's power. The underlying fear of Western economies regarding Huawei as the only company mastering 5G technologies is the reinforcement of China's geopolitical and economic leadership.[7]

Furthermore, China's high-tech intellectual monopolies have overall good relationships with the Chinese state and have exercised a strong influence on Chinese digital policy (Azmeh et al., 2019; de Graaff, 2020). Baidu and Tencent have a seat in China's national political advisory body and the founders and CEOs of Huawei and Alibaba are affiliated to China's

Communist Party. An overall result of the consolidation of China's national innovation system has been the strengthening of its military[8] and economic power in close partnership with China's intellectual monopolies, in particular Huawei and ZTE (Tejeda Canobbio, 2011), a story that looks much similar to the US one but with fewer visible frictions given the strength of the Communist Party.

Chinese corporate leaders have had a clear strategy of expanding by acquiring technologically advanced businesses of Western global leaders, thus contributing to China's state "go out policy". Lenovo acquired IBM computers' business in 2005 and Motorola's business – previously acquired by Google – in 2014. Chinese companies have also been actively acquiring German innovative firms, such as Kuka and KraussMaffei. In 2017, the Zhengzhou Group and Renaissance Capital Investment acquired the engine division of Bosch (Slipak, 2018). Besides acquiring full businesses, purchasing equity in technologically advanced companies is also frequent among China's intellectual monopolies. It has been Alibaba and Tencent's main globalization strategy (Jia et al., 2018). Moreover, these tech giants and Baidu cooperate with Audi and the joint venture between FAW Group Corporation and Volkswagen in data analysis, internet-vehicle platform building and intelligent urban transport.[9]

However, to this point, China is still far from the US in most technologies. Indeed, China's second place in terms of corporate profit share in Forbes Global 2000 is mostly driven by two sectors: digital and finance. In terms of top corporations in market capitalization, by December 31, 2019 China ranked third after Europe with 14 companies (in 2009, China had 11 companies in this ranking) (PWC, 2020). What gives further proof of the still undisputed US S&T supremacy – which of course stands with exceptions like 5G – is that China had only three global innovators in the 2020 edition of Derwent Top 100 global innovators, while the US had 39 (Clarivate Analytics, 2020).

Anyway, and regardless of its enduring leadership, the US trade war with China that became visible in 2018 can be understood as a technological war. The US aims to constrain China's technological catching-up, precisely targeting the digital industries, where China has advanced the most. The US is once again proactive in defending its global technological leadership and political hegemony from its most serious technological contender (Ciuriak, 2019; Ernst, 2020; García-Herrero, 2019). According to a Deutsche Bank report, we are in the midst of a global tech cold war with its own wall: two parallel tech regimes (Walia, 2020). However, the difference with the previous Cold War is the high level of co-dependence between the tech regimes led by the US and China, respectively. The report presents a China/US tech geopolitical capacity ratio over time. Until 2018, China narrowed is technological distance with the US at a rate that – if maintained – would have led to tech parity at some point between

2025 and 2030. However, in 2019, the ratio worsens, probably as a result of the US state strategy to slowdown China's catching-up.

Clearly, each country's intellectual monopolies are critical players in this conflict since they are major sources of technological leadership. Notwithstanding the deal achieved by the end of 2019, there are certain possibilities of not only tech regimes but also global value chains' decoupling, some of them organized around the US and others around China.[10] This speculation has gained ground since the Covid-19 pandemic.

4 Clashes of power between states and intellectual monopolies

As Strange (1996) anticipated, the decline of the state's power vis-à-vis corporations can be partly explained by the acceleration of technological change, which tilts the scale in favour of corporations. As identified by Feenberg (2010, p. 5) "political democracy is largely overshadowed by the enormous power wielded by the masters of technical systems". Indeed, we should consider that powerful intellectual monopolies pass over their home states in specific contexts or respects.[11] With this in mind we reconceived core states as one of capitalism's multiple powerful actors.

Beyond explicit confrontations, since intellectual monopolies organize and plan production and innovation networks taking place in different countries, they generate an overlap of political realms with sometimes contradictory rules and norms. Who oversees production and innovation inside the networks organized by intellectual monopolies? The latter or the different states where intellectual monopolies' production or innovation networks are based? To whom subordinate firms and other organizations are accountable for their actions? Their state or the intellectual monopoly coordinating the network? The simple answer is both. The complicated part is to identify what happens when they are in contradiction, and what are the consequences of this complex set of power structures for workers and subordinated organizations.

Intellectual monopolies have replaced state functions as policymakers. An extreme example recently disclosed is Eric Schmidt, Alphabet's former executive chairman, advising the US federal government while still managing Alphabet. He was the chair of the US Defense Innovation Board, which recommended the use of artificial intelligence to the US Department of Defense. He also chaired the National Security Commission on Artificial Intelligence which advises the US Congress on analogous topics (Klein, 2020).

The government's threat over China is – at least to some extent – driven by US data-driven intellectual monopolies' concern over Chinese rivals like Alibaba, Tencent and Huawei. The CEOs of Google, Amazon, Facebook and Apple made this clear in their testimonies in the 2020 US Congress Hearing. As a remedy, Schmidt had been pushing for more public investment in research related to artificial intelligence and tech-enabling infrastructure (such as 5G) (Klein, 2020). Furthermore, these data-driven intellectual monopolies make their own rules and norms for their *digital republics* and, to some degree, replace the role of states. Facebook's founder and chief executive, Mark Zuckerberg, states it clearly

> Every day, platforms like Facebook have to make trade-offs on important social values – between free expression and safety, privacy and law enforcement, and between creating open systems and locking down data.[12]
>
> (Mark Zuckerberg, Feb 16, 2020)

And immediately afterwards, he advocates for more public regulations and informs that Facebook is working together with different governments to that end. A similar claim was raised by Sundar Pichai, arguing that artificial intelligence needs to be regulated.[13]

The division of power is not clear, given that corporate power and planning capacities go beyond national frontiers and beyond the capital they own. Overall, there is a legal vacuum in the reach of each state's power and where the power of the intellectual monopoly controlling a portion of global production and innovation begins. This vacuum allows intellectual monopolies to expand their power and profits.

Another source of conflict between intellectual monopolies and core states concerns the relative absence of the usual benefits of being home to big corporations: employment generation and tax payments. Considering their earnings, global leading corporations do not generate in their home countries expected employment due to outsourcing and offshoring (of production and innovation), which is particularly the case of US and also European intellectual monopolies. This has contributed to the rise in inequalities in these regions. The consequent social distress put pressure on stringent regulations. In the US, we referred in Section 2.1 to the 2017 Tax and Jobs Act (Public Law 115-97), but changes have not been significant.

US intellectual monopolies are masters of tax avoidance. As we mentioned before, operations leading to lower tax bills and financialized profits are easier for companies with higher shares of intangible over tangible assets. Offshoring IPRs to countries where corporations are not required to pay taxes for their intellectual property is a mechanism frequently used to divert profits to tax havens (Bryan et al., 2017) (see Chapter 7 on Apple's case). By the end of 2016, the top ten companies in terms of offshored savings were: Apple, Microsoft, Cisco, Oracle, Alphabet, Johnson & Johnson, Pfizer, Qualcomm, Amgen and Merck (Pozsar, 2018).

In China, whose global intellectual monopolies sprang from the sustained stimulus and protection of its state, the latter's central planning capacity is starting to find limits vis-à-vis new intellectual monopolies. These corporations were not born as the chosen ones by the state, but still enjoyed the benefits of China's protectionism. The recent case of Bytedance provides a good example. The company was spending its Chinese profits to expand its unprofitable business in the US when the US government banned its blockbuster TikTok app. Bytedance was not among Beijing's favoured companies, among others, because of the difficulties in controlling the videos uploaded to TikTok (Yang, 2020). Regardless of the end of the story between TikTok, the US and Chinese governments and US intellectual monopolies as potential buyers for part of TikTok's business, what the case put forward was a possible surge of clashes between emerging Chinese (data-driven) intellectual monopolies and their state. Indeed, in late 2020 the Chinese state delayed Ant Group's IPO, followed by the introduction of antitrust regulation for digital companies.

Meanwhile, Europe remained focused on increasing regulations on foreign data-driven intellectual monopolies, including different accusations of excessive market power and unfair competition. Unlike previous stages in capitalism, Europe risks playing in the subordinate side, where the peripheries have historically been and generally remain. Germany's fear of falling behind the US and China's tech giants should also be read as a broader European concern to lag (far) behind those core economies.[14] Overall, Europe and Japan are latecomers of the digital economy, and this space is being filled primarily by China, emerging as a digital technological power (UNCTAD, 2019). Moreover, with a drop of eight companies between March 2009 and December 2019, Europe's share of global top 100 corporations in market capitalization fell from 27% to 15%. This drop was taken over by the US (PWC, 2020). Regulating the digital economy could thus be seen as Europe's geopolitical rebalancing move.[15]

5 Final remarks

In this chapter, we argued that core states and certain corporations built a mutually beneficial relationship. We identified US and Chinese policies that contributed to the emergence and spread of global intellectual monopolies. Likewise, we elaborated on how these corporate leaders sustain and expand their respective countries' geopolitical power. Nevertheless, we also addressed states' concerns and the overall tensions of the juxtaposition of power between core states and intellectual monopolies.

The US state cannot afford to lose its intellectual monopolies since its global hegemon power significantly depends on those companies. Likewise, it cannot afford to let its intellectual monopolies be given their consequences for income and wealth concentration resulting in increasing social unrest. From the US state perspective, the technological war with China is necessary to remain the only superpower. Nevertheless, this conflict is also a powerful device to redirect public attention and blame – as it has always been the case of the United States – an "other" of the internal consequences of home (and global) capitalism.

Neither can the Chinese state afford to lose its alliance with its intellectual monopolies. Its national innovation system and geopolitical power are based on a strong partnership – although not without tensions – between China's state and intellectual monopolies, the only ones challenging the US and its intellectual monopolies.

All in all, the US and Chinese states have benefited from their respective intellectual monopolies to build and reinforce their geopolitical power. Meanwhile, in the rest of the world, knowledge and data extractivisms are further expanding inequalities, diminishing social well-being and curtailing development opportunities (see Chapters 11–13). The resulting world scenario is a ticking bomb.

A missing piece in this puzzle that will be addressed in future research concerns integrating international organizations to our analysis, seeking to understand how intellectual monopolies influence them and their role as arenas of core states' contest for global hegemony. Let us just point out that each time the US withdraws from international coordination, China moves forward. Remarkably, during Trump's administration, the US withdrew from international treaties and organizations, putting into question its historical openness. A possible interpretation could be that the hegemon fosters an open world economy but as far as it benefits from it.

To conclude, beyond the focus on the US and China, this chapter has also made self-evident that unfolding the interplay between state and corporate power is always context-dependent. While in some contexts the state rules over global leader corporations, the latter overcome even core states' power in other contexts. As capitalism develops through the interplay of its powerful actors, it is not possible to anticipate concrete outcomes of such a multifaceted relationship. Neither can we anticipate the counter-hegemonic tendencies that, as Cox (1981) emphasized, generally emerge to oppose the state and world order structures of capitalism. The institutions that will lead the counter-offensive to intellectual monopoly capitalism remains to be seen.

Notes

1 The US state not only acts as venture capital itself but has also inspired the creation of venture capitalism. The first venture capital firm, American Research and Development, dates from 1946. It was created by General Georges Doriot, a former manager of procurement and head of R&D in the US Military Planning Division during the Second World War who recognized that his past experience had been instrumental in the creation of its venture capital firm (Weiss, 2014).

2 In a nutshell, a Dutch company receives royalties from sales done in the US. Royalties do not pay taxes in The Netherlands, but profit does. So, these earnings are paid to the Irish subsidiary as a payment for the license of the IPRs because it is said that actually the Irish subsidiary owns the intangible assets and that has licensed them to the Dutch subsidiary.

3 China's household registration (hukou) system played a central role in sustaining low wages in China. This system links access to social services and benefits to the place of birth, distinguishing between agricultural and non-agricultural residency status. In several cases, large corporations' workforce installed in SEZs are migrant workers from rural areas who, given their hukou, accept extremely precarious working conditions. This system persists and contributes significantly to the heterogeneity among workers (Chan & Pun, 2010).
4 https://www.reuters.com/article/amazon-cloud-idUSN1E7A727Q20111109.
5 In the last year, the US growth in the 100 global innovators ranking mirrored the fall of Japan (Clarivate Analytics, 2020).
6 https://www.theguardian.com/world/2013/jun/06/us-tech-giants-nsa-data.
7 https://www.ft.com/content/24b01f0e-441e-11ea-a43a-c4b328d9061c.
8 China has the second largest defence budget, accounting for 13.1% of the global total (SIPRI, 2018).
9 https://www.audi-mediacenter.com/en/press-releases/audi-strengthens-partnerships-with-chinese-tech-giants-6711.
10 https://www.ft.com/content/f23d8854-11fa-11ea-a225-db2f231cfeae.
11 An illustration of this point is that among the 30 biggest revenues combining companies and governments in 2015, there are ten companies (Zingales, 2017).
12 (https://www.ft.com/content/602ec7ec-4f18-11ea-95a0-43d18ec715f5?segmentId=b0d7e653-3467-12ab-c0f0-77e4424cdb4c)
13 https://www.ft.com/content/3467659a-386d-11ea-ac3c-f68c10993b04?segmentId=b0d7e653-3467-12ab-c0f0-77e4424cdb4c.
14 https://www.ft.com/content/6f69433a-40f0-11ea-a047-eae9bd51ceba.
15 By 2019, Europe had 3.6% of the market capitalization value of the world's 70 largest digital platforms (UNCTAD, 2019).

References

Arocena, R. (2018). Power, innovation systems and development. *Innovation and Development*, *8*(2), 271–85.

Azmeh, S., Foster, C., & Echavarri, J. (2019). The international trade regime and the quest for free digital trade. *International Studies Review, 22*(3), 671–92.

Babic, M., Fichtner, J., & Heemskerk, E. M. (2017). States versus corporations: Rethinking the power of business in international politics. *The International Spectator*, *52*(4), 20–43.

Berman, E. P. (2011). *Creating the market university: How academic science became an economic engine.* Princeton University Press.

Bethell, J. T., Hunt, R. M., & Shenton, R. (2009). *Harvard A to Z.* Harvard University Press.

Block, F. (2008). Swimming against the current: The rise of a hidden developmental state in the United States. *Politics & Society*, *36*(2), 169–206.

Braun, B. (2020). *American asset manager capitalism.* SocArXiv, 18 June 2020. Web. doi:10.31235/osf.io/v6gue

Bryan, D., Rafferty, M., & Wigan, D. (2017). Capital unchained: Finance, intangible assets and the double life of capital in the offshore world. *Review of International Political Economy*, *24*(1), 56–86.

Bush, V. (1945). Science: The endless frontier. *Transactions of the Kansas Academy of Science (1903-)*, *48*(3), 231–64.

Bustelo Gómez, P., & Fernández Lommen, Y. (1996). *La economía china ante el siglo XXIveinte años de reforma*. Síntesis.

Castro, D., McLaughlin, M., & Chivot, E. (2019). *Who is winning the AI race: China, the EU or the United States?* Center for Data Innovation.

Chan, J., & Pun, N. (2010). Suicide as protest for the new generation of Chinese migrant workers: Foxconn, global capital, and the state. *The Asia-Pacific Journal, 37*(2), 1–50.

Chen, X., & Ogan, T. L. (2017). China's emerging Silicon Valley: How and why has Shenzhen become a global innovation centre. *European Financial Review*, 55.

China Clarivate Analytics. (2018). *2018 top 100 Chinese innovators*. Clarivate Analytics.

Ciuriak, D. (2019). A trade war fuelled by technology. *Opinion, January, 11*. https://www.cigionline.org/articles/trade-war-fuelled-technology

Clarivate Analytics. (2020). *Derwent top 100 global innovators 2020*. Clarivate Analytics.

Clausing, K. A. (2020). Profit shifting before and after the tax cuts and jobs act. *SSRN 3274827*

Cox, R. W. (1981). Social forces, states and world orders: Beyond international relations theory. *Millennium, 10*(2), 126–55.

Dasgupta, P., & David, P. A. (1994). Toward a new economics of science. *Research Policy, 23*(5), 487–521.

de Graaff, N. (2020). China Inc. goes global. Transnational and national networks of China's globalizing business elite. *Review of International Political Economy, 27*(2), 208–33.

Delgado-Ramos, G. C. (2007). Alcances y límites del sistema científico tecnológico chino. *CONfines de Relaciones Internacionales y Ciencia Política, 3*(5), 35–48.

Drahos, P. (1995). Global property rights in information: The story of TRIPS at the GATT. *Prometheus, 13*(1), 6–19.

Durand, C., & Milberg, W. (2020). Intellectual monopoly in global value chains. *Review of International Political Economy*, 27(2) 404–429. doi:10.1080/09692290.2019.1660703

Ernst, D. (2020). *Competing in artificial intelligence chips: China's challenge amid technology war*.

European Commission. (2019). *EU R&D scoreboard*. European Commission.

Farrell, H., & Newman, A. L. (2010). Making global markets: Historical institutionalism in international political economy. *Review of International Political Economy, 17*(4), 609–38.

Feenberg, A. (2010). *Between reason and experience: Essays in technology and modernity*. MIT Press.

Fichtner, J., & Heemskerk, E. M. (2018). The new permanent universal owners: Index funds, (Im) patient Capital, and the Claim of Long-termism. *SSRN 3321597*

García-Herrero, A. (2019). Europe in the midst of China-US strategic competition: What are the European Union's options? *Bruegel Working Papers* No. 2019/03. Brussels

Girado, G. A. (2017). *¿Cómo lo hicieron los Chinos?: Algunas de las causas del gran desarrollo del gigante asiático*. Astrea.

Glick, M. (2019). Antitrust and economic history: The historic failure of the Chicago school of antitrust. *The Antitrust Bulletin*, *64*(3), 295–340.

Glick, M., & Ruetschlin, C. (2019). Big tech acquisitions and the potential competition doctrine: The case of Facebook. *Institute for New Economic Thinking Working Paper Series*, *104*, 1–60.

Godin, B. (2006). The linear model of innovation: The historical construction of an analytical framework. *Science, Technology, & Human Values*, *31*(6), 639–67.

Godinho, M. M., & Ferreira, V. (2012). Analyzing the evidence of an IPR take-off in China and India. *Research Policy*, *41*(3), 499–511.

Gu, S., Schwaag Serger, S., & Lundvall, B. A. (2016). China's innovation system: Ten years on. *Innovation*, *18*(4), 441–48.

Hager, S. B., & Baines, J. (2020). The tax advantage of big business: How the structure of corporate taxation fuels concentration and inequality. *Politics & Society*, *48*(2), 275–305.

Jia, K., Kenney, M., & Zysman, J. (2018). Global competitors? Mapping the internationalization strategies of Chinese digital platform firms. In Tulder, R., Verbeke, A. and Piscitello, L. (Eds.) *International business in the information and digital age*. 187–216. Emerald Publishing Limited.

Klein, N. (2020). Screen new deal. *The Intercept*. https://theintercept.com/2020/05/08/andrew-cuomo-eric-schmidt-coronavirus-tech-shock-doctrine/

Lane, C. (2007). National capitalisms and global production networks: An analysis of their interaction in two global industries. *Socio-Economic Review*, *6*(2), 227–60. doi:10.1093/ser/mwm010

Lee, K., Gao, X., & Li, X. (2016). Industrial catch-up in China: A sectoral systems of innovation perspective. *Cambridge Journal of Regions, Economy and Society*, *10*(1), 59–76.

Lopez Giron, A. J., & Vialle, P. (2017). *A preliminary analysis of mergers and acquisitions by Microsoft from 1992 to 2016: A resource and competence perspective*. Proceedings 28th European Regional Conference of the International Telecommunications Society (ITS): "Competition and Regulation in the Information Age".

Marginson, S. (2014). University research: The social contribution of University research. In Shin, J and Teichler, U. (Eds.) *The future of the post-massified University at the crossroads* (pp. 101–17). Springer. http://link.springer.com/chapter/10.1007/978-3-319-01523-1_8

Mazzucato, M. (2015). *The entrepreneurial state: Debunking public vs. private sector myths* (Vol. 1). Anthem Press.

Milberg, W., & Winkler, D. (2013). *Outsourcing economics: Global value chains in capitalist development*. Cambridge University Press.

Montalban, M., & Sakinç, M. E. (2013). Financialization and productive models in the pharmaceutical industry. *Industrial and Corporate Change*, *22*(4), 981–1030.

Mueller, M. L. (2011). China and global Internet governance: A tiger by the tail. *Access Contested: Security, Identity, and Resistance in Asian Cyberspace*, 177–94.

Muscio, A., Quaglione, D., & Vallanti, G. (2013). Does government funding complement or substitute private research funding to universities? *Research Policy*, *42*(1), 63–75.

National Science Foundation. (2020). *2020 the state of U.S. science & engineering.* National Science Foundation.

Noh, H., & Lee, S. (2019). Where technology transfer research originated and where it is going: A quantitative analysis of literature published between 1980 and 2015. *The Journal of Technology Transfer, 44*(3), 700–40.

Nolan, P. (2012). Is China buying the world? *Challenge, 55*(2), 108–18.

Pestre, D. (2003). *Science, argent et politique: Un essai d'interprétation: une conférence-débat orgnanisée par la groupe Sciences en questions, Paris, INRA, 22 novembre 2001.* Editions Quae.

Pozsar, Z. (2018). Repatriation, the echo-taper and the€/$ basis. *Global Money Notes, 11.*

PWC. (2020). *Global top 100 companies by market capitalisation.* PWC.

Rose, H., & Rose, S. P. R. (2014). *Genes, cells, and brains: The promethean promises of the new biology.* Verso Trade.

Ruttan, V. W. (2006). *Is war necessary for economic growth?: Military procurement and technology development.* Oxford University Press.

Schwartz, H. M. (2019). American hegemony: Intellectual property rights, dollar centrality, and infrastructural power. *Review of International Political Economy, 26*(3), 490–519. https://doi.org/10.1080/09692290.2019.1597754

Shubber, K. (2019, November 5). US price-fixing prosecutions at historic low for third straight year. *Financial Times.* https://www.ft.com/content/a3b75c80-fe74-11e9-be59-e49b2a136b8d

Slipak, A. (2018). Las relaciones entre China y Alemania en el tablero de la Economía Política Internacional. Una mirada desde América Latina. *Realidad Económica.*

Slipak, A., & Ghiotto, L. (2019). América Latina en la Nueva Ruta de la Seda; El rol de las inversiones chinas en la región en un contexto de disputa (inter) hegemónica. *Cuadernos de Estudios Latinoamericanos (CEL), 4*(7), 26–55.

Starrs, S. (2013). American economic power hasn't declined—It Globalized! Summoning the data and taking globalization seriously. *International Studies Quarterly, 57*(4), 817–30.

Strange, S. (1993). Big business and the state. In Eden, L. and Potter, E. (Eds.) *Multinationals in the global political economy* (pp. 101–7). Springer.

Strange, S. (1996). *The retreat of the state: The diffusion of power in the world economy.* Cambridge University Press.

Svampa, M., & Slipak, A. (2018). Amérique latine entre vieilles et nouvelles dépendances: Le rôle de la Chine dans la dispute (inter) hégémonique. *Hérodote. Revue de Géographie et de Géopolitique, 4,* 153–66.

Tejeda Canobbio, E. (2011). Lecciones de política económica e industrial para México. China, industria electrónica y derechos de propiedad. *Cuadernos de Trabajo Del Cechimex, 7,* 1–16.

Ting, A. (2014). ITax – Apple's international tax structure and the double non-taxation issue. *British Tax Review, 1.* https://scholar.google.com/scholar?hl=en&as_sdt=0%2C5&q=iTax+%E2%80%93+Apple%E2%80%99s+International+Tax+Structure+and+the+Double+Non-taxation+Issue%E2%80%99.&btnG=

UNCTAD. (2019). *Digital Economy Report 2019: Value creation and capture–Implications for developing countries.* United Nations.

Veugelers, R. (2018). *Are European firms falling behind in the global corporate research race?* Bruegel Policy Contribution.

Wade, R. H. (2017). The American paradox: Ideology of free markets and the hidden practice of directional thrust. *Cambridge Journal of Economics*, *41*(3), 859–80.

Walia, A. (2020). *The coming tech wall and the covid dilemma*. Deutsche Bank.

Weinhardt, C., & ten Brink, T. (2020). Varieties of contestation: China's rise and the liberal trade order. *Review of International Political Economy*, *27*(2), 258–80.

Weiss, L. (2014). *America Inc.? Innovation and enterprise in the national security state*. Cornell University Press.

Wen, Y. (2017). *The rise of Chinese transnational ICT corporations: The case of Huawei* [PhD Thesis]. Communication, Art & Technology: School of Communication.

Wu, X., & Gereffi, G. (2018). Amazon and Alibaba: Internet governance, business models, and Internationalization strategies. In Tulder, R., Verbeke, A. and Piscitello, L. (Eds.) *International business in the information and digital age* (pp. 327–56). Emerald Publishing Limited.

Yang, Y. (2020, August 3). Why TikTok owner ByteDance is no Huawei for Beijing. *Financial Times*. https://www.ft.com/content/0c42dc7c-b927-477a-90b7-a202bbe4bc50

Zeng, D. Z. (2010). *Building engines for growth and competitiveness in China: Experience with special economic zones and industrial clusters*. The World Bank.

Zingales, L. (2017). Towards a political theory of the firm. *Journal of Economic Perspectives*, *31*(3), 113–30.

5

RESEARCH UNIVERSITIES

Between subordination and intellectual monopoly*[1]

1 Introduction

Universities have historically been conceived as detached from the economic realm. Even if their "products" (trained professionals and knowledge) have always been indispensable inputs for capital accumulation, their role as a productive engine for technical change is a 20th-century outcome. Indeed, innovation was not always conceived, as it is today, as "science applied" to industry. By the end of the 19th century, thinkers still considered innovation as the connection of science with the useful arts (Godin, 2014).

Far from that scenario, frontiers between science and industry are fuzzier than ever. Since the 1990s, academic capitalism accelerated in the United States and around the world. It consolidated a new knowledge and learning international regime, including world university rankings shaping internal academic behaviours and university-industry links beyond national borders, in line with the progressive transnationalization of innovation networks. For Münch (2014), in this new regime, the sharp differentiation between science and economy ceased. As universities became marketers, academic research internally transformed its logics and practices, amalgamating traditional Western academic culture and its specific forms of competition with behaviours and demands previously exclusive of the private spheres of capital accumulation (Slaughter & Rhoades, 2004). In countries like China, where there was not such a tradition of academic freedom for research (Marginson, 2011), universities spread in these decades already integrated into corporate innovation networks, intertwined with enterprises.

In this chapter, we will argue that universities' adoption of enterprise characteristics gave rise to different types of academic capitalism universities, according to the type of firm they could emulate. We will dig into how research universities (and their researchers) contribute with their research to produce science-based innovations and what consequences this brings to academic labour. To do so, we analytically distinguish two intertwined

* This chapter is co-authored with Prof. Hugo Harari-Kermadec (IDHES, Université Paris Saclay).

transformations: "internal" academic labour changes, adapting itself to capitalist production processes and the "external" exchanges of research outcomes, considering universities' different bargaining power to decide the conditions of those exchanges.

Concerning academic labour, the blurring frontiers between public and private are affecting working conditions just as it occurred with labour in general. Competition to retain and obtain the few remaining permanent positions or relatively good jobs is fostered by an overall scenario of casualization, precarious working conditions and an extreme focus on individual performances. This scenario raises mental illnesses and weakens workers' position in class struggle (Hall & Bowles, 2016; Roggero, 2011).

Regarding the "external transformation", partly driven by the pressure to link academic research to innovation, research universities regularly participate in innovation networks planned and organized by intellectual monopolies. These monopolies predate knowledge that is assetized, triggering intellectual rents at the expense of subordinated firms and, what interests us in this chapter, at the expense of research universities.

The rest of our chapter is organized as follows. Section 2 argues that the adoption of private firms' charactertistics by universities can be better understood as a differentiated process. In particular, since we are interested in universities' transformation from public or commons to private knowledge producers, we suggest two types of research universities. We analyse how these two ideal types participate in intellectual monopolies' innovation networks. Next, we present the internal transformations taking place at university laboratories or research centres understood as a process of commodification of academic labour, thus looking at its effects on scholars, their salaries and working conditions. The role of public policy fostering these transformations is also considered. Concluding remarks and further research questions are presented in the final section, together with some nuances concerning the general transformations developed throughout the chapter.

2 The academic intellectual monopoly and subordinate research-universities

Intellectual monopolies partner with universities and public research organizations, even by installing facilities and joint research centres in their perimeters. An example is CREATE initiative in Singapore, which involves intellectual monopolies, local and core countries' research universities (see Chapter 12). Nikon has Imaging Centers or Centers of Excellence in 15 academic institutions.[2] Microsoft established the "MSR-INRIAMicrosoft Research Inria Joint Centre" at France's National Institute for Research in Digital Science and Technology (INRIA) and has a "CUHK MoE-Microsoft Key Lab" at the City University of Hong Kong. Siemens has eight Centers of Knowledge Interchange (CKI), four in Germany and the other four in

Graz University of Technology (Austria), Tsinghua University (China), UC Berkeley (USA) and Georgia Tech (USA).[3] And the list continues.

Overall, the nature of academic research changed. In its most extreme form, focusing on the economic value of knowledge demands to replace fundamental research – detached from possible applications – with research oriented towards producing innovations (Pestre, 2003). Even basic research became, as its name implies, the basis of future applications. It is produced with applicability as a long-term aim, as in Stokes' (1997) Pasteur quadrant. Slaughter and Leslie (1997) call this transformation the emergence of technoscience, which is at once science and product. This change took place together with a transformation of the scientific production regime: from a handicraft activity requiring a small investment in equipment and facilities, towards big (expensive and industrialized) science (Rose & Rose, 2014). The availability of funds further contributes to differentiate universities and research groups.

Both private funding and competitive public grants influence research lines and reinforce market logic (Arocena et al., 2015; Pavlidis, 2012; Rikap, 2017a; Slaughter & Leslie, 1997; Vincent-Lancrin, 2006). Public and private frontiers vanish because there is a unification of the senses and motives beneath academic research and funding orientation. However, even if the origins of the monies and research aims are confounded between public and private, are both public and private benefiting from successful results? Furthermore, are all research universities equally enjoying economic benefits of this turn towards assetization? Both questions have a negative answer.

The turn of academic knowledge into assets included an adaptation to quantitative evaluation criteria. Quantification amalgamates knowledge with commodities, which can be industrially reproduced thus uniformed and normalized. World university rankings are the most extreme form of academic quantification, as we show in Section 3. All over the world, but especially in Asia, policies were put in place to transform most prestigious universities into world-class institutions. The definition of a world-class institution is, in itself, the result of quantitative indicators that privilege research over teaching and that evaluate research results with indicators that reduce knowledge to homogeneous and comparable units (Hazelkorn, 2011; Ziguras, 2016). Altbach (2013) has fostered the world-class recommendation for developing countries stating that those research universities would contribute to their countries' economic growth. The author emphasizes that they could generate significant incomes from tuition and fees, intellectual property rights (IPRs) and other discoveries with market value.

Meanwhile, in core countries, public R&D also became strongly linked to universities' stratification. The replacement of block-grants with competitive grants led to a self-reinforcing scheme where winning increases the chances to keep winning in the future. Winning competitive research grants confers status and revenues, while it fosters national competition (Marginson, 2016; Taylor, 2016). As Münch (2014) explains, the so-called entrepreneurial universities compete for a higher-ranking position, grants, scholars and students. An extreme example is that of the Nanyang Technological University. It fired 200 tenured faculty members aged between 55 and 65 because their performance was not aligned with the university's research benchmarks.

This section aims to make sense of the transformations mentioned above within the general picture of intellectual monopoly capitalism, which is the backbone of this book. Considering the taxonomy of firms presented in Chapter 2, we distinguish between two types of research universities according to their place in global innovation networks. If they have certain bargaining power and harvest intellectual rents, to some extent emulating (corporate) intellectual monopolies, we call them academic intellectual monopolies. On the contrary, if they participate in subordinate positions, we will refer to them as subordinate research universities copying features of innovating companies. As it was explained in Chapter 2, start-up companies, frequently university spin-offs, are the typical example of innovating companies.

Every university copying private firms' features may try to become an intellectual monopoly, thus steering knowledge production according to its own economic needs and collecting resulting benefits. However, most universities will not have the required enforcement capacity and resources. As was concluded by Link (2015, p. 199) for the case of projects funded by US federal agencies, "when a firm engages in a Phase II project along with a university research partner, it can appropriate the knowledge flows from university in terms of a greater likelihood of patenting and in terms of greater employee growth".

As further explained in Chapter 2, being an intellectual monopoly entails to systematically plan and organize innovation networks and be capable of garnering intellectual rents from successful results. Hence, it demands a history of past successive innovations, meaning that knowledge results should be successfully integrated into planned production networks expanding capital accumulation. In other words, the build upon their previous innovations. Moreover, financial strength is required to keep that innovative pace. In addition, once established as an intellectual monopoly, the corporation should be capable of outsourcing innovation modules and still profit from their successful results, while transferring the risk (associated with knowledge uncertainty) to other organizations.

Many research universities have a successful tradition of knowledge accomplishments. However, most research universities are under severe budget constraints. Remarkably, those with a history of scientific breakthroughs, in general, lack an equally successful history of monetizing those breakthroughs. Spin-off companies' most common destiny is bankruptcy. In the few cases where they are successful, they often end up being acquired (generally by an intellectual monopoly). If even in Silicon Valley success rates are extremely low,[4] what are the chances left for university spin-offs?

It makes sense to think that most research universities will behave as innovating companies, subordinating to intellectual monopolies. At least to some extent, their research becomes planned by intellectual monopolies (or by academic intellectual monopolies). Their research laboratories and individual scholars engage in the production of innovations. However, knowledge is assetized by intellectual monopolies who seldom share the ownership of resulting IPRs, when they participate in experimental steps, as we show in the next section. Anyway, formally co-owning IPRs does not necessarily mean that intellectual monopolies share the associated rents, as Chapter 12 shows for Singapore's world-class universities. As explained by Birch (2017), knowledge becomes capitalized property when IPRs transform it into an asset. It is a revenue-generating resource that allows its owner to collect rents, even if no commodity is being sold on the market with the achieved result.

Concerning the few cases of academic intellectual monopolies, drawing on Münch and Baier (2012), we argue that oligopolistic structures have emerged in the scientific realm. A small number of institutions appropriate most of the research funds. For them, a virtuous circle emerges (which is a vicious circle for those left behind). Past research and development successes better position them for future innovation projects. This small group of academic research institutions monopolized the capacity to produce cutting-edge knowledge integrated into different innovation circuits. They have become (academic) intellectual monopolies garnering part of the resulting intellectual rents of the innovation circuits they contribute to organizing and where other (subordinate) research institutions participate without significant profits. Chapter 13 exemplifies this practice, including the case of joint patents between Columbia University and the University of Buenos Aires, where the former keeps all the royalties.

Academic intellectual monopolies also enjoy – when this is legally authorized – large endowments. Endowments induce financialization. Cantwell (2016) has argued that university endowment management is a form of financial-academic capitalism where the priority is the management of those funds in order to maximize returns rather than managing them according to the university's internal requirements. Kantor and Whalley (2014) observed that many US universities tend to spend between 4% and 5% of the market value of their endowment each year. So, if their stocks grow (decrease), they spend more (less), independently of internal requirements.[5]

Chapters 12 and 13 present study cases of subordinate research universities, as we said, the most frequent university type among research universities engaging in innovation activities. The Fraunhofer Society,

Germany's major public applied research organization – with more than 70 research institutes – is another compelling example. Created after the Second World War, military or defence research played an essential role in its beginnings, but now represents less than 5% of total research funds. Since the 1960s, Fraunhofer Society changed its budget structure. The public sector provides around 30% as a block-grant, and the rest depends on each institute's ability to attract its own funding sources. The latter include public and European Union grants, but also private sources. By 2018, contracts with industry represented one-third of its total research budget (The Fraunhofer Society, 2019). This funding scheme influences research priorities and results in privileging IPRs over publications. At least since 2008, the Fraunhofer Society is among Germany's 20th most prolific patent applicants. However, licence-fees revenue represented less than 4% of its total budget in 2018, a figure that Fraunhofer's annual report claims to be going down due to the expiration of licensed patents.

In an interview with a former Fraunhofer researcher, we verified that prioritizing IPRs means that every significant result must first be provided to the patent office to assess whether it should be patented before publication. The interviewee also claimed that this institution struggles when it comes to commercializing R&D results. The researcher mentioned the case of a promising patent granting a monopoly over a product that was required to comply with an international standard. The patent was sold to a company instead of licensing it or starting a spin-off company, which resulted in fewer revenues for Fraunhofer. As the public sector still funds around 66% of Fraunhofer's research contracts through block-grants and competitive calls at the local, national or EU level, it might be said that through Fraunhofer the state subsidizes private firms. Indeed, Comin et al. (2019) found that firms' performance in Germany is positively related to interacting with Fraunhofer and becomes stronger the more often firms establish those links. Although an in-depth analysis should be conducted to validate this assertion, Fraunhofer could be considered as an example of a subordinate research university.

Examples of research universities that qualify as academic intellectual monopolies are Columbia University and Harvard. Concerning the former, its network of Alumni in the United States, which includes federal judges, contributes to guarantee compliance with its IPRs, which strengthens its deterrence capacity. Harvard also enjoys this type of advantange. Moreover, it keeps the economic profits of its performed research, even when private sources have significantly sponsored it. Harvard is always the exclusive owner of possible results. It is also financially autonomous. It succeeds both in terms of private sponsorship and competitive public funds for research and has the biggest university endowment fund (Taylor et al., 2013). Nevertheless, its research priorities are defined following a top-down structure. Its board of trustees includes Google (Kent Walker, Senior Vice President, Global Affairs and Chief Legal Officer) and Snap Inc (Michael M. Lynton, Chairman) representatives, evidencing how intertwined these types of universities are with corporate intellectual monopolies.

We analyse next how the emergence of these two types of universities affects academic freedom and the orientation of research agendas.

2.1 Academic freedom and the definition of research agendas under intellectual monopoly capitalism

Although academic intellectual monopolies are not constrained by their budgets, this is not enough to guarantee their researchers' academic freedom. Under intellectual monopoly capitalism, academic freedom is subordinated to profiting from knowledge. Researchers in private R&D laboratories may enjoy some degrees of academic freedom to decide their research topics and methods, as far as that research contributes to higher profits. Take, for instance, Google's working scheme. Workers are encouraged to dedicate 30% of their time to non-core duties to stimulate innovation (Steiber, 2014). Hence, further developing the idea of fuzziness between science and economy, as intellectual monopolies encourage what we could rename as R&D autonomy, research universities subordinate academic freedom to economic goals.

As in a corporation, senior officials occupying top positions of a hierarchical decision-making structure define research lines in academic intellectual monopolies. These managers guide research towards preserving their universities' leadership, usually in line with corporate needs. As shown by Barringer and Slaughter (2016), the board of trustees of elite private universities in the United States orients research according to the needs of the enterprises they also represent. Furthermore, in these institutions, the criteria applied to define who is a top researcher to be hired is associated with her capacity to attract private resources, which implicitly benefits researchers that are less attached to historical academic freedom principles.

Participating in innovation networks is as crucial for an academic intellectual monopoly as it is for the subordinate research university. What differentiates these types of universities is the capacity of the former to plan and organize its innovation circuits and networks that is absent in the latter, which participates but subordinating to intellectual monopolies. Subordination is both a knowledge and economic relation. Concerning the former, subordinate research universities have little to no say in the organization and definition of research priorities when they join innovation networks. Regarding the latter, they have limited chances to monetize their creative results, which are transformed into assets by intellectual monopolies.

Let us consider the case of private sponsorship of research. Typically, the academic intellectual monopoly receives private sponsorship without looking for it. In contrast, the subordinate research university seeks private sponsorship and is more prone to accept these sponsors' external research orientations. When successful, it delivers research results to sponsors that generally did not pay an innovation rent as part of that agreement, but only part of the associated costs. By fulfilling these private needs, academic freedom is jeopardized. Academic freedom is also endangered due to budget shortfalls because they may directly condition research questions, adapting to those that might be economically feasible, thus limiting creativity and negatively impacting on global knowledge production. In some cases, primarily when these institutions are located in the peripheries, they may not even have the resources to pay international publishers – another example of intellectual monopolies – for access to frontier research. If they do so, the economic burden will go at the expense of other research expenses.

Academic intellectual monopolies also steer research agendas of subordinate research universities. From a dependency theory perspective, uneven relations between universities have been conceived as a form of academic dependency (Beigel, 2010, 2017) or subordinated integration (Kreimer, 2006, 2014). Drawing on these contributions, we argue that current forms of academic dependency happen at the institutional and not at the country level. The gap between universities from the same country has widened; they are not all equally dependent. The role played by each university is also conditioned by the types of institutions that are working together. An academic intellectual monopoly and a subordinate research university working together to achieve market innovations will not relate on equal terms regardless of their country of origin. The former will lead the project, orient it and retain most of the profits.[6] Nevertheless, as far as academic intellectual monopolies are based in core countries, the centre-periphery unequal circulation and production of knowledge is reinforced.

Academic freedom discussions directly point to the impact of these transformations on scholars. In the next section, we concentrate on labour, considering the differences between the two introduced types of research universities.

3 Academic labour commodification

Academic work has adopted commodity-producing labour characteristic *pari passu* with universities' reconfigurations. To some extent, these changes were fostered by the quantitative modalities of the new public management (Bruno, 2009). Elaborating on Harvie (2006), diverse activities like teaching and research are becoming commensurable activities due to the imposition of metrics whose underlying aim is to transform academic work into alienated and commodified labour. Here, we unpack this transformation concentrating on the effects of quantification on academic labour. A summary is presented in Table 5.1.

Table 5.1 Summary firms, university types and impact on academic labour

Type of firms (see Chapter 2)	*Resulting research university type*	*Position in innovation networks*	*Main market activities*	*Academic labour*
Intellectual monopoly	Academic intellectual monopoly	Dominant	Organizes innovation circuits and networks and is capable of harvesting rents from them, enjoying the funds provided by less powerful actors.	Highest salaries and best working benefits. More stable working conditions. Worktime allocation: mostly research. Limited teaching hours and university staff takes care of administrative tasks (such as writing applications for grants).
Innovating company	Subordinate research university	Subordinate	It participates in innovation circuits but subordinated to intellectual monopolies, without significantly profiting from successful results.	Maximum pressure from university management (and state) to go up in rankings, thus to outperform in research (imposition of quantitative evaluations: number of published papers and citations in top journals).

3.1 Evaluation as a process that transforms academic labour

The traditional form of the academic relation has been conceptualized in alternative ways. Humboldt (1810) stated that masters and students (together) should carry out collaborative research. Masters were expected to convey the spirit of fundamental research, to inspire passion for knowledge production and to contribute to the organization and transformation of human experience (Schleiermacher, 1808). In Humboldt's project for the University of Berlin, freedom to learn and to teach was supposed to be granted (Anderson, 2004; Bermejo Castrillo, 2008; Morgan, 2011). The Humboldtian University model expanded beyond Germany to the whole Western world and prevailed as a guiding principle for universities until the irruption of economic accountability (Rikap, 2017b).

The centrality given by Western scholars to the development of science, which is a legacy of this Humboldtian University model, prevailed during most of the 20th century and led Merton (1973) to conceptualize science as a specific social institution, with its norms acting as the moral authority. Advancing knowledge was supposed to be scholars' primary role, hence in this ethos, priority in discoveries was paramount and should be rewarded as such.

These detached logics and practices clashed with the new economic role given to universities and science. Therefore, as their very meanings were changing, an internal transformation took place in the academic relation between researchers, compatible with the intertwined new reality that combined scientific and economic aims. The spread of evaluation criteria as the quantification of achievements influenced this transformation.

With the proliferation of competitive calls for public grants, the state abandoned its benevolent form (characterized by providing block-grants without further control over universities' expenses) towards what Neave (1988, 1998, 2012) dubbed the Evaluative State. In short, the Evaluative State promotes the use of metrics. Thus, they steer the quantification process. Nevertheless, as shown by Hazelkorn (2011), quantitative criteria prevail not only in the state's assessment of university results but also as means used internally. Once science and economy intertwine, evaluation spreads everywhere (to universities, research institutions or departments, scholars and scientific publications) based on quantified indicators, which, in line with Faure et al. (2005, pp. 115–6), result from codifying, standardizing and even taylorizing academic tasks.

Evaluation is an active process that contributes to shaping the evaluated subject according to the assessment criteria. Thus, the introduction of quantitative criteria to evaluate universities (and their productive relations and products) is actively transforming academic labour. While it kept some of its specificities, it merged them with the commodity production relation. Furthermore, evaluation results are signals for potential students but also for firms, in particular for intellectual monopolies that will quickly identify cutting-edge research. Academic quantification facilitates intellectual monopolies *know-who* should be contacted for each step of their innovation networks.

3.2 A change in the benchmark from the average to the top

Quantitative indicators could consider averages as benchmarks when applying a metric to a set of comparable objects. Averages were the norm under Taylorism and Fordism; tasks were standardized, split into short, homogeneous and timed parts (Braverman, 1998). Workers had to avoid deviations from the planned process placed in the middle. But the norm changed and is no longer placed at the middle or average, but at the top (Desrosières, 2003; see also Jany-Catrice, 2012). Rankings have a normalizing power over universities in terms of their aims and strategies (Kauppinen et al., 2016).

As quantitative evaluations spread in university systems around the world, world rankings stood out. Among them, the Shanghai ranking has contributed to defining a new norm for research universities. The categories of "world universities" or "world class universities" (Salmi, 2009) lack a specific definition. They are also abstract because they implicitly assume that every university should have the same goal whatever its history or focus, and that the accomplishment (or not) of this goal can be numerically measured.

In general, quantification is a double act leading to a numeric representation of something: an act of convention and measure (Desrosières, 2008). First, quantification contains the sociologically and politically situated intension of the measure. It defines what will be measured and what will not. Measuring requires redefining the object that will be measured. It needs to be deprived of its particular traits, thus becoming abstract (Endnotes, 2010, p. 135), as with universities in world rankings. The degree of abstraction will define the limits of what fits in the newly proposed category. In this process, the use of numbers conveys in itself a "universalist aim": to measure, the specificities of the object, and the subjectivity of those involved must be left behind (Desrosières, 2008, p. 13).

Nonetheless, every measure is a human act and entails decisions on priorities. In our example, the very rough methodology used for the Shanghai (as well as other) ranking is not purely objective as it is mistakenly assumed just because it is the result of statistic indicators. To measure means to choose what counts and actively abstract differences.

Most research universities and their members (administrative staff, scholars and students) take rankings into account because they influence funding opportunities. Governments, university presidents and managers internally impose the ranking's metric as the new norm and adapt the practices and self-representations of their faculty to be closer to the top, which is the benchmark. It follows that while rankings neglect the vast diversity of universities and the creative nature of science, quantification is actively transforming reality.

More in general, using quantitative indicators to evaluate science is another abstraction process within and beyond world rankings. It assumes that scientific publications are comparable units. Thus, that scientific results are quantitatively comparable. Even differentiating according to the journal where papers are published, it would still assume that two different papers in object, scope, framework and method but published in the same journal, or in a journal with a similar impact factor (another example of a measure that shapes academic labour), are comparable units. Providing the same numeric representation to two different activities assumes – explicitly or not – their common categorization, which assumes that they share a common nature. In the end, for the evaluator, every university activity can be measured and quantitatively compared.

On top of the effects of quantification itself, the definition of the new university benchmark should be scrutinized. Top universities will be those with more published papers in journals with high impact factors. To publish more, researchers need more money and more straightforward ideas that can be packed as a paper in a shorter period without significantly challenging status-quo so that publication is much guaranteed. The former opens the door for private sponsorship, while the latter diminishes the historical aim of the scientific work: a relentless contribution to the advancement of knowledge.

3.3 Harmful consequences on academic labour

Overall, university rankings and other quantitative indicators such as impact-factors and the H-Index, intentionally or unintentionally, contribute to leaving behind former norms of science. They created a new discursive space of representations, hierarchic and numerical, that is well structured for consumers (both students and firms), to orient themselves quickly, and for managers, to *manage* academics. This context poses severe consequences for scholars.[7]

Various authors have shown that faculty working conditions have been deteriorating. Flexible or precarious forms of contracting pile with pressures to deliver measurable results. Severe consequences for scholars' mental health and reduced academic freedom are two salient consequences (Currie & Vidovich, 2009; Enders & De Weert, 2004; Gregory & Winn, 2016; Rikap, 2016; Schapper & Mayson, 2005). Our typology allows us to explain why worse labour conditions are not equally distributed among universities. Academic intellectual monopolies still assure traditional scholars' benefits, at least for a significantly higher percentage of their faculty and restricted to tenure positions, which excludes Ph.D. and postdoctoral fellows.[8]

Both university types, when they are public institutions, are further urged by their corresponding states to outperform globally. This is accomplished by academic intellectual monopolies but is not always the case of subordinate institutions. Subordinate research universities suffer the most from the effects of world rankings. In the quest to become an academic intellectual monopoly, they work to comply both with state's evaluations and world rankings' quantitative criteria. Both leading universities in Singapore are good examples of the latter (see Chapter 12). Internal performance indicators become indistinguishable from those set by world rankings. "Publish or perish" (which in fact should be updated to "publish in high-impact factor journals or perish") and "apply or die" mottos rule in this type of intitution.

Among other examples, as stated by De Angelis and Harvie (2009), the United Kingdom (UK) is a frontline of academic capitalism. There, quantification contributes to reallocate funds according to university metrics. Its Research Excellence Framework (REF) introduced in 2014 is a synthetic score aimed at measuring the quality of university research. It particularly values publications in top journals defined by high-impact factor. Once the REF score is ready, it is multiplied by a cost coefficient specific for each field to define the total public research funding each university will receive. This scaling contributes to remove the specificities of academic work and to subordinate the production of knowledge to the production of exchange values. In other words, academic labour is progressively reorganized to produce more and more *commodities* in the same period.

In this framework, the power relation between universities and the state is reconfigured: academic freedom shrinks for most UK institutions because funding depends on the adaptation of research lines to an external agenda, and on the external evaluation of researchers' productivity. This reinforces the bargaining power of academic intellectual monopolies since they already excel in the considered criteria, and thus take advantage of this situation, accumulating more public resources. Still, as we have already stated, it is in this type of university where the economic transformation has gone the furthest. Successful results in terms of available budget and an assured demand for their products encourage that transformation, which entails pernicious consequences for its workers' academic freedom while inducing them to become publication-machines.

Meanwhile, the rest of the UK system is drowning in budget shortfalls and desperately seeks more customers (students and companies). Consequences are so pervasive that even the most progressive universities, such as SOAS whose disciplines are particularly punished by academic capitalism, are unloading the weight of performing far from the benchmark on scholars. A recent *solution* to budget shortfalls proposed by SOAS management included firing its precarious academics.[9]

Overall, in both types of research universities, the pressures to quickly achieve publishable and patentable results become a huge burden for academic workers. Anxiety and other psychiatric diseases become common pathologies due to an extremely competitive job where each step forward represents a more significant bottleneck. Those succeeding have higher chances of being recruited by an academic intellectual monopoly.

However, once recruited, requirements to keep up to the highest expectations remain both in terms of papers and economic valorization of research. In subordinate research universities, uncertainties on future job possibilities and relative failures (judging by the results of academic intellectual monopolies) also make academic workers more docile to external opportunities. This includes both private sponsorships of research and the possibility to start their own company, despite extremely low success rates.

4 Final remarks

In this chapter, we argued that research universities integrate global innovation networks led by intellectual monopolies in different positions. While a few can bargain with intellectual monopolies, most of them subordinate. Moreover, researching is becoming a more precarious and stressful job driven by the introduction of quantitative metrics and fix-term positions.

Quantification – as in the case of world rankings – evidences the attempt to homogenize academic work. However, universities are more heterogeneous than ever before, their ability as almost private firms to keep their profits and start an amplified accumulation process depends on their role in capitalist dynamics. Here, our distinction between the academic intellectual monopoly and the subordinate research univeristy sheds light. Their differences arise from the capacity of the former to control and organize innovation networks, thus profiting from their results. At the same time, the latter participates in those networks but, like innovating companies, it does not collect rents from its creative endeavour. It sells its research as a one-time product where the price is determined by adding measurable costs, thus not considering a an additional ammount (i.e., an intellectual rent) for the required creativity.

Participating in innovation circuits and networks curtails academic freedom for both research-university types. Although the academic intellectual monopoly has its own resources to balance capital accumulation needs with its internal academic demands, in order to keep its leadership, research tends to be steered towards the interests of corporate intellectual monopolies.

Nonetheless, this is not a unilateral trend. Research universities continue to serve their communities, which is an example of how they fulfil social demands and contribute in a non-commodified way to social and economic development (Arocena et al., 2015). Furthermore, students and faculty in many universities resist and suggest alternative agendas. In the case of quantification, it is noteworthy that some universities – like the University of Hamburg in Germany – have refused to provide their data to be ranked, as an attempt to undermine rankings' power. In Latin America, CLACSO is piloting an initiative called FOLEC aimed at transforming evaluation criteria, deprioritizing papers and acknowledging different research profiles.

The rest of this book will illustrate the framework anticipated in this first part. In every chapter, research universities will be a central player but generally joining intellectual monopolies' innovation networks in subordinated places.

Notes

1 Some sections of this chapter are partially based on the paper "The direct subordination of universities to the accumulation of capital" published by Capital & Class (doi:10.1177/0309816819852761).
2 https://www.microscope.healthcare.nikon.com/imaging-centers.
3 https://new.siemens.com/global/en/company/innovation/collaborations-partnerships.html.
4 https://www.startups.com/community/questions/396/for-every-success-story-in-silicon-valley-how-many-are-there-that-fail.
5 That fixed percentage was dubbed the Bengen rule. Bengen was a financial adviser who estimated that spending around 4% of an endowment or pension fund market value made it sustainable in the long run (Haskel & Westlake, 2018).
6 Please note that, as we previously remarked, we are focusing on the enterprise traits adopted by universities. We are not considering its surviving autonomy, Humboldtian or Mertonian ways of producing knowledge. These features highlight cooperation and the global nature of knowledge, detached from national or any other boundaries.
7 It also harms students, turning them into mere passive consumers instead of active, critical and engaged humans in a continuous learning process.
8 Of course, in countries where scholars are public servants, like France, their working conditions remain more protected. However, even this is changing with the introduction of bonuses for those who excel in their quantitative evaluations.
9 https://www.counterfire.org/news/20841-soas-just-effectively-sacked-all-of-its-casualised-academic-staff-in-one-go.

References

Altbach, P. G. (2013). *The international imperative in higher education*. Springer Science & Business Media.

Anderson, R. D. (2004). *European universities from the enlightenment to 1914*. OUP Oxford.

Arocena, R., Göransson, B., & Sutz, J. (2015). Knowledge policies and universities in developing countries: Inclusive development and the "developmental university." *Technology in Society*, *41*, 10–20.

Barringer, S. N., & Slaughter, S. (2016). University trustees and the entrepreneurial university: Inner circles, interlocks, and exchanges. In Slaughter, S. and Taylor, B. (Eds.) *Higher education, stratification, and workforce development* (pp. 151–71). Springer. http://link.springer.com/chapter/10.1007/978-3-319-21512-9_8

Beigel, F. (2010). *Autonomía y dependencia académica: Universidad e investigación científica en un circuito periférico: Chile y Argentina, 1950–1980*. Editorial Biblos.

Beigel, F. (2017). Científicos Periféricos, entre Ariel y Calibán. Saberes Institucionales y Circuitos de Consagración en Argentina. Las publicaciones de los Investigadores del CONICET. *Dados*, *60*(3), 825–65.

Bermejo Castrillo, M. Á. (2008). La universidad europea entre ilustración y liberalismo: Eclosión y difusión del modelo alemán y evolución de otros sistemas nacionales. In F. Oncina Coves (Ed.), *Filosofía para la universidad, filosofía contra la universidad:(de Kant a Nietzsche)* (pp. 49–165). Dykinson. https://dialnet.unirioja.es/servlet/articulo?codigo=2945241

Birch, K. (2017). Rethinking value in the bio-economy: Finance, assetization, and the management of value. *Science, Technology, & Human Values, 42*(3), 460–90.

Braverman, H. (1998). *Labor and monopoly capital: The degradation of work in the twentieth century.* Monthly Review Press.

Bruno, I. (2009). The "indefinite discipline" of competitiveness benchmarking as a neoliberal technology of government. *Minerva, 47*(3), 261. doi:10.1007/s11024-009-9128-0

Cantwell, B. (2016). The new prudent man: Financial-academic capitalism and inequality in higher education. In Slaughter, S. and Taylor, B. (Eds.) *Higher education, stratification, and workforce development* (pp. 173–92). Springer.

Comin, D., Licht, G., Pellens, M., & Schubert, T. (2019). Do companies benefit from public research organizations? The impact of the Fraunhofer Society in Germany. *The Impact of the Fraunhofer Society in Germany*, SSRN Electronic Journal 19-006. doi:10.2139/ssrn.3354365

Currie, J., & Vidovich, L. (2009). The changing nature of academic work. In Tight, M., Mok, K., Huisman, J. and Morphew, C. (Eds.) *The Routledge international handbook of higher education* (pp. 441–52). Routledge.

De Angelis, M., & Harvie, D. (2009). "Cognitive capitalism" and the rat-race: How capital measures immaterial labour in British universities. *Historical Materialism, 17*(3), 3–30.

Desrosières, A. (2003). Managing the economy. In T. M. Porter & D. Ross (Eds.), *The modern social sciences* (pp. 553–64). Cambridge University Press.

Desrosières, A. (2008). *L'argument statistique; 2: Gouverner par les nombres.* Mines ParisTech-Les Presses.

Enders, J., & De Weert, E. (2004). Science, training and career: Changing modes of knowledge production and labour markets. *Higher Education Policy, 17*(2), 135–52.

Endnotes. (2010). The history of subsumption. *Endnotes, 2*, 144–52.

Faure, S., Millet, M., & Soulié, C. (2005). *Enquête exploratoire sur le travail des enseignants chercheurs. Vers un bouleversement de la 'table des valeurs académiques'?* https://halshs.archives-ouvertes.fr/halshs-00602398/document

Godin, B. (2014). *Innovation and science: When science had nothing to do with innovation, and vice-versa.* Project on the Intellectual History of Innovation, Montreal: INRS, Forthcoming.

Gregory, K. L., & Winn, J. (2016). Marx, Engels and the critique of academic labor. *Workplace: A Journal for Academic Labor, 0*(28). http://ices.library.ubc.ca/index.php/workplace/article/view/186209

Hall, R., & Bowles, K. (2016). Re-engineering higher education: The subsumption of academic labour and the exploitation of anxiety. *Workplace: A Journal for Academic Labor, 28*, 30–47. doi:10.14288/workplace.v0i28.186211

Harvie, D. (2006). Value production and struggle in the classroom: Teachers within, against and beyond capital. *Capital & Class, 30*(1), 1–32.

Haskel, J., & Westlake, S. (2018). *Capitalism without capital: The rise of the intangible economy*. Princeton University Press.

Hazelkorn, E. (2011). *Rankings and the reshaping of higher education: The battle for world-class excellence*. Palgrave

von Humboldt, W. (1810). Sobre la organización interna y externa de los establecimientos científicos superiores en Berlín. In von Humboldt, W. *Escritos Políticos* (pp. 165–75). Fondo de Cultura Económica.

Jany-Catrice, F. (2012). *La performance totale: Nouvel esprit du capitalisme?* Presses Univ. Septentrion.

Kantor, S., & Whalley, A. (2014). Knowledge spillovers from research universities: Evidence from endowment value shocks. *Review of Economics and Statistics, 96*(1), 171–88.

Kauppinen, I., Coco, L., Choi, H., & Brajkovic, L. (2016). Blurring boundaries and borders: Interlocks between AAU institutions and transnational corporations. In Slaughter, S. and Taylor, B. (Eds.) *Higher education, stratification, and workforce development* (pp. 35–57). Springer.

Kreimer, P. (2006). Dependientes o integrados?: La ciencia latinoamericana y la nueva división internacional del trabajo. *Nómadas, 24*, 199–212.

Kreimer, P. (2014). "Citizen of the world" or a local producer of useful knowledge? That's the question. In H. Sabea & F. Beigel (Eds.), *Academic dependency and professionalization in the south: Perspectives from the periphery* (pp. 151–66). EDIUNC- Sephis.

Link, A. N. (2015). Capturing knowledge: Private gains and public gains from university research partnerships. *Foundations and Trends® in Entrepreneurship, 11*(3), 139–206.

Marginson, S. (2011). Higher education in East Asia and Singapore: Rise of the confucian model. *Higher Education, 61*(5), 587–611.

Marginson, S. (2016). Global stratification in higher education. In Slaughter, S. and Taylor, B. (Eds.) *Higher education, stratification, and workforce development* (pp. 13–34). Springer. http://link.springer.com/chapter/10.1007/978-3-319-21512-9_2

Merton, R. K. (1973). *The sociology of science: Theoretical and empirical investigations*. University of Chicago Press.

Morgan, K. J. (2011). Where is von Humboldt's University now? *Research in Higher Education, 42*, 325–44.

Münch, R. (2014). *Academic capitalism: Universities in the global struggle for excellence*. Routledge.

Münch, R., & Baier, C. (2012). Institutional struggles for recognition in the academic field: The case of university departments in German chemistry. *Minerva, 50*(1), 97–126.

Neave, G. (1988). On the cultivation of quality, efficiency and enterprise: An overview of recent trends in higher education in Western Europe, 1986–1988. *European Journal of Education, 23*(1/2), 7–23.

Neave, G. (1998). The evaluative state reconsidered. *European Journal of Education, 33*(3), 265–84.

Neave, G. (2012). *The evaluative state, institutional autonomy and re-engineering higher education in Western Europe: The prince and his pleasure*. Palgrave Macmillan.

Pavlidis, P. (2012). The antinomic condition of the University: "universal labour" beyond "academic capitalism." *The Journal for Critical Education Policy Studies, 10*(2), 139–59.

Pestre, D. (2003). *Science, argent et politique: Un essai d'interprétation: une conférence-débat orgnanisée par la groupe Sciences en questions, Paris, INRA, 22 novembre 2001.* Editions Quae.

Rikap, C. (2016). Heterogeneidades y condiciones de trabajo de los docentes universitarios en la Universidad de Buenos Aires: Un estudio comparado de las Facultades de Farmacia y Bioquímica, y Ciencias Económicas. *Trabajo y Sociedad, 27*, 109–37.

Rikap, C. (2017a). The differentiated market-university. Structural differences among university's commodification processes. In M. Tight & J. Huisman (Eds.), *Theory and method in higher education research* (Vol. 3, pp. 179–96). Emerald Group Publishing.

Rikap, C. (2017b). The meanings of university's autonomy in Western history as a clue to understand the consequences of universities' differentiated adoption of enterprise features. *Journal for Critical Education Policy Studies (JCEPS), 15*(3), 266–304.

Roggero, G. (2011). *The production of living knowledge: The crisis of the university and the transformation of labor in Europe and North America.* Temple University Press.

Rose, H., & Rose, S. P. R. (2014). *Genes, cells, and brains: The promethean promises of the new biology.* Verso Trade.

Salmi, J. (2009). *The challenge of establishing world-class universities.* World Bank Publications.

Schapper, J., & Mayson, S. (2005). Managerialism, internationalization, Taylorization and the deskilling of academic work: Evidence from an Australian university. In P. Ninnes & M. Hellstén (Eds.), *Internationalizing higher education: Critical explorations of pedagogy and policy* (Springer, pp. 181–97). Springer. http://link.springer.com/content/pdf/10.1007/1-4020-3784-8_10.pdf

Schleiermacher, F. (1808). *Pensamientos ocasionales sobre universidades en sentido alemán, con un Apéndice sobre la erección de una nueva.* De Gruyter.

Slaughter, S., & Leslie, L. L. (1997). *Academic capitalism: Politics, policies, and the entrepreneurial university.* ERIC. http://eric.ed.gov/?id=ED409816

Slaughter, S., & Rhoades, G. (2004). *Academic capitalism and the new economy: Markets, state, and higher education.* JHU Press.

Steiber, A. (2014). *The Google model: Managing continuous innovation in a rapidly changing world.* Springer Science & Business Media.

Stokes, D. E. (1997). *Pasteur's quadrant: Basic science and technological innovation.* Brookings.

Taylor, B. J. (2016). The field dynamics of stratification among US research universities: The expansion of federal support for academic research, 2000–2008. In Slaughter, S. and Taylor, B. (Eds.) *Higher Education, Stratification, and Workforce Development* (pp. 59–79). Springer. http://link.springer.com/chapter/10.1007/978-3-319-21512-9_4

Taylor, B. J., Cantwell, B., & Slaughter, S. (2013). Quasi-markets in US higher education: The humanities and institutional revenues. *The Journal of Higher Education, 84*(5), 675–707.

The Fraunhofer Society. (2019). *Annual Report 2018: 70 years of Fraunhofer, 70 years of future. What's next.* The Fraunhofer Society.
Vincent-Lancrin, S. (2006). What is changing in academic research? Trends and futures scenarios. *European Journal of Education*, *41*(2), 169–202.
Ziguras, C. (2016). Globalization and the transformation of Asian higher education. In C. Collins, M. Lee, J. Hawkins, & D. Neubauer (Eds.), *The Palgrave handbook of Asia Pacific higher education* (pp. 73–88). Springer. http://link.springer.com/chapter/10.1057/978-1-137-48739-1_5

Part 2

GLOBAL INTELLECTUAL MONOPOLIES. ILLUSTRATIVE CASES

6

TECHNOLOGICAL COOPERATION AND COMPETITION AMONG BIG PHARMACEUTICALS[1]

1 Introduction

The main contribution of this chapter is to show how intellectual monopoly's innovation networks are alternatively in technological cooperation or technological competition with each other. This is illustrated by studying the pharmaceutical industry, focusing on big pharmaceuticals selling patented prescription drugs, vaccines, and treatments. We also show that big pharmaceuticals predate from their innovation networks, turning into intangible assets knowledge that was at least partly created by other participating organizations, particularly universities. The chapter presents a two-step model for the inception of intellectual monopolies and mobilizes it to study Roche, Novartis and Pfizer's innovation networks.

Intellectual monopolies modularize knowledge production, distinguishing between competing steps of their innovation processes and steps where they collaborate for technology. For instance, generic modules can be co-produced between several intellectual monopolies and then integrated and combined with other equally generic or more specific modules from each of these leaders' different innovation circuits.

Concerning technological competition, as it was explained in Chapter 2, intellectual monopolies rely on their internal Research & Development (R&D) capabilities as well as on innovation outsourcing to reinforce their knowledge monopoly. In the case of pharmaceutical intellectual monopolies, universities and their hospitals, together with small R&D laboratories and public agencies, participate in this process, and this chapter argues that they do so in a subordinated way. These subordinate organizations can be conceived as subordinate research universities (see Chapter 5) and innovating companies (see Chapter 2) because they participate in innovation networks but without garnering significant associated intellectual rents, which are mostly appropriated by the intellectual monopoly.

The pharmaceutical industry is paradigmatic for studying technological cooperation and competition dynamics between intellectual monopolies. Big pharmaceuticals outsource most of the innovation processes as an answer to the recent exhaustion of the blockbuster model (Collier, 2011; Khanna, 2012; Lazonick et al., 2017). Moreover, since the 1990s, even if the biotechnology revolution resulted in more firms, its core concentration ratio increased. This core has an autonomous capacity to steer the industry, organizing from discovery to the distribution of new drugs (Baranes, 2016).

In this chapter, we focus on Roche, Novartis and Pfizer. Two outputs are considered in order to proxy their innovation networks: scientific publications and patents. Indeed, not every scientific publication leads to innovations, and probably most will not. Nevertheless, corporations get involved in scientific research when it contributes to their innovation goals. Hence, we argue here as well as in other chapters that the networks of most frequent scientific publications' co-authoring institutions provide information about intellectual monopolies' institutionalized innovation networks. By comparing these networks with those of patent co-ownership, we can infer dynamics within innovation networks in terms of who contributes and who assetizes successful results. This analysis is complemented by studying the funding sources of chosen big pharmaceuticals' scientific publications.

Anticipating our findings, each co-publication network map depicts a cluster of big pharmaceuticals, thus providing evidence of the strong engagement of these corporations in technological cooperation. Simultaneously, we find multiple clusters where they mostly outsource innovation modules to universities, and in fewer cases to hospitals and small R&D laboratories. These could be described as clusters that are in a technological competition with those organized by other big pharmaceuticals researching the same topics.

By comparing co-publications and co-patenting networks, we show that big pharmaceuticals outsource stages of their innovation networks to subordinate institutions because, albeit they contribute to innovation processes, they do not co-own their patents. These results support the assumption of big pharmaceuticals as intellectual monopolies that excercise a predatory relationship with the participants of their innovation networks. Furthermore, we find that the US National Institutes of Health, as well as other core countries' public funding agencies, are main supporters of big pharmaceuticals' research, as declared in publications' funding sources. This result goes beyond previous findings, such as Mazzucato (2015), that showed that big pharmaceuticals innovated using previous knowledge results that had been funded by the US public sector because we show that the public sector also directly finances these intellectual monopolies' current R&D.[2]

All in all, this chapter provides evidence on how big pharmaceuticals compete and cooperate for technology to reinforce their intellectual monopolies, which are significantly based on public funding. Next, we further elaborate on the intellectual monopoly capitalism framework developed in the previous section of this book, focusing on technological cooperation and competition between intellectual monopolies. Section 3 presents our methodology, and findings are introduced and discussed in Section 4. Section 5 concludes.

2 Innovation conceived as an asymmetric social relation

In line with the overall argument of this book, once a firm systematically wins the innovation race, the resulting gap with its industry widens. As explained in Chapter 2, driven by knowledge (and innovation) cumulative causation, intellectual monopolies systematically turn knowledge into intangible assets garnering associated intellectual rents. Simultaneously, since rents are a redistribution and not genuine value creation, they lower profits for the rest of the supply chain or platform and diminish catching up opportunities.

Established intellectual monopolies have a wide variety of knowledge management strategies at their disposal. These include outsourcing innovation steps, acquiring technology (typically through mergers and acquisitions, hereon M&A), and profiting from knowledge commons, as Chapter 3 showed for big pharmaceuticals and tech giants. In this chapter, we delve into R&D outsourcing and briefly refer to M&A.

Intellectual monopolies plan R&D beyond their capital legal ownership. Planning is understood here as a relationship of both technological and economic domination exercised by the intellectual monopoly on subordinate organizations. Chapter 2 presented two complementary conceptualizations of R&D outsourcing: innovation circuits (Levín, 1977) and global innovation networks (Ernst, 2009; Liu et al., 2013). For each particular innovation, we build on Levín (1977) to say that the intellectual monopoly is organizing a specific innovation circuit, which is integrated by all the organizations involved in that specific innovation process. In turn, global innovation networks' literature highlights the institutionalization of those relationships showing how certain actors have become systematic participants of a leader's innovation processes, thus creating an innovation network (Ernst, 2009). In simple terms, we argue that an innovation network is built once the same institutions integrate multiple innovation circuits.

When organizing innovation circuits and networks, intellectual monopolies outsource associated risks while still deciding the general orientations and desired results. In these structures, intellectual monopolies keep exclusive know-who (Johnson & Lundvall, 1994). They have exclusive knowledge covering the capacities of each and every participating organization. Therefore, they can coordinate the modularization of knowledge and its integration once results are achieved, assuring network complementarities. To this end, specific in-house knowledge management capabilities are required. As observed by Montalbán and Sakinc (2013), leader pharmaceutical corporations attract top talent, promote their autonomy, and reward them with higher wages and primes on results. However, beyond internal R&D capabilities, big pharmaceuticals foster collaborations with leading academic institutions and promising start-ups.

Among these collaborations, we are particularly interested in the intersection of phases or modules of innovation circuits and networks planned by different intellectual monopolies. Chapter 2 defined them as forms of technological cooperation. Intellectual monopolies also undertake a fierce technological competition with each other, aiming at continuous innovations to keep their privileged position, thus expanding (or at least sustaining) garnered intellectual rents. Here, this is illustrated by the multiple innovation networks planned by each big pharmaceutical independently, identified as clusters in each of their respective network maps that do not include other corporations (see Section 4.1).

Next, we propose a two-step model that synthesizes intellectual monopolies' knowledge management strategies, focusing on technological cooperation and competition between them.

2.1 Technological cooperation and competition between intellectual monopolies

Our two-period model (t=1 and t=2) distinguishes between knowledge management during the emergence of a new intellectual monopoly and once it is fully constituted as such. The main characteristics of this model are synthesized in Table 6.1.

T=1 corresponds to the inception of an intellectual monopoly, the wannabe Intellectual Monopoly "A". This period is characterized by high technological competition and in-house innovation. To become an intellectual

Table 6.1 A preliminary two-period model for understanding intellectual monopoly's knowledge management

	t=1 (Wannabe intellectual monopoly "A")	*t=2 (Intellectual monopoly "A")*
Innovation strategy (knowledge management)	Systematic in-house R&D	In-house R&D is complemented by outsourcing innovation modules, M&As and profiting from knowledge commons.
Associated risk	Mainly taken by "A"	Mainly taken by other participants of "A" innovation circuits/networks.
Relation with other intellectual monopolies	Technological competition	Technological competition and Technological cooperation.
Intellectual rents	Triggered from in-house R&D	Triggered from in-house R&D and predates knowledge from its innovation circuits/ networks.

monopoly, a one-time successful innovator must use associated intellectual rents to expand its investment in R&D. If successful, it will keep accumulating rents and further differentiate from other firms in its industry.

At this stage, cooperation with established or wannabe intellectual monopolies is usually not the best alternative. Already established intellectual monopolies will not cooperate with "A" on equal terms. They will probably use their monopoly power to subordinate "A" and appropriate resulting rents. Moreover, at this stage, it is hard for "A" to anticipate the degree of intellectual monopoly of other companies. If they are closer to T=2, "A" may end up subordinating. This would mean that the other corporations will mostly appropriate the resulting intellectual rents. At the same time, if they are behind "A", they may not be willing to co-produce knowledge with "A", which may end up subordinating them. A wannabe intellectual monopoly must enjoy sufficient internal capabilities to complete innovation processes in-house. Hence, in T=1, the smartest strategy is to attempt to innovate in-house continuously.

T=2 begins if "A" becomes an established intellectual monopoly. At this state, "A" can apply a variety of knowledge management strategies that will sustain its power and allow to appropriate knowledge from subordinate organizations with whom it establishes a predatory relationship. This practice will potentially expand its intellectual rents. Given knowledge modularity, knowledge management will include organizing innovation circuits, acquiring innovations (through M&A), and profiting from knowledge commons. In all these cases, "A" outsources several or even all the innovation modules. Outsourcing will diminish the risks associated with innovation's uncertainty.

In T=2, "A" competes with other intellectual monopolies but not mainly in terms of prices, which are secondary to technological differentiation. The most innovative product will garner higher intellectual rents, resulting in greater profits and profit rate. "A" specific modules or innovation circuits are in technological competition with those of other intellectual monopolies in the same industry (or in a close industry because innovation disrupts industry's frontiers).

Analogously, cooperation or collusion between intellectual monopolies will also prioritize the co-production of knowledge modules over agreements on prices and quantities, terms of sales, or dates of payments as it was previously the case (Baran & Sweezy, 1966). For more generic knowledge modules, cooperation between intellectual monopolies reduces associated risks and increases chances of success. If it becomes a sufficiently frequent partnership over multiple innovation circuits, technological cooperation will become a regular innovation network. Each intellectual monopoly may have more than one innovation network where it establishes technological cooperation with other intellectual monopolies. This depends on its degree of multi-technology and the level of interconnection between the other intellectual monopolies. These networks may include subordinated organizations as well as academic intellectual monopolies (see Chapter 5) and core state agencies or public research organizations (see Chapter 4).

Depending on the characteristics of the innovation and the industry, innovations may or may not be protected with intellectual property rights (IPRs). After reviewing multiple studies on the effects of patents on innovation incentives, Sampat (2018) concludes that the effects are highly sector-specific. For the pharmaceutical and chemical industries, patenting is the essential appropriability mechanism to assure intellectual rents.

In *T*=2, "A"'s capacity to simultaneously organize multiple innovation networks can be depicted as a network map with multiple (and to some degree interconnected) clusters, each representing an innovation network. This map should depict technological cooperation and competition clusters with other intellectual monopolies. The latter corresponds to all the clusters where "A" subordinates other organizations in order to innovate before its rivals. These multiple clusters may be organized to produce both more fundamental and more applied knowledge. The next section elaborates on our chosen network analysis methodology, which is also the basic methodology used in Chapters 7–9.

3 Methodological approach

We retrieved chosen pharmaceuticals' scientific publications and patents between 2008 and 2017 from the Web of Science and Derwent Innovation[3] databases. We studied the co-occurrences of authors' affiliations and the co-occurrences of patent assignees.

We have chosen two pharmaceuticals from Switzerland and one from the United States because they had the highest business expenditure in R&D of the industry for the studied period.[4] They are also among the largest pharmaceutical companies in the world in terms of revenues and profits and belong to this industry's core (Baranes, 2016) (see Table 6.2).

We retrieved all the patents and publications that corresponded to each big pharmaceutical's corporate tree considering M&A and the different names used by these companies to operate. For instance, Roche's corporate tree includes Genentech, while Alcon, Sandoz and Ciba-Geigy are examples of enterprises that were acquired by Novartis. Pfizer's corporate tree includes, among others, Medivation Prostate Therapeutics and Wyeth.

Table 6.2 Basic figures for chosen big pharmaceuticals (in USD)

	Position in 2017 business R&D global ranking	*Cumulative sales revenues (2008–17)*	*Cumulative R&D investment (2008–17)*	*Scientific publications (2008–17)*	*Corporate tree granted patents (2008–17)*
Roche	7th	505,412 b$	98,305 b$	17,717	8,518
Novartis	10th	509,056 b$	87,406 b$	10,895	5,948
Pfizer	14th	547,887 b$	81,774 b$	20,170	3,332

Source: Compustat, Web of Science, and Derwent Innovation.

Publications and patents data were processed using the CorText platform to build co-occurrence maps.[5] We used proximity algorithms that associate entities (institutional affiliations for publications and assignees for patents) according to their co-occurrence frequency. As in the other chapters of this book where this technique is applied, the procedure used to draw these maps, including our corpuses cleaning, follows Tancoigne et al. (2014).

Social network analyses using co-patenting and co-publication data allow mapping relations between actors within networks (Wasserman & Faust, 1994). Grassano et al. (2019) systematized the literature on why firms publish scientific articles. Reasons include attracting and retaining researchers, show technological and scientific proficiency, and improve their reputation. The authors also found that corporate publishing supports or complements intellectual property strategies and can be used to support the commercialization of innovative products resulting from new technologies. Even when publications are used to retain or attract researchers, their content will be aligned with their investigations and the publication will have to be pre-approved by the firm.

Building on this literature, we built each big pharma's co-authorship network map considered as a proxy of its innovation networks. Nodes represent authors' affiliations (universities, firms, etc.). In the case of patents, nodes are defined as different assignees. Their sizes represent the frequency of co-authorship or co-ownership with the corresponding big pharmaceutical. We always prioritized the top 150 nodes, meaning that the maps include for each chosen pharmaceutical its top 149 partners (or less if there are not at least 149 partners with a minimum proximity threshold of 0.1).

Due to the high density of the links and in order to concentrate on the most important ones, we used a chi-square (hereon Chi^2) metric for determining nodes proximity (Figures 6.1–6.3). Chi^2 considers actual co-occurrences between entities and automatically constructs clusters by focusing on the most frequent co-occurrences. In our framework, this means that the chosen algorithm privileged established innovation networks over occasional innovation circuits. In the resulting network maps, we interpret each cluster as an innovation network and all the network map as the correponding big pharma corporate innovation system.

Co-authorships and co-ownerships are depicted as direct but also indirect links. Indirect links are mediated by bridging institutions and take place when co-authorship between two organizations always involves a third co-authoring institution. The latter is the bridge, especially when it also co-authors with any or both of the first two independently. For our framework, bridges are particularly relevant when they connect institutions that belong to different clusters, thus contributing to the overall integration of the intellectual monopoly's corporate innovation system.

An alternative to Chi^2 could have been to use a raw metric. We would have thus considered the raw numbers of co-occurrences between every possible pair of nodes and shown every link above a selected threshold

(Wu & Leahy, 1993). However, this would not privilege any type of link. Hence, the resulting maps would show very dense networks where every institution is linked to big pharma. Distinguishing between sporadic innovation circuits and established innovation networks would have been impossible. The excess of data would have limited our understanding.

The comparison between both types of network maps (co-authorship and co-ownership) for each chosen corporation allows us to distinguish between who participates in big pharmaceuticals' innovation networks and who owns resulting intellectual rents. Co-ownership network maps also provide evidence of the relevance of M&A as a tactic to acquire technology and garner higher intellectual rents.

Finally, we extracted declared "funding sources" from scientific publications and built a list of the most frequent institutions funding each big pharmaceutical's corpus of publications.

Overall, a limitation of our chosen sources of information is that we will not capture all the stages or modules of chosen big pharmaceuticals' innovation networks, but only those that have a publication or patent as a result. For instance, we are not considering where the clinical trials take place. In the United States, organizations are supposed to record their clinical trial results in a federal database. However, it was recently shown that only 25% of big pharmaceuticals fully met this data sharing requirement (Miller et al., 2019). Hence, retrieving this type of information would be incomplete and probably misleading since big pharmaceuticals tend to hide unsuccessful clinical trials. These and other *ghost-management* strategies, such as promotional activities (Gagnon, 2015) referred to in Chapter 3, are beyond the scope of this chapter.

4 Main findings

The pharmaceutical industry is among the most innovative, both in terms of the number of patents and worldwide investment in R&D (Clarivate Analytics, 2019; European Commission, 2019). In line with our conceptualization of established intellectual monopolies in $T=2$, big pharmaceuticals outsource steps or modules of their innovation processes to universities, hospitals (often affiliated to the former) and start-ups.

From a historical perspective, even if collaborations between pharmaceuticals and public or academic research institutions date from the beginning of the last century, according to the pharmaceutical industry expert Khanna (2012), the nature of this relationship has recently changed. The 2000s transformed the neat division of intellectual labour between universities working on basic research that could eventually be transferred to pharmaceuticals who then used it to innovate in new marketable drugs. Universities were seeking to increase their collaborations with pharmaceuticals in part due to tightened research budgets (see Chapter 5). At the same time, outsourced R&D offset associated risks for big pharmaceuticals at a time when blockbuster patents' were expiring, with a consequent growth of generics' markets (Baranes, 2016; Collier, 2011; Dolgin, 2010; Lazonick et al., 2017).

The result is a more intertwined innovation process where, as we show in the rest of this section, research universities directly collaborate with pharmaceutical intellectual monopolies. However, the latter does not share the resulting patents with the former.

4.1 Scientific publications' co-authorship

We start our empirical analysis of big pharmaceuticals' innovation networks by studying scientific publications network maps, which were also complemented with a semantic analysis of each cluster's main research topics (Figures 6.1 to 6.3).[6]

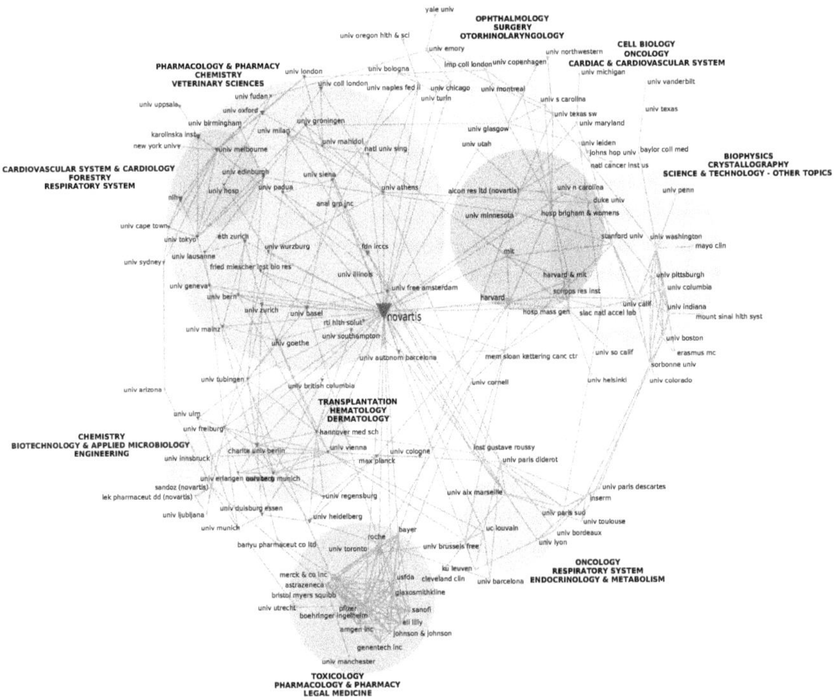

Figure 6.1 Network map. Novartis's top 150 co-authors (2008–17).
Source: Author's analysis based on Web of Science data extraction.

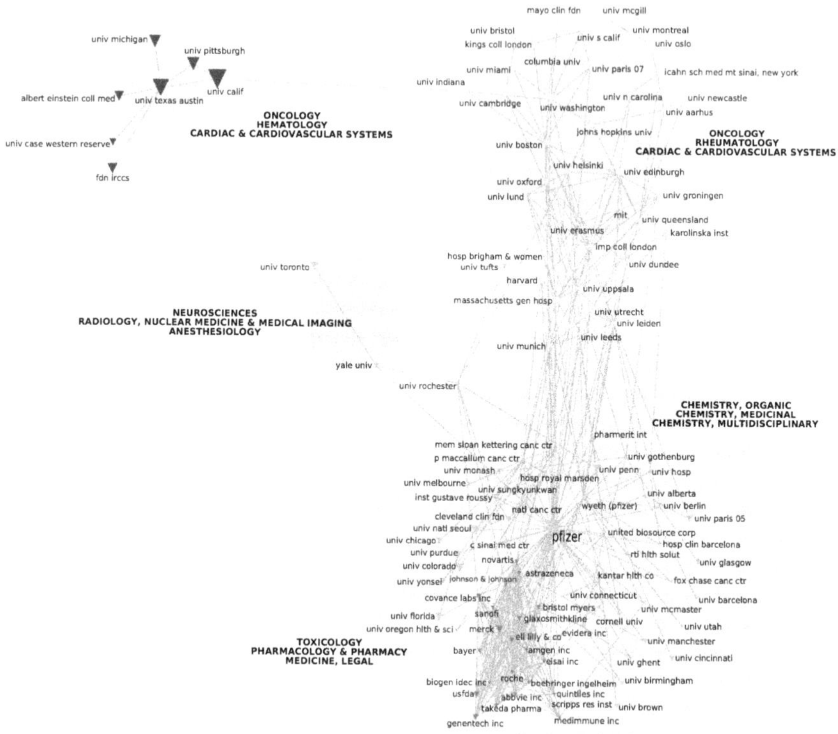

Figure 6.2 Network map. Pfizer's top 150 co-authors (2008–17).
Source: Author's analysis based on Web of Science data extraction. (Some names were colored only to make reading easier.)

The three maps provide evidence of technological cooperation between intellectual monopolies depicted as a single cluster integrated by big pharmaceuticals. Among Pfizer's top 50 partners, there are 11 big pharmaceuticals co-authoring 9.9% of the former scientific publications. In the case of Novartis, also 11 big pharmaceuticals belong to its top 50 co-authors (led by Roche and Pfizer with a 2.9% and 2.5% co-authoring frequency, respectively). This figure is 8 for Roche, with Novartis as its most frequent corporate co-author with a 2.1% frequency. The existence of only one cluster condensing technological cooperation between intellectual monopolies reflects that, to some extent, these co-produced knowledge modules are isolated from the other innovation networks that each of the

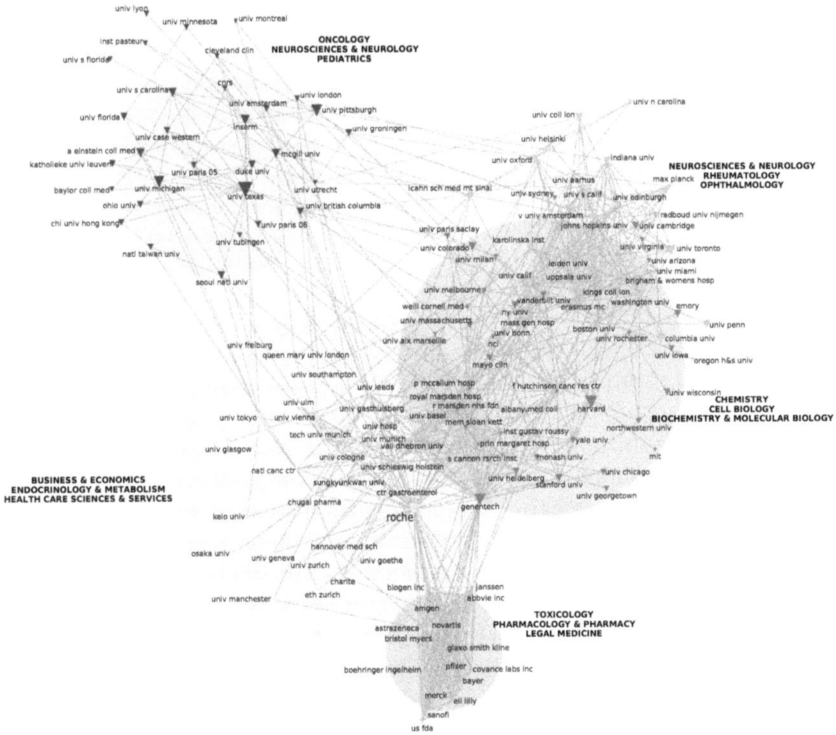

Figure 6.3 Network map. Roche's top 150 co-authors (2008–17).
Source: Author's analysis based on Web of Science data extraction.

chosen big pharmaceuticals builds with other organizations. Moreover, it reflects the strong technological cooperation of the whole pharmaceutical industry core.

In this industry, it is pretty clear that the level of required R&D investments justifies working together on generic stages of knowledge production, colluding technologically, instead of attempting to achieve those results separately. This is also the case of major initiatives conducted together with the public sector. An example of the latter is the Innovative Medicines Initiative (IMI), the largest public-private consortium in life sciences.[7]

Big pharmaceuticals also cooperate for process innovations that belong to what could be considered as pre-competitive or pre-market stages. In simple terms, they generally compete for the molecules but cooperate when it comes to determining the most efficient processes to manufacture prescribed drugs. Adopting the same technology platforms is less costly and facilitates approval from regulatory agencies. Furthermore, these process innovations' collaborations push the whole industry to adopt the new manufacturing processes.

Cooperation between big pharmaceuticals includes setting new regulations for the whole industry. In this respect, it is noteworthy that the United States Food and Drug Administration (USFDA) participates in the big pharma cluster in the three maps, and with a significant level of co-occurrences. It co-authored 0.82%, 0.92% and 1.25% of Roche, Novartis and Pfizer's scientific publications, respectively. Technological cooperation between a public agency and the industry it regulates adds another layer to the already blurred frontiers between public and private that result from lobbying and "revolving doors" – defined in this case as employees that go from big pharmaceuticals to the USFDA and back – (Davis & Abraham, 2013).

Besides these different forms of technological cooperation between powerful organizations, co-publications' network maps (Figures 6.1–6.3) also provide evidence of technological competition between chosen pharmaceutical companies. Technological competition is identified by the clusters that do not include other big pharmaceuticals. In these figures they are mostly integrated by academic research institutions working on related topics.

To find clues of technological competition between clusters from different (and even from the same) network maps, we identified the most frequent research topics of each cluster. A third variable was depicted in each network map showing the three most frequent topics of each cluster. For instance, "oncology" and "cardiac and cardiovascular systems" are two of the three most frequent topics of the cluster led by Harvard in Novartis's map and of the two clusters on the top of Pfizer's map. It is also possible to find that even these two latter clusters are in technological competition with each other.

Remarkably, the different technological competition clusters from each chosen company share many of the most frequent partners. Thirty-two universities co-authoring 25.5% of Pfizer's total publications integrate its 50 most frequent co-authors. The first two are the University of California (4.89%) and Harvard (3%). In the case of Roche, 36 universities are among its top 50 co-authoring institutions. These universities co-authored 31.6% of Roche's total publications in the analysed period. Novartis, for its part, has 31 universities among its 50 most frequent co-authors, co-authoring with them 31.8% of its total publications between 2008 and 2017. As well as Pfizer, both the University of California and Harvard are the most frequent co-authors of Novartis and Roche. The former co-authored 5.9% of Novartis's and 8.3% of Roche's publications, while Harvard co-authored 5.2% of Novartis's and 3.9% of Roche's publications. Furthermore, Harvard plays a bridging role in Novartis's network map, and the University of California does so for Roche. The University of Texas and the University of Washington are also among the top 20 co-authoring institutions of the three chosen pharmaceuticals, as well as Basel University for Roche and Novartis.

It is interesting to highlight that even if the most relevant universities within each of the big pharma networks coincide, these universities do not belong to the big pharma cluster in any of the maps. Each university – possibly but not exclusively through different research teams – relates separately with each of the analysed big pharma.[8] In other words, big pharmaceuticals' innovation networks exhibit a high reliance on the same institutions, but those collaborations are not jointly developed.

Summing up, co-authorship network maps have shown both technological cooperation and competition between big pharmaceuticals. Results also highlighted the role of universities, in particular leading universities, as most frequent co-authors. By researching with universities, pharmaceutical companies can control, or at least influence, the research done by scholars and spin-offs (such as biotechnology firms). In the next sub-heading, we present patent co-ownership network maps and compare them with results from Figures 6.1 to 6.3.

4.2 Patents' co-ownership analysis

Although big pharmaceuticals organize innovation circuits with multiple organizations that lead to patented results, we found that their patents are generally not shared with these organizations (Figures A6.1–A6.3 in the Appendix). Overall, patent co-ownership network maps show that big pharmaceuticals rarely share the ownership of their patents with other stakeholders.

In terms of other organizations, Roche's most frequent co-owner is the clinical trials company Array Biopharma (0.57% of Roche's patent portfolio). It is followed by a biotechnology company called Curis Inc that shares 0.3% of Roche's patents (Table A6.1, Appendix). Focusing on big pharmaceuticals, Roche's most frequent co-owner is Novartis (nine, 0.1% of Roche's granted patents in the analysed period). Similar results are observed for Pfizer and Novartis (see Tables A6.2 and A6.3 in Appendix). In terms of universities, Pfizer shared 0.7% of its portfolio with the University of Iowa. Moreover, two academic institutions appear in Novartis's map (Scripps Research Institute and Harvard). Among Novartis's top 50 co-owners, there are 42 individuals, 4 corporations and 2 academic institutions.

Most co-owners in the three patents' network maps are individuals. ResearchGate and LinkedIn data confirm that most of those co-owning more than 20 patents with any of the selected corporations, works or worked for that company or its subsidiaries.[9]

The comparison between co-publications and co-patenting networks sheds light on who collaborates with pharmaceutical innovations and who profits from them. Universities (as well as smaller companies) occupy an almost neglected position as big pharmaceuticals' patent co-owners, while they are indispensable in these companies' innovation networks. From our perspective, these results highlight that big pharmaceuticals secure and appropriate legal intellectual rents predating knowledge produced or co-produced with multiple organizations, in particular with research universities. Moreover, the risk of drug failure is significantly reduced by outsourcing R&D. From the standpoint of universities participating in big pharmaceuticals' innovation networks, these results are in line with the subordinate research university type, as discussed in Chapter 5.

Co-patenting network maps also provide information on the importance of each M&A in relation to acquired patents. Acquired companies with relatively big patent portfolios appear in the map leading different clusters that are barely connected to each big pharmaceutical's central cluster. For our analysed period, some of the purchased companies had significant patent portfolios in comparison with the overall patent portfolio of the big pharma acquiring it. Thus, they appear in a central place in the network. By acquiring smaller companies with already proven technologies, big pharmaceuticals significantly increase their patent portfolios, thus their intellectual rents, without incurring in R&D risks. Furthermore, big pharma investments are lower by purchasing already successful innovating companies.

Sometimes, both companies had no shared patent before the acquisition. Acquired companies appear in a cluster detached from the map's main clusters, such as Bind Therapeutics in Pfizer's map (Figure A6.3). Moreover, Pfizer's major deals included the acquisitions of Warner-Lambert (USD 122.8 bn, in 1999), Pharmacia (USD 64.3 bn, in 2002) and Wyeth (USD 64.2 bn, in 2009). Together with Hospira (acquired for USD 17 bn, in 2015), these were Pfizer's most significant patent acquisitions in our analysed period (Table A6.2 in Appendix).

In other cases, clusters are connected, pointing to collaborations before the acquisition. They may also reflect another common practice between intellectual monopolies: companies that are acquired for their technology are sometimes kept, at least for some time, as separate entities. The acquirer corporation may still apply for patents under the name of its acquired company if the results were achieved in the latter's laboratories even after acquiring it. Roche's Genentech, acquired in 2009 in a USD 44 bn deal, is an example of the latter (Figure A6.1).

Big pharmaceuticals illustrate how intellectual monopolies combine vertical deconcentration (outsourcing manufacturing and R&D), with horizontal centralization (M&A). Both strategies enlarge their intellectual monopoly rents. At the same time, they limit rivals and distribute more value to shareholders (Lazonick et al., 2017; Montalban & Sakinç, 2013). Both knowledge management tactics show a shared feature of already established intellectual monopolies (in T=2). As far as they can collect resulting rents, it is best to wait for others' earlier research success before engaging. This *mantra* is complemented by profiting from public funding sources, as we show next.

4.3 Funding sources

In the pharmaceutical industry, once a drug is discovered, its reproduction tends to be easy to copy. Therefore, pharmaceutical companies historically argue for tightening IPRs claiming that they are required to compensate for their investments in R&D. However, by looking at most frequent funding sources of their scientific publications (Table 6.3), we provide evidence of their high dependence on public funds for R&D, thus at least partially refuting that argument.

Table 6.3 gives further proof of big pharma's technological cooperation, given that they are among each other's publications most frequent funding sources. Still, the most striking result is that the US National Institutes of Health (NIH) is, for the three studied big pharmaceuticals, the most frequent external funding source of published papers. Similar agencies from other core countries are also among their most frequent funding sources. For instance, the European Commission and the UK Innovation and Research agency are top funding institutions in the three analysed cases.

Overall, funding sources come mostly from the countries of origin of big pharmaceuticals' main university co-authors. Probably these universities (in some cases together with big pharmaceuticals) apply for public funds that are being used for joint research. In other cases, such as the technological cooperation cluster between big pharmaceuticals, it may be that intellectual monopolies themselves are granted with funds from these science and technology agencies.

Our results to some extent differ from Cleary et al. (2018). The authors showed that the NIH was among published research funding sources of at least one paper of those related to each of the 210 new drugs approved by the USFDA between 2010 and 2016. However, since they found that most of the NIH funded papers corresponded to biological targets – classified by the authors as basic research – and not drugs themselves, they conclude that NIH funds complement industry investment in R&D, focused mostly on applied research. By focusing on big pharmaceuticals, our results show that the NIH is not only funding most of the "basic research" associated with new drugs, as shown by Cleary et al. (2018), but also industry R&D.

Hence, our results go beyond the accepted idea that states, in particular the United States, have been significant R&D investors of the most radical and path-breaking discoveries of this industry without enjoying their associated profits (Barringer & Slaughter, 2016; Mazzucato, 2015, Chapter 3). Besides the latter, public agencies keep funding intellectual monopolies, thus further contributing to expanding their rentiership and predation. Nevertheless, this result should not be interpreted as a direct subordination of most powerful states to (global) intellectual monopolies. Chapter 4 has argued that core states have also benefited from their intellectual monopolies. They establish a dialectical relationship since intellectual monopolies reinforce their geopolitical power while increasing inequalities and polarization.

Table 6.3 Selected big pharmaceuticals' main funding sources as declared in their scientific publications (2008–17)

Pfizer	*Novartis*	*Roche*
Pfizer	Novartis	Roche
NIH	NIH	NIH
UK Research and Innovation	European Commission	European Commission
Merck & co	UK Research and Innovation	Novartis
Novartis	GlaxoSmithKline	Pfizer
GlaxoSmithKline	Pfizer	Merck & co
Bristol-Myers Squibb	Merck & co	UK Research and Innovation
Johnson & Johnson	Swiss National Science Foundation	German Research Foundation
AstraZeneca	Roche	GlaxoSmithKline
Eli Lilly	German Research Foundation	Bristol-Myers Squibb
Roche	Wellcome Trust	Swiss National Science Foundation
European Commission	AstraZeneca	Johnson & Johnson
Sanofi	Sanofi	AstraZeneca
Wellcome Trust	UK National Institute for Health Research	Sanofi
Boehringer Ingelheim	Takeda	US Dept of Energy
National Science Foundation	Eli Lilly	Eli Lilly
Takeda	US Dept of Energy	Wellcome Trust
Abbott	National Science Foundation	Amgen
Bayer	Boehringer Ingelheim	National Science Foundation
Amgen	Bayer	Takeda
Teva Inc	Bristol Myers Squibb	Japan MEXT
Canadian Institute of Health Research	Johnson & Johnson	Canadian Institute of Health Research
Astellas Pharma	Teva Inc	UK National Institute for Health Research
Eisai, Inc.	Amgen	Federal Min of Education and Research (BMBF)
Innovative Medicines Initiative	Federal Min of Education and Research (BMBF)	Abbott

Source: Author's analysis based on Web of Science data extraction.

Under intellectual monopoly capitalism, at least part of global hegemony is defined in the intellectual monopoly contest. Countries hosting and partnering with more intellectual monopolies will thus be in a better bargaining position. It seems that the US state prefers to remain as global hegemon, at the expense of losing intellectual rents of publicly funded research.

5 Final remarks

This chapter has contributed to our understanding of innovation as a power relation. We have elaborated on technological cooperation and technological competition dynamics between intellectual monopolies, illustrated by analysing the innovation strategies of selected big pharmaceuticals. We found neat clusters of technological cooperation in scientific publications' network maps.

Intellectual monopolies decide in which knowledge modules compete or collaborate for technology. This influences global capital accumulation, industrial organization and knowledge production and circulation. Big pharmaceuticals' scientific publications provided a more accurate depiction of the variety of stakeholders involved in their innovation networks. The comparison between network maps, corresponding to scientific co-publication and patent co-ownership, points to the subordination of universities, public research organizations and start-ups. They have a fundamental role in big pharmaceuticals' innovation networks, but almost negligible participation in the distribution of intellectual rents. By keeping exclusive ownership of their patents, and considering that pharmaceutical companies' high prices are an apparent fact, this chapter has provided convincing evidence of big pharmaceuticals' knowledge predation from their innovation networks.

Furthermore, the reappearance of the same institutions in the three maps points to the higher R&D capabilities of some but not all (nor most) of the research institutions from core countries reflecting these countries' internal heterogeneities. Our results also provide evidence of a persistent technological gap between cores and peripheries. Innovation flows are not constrained by national boundaries but are still limited to certain organizations from a few countries. The absence of the peripheries in our maps could be pointing to their technological gap but may also be hiding knowledge extractivism, as we argue in the last section of this book. For instance, Chapter 13 studies different dimensions of pharmaceutical knowledge extractivism that complement this chapter.

To conclude, our results call for rethinking policy advice. Recommendations should be derived from a general analysis of capitalism's dynamics, also acknowledging the different hierarchies between states and, thus, their different enforcement capacities. Moreover, our results provided examples of subordinate research universities (see Chapter 5), which call for a discussion of the aims and priorities of academic research, considering the premise of knowledge as a public good.

Notes

1 This chapter is based on the paper "Asymmetric Power of the Core: Technological Cooperation and Technological Competition in the Transnational Innovation Networks of Big Pharma" doi:10.1080/09692290.2019.1620309 published by the *Review of International Political Economy* (https://www.tandfonline.com/toc/rrip20/current).
2 Covid-19 pandemic has made all the more apparent the engagement of core states funding big pharmaceuticals' vaccines.
3 This database includes all the information from the following patent offices: USPTO, WIPO, European, Japan, Australian, British, Canadian, French, German, Russian and Korean patent offices.
4 In fact, considering cumulative R&D expenses for our chosen period (2008–17), Roche, Novartis and Johnson and Johnson are the top three companies. However, the latter is not strictly a pharmaceutical company (it produces also medical devices and consumer packed goods) thus choosing it could lead to misleading results. Therefore, we will consider Pfizer that ranked fourth. We verified the relevancy of chosen corporations by looking at their rank in terms of sales revenues for the same period and they remain among the top five big pharmaceuticals.
5 CorText is an open platform for performing bibliometric and semantic analysis that uses the spatial algorithms that draw on classic graph visualization methods for depicting the network maps (Fruchterman-Reingold). It can be accessed online at https://www.cortext.net/.
6 This was achieved by introducing another variable to our maps on the main topics or subjects characterizing each paper. This information is provided by Web of Science and we used Cortext to include it in the network map by producing tags that are associated with each cluster. For this new dimension taken from our data set, we also used a chi^2 metric. Only top three closest tags are associated with each cluster on the maps.
7 https://www.imi.europa.eu/.
8 Strict confidentiality agreements enable big pharmaceuticals to work with the same institutions separately. Furthermore, subordinate research institutions may not know all the modules or stages of the innovation circuits they join.
9 We presume the same holds for the rest of the individuals, but we only checked their affiliations/working place if they had more than 20 patents co-owned with a big pharmaceutical.

References

Baran, P. A., & Sweezy, P. M. (1966). *Monopoly capital*. NYU Press.
Baranes, A. I. (2016). *An original institutionalist approach to the structure, conduct, and performance of the pharmaceutical industry: The importance of intangible assets* [PhD Thesis]. University of Missouri-Kansas City.
Barringer, S. N., & Slaughter, S. (2016). University trustees and the entrepreneurial university: Inner circles, interlocks, and exchanges. In Slaughter, S. and Taylor,

B. (Eds.) *Higher education, stratification, and workforce development* (pp. 151–71). Springer. http://link.springer.com/chapter/10.1007/978-3-319-21512-9_8
Clarivate Analytics. (2019). *Top 100 global innovators 2018–2019.* Clarivate Analytics.
Cleary, E. G., Beierlein, J. M., Khanuja, N. S., McNamee, L. M., & Ledley, F. D. (2018). Contribution of NIH funding to new drug approvals 2010–2016. *Proceedings of the National Academy of Sciences, 115*(10), 2329–34.
Collier, R. (2011). *Bye, bye blockbusters, hello niche busters.* Can Med Assoc.
Davis, C., & Abraham, J. (2013). *Unhealthy pharmaceutical regulation: Innovation, politics and promissory science.* Springer.
Dolgin, E. (2010). Big pharma moves from "blockbusters" to "niche busters." *Nature Medicine, 16*, 837.
Ernst, D. (2009). *A new geography of knowledge in the electronics industry? Asia's role in global innovation networks.* https://papers.ssrn.com/sol3/papers.cfm?abstract_id=2742923
European Commission. (2019). *EU R&D scoreboard.* European Commission.
Gagnon, M. A. (2015). *Shaping the social determinants of value through economic ghostmanagement: An institutionalist approach to capital accumulation.* In Jo, T and Lee F. S. (Eds), *Marx, Veblen and the Foundation of Heterodox Economics.* (pp. 228–51) Routledge.
Grassano, N., Camerani, R., & Rotolo, D. (2019). Do firms publish? A multi-sectoral analysis. *DRUID Working Paper, 21.*
Johnson, B., & Lundvall, B. A. (1994). The learning economy. *Journal of Industry Studies, 1*(2), 23–42.
Khanna, I. (2012). Drug discovery in pharmaceutical industry: Productivity challenges and trends. *Drug Discovery Today, 17*(19), 1088–102.
Lazonick, W., Hopkins, M., Jacobson, K., Sakinç, M. E., & Tulum, Ö. (2017). *US pharma's financialized business model.* Institute for New Economic Thinking.
Levín, P. (1977). Circuitos de innovación. *Revista Interamericana de Planificación, XX*(44). http://www. revistaespacios.com/a81v01n01/81010120.html
Mazzucato, M. (2015). *The entrepreneurial state: Debunking public vs. private sector myths* (Vol. 1). Anthem Press.
Miller, J., Ross, J. S., Wilenzick, M., & Mello, M. M. (2019). Sharing of clinical trial data and results reporting practices among large pharmaceutical companies: Cross sectional descriptive study and pilot of a tool to improve company practices. *British Medical Journal, 366*, 14217.
Montalban, M., & Sakinç, M. E. (2013). Financialization and productive models in the pharmaceutical industry. *Industrial and Corporate Change, 22*(4), 981–1030.
Sampat, B. N. (2018). *A survey of empirical evidence on patents and innovation.* National Bureau of Economic Research.
Tancoigne, E., Barbier, M., Cointet, J. P., & Richard, G. (2014). The place of agricultural sciences in the literature on ecosystem services. *Ecosystem Services, 10*, 35–48.
Wasserman, S., & Faust, K. (1994). *Social network analysis: Methods and applications* (Vol. 8). Cambridge University Press.
Wu, Z., & Leahy, R. (1993). An optimal graph theoretic approach to data clustering: Theory and its application to image segmentation. *IEEE Transactions on Pattern Analysis and Machine Intelligence, 15*(11), 1101–13.

Appendix

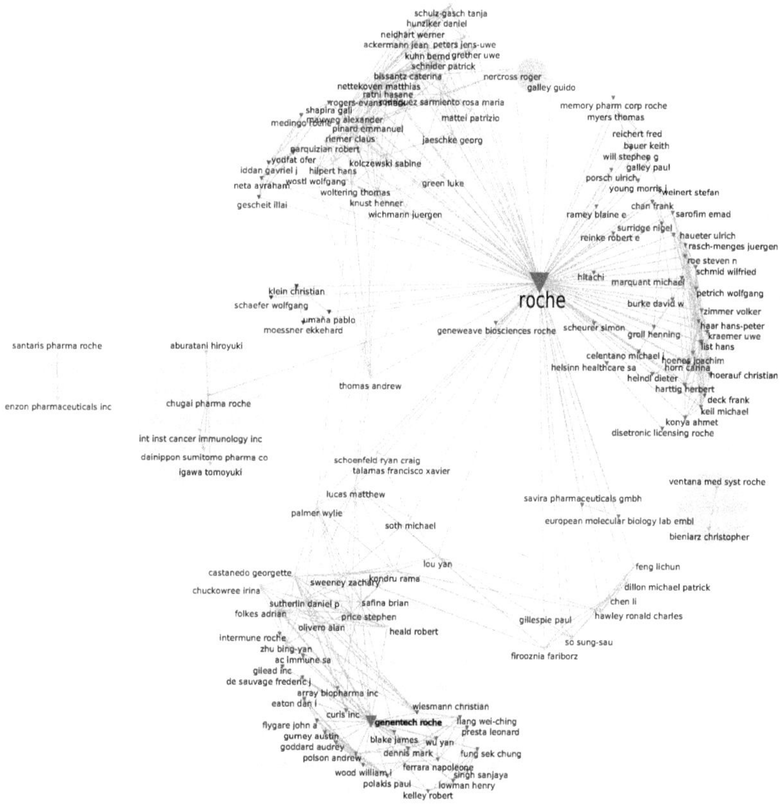

Figure A6.1 Roche corporate tree granted patents assignees (2008–17).
Source: Author's analysis based on Derwent Innovation data extraction.

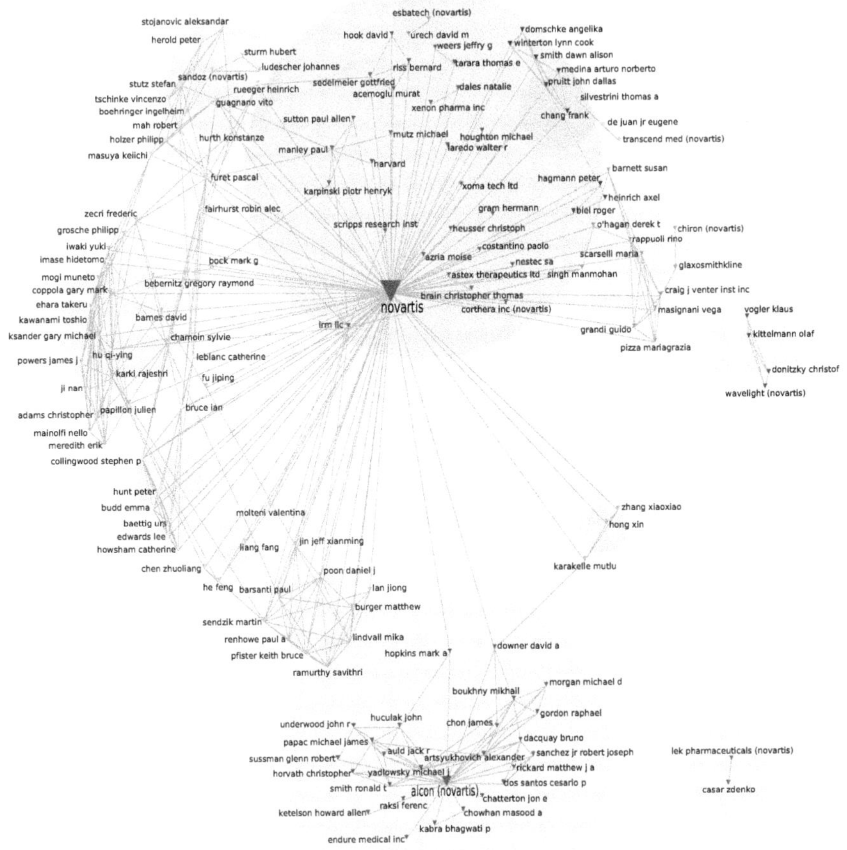

Figure A6.2 Novartis corporate tree granted patents assignees (2008–17).
Source: Author's analysis based on Derwent Innovation data extraction.

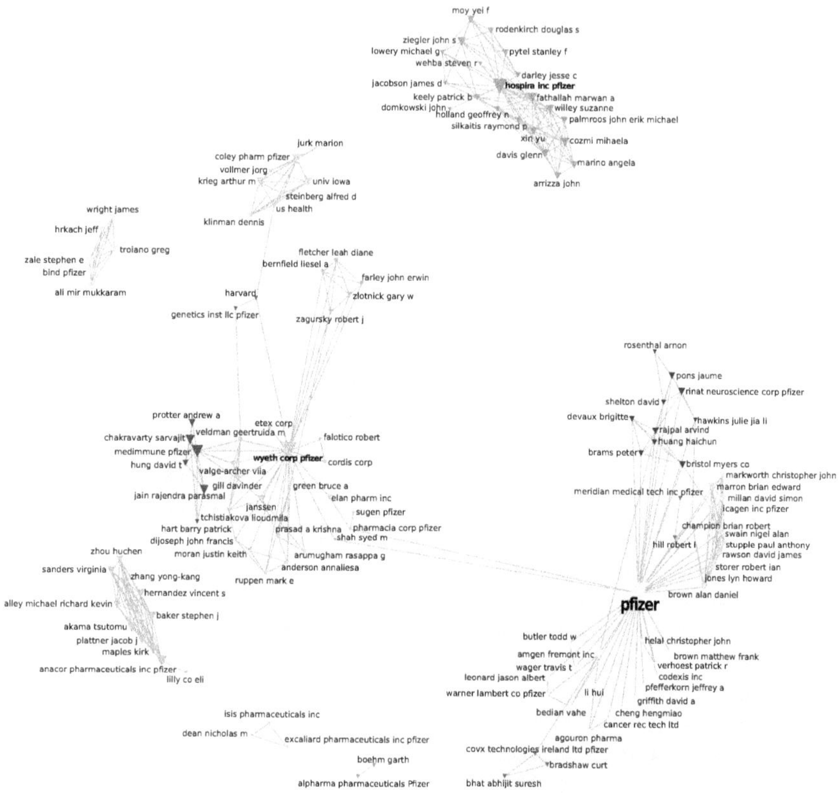

Figure A6.3 Pfizer corporate tree granted patents assignees (2008–17).
Source: Author's analysis based on Derwent Innovation data extraction.

Table A6.1 Roche Corporate Tree Granted Patents 2008–17: top 15 assignees' frequencies

Entity	*Number of granted patents*	*Type of Stakeholder*
ROCHE	5610	Roche
GENENTECH	1636	Roche
CHUGAI PHARMA	521	Roche
VENTANA MED SYST	183	Roche
SANTARIS PHARMA	66	Roche
INTERMUNE	59	Roche
YODFAT OFER	54	Individual
ARRAY BIOPHARMA INC	49	Firm
LIST HANS	49	Individual
ANADYS PHARMA	48	Roche
MEMORY PHARM CORP	44	Roche
MEDINGO Roche	39	Roche
WU YAN	33	Individual
454 LIFE SCIENCES	31	Roche
DISETRONIC LICENSING	30	Roche

Source: Author's analysis based on Derwent Innovation data extraction.

Table A6.2 Pfizer Corporate Tree Granted Patents 2008–17: top 15 assignees' frequencies

Entity	*Number of granted patents*	*Type of stakeholder*
PFIZER	1137	Pfizer
WYETH CORP	1071	Pfizer
HOSPIRA INC	129	Pfizer
WARNER LAMBERT CO	99	Pfizer
PHARMACIA CORP	88	Pfizer
COLEY PHARM	64	Pfizer
MEDIMMUNE	76	Pfizer
GENETICS INST LLC	66	Pfizer
ANACOR PHARMACEUTICALS INC	62	Pfizer
ICAGEN INC	60	Pfizer
BIND	44	Pfizer
RINAT NEUROSCIENCE CORP	45	Pfizer
ZOETIS LLC	43	Pfizer
AMGEN FREMONT INC	43	Firm
MERIDIAN MEDICAL TECH INC	38	Pfizer

Source: Author's analysis based on Derwent Innovation data extraction.

Table A6.3 Novartis Corporate Tree Granted Patents 2008–17: top 15 assignees' frequencies

Entity	*Number of granted patents*	*Type of stakeholder*
Novartis	4125	Novartis
Alcon	942	Novartis
Sandoz	217	Novartis
Lek Pharmaceuticals	188	Novartis
Wavelight	142	Novartis
GlaxoSmithKline	56	Firm
Esbatech	44	Novartis
Hexal	44	Novartis
Transcend Med	43	Novartis
Furet Pascal	36	Individual
IRM LLC	32	Firm
Wavetec Vision Systems Inc	31	Novartis
Xoma Tech Ltd	30	Firm
Smith Ronald T	28	Individual
Boukhny Mikhail	28	Individual

Source: Author's analysis based on Derwent Innovation data extraction.

7

APPLE

From legal towards data-driven intellectual rentiership

1 Introduction

Apple first hit the top of the world's market capitalization ranking in 2011. It was the the company with the largest market capitalization between 2014 and late 2018. Since then, it remained in the top three, castling with Microsoft, Amazon and, more recently, Saudi Aramco. By 2020, it took back the podium that the latter had got since its IPO. Within the smartphone industry, Apple concentrates its sales in the high-end phone segment, which contributes to explaining why, by 2015, it captured around 90% of this market's profits, albeit that year it only sold 12% of the total units sold (WIPO, 2017). No wonder why Apple has called the attention of the academic literature.

Apple has been typically taken as an illustrative example of a global value chain (GVC) leader (Bergvall-Kareborn & Howcroft, 2013; Dedrick et al., 2009; Kraemer et al., 2011; Satariano & Burrows, 2011). The GVC approach was criticised due to its lack of a conceptual explanation for the emergence of such leaders (Rikap, 2018; Starosta, 2010a, 2010b). Alternatively, this book and my past research have pointed to intangibles' monopolization as the genesis of leaders, in this context renamed intellectual monopolies (see Chapter 2). From this framework, Apple was reconceived as a corporation that underpins its GVC power in its knowledge monopoly, with particular focus on the concentration of intellectual property rights (IPRs) (Durand & Milberg, 2020; Rikap, 2018).

Apple was also the witness case used to show how big corporations offshore IPRs and financialize their intangible assets (Froud et al., 2012; Lazonick et al., 2013; Pozsar, 2018). By 2016, Apple was the top company in offshore savings, offshoring over $200 billion (90% of its total savings), mostly in corporate bonds managed by Braeburn Capital, its asset management subsidiary (Pozsar, 2018).

In this chapter, we first elaborate on Apple's history as an intellectual monopoly by identifying the different types of intellectual rents it has collected throughout time. Building on Durand and Milberg's (2020) taxonomy, Apple's intellectual rents originally came from its vertical natural monopoly as well as from its innovation monopoly. We also elaborate on how Apple – as Microsoft, Amazon, Google and Facebook had done – is currently diversifying its business, deprioritizing the iPhone, aiming to become a data-driven intellectual monopoly. Overall, Apple's case shows how different types of intellectual rents accumulate, reinforcing intellectual monopolies. This analysis is complemented with a preliminary discussion of the interplay between its intangibles' concentration and financial rentierism.

The rest of this chapter is organized as follows. In Section 2, we further develop the intellectual monopoly capitalism framework. Section 3 analyses Apple's intellectual monopoly distinguishing types of garnered intellectual rents, and Section 4 elaborates on the complementarities between intellectual and financial rents for the case of Apple. Final remarks are presented in Section 5.

2 Further conceptualizing intellectual monopolies: types of intangible rents

Pagano's (2014) intellectual monopoly capitalism concept refers to the high concentration of IPRs. In this book, we moved beyond this narrow definition. We conceived intellectual monopoly capitalism as an era where capital accumulation is driven by corporations that have monopolized knowledge in multiple and complementary ways, transforming it into assets, including but not restricting intellectual monopoly to the concentration of IPRs (see in particular Chapter 2). Continuous innovations (both science-based and not, such as creating a new market from brand-building) are the most straightforward and possibly most studied ways to conceive these monopolies.

Once intangibles are turned into assets, their owners garner intellectual rents. These rents, also called knowledge or technoscientific rents, arise from the private appropriation or control of intangibles (Birch, 2019; Durand & Milberg, 2020; Foley, 2013; Pagano, 2014; Schwartz, 2016; Teixeira & Rotta, 2012). Drawing on Christophers (2019), rent-baring assets are also characterized by limited or no competition, thus providing significant market power.

Here, in order to provide a comprehensive understanding of Apple as an intellectual monopoly, we build on Durand and Milberg's (2020) taxonomy of intellectual rents: vertical natural monopoly, legal monopoly, data-driven innovation and intangibles-differential rents. We depart from this classification but with two essential revisions.

First, we will not consider intangibles-differential economies of scale as a rent, even if Apple enjoys this source of higher profits at least since 2004 – as we argue in Section 3.1 – when it completely outsourced manufacturing. Durand and Milberg (2020) defined intangibles-differential rents as a rent emerging from the difference in endless economies of scale for intangible assets versus at most temporary economies of scale of tangible assets. We leave this aside because we conceive this difference in economies of scale as an industrial organization difference. It leads to differential profits (higher for the company relatively more intensive in intangibles), but that should not be conceptualized as a rent. Rents, as much discussed in Chapter 2, refer to the payment or sum received after holding the monopoly over a natural or artificially scarce resource or product. Hence, counting as rent intangibles' more significant economies of scale would be to confuse knowledge privatization and assetization with another quality of intangibles: lower (sometimes close to zero) marginal cost (Haskel & Westlake, 2018). The latter increases profits and increases entry barriers, but it is not rent-bearing.

Second, we will reconceptualize intangibles' legal monopoly rents as a specific case of innovation monopoly. Innovations can be protected with IPRs but can also be kept in secret or as tacit knowledge, among other mechanisms (Ambrosini & Bowman, 2001; Howells, 1996; Johnson & Lundvall, 1994). All the latter escaped from Durand and Milberg's (2020) taxonomy.

2.1 Vertical natural monopoly intangible rents

In an early conceptualization of what was afterwards dubbed GVC, Cox (1981, p. 47) refers to the internationalization of production as a "globally organised production process planned and controlled by the source of the technology". The author continued explaining that formal ownership was not as important as how elements are integrated into the production system. Building on Johnson and Lundvall (1994) know-who and know-how, every GVC leader must know-who can do what within the chain and know-how to integrate those dispersed stages of the overall production process. Their exclusive know-how also includes how to handle inventories and data along the supply chain. All this knowledge is an advantage that enables the leader to be the only one that can organize and plan the GVC. Its capacity to be the only one knowing the whole chain is an intangible asset. Following Durand and Milberg (2020), this intangible asset triggers vertical natural monopoly rents from network externalities that raise entry barriers.

By overseeing the whole network or chain, the leader assures its complementarities. Beyond GVC, the same know-who and know-how as a single quality of the leader can be extended to corporate innovation systems (Granstrand, 2000) or global innovation networks (Ernst, 2009; Linden et al., 2009; Liu et al., 2013). Intellectual monopolies have the exclusive knowledge on how to integrate, organize and even plan their innovation system or networks, which includes knowledge on who can perform each step. As Orazbayeva (2015, p. 7) – who is a manager at Siemens Science-to-Business Marketing Research Centre – explains for Siemens, the company's Corporate Technology unit uses "Big Data applications (Academic Research

Intelligence, e.g. Elsevier's SciVal) to identify and access the main fields of scientific research at all major universities worldwide." Thus, Siemens – as any intellectual monopoly – *knows whom* to contact for each step of its global innovation networks.

2.2 Intangibles' legal monopoly rents and the innovation monopoly

In the case of intangible rents driven by a legal monopoly, Durand and Milberg (2020) follow Pagano's (2014) intellectual monopoly concept of a corporation that concentrates IPRs. However, the capacity to monopolize knowledge, thus extracting rents, goes beyond patents, trademarks and copyright. The literature review conducted by Sampat (2018) highlights that patenting is not the most important appropriability mechanism to assure intellectual rents, except for specific industries. The same results are achieved by Comino et al. (2019) but focused on ICT. In Chapter 3, we also showed that innovation monopoly could rely on alternative forms of producing knowledge detached from or even opposite to IPRs (open access and knowledge commons). Hence, we conceptualize legal monopoly rents as a specific form of innovation monopoly rents defined as rents triggered after the systematic concentration of innovations. Besides the concentration of IPRs, secrecy is a widespread mechanism and forms of tacit knowledge concentrated in a single firm may also be included within the broader innovation monopoly rent concept.

As Chapter 6 highlighted, innovation monopoly rents, in particular in the form of IPRs, are of utmost importance for sustaining big pharmaceuticals' intellectual monopolies. However, these companies also *know who* can perform each step of their global innovation networks. As we showed in Chapter 6, this includes multiple research universities and start-ups. Therefore, they accumulate both types of rents from intangibles. As we will argue later in this chapter, these two were also Apple's first sources of rent.

2.3 Data-driven intellectual monopoly

A central argument in this chapter is that Apple aims to evolve from an intellectual monopoly based on vertical natural monopoly and innovation monopoly rents (the latter highly dependent on IPRs), towards also becoming a data-driven intellectual monopoly. These monopolies use processed data, called digital intelligence, to orient future innovations and also innovate in ways to extract new sources of data (see Chapter 2, Section 2.1).

Individuals and organizations may get full access to their respective data. However, since it is aggregated data, which is accumulated in private repositories, what can be turned into intangible assets, knowledge extractivism as a specific form of accumulation by dispossession takes place (see Chapters 11 and 13 on how this impacts the peripheries). In fact, it is not just the capacity to centralize new (big) data that triggers data-driven rents. Data needs to be processed and analysed with powerful machine learning algorithms to become digital intelligence (Nuccio & Guerzoni, 2019; UNCTAD, 2019). The constant flux of new centralised data is currently mostly processed by a specific machine learning approach that combines deep learning and neural networks. These are algorithms that learn as they process that data and improve by themselves. In this sense, they can be conceived as a general method for invention (Cockburn et al., 2018). Digital intelligence gives direction to further innovations and orients data-driven intellectual monopolies' overall business.

Hitherto – and unlike the aforementioned intellectual rents in the taxonomy – this has been a more exclusive source of monopoly power. Among data-driven intellectual monopolies, Microsoft, Amazon, Google and Facebook, together with their Chinese counterparts (Baidu, Tencent and Alibaba), stand out. Tech giants centralize both organizations' and individuals' data. The latter are partially generated in private spheres or non-economic spheres of sociability – such as social networks. Once these data are assetized, it may even be said that the result is a commodification of private relations.

In the following section, Apple's recent history is reviewed through the lenses of the three different types of intellectual rents we have presented in this section, mainly focusing on Apple's predatory practices and quest for data-driven rents.

3 Apple's intellectual monopoly

In this section, we consider the types of rents from intangibles that we built on the basis of Durand and Milberg's (2020) taxonomy to assess the recent evolution of Apple's intellectual monopoly.

3.1 Apple's GVC through the lenses of vertical natural monopoly rents

Apple is a GVC leader with a superior profit rate compared to that of its suppliers (Chan et al., 2013; Kraemer et al., 2011; Linden et al., 2009; Rikap, 2018). It was considered by Durand and Milberg (2020) as an example of a company garnering vertical natural monopoly rents from its GVC. Apple knows who can produce each step of its different value chains and has the exclusive knowledge to oversee and integrate the whole chain. This knowledge allows Apple to plan the value chains of each and every of its products.

Which enterprises participate in a GVC is not set once and for all. Rikap (2018) reconstructed Apple's GVC by 2011 and used Compustat firm-level information for listed US and Rest of the World corporations to compare Apple and its subordinate companies' profit rates. Apple's hardware manufacturing is outsourced, primarily to Asia, and the rest is produced in the

United States and Ireland (Apple Inc, 2019). This strategy differentiates it from other GVC leaders of the smartphone market (Huawei and Samsung) that internally produce or assemble some components (WIPO, 2017).

Apple exercises extreme control over its subcontractors and suppliers, which results in the appropriation of part of their value (Chan et al., 2013; Froud et al., 2012; Haslam et al., 2013; Kraemer et al., 2011; Linden et al., 2009; WIPO, 2017; Xing, 2019). An illustrative example is how Apple changed the screen of the iPhone weeks before it was launched, forcing an overhaul of the assembly line, and how Foxconn, Apple's main contractor, reacted to produce it, waking up workers in the middle of the night to fulfil Apple's requirement (Rikap, 2018). Chan et al. (2013) interviewed Foxconn employees that pointed out that Apple monitors onsite production processes and delivery times. These are characteristics that evidence Apple's planning capacity over Foxconn. In fact, according to former employees and suppliers interviewed by Satariano and Burrows (2011, p. 50), Apple controls every bit of its supply chains, building a "closed ecosystem".

Foxconn can be conceived as a complier company. Complier firms, as we explained in Chapter 2, are subordinate companies because they are not producers of new technologies but only their early adopters. They produce with the most updated techniques, but those techniques are defined by the intellectual monopolies whose production system they integrate. Foxconn's technological levels are in line with those of advanced manufacturers from the United States.[1] In these cases, where multiple companies are ready to comply, intellectual monopolies increase their profits by privileging those accepting to be paid the lowest price. Extreme working conditions and lower wages contribute – as it is the case of Foxconn – to guarantee lower prices (see Chapter 10 on the effects of intellectual monopoly capitalism on workers).

Foxconn takes the risks and accepts being planned by Apple, while the latter gets even higher profit rates by appropriating part of the value produced in its colossal subcontractor. In line with the expected (big) size of complier firms that concentrate the tangible capital investment that is outsourced by leaders, Foxconn is a gigantic corporation. Hon Hai Precision Industry (Foxconn's company name in Taiwan Stock Exchange) was ranked 23rd in Global 500 by *Fortune Magazine* in 2019, which ranks enterprises according to their revenues.

Also in accordance with complier firms, Foxconn enjoys a positive – but lower than Apple's – profit rate (Apple Inc, 2020; Hon Hai Precision Industry, 2020). As explained by Chan et al. (2013), Foxconn's profit rate remains positive precisely, in part, by reducing labour expenditures both in terms of wages and benefits, which even led to a suicide wave as a protest measure. Driven by wages rise in China, Foxconn started replacing labour with robots. Moreover, Foxconn is considering opening facilities in Brazil and Vietnam, a decision accelerated by the recent trade war between the United States and China.[2]

3.2 Apple's innovation monopoly rents

Besides vertical natural monopoly rents, Apple collects intellectual rents from its innovation monopoly. The latter results from two complementary sources, both highly reliant on IPRs in the case of Apple: technological innovation and brand-building. Concerning technological innovations, Figure 7.1 presents the evolution of Apple's granted patents. We also perform a network mapping analysis of its innovation networks, including a lexical analysis of its scientific publications.[3] The latter will provide evidence of the multi-technology base of its innovations. The comparison between co-authorship and co-ownership will highlight the subordinate role played by companies and universities participating in Apple's innovation networks.

A steppingstone in Apple's intellectual monopoly was the introduction of the iPod in 2004, but its dominance was boosted after its major science-based innovation, the iPhone, in 2007. It was followed by consecutive improvements every year since then and by other innovative products like the iPad in 2009, which contributed to a further soar in profits and profit rate (Figure 7.2).[4] Both innovations heavily relied on technologies funded and developed by the US state, such as the Internet and touch-screen displays (Mazzucato, 2015). Apple's profit rate evolution can be explained as the result of a twofold process: rentiership and extraordinary profits due to its relatively higher intangible capital intensity. Concerning the former,

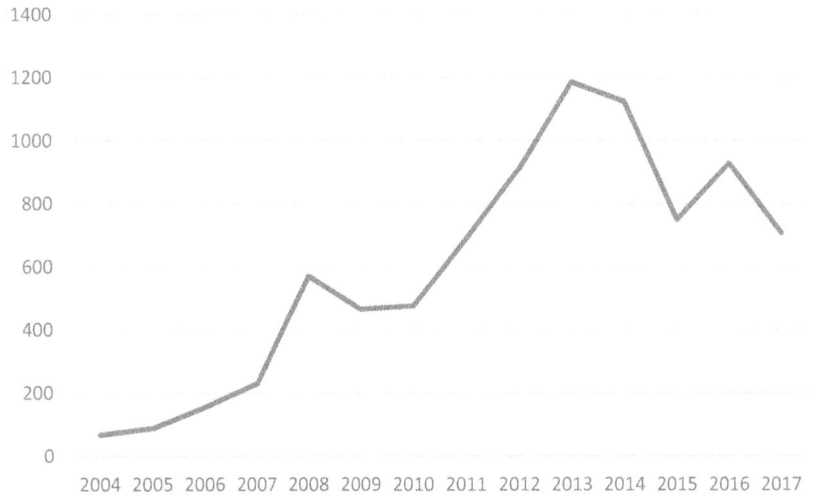

Figure 7.1 Evolution of Apple's granted patents (all major patent offices).
Source: Derwent Innovation.

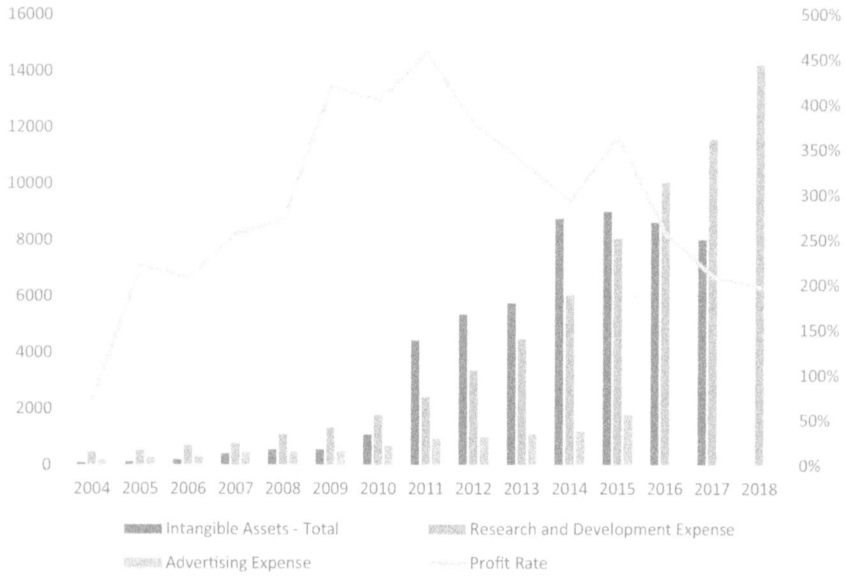

Figure 7.2 Evolution of Apple's profit rate, R&D investment, intangible assets and advertising expense (millions USD).[5]

Source: Compustat.

both a constant flow of innovations and vertical natural monopoly rents expanded intellectual rents over time. Financial rents are also part of this story, as we show in Section 4.

Since the iPhone was launched, Apple's investment in R&D grew systematically, consistent with its skyrocketing profit rates until 2011 (Figure 7.2). Probably, the dramatic increase in profit rate allowed Apple to reinvest gigantic sums in R&D driven by its – back then – retain and reinvest strategy (Lazonick et al., 2013), while further investing in advertising was not the chosen strategy (Figure 7.2). As an intellectual monopoly, in order to keep its leadership, Apple needed to increase its R&D investment looking for further innovations.

The co-evolution of Apple's margin and investment in R&D is quite telling in this respect. Just before the iPhone was launched, Apple increased its share of R&D investment over revenues, compatible with the quest for innovation monopoly rents, in this case, mostly based on IPRs (see Figure 7.1). Margins, as they are calculated in annual reports subtracting R&D as an expense instead of considering it an investment, were negatively affected but eventually led to the iPhone, thus paid-off enormously (Figure 7.3).

Additional R&D investments gave fruitful creative results judging by Apple's intangible assets growth (Figure 7.2) and by the evolution of its granted patents (Figure 7.1). Interviews performed for a WIPO report stressed that "companies in the smartphone industry appear to consider their patent portfolios as central to maintaining a competitive advantage in a dynamic marketplace" (WIPO, 2014, p. 32). Still, as shown in this report, it is innovation rather than patents which is the key driver behind leading companies. Granted patents gather part of innovations' effect, which is why they usually follow the same trend. Moreover, Apple has been fragmenting its innovations in multiple patents; a strategy called patent thickets that evidence Apple's technological competition with rival intellectual monopolies. Patent thickets increase enforcement transaction costs and companies' chances to threaten those trying to copy them (Ernst, 2016; Noel & Schankerman, 2013).

Figure 7.3 also shows that, in recent years, as iPhone-related innovations peaked, Apple increased its R&D investments *vis-à-vis* revenues. Therefore, margins that consider R&D as an expense show a more significant decrease than the alternative calculation that considers R&D as an investment (Rikap, 2020). In the next section, we will argue that Apple's ambition to catch-up with other tech giants in data-driven innovation rents drives this second wave of relatively higher R&D efforts in relation to margins.

Together with technological innovations, we explained in Chapter 2 that brands are intangible assets that appropriate value in the form of intellectual rents. They do not contribute to value creation but enable value appropriation by segmenting markets, creating new ones, thus included in the

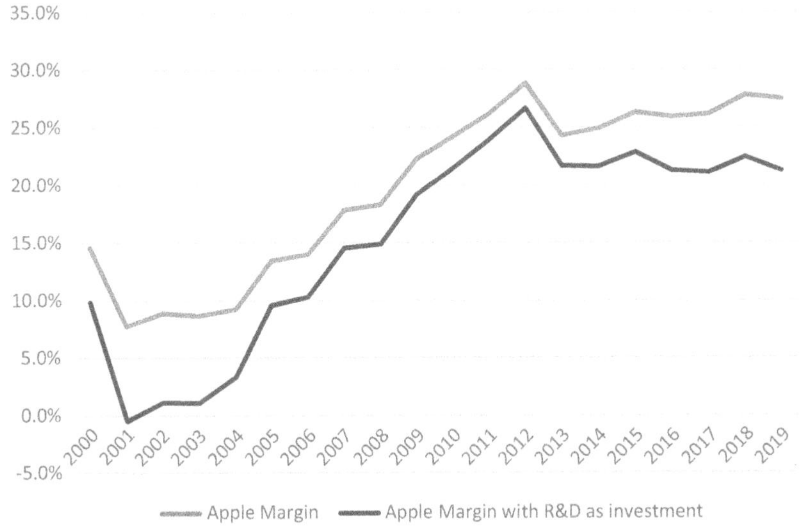

Figure 7.3 Apple's margins over time, with and without R&D as an investment.
Source: Compustat.

innovation concept mobilized in this book. "Apple" is the world's most valuable brand, according to Forbes.[6] Regardless of the specific calculation used to achieve this result, it is clear that a fraction of Apple's innovation monopoly rents corresponds to its brand-building, which led to creating a somehow separate market for Apple products. Haskel and Westlake (2018, Chapter 4) claim that Apple's brand is indeed beneath part of the iPhone's success. The iPhone was not the first smartphone, but Apple's brand implied stylish and user-friendly devices, which was in sharp contrast with already existing devices.

3.2.1 Apple's corporate innovation system

Apple's innovation strategy is a combination of in-house and outsourced knowledge modules. As explained in Chapter 2, each intellectual monopoly organizes a corporate innovation system. This system is integrated by multiple global or transnational innovation networks working on different technologies or steps of different innovation processes. They are integrated by different organizations that participate in subordinated positions and some innovation networks may intersect with those of other intellectual monopolies, thus engaging in technological cooperation. In Apple's innovation system, subordinate organizations include innovating companies, defined as companies participating in innovation networks in a subordinated position, without garnering significant rents (see Chapter 2), research universities and public research organizations (see Chapter 5).

Apple's innovation system can be partially depicted by building a network map where the nodes are the affiliations of its scientific publications' co-authors[7] (Figure 7.4). Apple's published papers between 2004 and 2019 were retrieved from the Web of Science (WoS) and processed using the CorText platform.[8] In the map, each cluster can be conceived as an innovation network while the whole map represents its corporate innovation system. Apple shared publications with 494 institutions. In order to concentrate on the most important links, Figure 7.4 was built using a Chi-square metric for determining nodes proximity. We prioritized the top 101 nodes, meaning that the map depicts Apple and its 100 most frequent co-authors. Since Apple is authoring every publication, the network map places Apple in a central place. Those institutions that are its most frequent co-authors within its top 100 co-authoring organizations appear directly connected to Apple, either in its cluster or in another one but still directly linked. There are 31 direct links with Apple on the map, mostly universities but also companies.

This map includes the WoS "subject category" as a third variable in order to show the most frequent research topics of each cluster. The diversity of covered subjects points to Apple's strategy to become a multi-technology and multi-product intellectual monopoly, beyond the iPhone, as we further discuss in the next sub-heading.

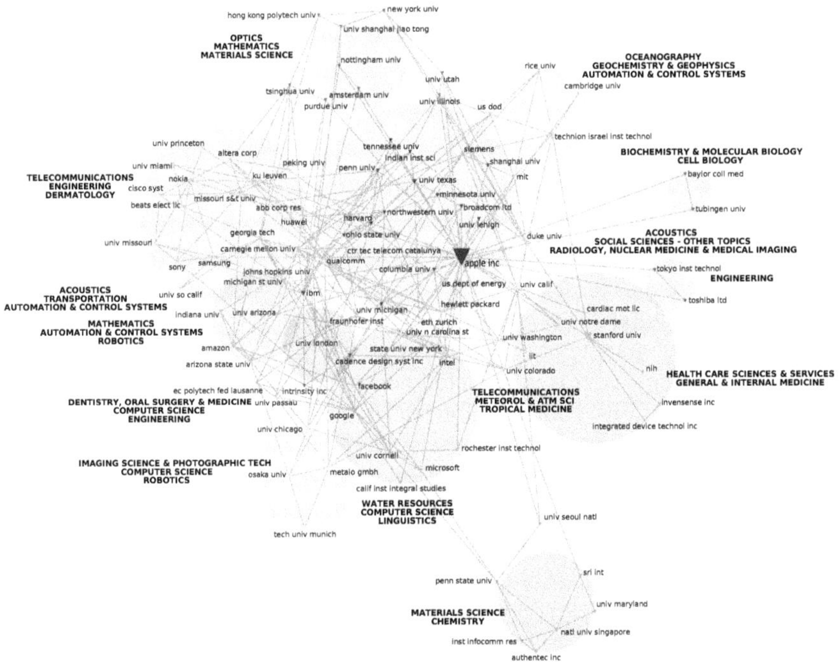

Figure 7.4 Network map. Apple's top 100 co-authors (2004–19).
Source: Author's analysis based on Web of Science data extraction.

Figure 7.4 is a compelling depiction of the scope of an intellectual monopoly's innovation system. It includes top research universities, innovating companies and other intellectual monopolies. Seventy-two percent of Apple's publications were co-authored with at least one research university and, within total co-authoring institutions, 49% were universities. Stanford University and the University of California stand out. Among other projects, by the end of 2017, Stanford University School of Medicine and Apple launched a joint heart study on Apple Watch.[9] However, until 2017 included, the only university sharing patents (only two) with Apple was the University of Minnesota.[10] This comparison between co-authorship and co-ownership provides evidence of Apple's knowledge predation from universities participating in its innovation system. Thus, it also allows us to consider these universities as subordinate research universities (see Chapter 5), at least in their relationship with Apple. More generally, Apple's top patent co-owner, besides its employees, is SensoMotoric Instruments, a Free University of Berlin spin-off sharing 22 patents (0.3% of Apple's portfolio until 2017 included).

Figure 7.4 also shows that Apple has research ties with the US government. Both the US Department of Energy and the US Department of Defense are directly connected to Apple. Although it is highly likely that most of this research remains secret, US government offices co-authored almost 4% of Apple's total publications in the selected period. It should be recalled that the US public funds for blue-sky research significantly contributed to Apple's initial success (Mazzucato, 2015, Chapter 5).

Apple published papers with 168 companies between 2004 and 2019, including other intellectual monopolies. There are two main technological cooperation clusters between intellectual monopolies in Figure 7.4. As explained in Chapter 6, technological cooperation refers to rival intellectual monopolies sharing steps or modules of their respective innovation networks. In the map, this is depicted as rival intellectual monopolies co-authoring publications. Clusters plotting rival intellectual monopolies show that these companies not only compete all against each other but also collaborate for innovation. Overall, both behaviours are closely related, to the point that two intellectual monopolies can simultaneously quarrel at courts and share R&D projects.

In Figure 7.4, one of these clusters corresponds to the smartphone industry (topics associated with this cluster refer to telecommunications and engineering but also with dermatology due to touch screening technologies). This cluster is integrated by Apple's main technology and market rivals: Sony, Samsung, Huawei and Nokia. Samsung and Apple relationship is driven by technological cooperation and competition. When looking at the technologies required to produce an iPhone, technological interlinks with Samsung become clear, but these companies also conduct research together. Simultaneously, they have met in court countless times claiming IPRs infringements, a sign of their intense technological competition.

A similar story is that of Apple and Qualcomm – also included in Figure 7.4 – although the latter qualifies as an innovating company or eventually a wannabe intellectual monopoly but not as an established intellectual monopoly (see Chapter 6 for a distinction between wannabe and established intellectual monopolies). As developed in Chapter 2, innovating companies sell innovation (or innovation modules), losing intellectual rents in the hands of intellectual monopolies.

Qualcomm spends almost a quarter of its revenues in R&D (European Commission, 2019). Regardless of its high margins and position in the chip's market, Qualcomm's high dependence on profits coming from royalties is aligned to the innovating company type. The fact that Qualcomm is not a multi-product company, unlike ICT intellectual monopolies, further reinforces that claim.

Analysing 2016 figures, Dedrick and Kraemer (2017) have shown that although Qualcomm's operating margin was 22.4%, this figure was mostly driven by its licensing business, which has an 85% operating margin and explains a third of the company's revenues. The other two-thirds of its revenues corresponded to chip's sales with a 12% operating margin. Innovating companies, as we explained in Chapter 2, derive most of their profits from intellectual rents since their main business is to produce steps of intellectual monopoly's innovation circuits. A sign of Qualcomm's weaker bargaining power *vis-à-vis* Apple was that it kept providing chips to Apple while suing the latter for IPR infringement.[11] Furthermore, Dedrick and Kraemer (2017) also showed that Qualcomm's licensing revenues, albeit of utmost significance for the company, represented less than 2% of the total revenues of the smartphone industry.

Another proof of Qualcomm's weaker business is that Apple has replaced Qualcomm with Intel processors since the iPhone 7 (WIPO, 2017). The impact of being dropped by an intellectual monopoly – left outside its innovation system – after developing a mid- or long-term business relationship with the latter is a sign of innovating companies' subordinated position. For instance, when Apple announced that it would stop working with Imagination Technologies, this company's stocks plunged.[12] After years of struggling, the company was acquired by a Chinese equity fund for around a quarter of its peak market value. The company may recover in the near future because it reached a new licensing deal with Apple.[13]

The second cluster depicting technological cooperation between rival intellectual monopolies plots Google, Microsoft and Facebook.[14] Google and Microsoft – as well as IBM – are among Apple's top ten co-authors. Intel is also part of this cluster, another case of an innovating company. It is worth noting that Apple plans to replace Intel processors with its own designed processors in Mac computers, based on technology licensed from a Japanese firm, Arm, recently acquired by Nvidia.[15]

Broadcom is the only corporation that belongs to Apple's central cluster. This company provides improved chips and contributes to reconfigure the iPhone value chain by systematically providing new features to achieve the next iPhone generations. Broadcom chips include the provision of wireless charging, Wi-Fi, Bluetooth and GPS capabilities for the new models. Furthermore, Apple and Broadcom have been working together in innovation circuits for analogue interface and wireless charging.[16] Broadcom is frequently participating in Apple's innovation processes, evidenced by its place and direct connection with Apple in Figure 7.4. Broadcom and other firms in Apple's innovation system like Sri International or InvenSense can also be conceived as innovating companies. None of them share patents with Apple, which likely steers these companies' research according to its R&D agenda. Intellectual monopolies engage in research with start-ups (thus, innovating companies) as far as the latter investigate (or is willing to investigate) on topics that are within the former research agenda. The fact that these start-ups finally published papers with Apple points in that direction.

Finally, in terms of countries of origin, considering both Apple's history and home base, the predominance of American partners is not a surprise. Anyway, in the whole corpus of Apple's publications between 2004 and

2019, 9% was published with at least one German organization and 7% (including Metaio GmbH, an innovating company which was later acquired by Apple) with at least one Chinese organization. Huawei is Apple's 33rd co-author. Another example of an ongoing innovation network that goes beyond the United States involves Aarhus University in Denmark. In 2016, Apple agreed to install a mega data centre next to this university's Foulum research centre to collaborate on sustainable energy and computer science R&D.[17]

Beyond innovation networks illustrated in Figure 7.4, another example of how Apple simultaneously plans multiple innovation circuits is apps development. In their analysis of platforms and complementors, Lan et al. (2019) distinguished between lower and upper layers within platforms' architecture. Lower layers are responsible for foundational services, thus rendering their owners' higher power over the whole system. Microsoft's Windows, Apple's iOS and Google's Android platforms are examples of lower layers. These platforms' success depends on the diversity and proficiency of the applications they offer, which is guaranteed by opening the platform to millions of developers.

Since 2008, Apple's apps are based on a form of outsourcing called "crowdsourcing" because it is performed by a community attracted by an open call (Brabham, 2008). Apple provides developers a software development kit that explains the type of apps that can be made publicly available. Guidelines include technical information, information on privacy policies, trademarks, religion and sex matters. Apple controls the whole innovation process: the programming software to be used (iOS), the approval process, the distribution mechanisms, suggested pricing categories (in general predefined low prices) and the rewards scheme (Apple retains 30% of every in-app purchases plus in-app advertising). Hence, Apple decides which apps will be sold and when, without paying any direct remuneration to developers who actually afford all the associated production costs and risks (Bergvall-Kareborn & Howcroft, 2013).

Apple's role as gatekeeper is the main argument against the company in the US Congress tech giants' antitrust investigation opened in 2019 and became apparent with its fight with Epic (Fortnite game developer company) in 2020. The latter violated the 30% rule, Apple delisted its game from the Apple Store, and then Epic initiated a claim against Apple for monopoly practices. Apple replied giving the former two weeks to comply with its store rules. Otherwise, Apple would block Epic from accessing to Unreal Engine. The latter is a software tool kit developed by Epic and used by hundreds of other developers that provides shortcuts for programming and making more realistic graphics. Epic charges 5% royalty on every game sold that relies on Unreal Engine.[18]

Developers can be conceived as innovating companies. They participate in Apple's innovation system but taking all the risk and capital commitment and accept every clause imposed by Apple. When successful, they must share profits with Apple. In particular for the case of self-employed developers (unlike established firms like Epic), this is a business that, more often than not, provides no remuneration at all. Still, those consistently successful in creating highly purchased apps garner part of the associated intellectual rents, thus enjoying significant profit rates (see Chapter 2).

While Apple minimizes its risks and significantly avoids software development costs, developers are even required to adapt their apps to Apple's new products or features, ensuring compatibility if they want to keep their apps on offer. As a result, Apple profits from the productivity of its crowdsourced workforce.

Summing up, Apple's innovation monopoly and vertical natural monopoly rents complement each other and explain its intellectual monopoly, providing Apple higher profits and profit rate. By developing planning relations with developers, start-ups, universities and public bodies that participate in Apple's innovation system, all these organizations reinforce Apple's dominance. By predating knowledge from them, which Apple turns into intangible assets, it increases its profit rate. However, Figure 7.2 shows that Apple's profit rate is falling since 2011, except for a rebound in 2015. What is behind this evolution and what is Apple doing to reinforce its intellectual monopoly?

3.3 Apple's quest for data-driven innovation rents

In order to keep their intellectual monopoly, corporations must continually reinforce their concentration of knowledge. Apple continued launching new iPhone models and other products after 2011. However, they do not seem to be breakthrough innovations because the impact on sales was not as outstanding as former innovations, while other intellectual monopolies – notably Huawei and Samsung – leapfrogged in the technological competition. In fact, in 2016, Apple's net sales decreased. Besides general macroeconomic conditions, the company recognized that its first fall in years was explained by "a lower rate of iPhone upgrades during 2016 compared to 2015" (Apple Inc, 2018, p. 23). As described in a WIPO report, the market-share of the smartphone market leaders depends on consumer preferences for their innovations (WIPO, 2014). As Huawei pioneered in 5G technology and Samsung in handsets' cameras, Apple lagged behind.

Moreover, the handset market is reaching a possible technological peak. In parallel, the high-tech industry was shifting from innovations in devices towards innovations in computing services. This revolution was driven by the development of new sources and repositories of constant fluxes of data. These repositories are owned by tech companies, in particular by the other four of the GAFAM acronym (Google, Amazon, Facebook and Microsoft). These four companies have monopolized multiple sources or original data, triggering data-driven innovation rents (Rikap, 2020).

Increasingly investing in R&D is a necessary but not a sufficient condition to win the innovation race, especially since high-tech intellectual monopolies follow multi-technology and multi-product strategies, favoured by their access to data, to widen their innovation success rates. In this context, Apple shifted its strategy, moving away from a paramount focus on the iPhone towards services (such as App Store, Apple Pay, iTunes and cloud services), and wearables (such as AirPods)[19] (Apple Inc, 2019). In terms of its intellectual monopoly, these are not only innovative products. They are also a means to harvest data-driven innovation rents since those services provide consumer's data to Apple that it can use to enhance that provision and further innovate. Morgan Stanley expects Apple's service business will grow to USD 100 billion by 2023.[20] Remarkably, this move from handset to the data value chain is also taking place in the Chinese company Xiaomi.[21]

This shift in strategy can be traced by looking at Apple's revenues per product. Even considering that each new iPhone historically meant a price-increase (thus, ceteris paribus, an increase in revenues),[22] Apple's total iPhone revenue fell in 2019 and the share of iPhone revenue within total Apple revenues went from 62% to 55% in only one year (Table 7.1). This fall is not only explained by iPhone's sales evolution but also by the growth in revenues from every other product, in particular services (16% increase) and "wearables, home and accessories" (41% increase). The latter's revenues almost doubled in two years. Furthermore, the financial market seems to also bet for a reconversion *à la Microsoft* (see Rikap and Lundvall, 2020), given Apple's market capitalization growth in 2019 and 2020.[23]

Besides broadening its business with a clear move into services, in what can be understood as an attempt to become a multi-product company centralizing data from services and producing digital intelligence, Apple is also expanding its technological reach. Apple's move to dominate digital

Table 7.1 Net sales disaggregated by significant products and services (in thousands of USD and shares)

	2019	*2019 share (%)*	*2018*	*2018 share (%)*	*2017*	*2017 share (%)*
iPhone	142,381	55	164,888	62	139,337	61
Mac	25,740	10	25,198	9	25,569	11
iPad	21,280	8	18,380	7	18,802	8
Wearables, home and accessories	24,482	9	17,381	7	12,826	6
Services	46,291	18	39,748	15	32,700	14
Total net sales	26,0174	100	265,595	100	229,234	100

Source: Author's compilation from Apple's Annual Reports.

technologies includes catching-up with the other GAFAM in artificial intelligence.[24] After acquiring Siri in 2010, Apple lagged behind in this technology. Its catching-up strategy included the acquisitions of Emotient in 2016 and, since 2018, Apple accelerated related acquisitions, including Drive.ai and Turi. Early in 2020, it acquired Xnor – whose machine learning algorithms are run on-device instead of in the cloud – paying USD 200 million for the latter, thus beating Microsoft and Amazon offers.[25] Overall, Apple became the second company in terms of artificial intelligence companies' acquisitions, after Alphabet and followed by Microsoft (World Intellectual Property Organization, 2019). Apple also recently joined a new artificial intelligence initiative called Partnership on AI, already integrated by Microsoft, Google, Amazon, IBM and Facebook, which illustrates technological cooperation between intellectual monopolies.[26]

Overall, by leveraging on the iPhone and its other devices as platforms, Apple is moving towards a data-driven intellectual monopoly. It seems Apple is applying the other GAFAM companies' strategy to offer services that generate big data.

In the next section, this analysis of Apple's history as an intellectual monopoly is complemented with a preliminary assessment of the interplay between its intellectual and financial rents.

4 Apple's interplay between intellectual and financial rentierism

Davis and Orhangazi (2019) and Auvray et al. (2018) have recently studied the interplay between intellectual and financial rentierism from a macroeconomic perspective. The size of profit shifting in the United States is so big that, by 2016, it generated losses of between 30% and 40% of the corporate tax base (Clausing, 2020a). Profit shifting is concentrated in large multinational firms, typically intellectual monopolies (Pozsar, 2018; Wier & Reynolds, 2018). The 2017 tax and jobs act (Public Law 115–97) pretended to reduce incentives for profit shifting. However, as noted by Clausing (2020b), as of 2019 third quarter, there was no evidence of such a reduction.

Apple is probably the most extreme case of intertwined intellectual and financial rentierism. Apple further increased its available earnings by allocating profits and R&D expenses in low tax jurisdictions. By 2013, this strategy allowed Apple to reduce its US tax bill by USD 10 billion. Apple's intellectual property is mostly registered in the United States, where protection is stronger and where almost all its R&D activity takes place (Ting, 2014). However, it declares part of its earnings before tax and IPRs ownership in two subsidiaries in Ireland. Then, by using a cost-sharing agreement, Apple assigns a portion of its international profits to those companies (Bryan et al., 2017). The Paradise Papers revealed that Apple enjoys a loophole between the US and Ireland's legislation.

Ting (2014) reconstructed Apple's international tax structure in detail, composed of multiple subsidiaries created to avoid corporate taxes. Apple Operations International and Apple Sales International are incorporated in Ireland. However, these corporations have their headquarters in the United States. Subsidiary companies managed from headquarters outside Ireland do not pay taxes there, and corporate taxes in the United States are supposed to be paid at the place of incorporation. Thus, due to the differences in each taxing system, Apple's wholly owned Irish subsidiaries escape from both legislations.[27] Apple then declares most of its earnings (64% between 2009 and 2012) in Ireland, a country where it has only 1% of its customers and 4% of total employees.

Operations leading to lower tax bills and financialized profits are easier for companies like Apple, which base their power and profits in intangibles (rather than tangibles) dominance. Intellectual monopolies have higher chances to profit from tax loopholes because intangible assets (such as IPRs) can easily be declared anywhere thus justifying profit shifting (see Chapter 10).

Once the money is allocated in tax havens, the next step is financialization. Apple's intellectual rents become intangible assets invested in financial markets. This intellectual monopoly's colossal cash flows and relatively limited needs in terms of increasing tangible capital commitment in the short term (thanks to its extreme outsourcing strategy) lead to a financialization scheme. By 2016, Apple was the company with the world's highest offshored savings. Through Braeburn Capital, Apple keeps most of these savings in corporate bonds and financially monetizes them (Pozsar, 2018). Apple's asset manager Braeburn Capital is, overall, a hedge fund (Bryan et al., 2017).

Profits in tax havens are retained earnings. So, in order to pay to shareholders without paying US taxes, Apple issues debt in the United States. With the cash from the debt, it pays dividends and does buybacks. Then the offshored savings end up being formally funded by debt (Pozsar, 2018). Apple started buying back stocks in 2012 (USD 10 billion). Since then, buybacks soared year on year, reaching USD 210 billion in 2017 and jumping to USD 310 billion in 2018 after 2017 Tax and Jobs Act.[28] In the first six months after the Act, Apple's announced buybacks accounted for a quarter of total of US corporations' buybacks.[29]

All in all, as explained by Bryan et al. (2017), finance and offshoring of intangible capitals augment the portion of these earnings kept by intellectual monopolies (since they pay lower taxes by declaring IPRs and earnings in tax havens). Moreover, by setting a financialization scheme, they further expand their profits. Intangibles, as concluded by these authors, play a double role as industrial and financial assets. In this respect, it should not be a surprise that the top ten companies in terms of offshored savings are high-tech and big pharma intellectual monopolies (Pozsar, 2018). Overall, we argue that intellectual monopolies' intangible intensity, robust economic position and global operations are used as leverage to make financial gains, aided by differences in national taxing systems.

5 Concluding remarks

This chapter illustrated how different sources of intellectual monopoly reinforce each other by looking at Apple's paradigmatic example. Apple was incepted as an intellectual monopoly based on vertical natural monopoly and innovation monopoly rents. However, its overreliance on the iPhone could have led to an eventual loss of its intellectual monopoly, outpaced by Huawei, Samsung and others in the smartphone market. Most importantly, it was outpaced by other GAFAM in terms of technological leadership in digital intelligence. We argued that these could be the underlying causes of Apple's move to a more diversified innovation portfolio, focusing on products and services that can provide original big data sources. Apple is becoming a data-driven intellectual monopoly. Chapter 8 delves into another – already established – data-driven intellectual monopoly: Amazon.

Furthermore, Apple's case points to the complementarities between intellectual monopolies and financialization dynamics. Apple plays on two rentier fronts to maximize its profits. Apple predates knowledge from its innovation networks garnering different types of intellectual rents, and its nature as an intellectual monopoly allows Apple to freely move its colossal earnings and use them as financial assets.

The consequences of these dynamics are greater inequalities at every possible level: between countries, between social classes, between workers, and between managers, stock owners and asset managers on the one side, and the rest of the population on the other. Chapters 10 and 14 will revisit these and other consequences of intellectual monopoly capitalism.

Notes

1 http://column.global-labour-university.org/2012/08/t-shirt-economics-labour-in-imperialist.html.
2 https://www.scmp.com/news/asia/southeast-asia/article/2176442/foxconn-considers-setting-factory-vietnam-response-us-china.
3 The methodology followed to draw these maps was presented in Chapter 6.
4 Profit rates were calculated dividing operating income after depreciation over property, plant and equipment – total (Net) (Basu & Vasudevan, 2012).
5 Since 2016, Apple stopped disclosing advertising expenses as a separate item in its annual reports and, since 2018, it includes intangible assets in other non-current assets. Therefore, these two series are incomplete in Figure 7.2.
6 https://www.forbes.com/powerful-brands/list/.
7 The frequency of co-authorship with Apple is represented by node's sizes.
8 Cortext is an open platform for performing bibliometric and semantic analysis. It can be accessed online at: https://www.cortext.net/.
9 https://med.stanford.edu/news/all-news/2017/11/stanford-medicine-to-collaborate-on-apple-heart-study.html.
10 Data on patent co-ownership was retrieved from the Derwent Innovation database.

11 https://www.cnet.com/news/qualcomm-didnt-have-all-the-license-negotiating-power-exec-testifies/; and https://www.theverge.com/2019/4/16/18410985/apple-qualcomm-settle-royalty-dispute-patent-licensing-terms-high-fees.
12 https://www.forbes.com/sites/laurengensler/2017/04/03/apple-drops-imagination-technology-stock-craters/#8ea1aa5599d3.
13 https://www.ft.com/content/73795ec8-2d2d-11ea-a126-99756bd8f45e.
14 Amazon is also depicted but does not belong to the same cluster.
15 https://www.bloomberg.com/news/articles/2020-06-09/apple-plans-to-announce-move-to-its-own-mac-chips-at-wwdc?cmpid=BBD060920_TECH&utm_medium=email&utm_source=newsletter&utm_term=200609&utm_campaign=tech.
16 https://www.cnbc.com/2018/06/05/broadcom-will-generate-10-in-revenue-from-every-new-iphone-jp-morgan-estimates.html.
17 http://dca.au.dk/en/current-news/news/show/artikel/aarhus-university-welcomes-apple-as-close-neighbour-to-its-foulum-research-centre/.
18 https://www.ft.com/content/f77b7979-c943-4b9d-b7b7-7953b63bea7e and https://www.ft.com/content/733e1730-868e-479b-88fe-f83d4111918a?segmentId=b0d7e653-3467-12ab-c0f0-77e4424cdb4c.
19 https://fortune.com/2019/08/06/apple-airpods-business/ and https://www.ft.com/content/31eec6d0-fb39-11e9-98fd-4d6c20050229.
20 https://appleinsider.com/articles/18/11/08/apples-services-will-grow-to-over-100-billion-per-year-in-2023-says-analyst.
21 https://www.businessinsider.com/xiaomi-reinvests-in-artificial-intelligence-powered-device-ecosystem-2020-1?r=US&IR=T.
22 The fact that Apple recently introduced a cheaper iPhone also provides evidence of how its innovations are not enough to accomplish its market goals, thus it broadened its product mix to include lower tiers.
23 https://www.ft.com/content/ef09a97a-fcea-44d7-a5c0-5dc67becf286?segmentId=b0d7e653-3467-12ab-c0f0-77e4424cdb4c.
24 In particular, Microsoft and Alphabet are in the top 10 artificial intelligence patent applicants (World Intellectual Property Organization, 2019).
25 https://www.ft.com/content/8ea5f6b2-37e0-11ea-a6d3-9a26f8c3cba4?segmentId=b0d7e653-3467-12ab-c0f0-77e4424cdb4c.
26 https://www.partnershiponai.org/2016/09/industry-leaders-establish-partnership-on-ai-best-practices/and https://www.partnershiponai.org/2017/01/partnership-ai-update/.
27 https://www.ft.com/content/991f11ae-2c51-11ea-bc77-65e4aa615551.
28 https://www.aboveavalon.com/notes/2019/4/24/apples-400-billion-buyback-program.
29 https://www.theguardian.com/business/2019/nov/08/how-big-tech-is-dragging-us-towards-the-next-financial-crash?utm_term=RWRpdG9yaWFsX1RoZUxvbmdSZWFkLTE5MTEwOQ%3D%3D&utm_source=esp&utm_medium=Email&utm_campaign=TheLongRead&CMP=longread_email.

References

Ambrosini, V., & Bowman, C. (2001). Tacit knowledge: Some suggestions for operationalization. *Journal of Management Studies*, *38*(6), 811–29.

Apple Inc. (2018). *Annual Report 2017.* Apple Inc.

Apple Inc. (2019). *Annual Report 2018.* Apple Inc.

Apple Inc. (2020). *Annual Report 2019.* Apple Inc.

Auvray, T., Durand, C., & Rabinovich, J. (2018). *Explaining the investment slowdown an empirical analysis of the relations between financialization, globalization and intangibles*. Congrès de l'AFEP.

Basu, D., & Vasudevan, R. (2012). Technology, distribution and the rate of profit in the US economy: Understanding the current crisis. *Cambridge Journal of Economics, 37*(1), 57–89.

Bergvall-Kareborn, B., & Howcroft, D. (2013). The Apple business model: Crowdsourcing mobile applications. *Accounting Forum, 37*, 280–9.

Birch, K. (2019). Technoscience rent: Toward a theory of rentiership for technoscientific capitalism. *Science, Technology, & Human Values, 45*(1), 3–33.

Brabham, D. C. (2008). Crowdsourcing as a model for problem solving: An introduction and cases. *Convergence, 14*(1), 75–90.

Bryan, D., Rafferty, M., & Wigan, D. (2017). Capital unchained: Finance, intangible assets and the double life of capital in the offshore world. *Review of International Political Economy, 24*(1), 56–86.

Chan, J., Pun, N., & Selden, M. (2013). The politics of global production: Apple, Foxconn and China's new working class. *New Technology, Work and Employment, 28*(2), 100–15.

Christophers, B. (2019). The problem of rent. *Critical Historical Studies, 6*(2), 303–23.

Clausing, K. A. (2020a). How big is profit shifting? *SSRN 3503091*

Clausing, K. A. (2020b). Profit shifting before and after the tax cuts and jobs act. *SSRN 3274827*

Cockburn, I. M., Henderson, R., & Stern, S. (2018). *The impact of artificial intelligence on innovation*. National Bureau of Economic Research.

Comino, S., Manenti, F. M., & Thumm, N. (2019). The role of patents in information and communication technologies: A survey of the literature. *Journal of Economic Surveys, 33*(2), 404–30.

Cox, R. W. (1981). Social forces, states and world orders: Beyond international relations theory. *Millennium, 10*(2), 126–55.

Davis, L., & Orhangazi, Ö. (2019). *Competition and monopoly in the U.S. economy: What do industrial concentration data tell?* University of Amherst.

Dedrick, J., & Kraemer, K. L. (2017). *Intangible assets and value capture in global value chains: The smartphone industry* (Vol. 41). WIPO.

Dedrick, J., Kraemer, K. L., & Linden, G. (2009). Who profits from innovation in global value chains?: A study of the iPod and notebook PCs. *Industrial and Corporate Change, 19*(1), 81–116.

Durand, C., & Milberg, W. (2020). Intellectual monopoly in global value chains. *Review of International Political Economy, 27*(2), 404–29. doi:10.1080/09692290.2019.1660703

Ernst, D. (2009). *A new geography of knowledge in the electronics industry? Asia's role in global innovation networks*. https://papers.ssrn.com/sol3/papers.cfm?abstract_id=2742923

Ernst, D. (2016). *Global strategic patenting and innovation–policy and research implications*. East-West Center Working Papers.

European Commission. (2019). *EU R&D scoreboard*. European Commission.

Foley, D. K. (2013). Rethinking financial capitalism and the "information" economy. *Review of Radical Political Economics, 45*(3), 257–68.

Froud, J., Johal, S., Leaver, A., & Williams, K. (2012). Apple business model. 'Financialization across the Pacific: Manufacturing cost ratios, supply chains and power. *Critical Perspectives on Accounting*, *25*(1), 46–57.

Granstrand, O. (2000). Corporate innovation systems: A comparative study of multi-technology corporations in Japan, Sweden and the USA. Chalmers University.

Haskel, J., & Westlake, S. (2018). *Capitalism without capital: The rise of the intangible economy*. Princeton University Press.

Haslam, C., Tsitsianis, N., Andersson, T., & Yin, Y. P. (2013). Apple's financial success: The precariousness of power exercised in global value chains. *Accounting Forum*, *37*, 268–79.

Hon Hai Precision Industry. (2020). *Annual Report 2019*. Hon Hai Precision Industry.

Howells, J. (1996). Tacit knowledge. *Technology Analysis & Strategic Management*, *8*(2), 91–106.

Johnson, B., & Lundvall, B. A. (1994). The learning economy. *Journal of Industry Studies*, *1*(2), 23–42.

Kraemer, K., Linden, G., & Dedrick, J. (2011). Capturing value in global networks: Apple's iPad and iPhone. University of California, Irvine, University of California, Berkeley, y Syracuse University. http://Pcic. Merage. Uci. Edu/Papers/2011/Value_iPad_iPhone. Pdf. *Consultado El*, *15*. https://pdfs.semanticscholar.org/9cb5/262a46e7c9131de43433b7c5f9b65386f8e2.pdf

Lan, S., Liu, K., & Dong, Y. (2019). Dancing with wolves: How value creation and value capture dynamics affect complementor participation in industry platforms. *Industry and Innovation*, *26*, 943–63. doi:10.1080/13662716.2019.1598339

Lazonick, W., Mazzucato, M., & Tulum, Ö. (2013). Apple's changing business model: What should the world's richest company do with all those profits? *Accounting Forum*, *37*, 249–67.

Linden, G., Kraemer, K. L., & Dedrick, J. (2009). Who captures value in a global innovation network?: The case of Apple's iPod. *Communications of the ACM*, *52*(3), 140–44.

Liu, J., Chaminade, C., & Asheim, B. (2013). The geography and structure of global innovation networks: A knowledge base perspective. *European Planning Studies*, *21*(9), 1456–73.

Mazzucato, M. (2015). *The entrepreneurial state: Debunking public vs. private sector myths* (Vol. 1). Anthem Press.

Noel, M., & Schankerman, M. (2013). Strategic patenting and software innovation. *The Journal of Industrial Economics*, *61*(3), 481–520.

Nuccio, M., & Guerzoni, M. (2019). Big data: Hell or heaven? Digital platforms and market power in the data-driven economy. *Competition & Change*, *23*(3), 312–28. doi:10.1177/1024529418816525

Orazbayeva, B. (2015). *Siemens research cooperation with universities*. Siemens AG.

Pagano, U. (2014). The crisis of intellectual monopoly capitalism. *Cambridge Journal of Economics*, *38*(6), 1409–29.

Pozsar, Z. (2018). Repatriation, the echo-taper and the €/$ basis. *Global Money Notes*, *11*.

Rikap, C. (2018). Innovation as economic power in global value chains. *Revue d'Économie Industrielle*, *163*, 35–75.

Rikap, C. (2020). Amazon: A story of accumulation through intellectual rentiership and predation. *Competition & Change*. doi:10.1177/1024529420932418

Rikap, C. & Lundvall, B.A. (2020). Big Tech, knowledge predation and the implications for development. Innovation and Development, 1–28. https://doi.org/10.1080/2157930X.2020.1855825

Sampat, B. N. (2018). *A survey of empirical evidence on patents and innovation.* National Bureau of Economic Research.

Satariano, A., & Burrows, P. (2011). Apple's supply-chain secret? Hoard lasers. *Bloomberg Businessweek*, 50–54.

Schwartz, H. M. (2016). Wealth and secular stagnation: The role of industrial organization and intellectual property rights. *The Russell Sage Foundation Journal of the Social Sciences*, *2*(6), 226–49.

Starosta, G. (2010a). Global commodity chains and the Marxian law of value. *Antipode*, *42*(2), 433–65.

Starosta, G. (2010b). The outsourcing of manufacturing and the rise of giant global contractors: A Marxian approach to some recent transformations of global value chains. *New Political Economy*, *15*(4), 543–63.

Teixeira, R. A., & Rotta, T. N. (2012). Valueless knowledge-commodities and financialization: Productive and financial dimensions of capital autonomization. *Review of Radical Political Economics*, *44*(4), 448–67.

Ting, A. (2014). ITax – Apple's international tax structure and the double non-taxation issue. *British Tax Review*, *1*. https://scholar.google.com/scholar?hl=en&as_sdt=0%2C5&q=iTax+%E2%80%93+Apple%E2%80%99s+International+Tax+Structure+and+the+Double+Non-taxation+Issue%E2%80%99.&btnG=

UNCTAD. (2019). *Digital Economy Report 2019: Value creation and capture–Implications for developing countries.* United Nations.

Wier, L., & Reynolds, H. (2018). *Big and "unprofitable": How 10% of multinational firms do 98% of profit shifting.* WIDER Working Paper.

WIPO. (2014). *The impact of the acquisition and use of patents on the smartphone industry.* WIPO and Center on Law and Information Policy at the Fordham University School of Law.

WIPO. (2017). *World Intellectual Property Report 2017: Intangible capital in global value chains.* World Intellectual Property Organization.

World Intellectual Property Organization. (2019). *WIPO Technology Trends 2019. Artificial intelligence.* WIPO.

Xing, Y. (2019). *How the iPhone widens the US trade deficit with China: The case of the iPhone X.* National Graduate Institute for Policy Studies.

8

AMAZON'S DATA-DRIVEN INTELLECTUAL MONOPOLY

1 Introduction

Amazon has reconfigured the retail industry. Since the 1990s, a group of retailers from core countries had opened stores around the world becoming big transnational corporations (Baud & Durand, 2012; Coe & Hess, 2005; Wrigley et al., 2005). Retailers "rationalized their supplier base to stabilise relations with a few 'preferred' producers" (Wood et al., 2016, p. 5). These retail giants fit Gereffi's (1994, 1996, 2001) buyer-driven commodity (later value) chain. It was said that buyer-driven chains hold a brand without the need to own factories because they control how, when and where production takes place (Gereffi, 2001).

However, since the 2000s, these retailers show a slowdown in their sales growth, signalling a potential loss of their leadership (Figure 8.1). This impression can be further confirmed by the flat – and for some of them decreasing – margins over net sales (Figure 8.2) in a context of rising corporate share and higher margins for leader corporations within each industry (see Chapter 1).

While transnational retailers were aching, e-commerce blossomed. Amazon is the paradigmatic example. It has systematically increased its sales at an average of 30% per year since 2000, with an impressive evolution in terms of "Technology and Content" investment (which primarily includes R&D investment) over net sales since 2010 (see Figure 8.3) and an exponential patent portfolio (Figure 8.4). Lichtenthaler (2018) shows that Amazon is the only company in the world that appears in the most diverse innovation rankings in terms of the indicators used to define innovative companies.

E-commerce meant a turn to data-driven innovation in retail. Not only new players like Amazon, Alibaba and MercadoLibre use processed market data to steer their business and further innovate. Walmart, the transnational retailer with the highest market capitalization, is also aware of the

Figure 8.1 Sales growth evolution. Selected transnational retailers.
Source: Compustat.

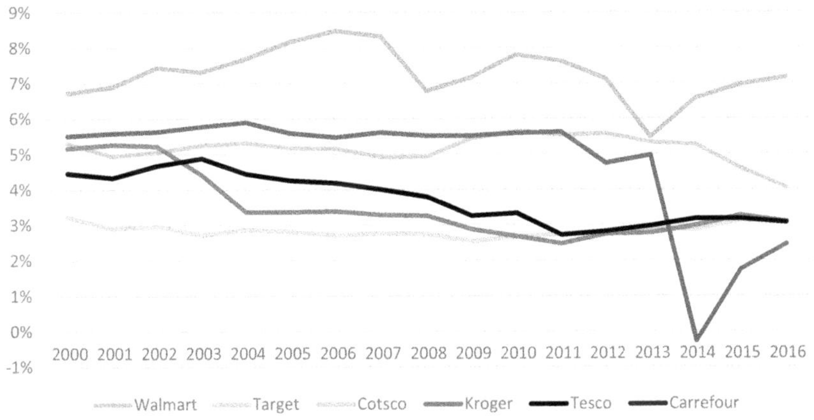

Figure 8.2 Margins over net sales. Selected transnational retailers.
Source: Compustat.

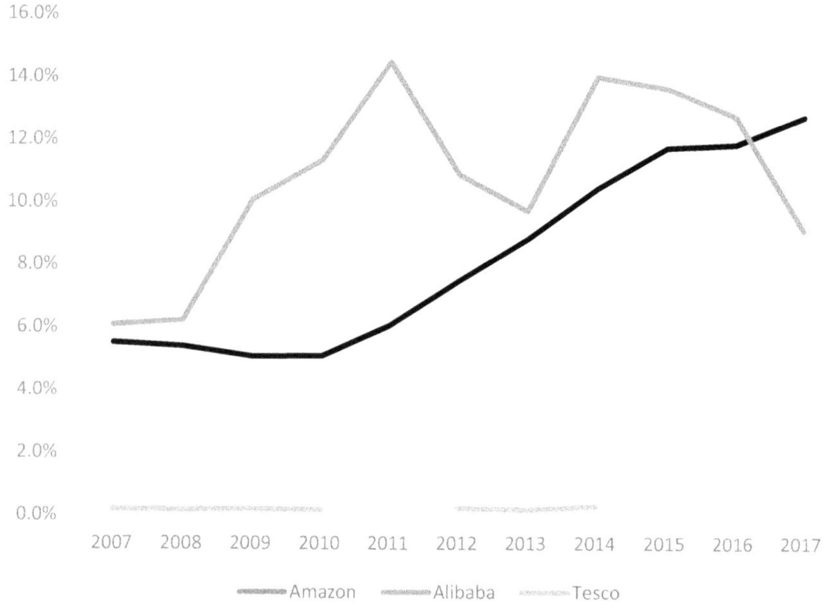

Figure 8.3 R&D over net sales. Selected transnational retailers.
Source: Compustat.
* Chosen retailers according to information availability: Amazon, Tesco,[1] Alibaba.

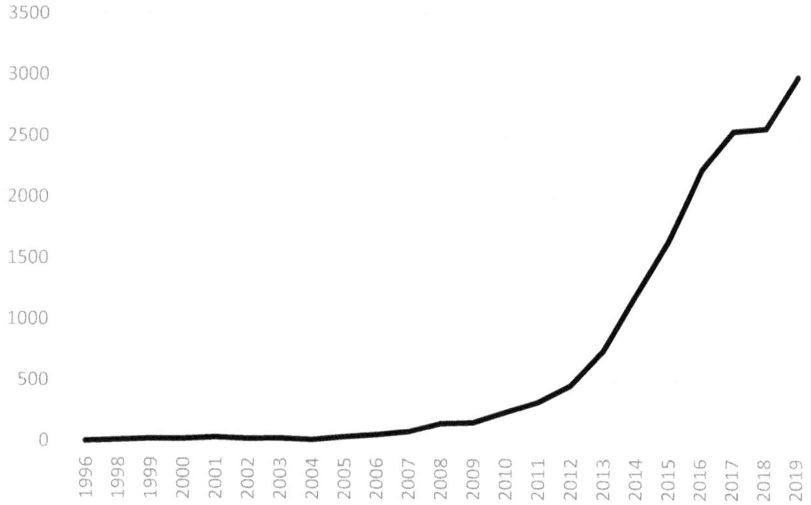

Figure 8.4 Amazon's granted patents per year.
Source: Derwent Innovation.

centrality of innovation and data for the retail industry in the 21st century.[2] This turn towards innovation and digital intelligence is in contradiction with buyer-driven chains' distinctive characteristics. According to Gereffi (1994), profits in producer-driven chains derived from scale economies and technological advances, while in buyer-driven chains they depended on a combination of other factors, such as design and marketing.

In this chapter, we argue that Amazon's revolution goes beyond disrupting the retail industry. Amazon is an illustrative example of how the most powerful corporations in this stage of capitalism are intellectual monopolies. Among intellectual monopolies, those that combine a monopoly over constant flows of original data with a state-of-the-art capacity to process and analyse these data with machine learning code, producing digital intelligence, will take the lead. In particular, Amazon relies on deep learning and neural networks, which are machine learning approaches where algorithms learn as they process data. As Cockburn et al. (2018) argue, these algorithms' learning capacity means the development of a new method for inventing, a general-purpose method of invention that is transforming how innovations take place. It significantly automates discoveries and also expands the types of problems that can be addressed through big data analysis and reshapes how scientific problems from diverse disciplines are framed. Therefore, tech giants like Amazon could eventually expand their intellectual monopoly without limits on the basis of innovations derived from their digital intelligence.

In the next section, we further elaborate on our intellectual monopoly framework by arguing that GVC and platform approaches fail to identify the specificity of contemporary global leading corporations as (data-driven) intellectual monopolies. Nonetheless, they are still relevant to explain particular traits of intellectual monopolies' operations. Section 3 provides evidence of Amazon as a data-driven intellectual monopoly by studying the content of its patents as well as its innovation networks. Section 4 complements this analysis by elaborating on other sources of economic power that Amazon mobilizes to strengthen its intangible assets' dominance. The power of data-driven intellectual monopolies dominating the digital economy goes beyond the economic realm. To give an account of this transformation, this section also elaborates on Amazon's political power *vis-à-vis* the US and Chinese states. Section 5 concludes.

2 The limits of GVC and platforms to understand emerging industrial organization patterns

This section argues that the literature on GVC and platforms should be articulated with broader understandings of the determinants of global leading corporations' inception as intellectual monopolies. In a nutshell, our main argument in this section is twofold. First, even if GVC leaders are intellectual monopolies, the latter is a more comprehensive concept to understand today's most powerful corporations. Some contemporary leader corporations do not organize value or supply chains but still enjoy an intellectual monopoly. Second, not every platform is a leading corporation. It should be distinguished between platforms that have become a data-driven intellectual monopoly and those that achieved one or few innovative hits. The latter will have, at most, a short-term extraordinary profit unless they build on those initial successes triggering a continuous process of knowledge monopolization.

When we say that GVC leaders are intellectual monopolies, we are building on Durand and Milberg (2020). According to these authors, GVC leaders enjoy vertical natural monopoly rents because they have exclusive knowledge covering the whole chain and thus the capacity to integrate it, assuring network complementarities. Therefore, leaders can be conceived as intellectual monopolies who have monopolized knowledge of the overall structure of the chain. GVC leaders are the only ones that can make sense of it by overseeing and planning, thus integrating all its parts. Furthermore, in line with Serfati (2008), GVC leaders control a significant share of the value creation process by capturing value produced in different parts of the chain. Vertical natural monopoly rents are not the only rent that can be extracted from monopolizing intangible assets, as identified by Durand and Milberg (2020) (see also Chapter 7). Thus, intellectual monopolies may emerge even for leading corporations that do not organize GVC if they concentrate intangible assets collecting, for instance, innovation rents or data-driven rents.

In particular, this leads us to consider leaders that organize platforms. This notion not only refers to how different producers relate with and rely on each other but also serves to define the creation of online marketplaces, from Uber or Airbnb – which are focused on selling a single product – to vast platforms such as Google or Amazon (Armstrong, 2006; Gawer, 2014; Rochet & Tirole, 2003). Platforms have also been defined as a new type of firm with a designed core architecture that (1) allows to provide – and governs the provision of – infrastructure that mediates between users, (2) has a monopoly tendency due to network effects and (3) often uses cross-subsidization to offer some products for free while charging for others (Srnicek, 2017).

Hence, platforms can be conceptualized as infrastructures that connect users, enabling market (and eventually also collaborative) exchanges. Platforms are often the marketplace connecting potential sellers and buyers, allowing them to exchange. In other cases, platforms are a showcase where sellers can promote their products. Even what Cusumano et al. (2019) call innovation platforms, like Android or iOS, are marketplaces aimed at selling applications. They could be reconceptualized as marketplaces for (product) innovations.

By providing indispensable digital connecting infrastructure, platforms provide privileged access to data (Srnicek, 2017). We argue that successful platform corporations are, as well as GVC leaders, intellectual monopolies. In the case of platform leaders like Amazon, their platforms are a means to monopolize a constant flow of diversified market data. Within most successful platforms, extracted data is not only vast (which is a result of network effects) but also quite diverse, which triggers economies of scope (chances to monetize data increase when different data sources are cross-referenced). Diversity amplifies these corporations' chances to expand their businesses and innovations. The result is a constant stream of what Durand and Milberg (2020) called data-driven innovation rents, inspired by Foley's (2013) informational rents.[3]

Thriving platforms are global intellectual monopolies, such as Amazon, Google, Microsoft and Facebook. Chapter 7 also argues that Apple is attempting to become a data-driven intellectual monopoly. US tech giants enjoy multiple and diverse sources of big data. These data are vital to improving their machine learning algorithms systematically. Likewise, it is through digital intelligence that these companies create new ways to extract data (Dolata, 2020; Kenney & Zysman, 2019; Rikap, 2020; Srnicek, 2017). Data-driven intellectual monopolies create new ways to expand and further diversify the data they centralize. In the case of Amazon, Amazon Web Services (AWS) is an example of the latter: a profitable business that, simultaneously, provides new flows of data (for instance on customers' use of computing services) that further nourish this and other businesses for Amazon. Digital intelligence leads successful platform companies to expand their businesses to adjacent platforms and also beyond platforms. Examples for Amazon are Fulfillment-by-Amazon (FBA), its storage and delivery service, which is not a platform, and Amazon Prime Video and the Kindle, which do operate as platforms.

On the contrary, less profitable platforms rely on a single (even if major) innovation that can be easily copied and whose associated data are not diverse enough to provide wider and multi-product innovation possibilities. Therefore, the chances of losing their innovative advantage in the short-term are high, and intellectual rents – if they are garnered – will also be limited in time. Uber and Airbnb (even before the pandemic) are paradigmatic examples of platforms based on single innovations and whose sources of new streams of data are relatively narrow.

Hence, there are both struggling and thriving platform companies (Montalban et al., 2019), with some promising platforms struggling since their IPOs.[4] Simultaneously, there are cases of global leaders that are not based on platforms such as big pharmaceutical companies (see Chapter 6). Furthermore, some global leaders neither organize extended GVC nor base their dominance on platforms, such as State Grid Corporation of China (Chapter 9). What these cases have in common with GVC leaders and successful platform corporations like Amazon is that they have all monopolized access to knowledge. Intellectual monopolies are corporations that have monopolized access to knowledge turned into intangible assets. They garner intellectual rents from their innovations but also predating from their innovation networks (see Chapters 2 and 10).

Hence, a conceptualization of the reasons underlying the success of companies like Amazon cannot only rely on their condition as platforms. We argue that the basis of Amazon's leadership is its intellectual monopoly. In particular, its data-driven intellectual monopoly emphasizing that it has centralized big data that are processed with deep learning and neural network algorithms to produce digital intelligence. The latter is used to further orient innovations and businesses (see Chapters 2 and 7). In the next section, we overview intellectual monopolies' specificities.

2.1 Intellectual monopolies' production and innovation networks[5]

By continuously monopolizing access to knowledge, intellectual monopolies sustain entry barriers that perpetuate their leadership. They do so in different ways, including GVC leader's exclusive knowledge of the chain they organize and integrate, technological platforms that harvest and process constant flows of users' data to innovate further and diversify their business, and, in line with Pagano (2014), corporations that concentrate on intellectual property rights (IPRs).

Intellectual monopolies organize innovation networks from which they appropriate knowledge through predatory relationships and garner intellectual rents. They outsource innovation steps to subordinate actors. As explained by Yeung and Coe (2015), once a firm innovates, it will try to perpetuate its leadership seeking to capture as much value as possible. It does so by unequally exchanging with those participating in its innovation networks. Moreover, drawing on Dolata (2013), intellectual monopolies can quickly and continuously adapt and anticipate new technologies, which is easier if some steps of the innovation process are outsourced. What to produce in-house and what to outsource depends – among others – on the nature of the intangible.

Unequal exchanges are also the norm in GVCs and platforms led by these companies. Within the GVC literature, the decision about internalization or outsourcing depends on the degree of power asymmetry between the leader and the rest of the chain, and on the degree of codifiability of the information needed to assure successful results from outsourcing (Strange & Humphrey, 2018). In the same vein, within platform's framework, Cusumano and Gawer (2002) had explained that leaders determine their scope by deciding what components will be produced in-house and what outsourced. They continue arguing that platform leaders seek consensus and control external firms. We rephrase the latter as consensus *through* control. In general, platform owners establish asymmetric relations with their complementors. Lan et al. (2019) add that this asymmetry deepens when the platform owner grows faster than its complementors. In cases like that of Amazon, where the platform owner competes with complementors in certain markets, the authors add that complementors' risk of value expropriation in the hands of the platform owner increases.

Outsourcing also depends on what is considered as a core activity by the intellectual monopoly, which cannot be universally defined. Unlike Walmart, who outsources warehouses to Schneider, Amazon has its own warehouses and manages its logistics. This decision, as we will see in the next section, is aligned to its innovation strategy since part of Amazon's patents concern storage and distribution, such as inventory management.

The next section explores Amazon's intellectual monopoly considering both how it uses data for continuous and technologically diverse innovations and how it does so by predating knowledge from its innovation networks with subordinate actors, garnering resulting intellectual rents.

3 Amazon's data-driven intellectual monopoly

Amazon's first innovative breakthrough, books' e-commerce, initiated its data-driven intellectual monopoly. Amazon collects customized data on consumer habits and personal information (past and present addresses, age, history of purchased goods, etc.) as well as of third-party sellers. Amazon uses digital intelligence to spot unsatisfied needs or profitable business opportunities in its marketplace.

The company advocates that it only uses aggregated (and not customized) data to steer its business (Sorokina & Cantu-Paz, 2016). However, its CEO Jeff Bezos declared in the US Congress Big Tech hearing that he could not assure that customized data were not being used by employees to favour Amazon.[6] Amazon uses collected and customized data to detect potential businesses (Galloway, 2017) while transferring the risks of new product failures to rival companies (Bensinger, 2012). Moreover, Amazon was also accused of price discrimination based on consumers' data (Khan, 2017).

Amazon has become a systematic innovator by centralizing and processing data. As explained in the previous section, it is digital intelligence defined as machine learning processed data that can be monetized. Our argument here is that Amazon became a multi-technology and multi-product corporation based on monopolizing and transforming data into intangible assets. A first sign of the relevance given to the data value chain is that the three most frequent multi-terms in Amazon's scientific publications corpus retrieved from the Web of Science database are "machine learning", "deep neural networks" and "neural network". Therefore, it may be said that most of Amazon's scientific publications deal with these topics.

To provide further evidence of this strategy, we performed a semantic analysis of the content of Amazon's patent portfolio until 2017 included. We extracted the most frequent multi-terms from its patents' titles and abstracts and performed a cluster analysis that plots, from that list of mined multi-terms, the 100 multi-terms with the highest frequency of co-occurrence (Figure 8.5). In the map, each multi-term is a node, and its size represents its corresponding frequency of occurrence in Amazon's patent portfolio. The methodology followed to build this, and the following network maps, is presented in Appendix 1.

Patents provide a good (although incomplete) depiction of Amazon's diversified innovation portfolio as well as of the relevance of data

Figure 8.5 Amazon's patents semantic analysis.
Source: Author's analysis based on Derwent Innovation data extraction.

management (storage and analysis). Topics range from patents associated with the Kindle and similar devices (top left cluster), thus product innovations, to process innovations for storage and logistics, where managing inventories appears as a frequent topic (top right cluster). Amazon uses drones for delivering packages, and its fulfilment centres are in part operated by robots.[7] Advanced automation is transforming the storage and delivery industry. In 2012 and after acquiring Kiva, Amazon pioneered the introduction of mobile robots that can carry up to 340 kilos and detect fallen items. Furthermore, machine learning solves inventory issues at Amazon.[8]

The number of multi-terms containing the word data (9) on the map provides evidence of its centrality for Amazon. Moreover, there is a specific cluster focused on data storage (with multi-terms like "data blocks" and "data storage") whose multi-terms have a connecting place in the network map, relating the data storage cluster with two more prominent clusters. One of the latter seems to concentrate patents on e-commerce and, more generally, on Amazon's marketplace. The other cluster could be identified as an AWS[9] cluster (at the bottom of the map), which includes multi-terms on virtual machines and web services. The data storage cluster is also connected to another cluster. This one deals with how to track data (including terms like "I.P. address" and "dns query") and is also related to the AWS cluster.[10]

Leveraging on its innovation (cum data) advantage and as shown by the diversity of its patent portfolio, Amazon has moved to multiple businesses. Moreover, innovations frequently include the creation of new sources of data, thus further expanding its data-driven intellectual monopoly. As we mentioned before, AWS is the paradigmatic example of this virtuous loop. Nevertheless, this success innovation story is based on outsourcing production as well as innovation steps to multiple types of organizations from which Amazon predates value and knowledge. In the cloud-servicing business, tech giants outsource analytics' consultancy to companies like 1Strategy, 47Lining and MightyHive. These companies are complier firms acting as an outsourced salesforce and helpdesk. They are big-data analytics consultants and trainers that expand AWS – and other tech giants' cloud computing – business. Concerning innovations, we show next that Amazon has instituted multiple innovation networks, with AWS related technologies occupying a central position.

3.1 Amazon's innovation networks[11]

In its initial stages, Amazon relied mainly on a closed innovation system based on a combination of secrecy and patenting. A former employee said that employees only attended scientific conferences to listen to stimulating, or potentially path-breaking ideas, but seldom presented their ongoing research.[12] Indeed, although Amazon's first scientific publication dates from 1996, its publishing activity was negligible until 2014.

As its intellectual monopoly matured, Amazon began to develop strong ties with different organizations, outsourcing modules of its innovation circuits while collecting resulting rents. In this respect, Amazon's experience is close to that of Google. Google, or more precisely Alphabet, can illustrate the transition from mainly in-house hits to outsourcing innovation steps or modules, in the sense of the two-step model introduced in Chapter 6 to distinguish between the knowledge management strategies of wannabe and already established intellectual monopolies. As explained by Steiber and Alange (2013, p. 251),

> Google's core business in the form of search and adwords/adsense was mainly based on internal innovations, while several of the new business areas have primarily depended on externally generated innovations. It emerged that Google's future growth will continue to depend on both internally and externally generated innovations.

We provide evidence of Amazon's move to outsourcing innovation steps by studying its network of most frequent co-authors. We retrieved its scientific publication until 2018 included from the Web of Science. We built Amazon's network map of 50 most frequent co-authors' affiliations (this is Amazon plus its top 49 co-authoring organizations). The frequency of co-authorship with Amazon is represented by each node's size (Figure 8.6).

Until 2018 included, Amazon had published with almost 600 different organizations, providing evidence of research and development outsourcing. Among them, we found other intellectual monopolies, start-ups, universities and public science and technology bodies. Institutions depicted in Figure 8.6 can be considered as belonging to Amazon's recurrent innovation networks. Less frequent co-authoring institutions (those not depicted) participate in Amazon's sporadic innovation circuits, but without being integrated into its institutionalized innovation networks. These results contrast with Amazon's patent portfolio structure, where only 13 out of its more than 10,000 patents until February 2018 were co-owned with other organizations, providing evidence of Amazon's predatory behaviour. Institutions that participate in its innovation networks are not co-owning its patents; therefore potential intellectual rents are exclusively in the hands of Amazon.

On top of these innovation networks, Amazon relies on outsourced innovation modules for app development for Alexa, Amazon's virtual assistant. Amazon (2020) recently stated that there are over 700,000 developers building skills for Alexa. It also harvests open-source software code and sometimes sponsors open software initiatives like the Linux Foundation to stay close to open source ecosystems, so that it can profit from the advantages highlighted in Chapter 3.

Figure 8.6 also shows different clusters plotting former (like Yahoo) and current intellectual monopolies (like Google and Microsoft). These clusters reflect technological cooperation between intellectual monopolies. Cooperation between platform leaders was described as a process where they support each other or use each other's platforms to innovate further (Gawer, 2014). In general, as presented in Chapter 6, the collaboration between intellectual monopolies occurs because, for specific innovation or knowledge modules, typically those more general and that require higher investments,

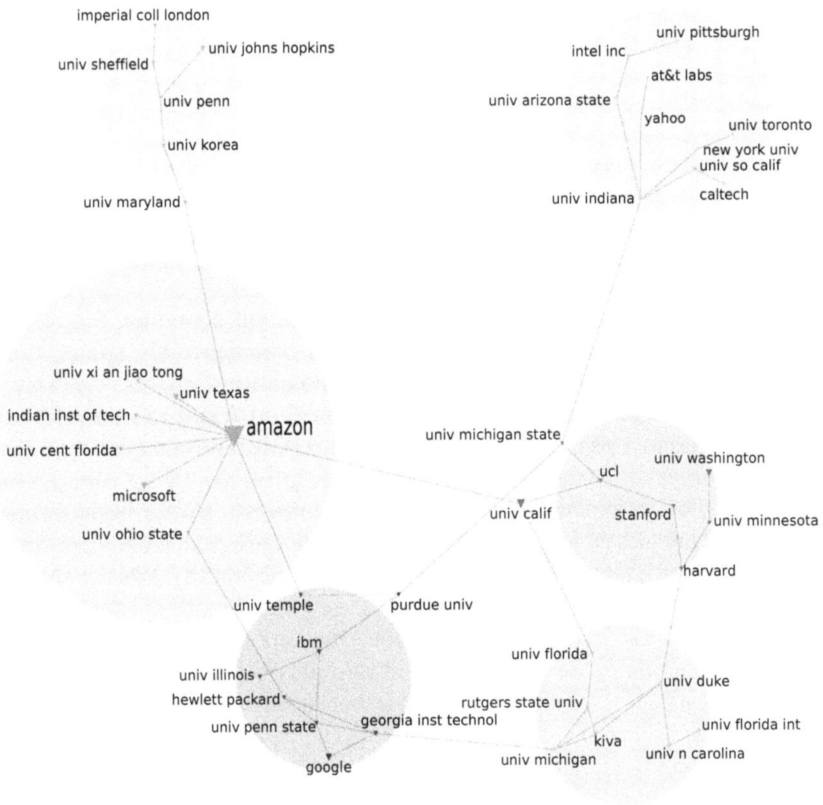

Figure 8.6 Network map. Amazon's top 50 co-authors (1996–2018).
Source: Author's analysis based on Web of Science data extraction.*
* This figure was originally published in Rikap (2020).

working together increases success rates and diversifies risks. At the same time, it does not diminish their eventually garnered rents since those results will not be directly applied to business but integrated into their respective innovation circuits. In the case of data-driven intellectual monopolies, when they cooperate for technology, they still retain exclusive access to their respective databases. Thus, they can share or even put in open source selected portions of the machine learning code that will be used to process them without the risk of losing associated rents.

While intellectual monopolies cooperate in specific steps of their innovation processes, they also undertake a fierce technological competition.

Continuous innovation is a preferred competition strategy over lowering prices among intellectual monopolies. In fact, in the high-tech and digital industry, competition is defined more by innovation than by price (Dolata, 2017; Shelanski, 2013). Still, lower prices, as well as other factors, reinforce Amazon's power. The next section elaborates on the interplay between intellectual monopoly and other sources of economic and political power.

4 Factors reinforcing Amazon's power as a data-driven intellectual monopoly

Scholars and media articles have identified different economic factors as sources of Amazon's dominance. Among them, we refer to low prices, tangible capital economies of scale, reputation and network effects. We briefly refer to the interplay between these arguments and Amazon's intellectual monopoly and focus afterwards on Amazon's political power as an intellectual monopoly.

Lowering prices below those of rival companies has always been among Amazon's strategies (Khan, 2017; Stone, 2013). They are enabled by Amazon's power to subordinate suppliers and companies offering in its marketplace. Deals with third-party sellers and suppliers are generally one-sided contracts where the latter can only accept or reject Amazon's conditions. This power to subordinate others, we argue, emerged from its intellectual monopoly that sprang from an idea (e-commerce of books) that ended up revolutionizing retail.

Since then, Amazon's knowledge monopoly has kept expanding. It is indispensable to explain its differential capacity to squeeze value from suppliers. Value is, in part, transferred to consumers to capture a greater share of the market. Greater market shares are key for Amazon because they mean greater data flows. Amazon is a technology company; its aim is not to be a retail or distribution company in itself but to expand its data-driven intellectual monopoly. It can afford to be only marginally profitable in its marketplace because its greatest advantage comes from expanding this business, which means expanding its access to data.

Low salaries paid to temporary workers at Amazon's warehouses further contribute to guarantee lower prices.[13] Low prices were also possible due to innovations that reduced costs. E-commerce itself reduces tangible capital commitment.

Likewise, Amazon's achieved scale relies on innovations, starting with the creation of an e-commerce marketplace. Additionally, process innovations in storage and distribution increased economies of scale. Amazon heavily invests in its fulfilment centres and warehouses (Wu & Gereffi, 2018). Economies of scale are, therefore, a result of interrelated factors where innovation is always paramount, as evidenced by the relevance of patents dealing with inventory-related innovation (Figure 8.5).

Another underpinning factor for Amazon's power could be its reputation, which drives platform users to enter and exchange (Thomas et al., 2014).

Reputation can reinforce Amazon's power but does not explain the origins of such a leading position. Indeed, reputation must be born from a concrete advantage from rivals, and we have argued that Amazon achieved such an advantage because its original innovations provided a constant stream of market data. Amazon's reputation depends on its greater knowledge about what each consumer wants and its low prices which, as we explained, rely on innovations and value predation from third-party sellers.

Finally, network effects also enhance Amazon's power. They are typically observed in platforms and lead to winner-take-all dynamics (Carballa Smichowski, 2018; Cusumano, 2010; Eisenmann, 2006). Nevertheless, consumer-side network effects are not that strong in the case of Amazon. Customers can look at its reviews but then buy elsewhere (Liebowitz, 2002). To limit this behaviour, Amazon introduced its loyalty program, Amazon Prime. On the supplier-side, network effects are strong for Amazon (Evans & Schmalensee, 2013). It was not since its beginning but only in 1999 when Amazon decided to open its – already successful – platform to third-party sellers. Over time, more third-party sellers became compelled to join Amazon.com, given the size of this marketplace. Still, as explained by Nuccio and Guerzoni (2019), network externalities by themselves cannot explain long-term entry barriers, whereas – in line with intellectual monopoly theory – the authors agree that continuous innovation and product quality can.

Amazon's intellectual monopoly also underpins its political power, which we explore next by briefly looking at its interplay with the US and Chinese states.

4.1 Amazon's political power

US high-tech giants have been recently denounced by their (mis)use of private data,[14] anti-competitive practices[15] and tax avoidance (Bryan et al., 2017; Pozsar, 2018). The US Congress is currently investigating Google, Amazon, Facebook and Apple, and the New York and California general attorneys joined the Federal Trade Commission to investigate Amazon for potential abuse of its market power.

Claims against Amazon started before this investigation. Early in 2018, Seattle's city council attempted to introduce a new tax to tackle homelessness. Initially, the proposed tax was USD 500 per employee to be paid by those corporations with more than USD 20 million revenues. Amazon complained, among others, by stopping a downtown expansion. Complying with Amazon's power, the city cut the tax to USD 275 per employee. Anyway, Amazon threatened to leave Seattle while pursuing an auction for its second headquarter. Finally, the tax was repealed due to Amazon's and other big companies' pressures. Other similar stories on how Amazon lobbies to benefit its business include its procurement deals with local governments in the United States to purchase office and classroom supplies through Amazon.com at no fixed prices. Prices depended on bids in Amazon's marketplace.[16]

Lobbying and the capacity to interfere in political decisions are not specific to intellectual monopolies but a regular practice among big corporations. On top of these forms of influence, as we introduced in Chapter 4, data-driven intellectual monopolies like Amazon dictate public policies. In line with Crouch (2011), they have become major insiders of the political realm. These monopolies are taking over what used to be conceived as state responsibilities. Data are a source of political power. States' sovereignty – at least formally – extends to national (or regional) borders, while data overflow them. Thus, Internet tech giants are introducing their own policies concerning cybersecurity, removing fake news and misinformation for the entire globe (Marcuzzi & Terzi, 2019.). Their ruling power over the internet is used to favour their own businesses. This became apparent when Facebook refused for some time to delete Trump's false posts while similar content from random individuals would have been banned.

Chapter 4 further discussed the different strategies that the US and Chinese states have undertaken. The United States has favoured a transnational and multi-stakeholder (including private sector) governance of the internet, facilitating the rule-making role of US data-driven intellectual monopolies. As Chapter 4 argues, the United States remains the global hegemon in part due to its global intellectual monopolies, which contributes to explain their higher tolerance with these corporations, unlike previous forms of monopoly capitalism.

China has been the only country seriously opposing Amazon and other tech giants like Google and Facebook. The protectionist policies of the Chinese state boosted the emergence of Alibaba, now Amazon's main global competitor. China's Great Fire Wall blocks companies like Amazon, therefore benefiting local corporations (Azmeh et al., 2020). The Chinese state's restriction over Amazon – and other high-tech intellectual monopolies – points to the limits of intellectual monopoly power when a core state is determined to control them. Since foreign ownership in e-commerce is forbidden, Amazon operates in China through third parties, at least partially owned by Chinese citizens.[17] Cloud services are also restricted to foreign companies, giving Alibaba's Ali Cloud a business advantage.[18]

Finally, data-driven intellectual monopolies are also providing key technologies to governments, such as Rekognition, Amazon's facial recognition technology, or Google and Apple's app for Covid-19 tracking. Programming code is never neutral; it is based on political decisions determined by tech giants. As these innovations underpin state power, they reinforce data-driven intellectual monopolies' (economic and political) power. It remains unclear, as noted by Wu and Gereffi (2018), how to conciliate global strategies of these corporations with states' attempts to regulate and govern the internet.

5 Final remarks

This chapter has further elaborated on a special type of intellectual monopoly that collects data-driven rents using Amazon as a case in point. Amazon's power relies on centralizing and analysing constant flows of data with machine learning algorithms. We argued that controlling a platform does not assure a company's leadership. Platforms that are born from a single breakthrough that is not followed by further hits will not become intellectual monopolies. This is the case, for instance, of Uber, WeWork and Airbnb. On the contrary, those that use their platforms to capture diverse sources of data that are transformed into digital intelligence will have the capacity to expand intellectual rents over time. The latter will become data-driven intellectual monopolies.

Our approach to innovation dynamics for Amazon's case has also provided insights on (1) the relevance of data for its multi-technology and multi-product innovations, (2) Amazon's knwoledge predation capacity, turning into assets knowledge from the innovation networks it organizes and (3) why other statements on the origin of Amazon's power either rely on innovations or are incapable by themselves to spawn leaders in a context of extreme technological competition.

The study of Amazon's intellectual monopoly has also contributed to our understanding of the interplay between intellectual monopolies and core states by focusing on Amazon's encroachment into the political sphere. A final caveat concerns the dynamics of these relationships. Political and corporate decisions are revised continuously by Amazon and the US and Chinese states. Hence, our highlighted examples must be considered as stages of an ongoing process. In this turf war, each outcome depends on multiple interlocking factors that exceed individual planning capabilities and individual power of any of the involved (corporate and state) superpowers. The next chapter continues exploring intellectual monopolies and states relationship by analysing a Chinese state-owned enterprise that became an intellectual monopoly relying on its home country national innovation system.

Notes

1 We could not include other multinational traditional retails because only Tesco presents R&D investment data in Compustat.

2 Walmart does not publish information on its R&D expenses but innovation's importance, particularly, the need to move fast with respect to innovation in data collection and analysis can be inferred from the following example. Data café is its data hub. They provide real-time analysis of transactional data plus 200 other sources "including meteorological data, economic data, Nielsen data, telecom data, social media data, gas prices, and local events databases" (https://www.forbes.com/sites/bernardmarr/2017/01/23/really-big-data-at-walmart-real-time-insights-from-their-40-petabyte-data-cloud/#427c546b6c10).

3 We have extensively discussed on data-driven intellectual rent in other parts of this book (see for instance Chapters 2 and 7).
4 https://www.economist.com/leaders/2019/04/17/techs-new-stars-have-it-all-except-a-path-to-high-profits.
5 Chapter 2 delves into intellectual monopoly theory. Here, we present a summary to frame Amazon's study case.
6 https://www.washingtonpost.com/technology/2020/07/29/apple-google-facebook-amazon-congress-hearing/
7 https://www.dailymail.co.uk/sciencetech/article-5808319/Amazon-100-000-warehouse-robots-company-insists-replace-humans.html.
8 https://www.ft.com/content/916b93fc-8716-11e7-8bb1-5ba57d47eff7 and https://spectrum.ieee.org/automaton/robotics/industrial-robots/interview-brad-porter-vp-of-robotics-at-amazon.
9 While Amazon's revenues mostly come from its ecommerce activity, AWS metrics are outstanding, it is this business where most of Amazon's profits concentrate (Amazon, 2019).
10 A more in-depth analysis of the evolution of Amazon's patent portfolio content is presented in Rikap (2020).
11 This section is based on Rikap (2020). "Amazon: A story of accumulation through intellectual rentiership and predation". Competition & Change. doi:10.1177/1024529420932418.
12 https://www.theregister.co.uk/2014/01/22/amazon_open_source_investigation/.
13 https://www.wired.com/story/meet-camperforce-amazons-nomadic-retiree-army/.
14 See for instance https://www.ft.com/content/4ade8884-1b40-11ea-97df-cc63de1d73f4?segmentId=b0d7e653-3467-12ab-c0f0-77e4424cdb4c.
15 See for instance https://www.ft.com/content/e56d2820-4cef-11ea-95a0-43d18ec715f5.
16 https://www.theguardian.com/business/2019/nov/08/how-big-tech-is-dragging-us-towards-the-next-financial-crash.
17 Restrictions inspired by the Chinese experience were introduced in India early in 2019 attempting to prevent foreign e-commerce companies like Amazon or Walmart to use their power to push down local business prices, also preventing them from selling goods that are "distributed by companies they have invested in". Amazon and Walmart tried but failed to delay these measures. https://edition.cnn.com/2019/01/31/tech/amazon-walmart-india-ecommerce-restrictions/index.html.
18 For instance, AWS services in China are provided by Beijing Sinnet Technology Co. While AWS is the absolute market leader globally, in China, it arrives third. There, Alibaba is the absolute leader with almost half of the market (https://www.analyticsinsight.net/alibaba-leads-asias-cloud-market-outshining-amazon-and-microsoft/)

References

Amazon. (2019). *Amazon Annual Report 2018*. Amazon Inc.

Amazon. (2020). *Small business success in challenging times. 2020 Amazon SMB Impact Report*. Amazon.

Armstrong, M. (2006). Competition in two-sided markets. *The RAND Journal of Economics*, *37*(3), 668–91.

Azmeh, S., Foster, C., & Echavarri, J. (2020). The international trade regime and the quest for free digital trade. *International Studies Review*, *22*(3), 671–92.

Barbier, M., Bompart, M., Garandel-Batifol, V., & Mogoutov, A. (2012). Textual analysis and scientometric mapping of the dynamic knowledge in and around the IFSA community. In I. Darnhofer, D. Gibbon, & B. Dedieu (Eds.), *Farming systems research into the 21st century: The new dynamic* (pp. 73–94). Springer.

Baud, C., & Durand, C. (2012). Financialization, globalization and the making of profits by leading retailers. *Socio-Economic Review*, *10*(2), 241–66.

Bensinger, G. (2012, June 27). Competing with Amazon on Amazon. *Wall Street Journal*. http://www.wsj.com/articles/SB1000142405270230444140457748290205582264

Bryan, D., Rafferty, M., & Wigan, D. (2017). Capital unchained: Finance, intangible assets and the double life of capital in the offshore world. *Review of International Political Economy*, *24*(1), 56–86.

Carballa Smichowski, B. (2018). Is ride-hailing doomed to monopoly? Theory and evidence from the main US markets. *Revue d'économie Industrielle*, *2*, 43–72.

Cockburn, I. M., Henderson, R., & Stern, S. (2018). *The impact of artificial intelligence on innovation*. National Bureau of Economic Research.

Coe, N. M., & Hess, M. (2005). The internationalization of retailing: Implications for supply network restructuring in East Asia and Eastern Europe. *Journal of Economic Geography*, *5*(4), 449–73.

Crouch, C. (2011). *The strange non-death of neoliberalism* (Polity). Polity.

Cusumano, M. A. (2010). Cloud computing and SaaS as new computing platforms. *Communications of the ACM*, *53*(4), 27–29.

Cusumano, M. A., & Gawer, A. (2002). The elements of platform leadership. *MIT Sloan Management Review*, *43*(3), 51.

Cusumano, M. A., Gawer, A., & Yoffie, D. B. (2019). *The business of platforms: Strategy in the age of digital competition, innovation, and power*. HarperCollins Publishers.

Dolata, U. (2013). *The transformative capacity of new technologies: A theory of sociotechnical change*. Routledge.

Dolata, U. (2017). *Apple, Amazon, Google, Facebook, Microsoft: Market concentration-competition-innovation strategies* [SOI Discussion Paper]. Stuttgarter Beiträge zur Organisations-und Innovationsforschung.

Dolata, U. (2020). *Platform-regulation. Coordination of markets and curation of sociality on the Internet* [SOI Discussion Paper]. Stuttgarter Beiträge zur Organisations-und Innovationsforschung.

Durand, C., & Milberg, W. (2020). Intellectual monopoly in global value chains. *Review of International Political Economy*, *27*(2), 404–29. doi:10.1080/09692290.2019.1660703

Eisenmann, T. R. (2006). Winner-take-all in networked markets. *Harvard Business School Technical Note*, 806–131.

Evans, D. S., & Schmalensee, R. (2013). *The antitrust analysis of multi-sided platform businesses*. National Bureau of Economic Research.

Foley, D. K. (2013). Rethinking financial capitalism and the "information" economy. *Review of Radical Political Economics*, *45*(3), 257–68.

Galloway, S. (2017). *The four: The hidden DNA of Amazon, Apple, Facebook, and Google*. Penguin.

Gawer, A. (2014). Bridging differing perspectives on technological platforms: Toward an integrative framework. *Research Policy*, *43*(7), 1239–49.

Gereffi, G. (1994). The organization of buyer-driven global commodity chains: How US retailers shape overseas production networks. In Gereffi, G. and Korzeniewicz, M. (Eds.) *Commodity Chains and Global Capitalism.* (pp. 95–122) Praeger.
Gereffi, G. (1996). Global commodity chains: New forms of coordination and control among nations and firms in international industries. *Competition & Change, 1*(4), 427–39.
Gereffi, G. (2001). Shifting governance structures in global commodity chains, with special reference to the internet. *American Behavioral Scientist, 44*(10), 1616–37.
Khan, L. (2017). Amazon's antitrust paradox. *The Yale Law Journal, 126*(3), 710–805. https://www.yalelawjournal.org/note/amazons-antitrust-paradox
Kenney, M., & Zysman, J. (2019). Work and value creation in the platform economy. In S. P. Vallas & A. Kovalainen (Eds.), *Work and labor in the digital age* (pp. 13–41). Emerald Publishing Limited.
Klein, N. (2020). Screen new deal. *The Intercept.* https://theintercept.com/2020/05/08/andrew-cuomo-eric-schmidt-coronavirus-tech-shock-doctrine/
Lan, S., Liu, K., & Dong, Y. (2019). Dancing with wolves: How value creation and value capture dynamics affect complementor participation in industry platforms. *Industry and Innovation, 26*, 943–63. doi:10.1080/13662716.2019.1598339
Lichtenthaler, U. (2018). The world's most innovative companies: A meta-ranking. *Journal of Strategy and Management. 11*(4), 497–511. doi:10.1108/JSMA-07-2018-0065
Liebowitz, S. (2002). *Rethinking the networked economy: The true forces driving the digital marketplace.* AMACOM Div. American Management Association.
Marcuzzi, S., & Terzi, A. (19 C.E., February). Are multinationals eclipsing nation-states? *Project Syndicate.* https://www.project-syndicate.org/onpoint/are-multinationals-eclipsing-nation-states-by-stefano-marcuzzi-and-alessio-terzi-2019-01?utm_source=Project%20Syndicate%20Newsletter&utm_campaign=0fba69ee69-sunday_newsletter_3_2_2019&utm_medium=email&utm_term=0_73bad5b7d8-0fba69ee69-93562901
Montalban, M., Frigant, V., & Jullien, B. (2019). Platform economy as a new form of capitalism: A Régulationist research programme. *Cambridge Journal of Economics, 43*(4), 805–24. doi:10.1093/cje/bez017
Nuccio, M., & Guerzoni, M. (2019). Big data: Hell or heaven? Digital platforms and market power in the data-driven economy. *Competition & Change, 23*(3), 312–28. doi:10.1177/1024529418816525
Pagano, U. (2014). The crisis of intellectual monopoly capitalism. *Cambridge Journal of Economics, 38*(6), 1409–29.
Pozsar, Z. (2018). Repatriation, the echo-taper and the €/$ basis. *Global Money Notes, 11.* Credit Suisse.
Rikap, C. (2020). Amazon: A story of accumulation through intellectual rentiership and predation. *Competition & Change.* doi:10.1177/1024529420932418
Rochet, J.-C., & Tirole, J. (2003). Platform competition in two-sided markets. *Journal of the European Economic Association, 1*(4), 990–1029.
Serfati, C. (2008). Financial dimensions of transnational corporations, global value chain and technological innovation. *Journal of Innovation Economics & Management, 2*, 35–61.
Shelanski, H. A. (2013). Information, innovation, and competition policy for the Internet. *University of Pennsylvania Law Review, 161*, 1663.

Sorokina, D., & Cantu-Paz, E. (2016). Amazon search: The joy of ranking products. *Proceedings of the 39th International ACM SIGIR Conference on Research and Development in Information Retrieval*, 459–60.
Srnicek, N. (2017). *Platform capitalism*. John Wiley & Sons.
Steiber, A., & Alänge, S. (2013). A corporate system for continuous innovation: The case of Google Inc. *European Journal of Innovation Management*, *16*(2), 243–64.
Stone, B. (2013). *The everything store: Jeff Bezos and the age of Amazon*. Random House.
Strange, R., & Humphrey, J. (2018). What lies between market and hierarchy? Insights from internalization theory and global value chain theory. *Journal of International Business Studies*, *50*, 1401–13.
Tancoigne, E., Barbier, M., Cointet, J. P., & Richard, G. (2014). The place of agricultural sciences in the literature on ecosystem services. *Ecosystem Services*, *10*, 35–48.
Thomas, L. D., Autio, E., & Gann, D. M. (2014). Architectural leverage: Putting platforms in context. *Academy of Management Perspectives*, *28*(2), 198–219.
Wood, S., Wrigley, N., & Coe, N. M. (2016). Capital discipline and financial market relations in retail globalization: Insights from the case of Tesco plc. *Journal of Economic Geography*, *17*(1), 31–57.
Wrigley, N., Coe, N. M., & Currah, A. (2005). Globalizing retail: Conceptualizing the distribution-based transnational corporation (TNC). *Progress in Human Geography*, *29*(4), 437–57.
Wu, X., & Gereffi, G. (2018). Amazon and Alibaba: Internet governance, business models, and internationalization strategies. In van Tulder, R., Verbeke, A. and Piscitello, L. (Eds.) *International business in the information and digital age* (pp. 327–56). Emerald Publishing Limited.
Yeung, H. W., & Coe, N. M. (2015). Toward a dynamic theory of global production networks. *Economic Geography*, *91*(1), 29–58.

Appendix: methodology

We retrieved information on every scientific publication authored by Amazon or any of its subsidiaries until 2018 included from the Web of Science, and its granted patents from 1996 (first year with data) until February 2018 from Derwent Innovation. Publications and patent data were processed with the CorText platform. We built co-occurrence maps using specific proximity algorithms that associate entities according to their co-occurrence frequency within a corpus of texts (Barbier et al., 2012). Entities were terms for the semantic analysis and research institutions for Amazon's publications co-authoring network. As in the rest of this book, the procedure used to draw these maps, including our corpuses cleaning, is adopted from Tancoigne et al. (2014). Resulting maps depicted entities grouped in interconnected clusters according to their co-occurrence frequency. This big data technique allowed us to detect communities in networks.

To analyse the content of Amazon's patents, we performed a lexical analysis of their abstracts and titles. We extracted the 1,000 most frequent phrases of up to six terms. Monograms were excluded to avoid words whose high frequency of occurrence responded to their grammatical function (such as "and" and "or"). The list was also refined to avoid phrases not related to the field and whose frequency responded to the level of grammaticalization within the innovation genre (such as "present invention", "preferred embodiment", "other uses", and "subject matter"). After cleaning, the resulting list contained 856 multi-terms. Next, a network map was constructed plotting the 100 multi-terms with the highest frequency of co-occurrence. The resulting map (Figure 8.5 in Section 3) grouped in clusters those multi-terms that were, in comparison with the total set of multi-terms' co-occurrences, most frequently connected. Each cluster was interpreted as referring to a specific technology or research priority (or to a set of closely interrelated technologies or research priorities). We chose a distributional metric for determining nodes' proximity. It accounts for the global distribution of co-occurrences of each pair of nodes with all the other nodes.

The same technique used for patents' multi-terms network map was applied to build Amazon's co-authorship network (Figure 8.6 in Section 3). As in the rest of this book, we proxied intellectual monopoly innovation networks with its co-publication network map. In Figure 8.6, nodes represented authors' affiliations, and their sizes represented their frequency of co-authorship with Amazon. A Chi-square proximity metric was used. This metric considers actual co-occurrences between entities, thus building clusters by privileging most frequent partners – which we interpreted as established innovation networks over occasional links. Co-authorships were depicted as direct but also indirect links. The latter refers to co-authorships that only take place when a third institution is also a co-author. When this third institution also published with at least one of the other two, it was plotted as a bridging or connecting node. In our corpus, every institution authored papers with Amazon. Hence, indirect links indicated institutions whose publications with Amazon always shared a third co-author who also publishes with Amazon independently.

Finally, to provide evidence on how Amazon is garnering intellectual rents from its co-authors, predating from organizations participating in its innovation networks, we compared co-authorships with its patent portfolio co-ownerships.

9

STATE GRID CORP

An intellectual monopoly relying on China's innovation system

1 Introduction

In a nutshell, this book has introduced an intellectual monopoly theory that argues a few corporations have systematically monopolized knowledge, undergoing a process of cumulative causation. The remaining companies that lack technical autonomy subordinate to them. Intellectual monopolies' economic power arises from their capacity to continuously transform knowledge into intangible assets, which allows them to capture most of the value produced in their production networks and the intellectual rents associated with the research and development (R&D) results of the innovation networks they organize. Concerning the latter, we have explained that intellectual monopolies plan innovation networks outsourcing knowledge modules to subordinate innovating companies, public research organizations and research universities. All the latter contribute to the innovation process. However, results are mostly transformed into intangible assets by the intellectual monopoly increasing its accumulation of intellectual rents. We referred to this relationship as knowledge predation.

Intellectual monopolies deter other companies from investing in R&D, thus reducing catching-up opportunities at the firm level. Noel and Schankerman (2013, p. 514) found that when technology rivals follow a systematic patenting strategy, the remaining firms diminish their R&D investments, patenting and market value. In this chapter, we argue that under intellectual monopoly capitalism, catching-up at the firm level implies joining the global elite of intellectual monopolies. This is an extremely complicated task for peripheral countries, regardless of the internal impacts in terms of industrial polarization that such a strategy will engender.

Nevertheless, the People's Republic of China (hereafter China) seems to be leapfrogging or catching up in various industries (Fan, 2006; Gu et al., 2016; Lee et al., 2016; Li et al., 2019). To understand this result, Chapter 4 has scrutinized the policies that China's state put in place since 1978 and how they contributed to the emergence of *made in China* intellectual monopolies. That chapter argued that China became a pole of attraction of foreign capital, which provided an unprecedented economic and geopolitical strength. The favourable conditions of China for that foreign capital investment (cheap labour and a huge and underexploited internal market) led corporations to accept the imposed conditions of technology transfer to local capitals. Together with the flexible implementation of the Trade Related Aspects of Intellectual Property Rights (TRIPS) agreement, all the latter contributed to the emergence of local leaders. China's protectionist measures limiting the power of intellectual monopolies from core countries, particularly in the high-tech industry, boosted their catching-up.

Beyond well-known success stories like that of Huawei, in this chapter, we show that China's catching-up goes beyond the ICT or high-tech industry. Aiming to lead the clean energy transition – thus further strengthening its geopolitical and economic power – (International Energy Agency, 2017), the state partnered with State Grid Corporation of China (SGCC). The goal was to turn this state-owned enterprise (SOE)[1] into a global leader in the provision of clean energy, an industry without global intellectual monopolies. SGCC became an intellectual monopoly by leading Ultra High Voltage (UHV) technologies and later reconfiguring the energy industry towards clean and efficient use of energy by using smart grids for its provision (Mah et al., 2017).

By the beginning of the century, SGCC was only a huge power supplier, ranking 40th in revenues worldwide (all industries considered). In 2018 it ranked second. Only in 2017, it invested USD 1.15 billion in R&D to produce breakthroughs within and beyond the energy industry (State Grid Corporation of China, 2018). Until 2017 included, it accumulated almost 17,000 granted patents and more than 100,000 patent applications. This impressive evolution allowed SGCC to integrate the top 100 Chinese innovators (China Clarivate Analytics, 2017). Moreover, from 1 scientific publication in 2003, its publishing frequency jumped to almost 1,000 in 2018.

To elaborate on the SGCC's inception as an intellectual monopoly, we will conceptually differentiate between national and global (or transnational) intellectual monopolies. We will argue that the former organizes innovation networks with mostly national organizations, while the latter extends its power beyond geopolitically close actors. We use network analyses of the SGCC's publications and patents to study its emergence as a national intellectual monopoly that is transitioning towards a transnational intellectual monopoly. We use cluster analyses of the affiliations of the SGCC's publications' co-authors to proxy its innovation networks. By coupling this analysis with that of the SGCC's patent portfolio, we also provide evidence that supports the hypothesis that SGCC, in line with the intellectual monopoly framework elaborated throughout the book, predates knowledge from its innovation networks, almost exclusively capturing rents from their successful results.

Summing up, the central question of this chapter is how global leaders emerge in the context of intellectual monopoly capitalism. To elaborate on this question, we argue that SGCC is succeeding in becoming a global intellectual monopoly because it first became a national intellectual monopoly. In this process, it relied on China's innovation system. SGCC profits from the R&D capacity of local research organizations and public support.

The rest of this chapter is organized as follows. Section 2 further develops the intellectual monopoly framework, particularly looking at the conditions that contribute to create a national intellectual monopoly and its transition to a global intellectual monopoly. Next, we delve into SGCC's stylized facts under the light of China's innovation and energy policies in Section 3. Section 4 presents our methodology and Section 5 illustrates and discusses our findings. Section 6 concludes.

2 How to become an intellectual monopoly

Monopolizing knowledge can be conceived as a lasting source of power relations between firms, one that can lead to globally unequal or asymmetrical market exchanges. We have expanded Pagano's (2014, p. 1413) definition of an intellectual monopoly as the "legal monopoly over some items of knowledge, which extends well beyond national boundaries" because knowledge can be systematically monopolized, even without a legal monopoly. Knowledge can be kept tacit or in secret, and data-driven intellectual rents emerged from innovations that rely on monopolizing access to original sources of data.

More in general, if a company manages to keep innovating before others adopt each past innovation, its advantage will hold even without intellectual property rights. Since innovation is cumulative and enjoys economies of scale, it demands minimum knowledge thresholds to allow copies, (Antonelli, 1999; Dosi, 1988). This leaves already innovative companies in a better position to garner rents from their own and others' knowledge results (see Chapter 2).

When outsourcing, intellectual monopolies do not necessarily exert direct control by commanding subordinate enterprises what to do and how to do it. As explained in Chapter 2, setting international standards reduces outsourcing costs. This is a mechanism that assures others will comply without directly controlling subordinate companies. In the case of SGCC, its chairman indicated that the company overcame its position as an international standards' adopter and that their technical standards increasingly became the international standards.[2] This move signals the transition that will be studied in this chapter.

As we have shown in previous chapters, intellectual monopolies also outsource steps of their innovation processes and still garner intellectual rents from successful results (see network analyses comparing publications with patents in Chapter 6 to 8). They are proactive organizers of portions of global capitalism beyond their own capital, controlling and planning both production and innovation networks. Our innovation network concept is inspired by global innovation networks (GINs) tradition (Ernst, 2009; Liu et al., 2013; Parrilli et al., 2013) and by Levín's (1977) innovation circuits' concept. While the latter looks at all the institutions and relationships established to achieve a single innovation, GINs concentrate on the institutionalization of certain actors as regular or frequent collaborators (see Chapter 2). Both when organizing these networks as well as for their internal R&D, intellectual monopolies leave degrees of autonomy to the researchers producing the different innovation modules or steps. As any creative activity, innovations cannot be anticipated entirely in advance and require a comfortable and stimulating working environment.

Here, we suggest a model which is a further development of the two-step model distinguishing between a wannabe and an established intellectual monopoly that was introduced in Chapter 6. The wannabe intellectual monopoly does mainly in-house innovation, competing for technology with other wannabe or already established intellectual monopolies. Once it becomes an intellectual monopoly, outsourcing innovation modules to subordinated companies or research institutions is sometimes preferred due to its planning capacity together with knowledge modularity. Outsourcing will diminish risks, which are even higher for innovation than for reproducing commodities. Furthermore, the intellectual monopoly will appropriate knowledge results profiting from intellectual rents from these innovation networks. The two-step model introduced in Chapter 6 also argued that cooperation between intellectual monopolies reduces innovations' inherent risks. In fact, it could increase success rates when alternative funding (such as public R&D investment that would free them from compromising capital) is not enough.

Here, and in order to study SGCC, we add an intermediate layer to integrate the vast contributions of the national and sectoral innovation systems' literature (see for instance, the pioneering work of Freeman, 1987; Lundvall, 1992; Malerba, 2002; Malerba & Orsenigo, 1997; Nelson, 1993). This literature has recognized the relevance of national and sectoral institutions and actors (besides firms' interactions) and their links for understanding innovation success or failure. Therefore, we propose an intermediate layer as the moment when a country's national innovation system is relevant for the inception and further expansion of its intellectual monopolies.

Hence, in a very schematic way, we suggest a three-step process for becoming a transnational intellectual monopoly. It starts with corporation "A" deciding to follow a strategy to become an intellectual monopoly (this is t_1). If and only if A systematically starts to monopolize intangible assets within a country, it will eventually become a national (or local) intellectual monopoly (this is $t_{1.5}$ since this is the step we add between steps 1 and 2 in the model presented in Chapter 6). Finally, if A manages to expand that monopoly at a transnational level, it will become a global (or transnational) intellectual monopoly (entering t_2). The main characteristics of each step are presented in Table 9.1.

We argue that during the formation of an intellectual monopoly, once a corporation starts accumulating intangibles, outsourcing innovation will initially rely on closer institutions that are easier to control, typically the institutions of its sectoral innovation system/s (Malerba, 2002; Malerba & Orsenigo, 1997). In other words, a possible strategy for becoming an intellectual monopoly is to rely on the R&D capabilities and funding of geographically, culturally and politically closer institutions. In line with Breschi and Lissoni (2001), proximity in terms of geographical distance, but also cultural affinity contributes to developing social bonds and face-to-face encounters that favour the circulation of knowledge. Indeed, following Lundvall (2017, Chapter 6), in a context of rapid technological change, meeting face-to-face is necessary to define and then solve problems.

Public research organizations (PRO) can perform state-of-the-art R&D, while the state provides funds that complement those of the wannabe intellectual monopoly. Historically, PROs, in particular universities, do not seek profit, which makes it easier for "A" to capture rents from their joint R&D. Research conducted in closer institutions is also easier to steer. Furthermore,

Table 9.1 Three-step model for becoming a transnational intellectual monopoly (IM)

	t_1 *(Wannabe IM A)*	$t_{1.5}$ *National IM A*	t_2 *(global IM A)*
Innovation strategy	Systematic in-house R&D	In-house R&D complemented by outsourcing innovation modules **at a national or local level**	In-house R&D complemented by outsourcing innovation modules **at a transnational level**
Associated risk	Mainly taken by the Wannabe IM A	Shared between IM A and other participants of IM A innovation circuits	Mainly taken by other participants of IM A innovation circuits
Relation with other IM	Technological competition	Technological competition, especially with transnational IM	Technological competition and Technological cooperation
Intellectual rents	Triggered from in-house R&D	Triggered from in-house R&D and predates knowledge from its innovation circuits/ networks	Triggered from in-house R&D and predates knowledge from its innovation circuits/ networks

Source: Author's elaboration.

governments promoting public–private partnerships for R&D foster collaborations within their borders. Even if already operating overseas, it will be more complicated for wannabe intellectual monopoly "A" to get public funds from other countries than its own. This may be especially true for SGCC since it comes from China, which is seen by core Western countries – particularly the United States – as a threat.

In more general terms, in the context of spread global intellectual monopolies seeking to monopolize access to knowledge in a growing number of sectors, policies could play a determinant role in the emergence of national intellectual monopolies as well as in their eventual globalization. Still, this is a double-edged sword since intellectual monopolies appropriate value and intellectual rents from their production and innovation networks, thus not leading to catching-up at the country level. The emergence of intellectual monopolies subordinates other companies that lose technical autonomy, widening the gap between firms.

In $t_{1.5}$, as far as a significant part of the R&D investments remain in-house, innovation risks will be shared between the national intellectual monopoly and the participants of its innovation circuits and networks. When the inception of such a monopoly is aligned to public policy – like that of SGCC –, we may expect the state will take care of a significant part of the potential risks. The states' protection when there are already global intellectual monopolies (as it was the case of Huawei or Alibaba), may contribute to raising barriers needed to keep accelerating A's innovation pace. Protectionism may last, at least, until "A" is capable of competing with global leaders on a more equal basis. This process, in a way, could be conceived as an adaptation of the dynamic "competitive advantages" notion (Amsden, 1997), which only applies to those corporations on the way to becoming intellectual monopolies as this may leave behind the rest of the companies.

Competition under intellectual monopoly capitalism is mostly based on a never-ending technological race. Once "A" becomes a transnational intellectual monopoly, it will be in a permanent technological competition with other intellectual monopolies innovating in the same or close fields. At this stage, keeping the pace of concentration of intangible assets, thus monopolizing knowledge, is mandatory for every intellectual monopoly to keep that position of power.

Another specificity of $t_{1.5}$ is that "A" would end up in a subordinate position if it collaborates for technology with global intellectual monopolies. While its innovative capacity is not that of global leaders, technological collaborations will favour the latter who will capture resulting intellectual rents. Nonetheless, it will profit from intellectual rents that will nurture its t_2 aspirations, if it focuses on organizing national innovation networks. The state's protection may even contribute to securing these rents (so that already existent global intellectual monopolies will see their actions limited in that country). When there is no global intellectual monopoly monopolizing knowledge in closer or the same fields, the self-expansion of A's intellectual monopoly power will face fewer challenges.

A final caveat should be stated. By no means, this three-step model implies that transitioning from t_1 to $t_{1.5}$, and from $t_{1.5}$ to t_2 are assured or natural processes. In fact, given innovation's uncertainty, becoming an intellectual monopoly is incredibly complicated. Hitherto, only a few corporations succeeded and now rule the world – sometimes hand in hand and sometimes in constant conflict – with core countries' states. Furthermore, transnational intellectual monopolies can lose their power position if they systematically lag in terms of innovations, degrading themselves into a national intellectual monopoly or eventually terminating their knowledge monopoly.

Moreover, it should be put into question the capacity of peripheral states to limit global intellectual monopolies from extracting and monetizing knowledge (and data) (see Chapters 11–14). In the case of the ICT industry, only China succeeded in limiting US intellectual monopolies like Apple, Google and Amazon. It has even been a challenge for the European Union (García-Herrero, 2019).

All in all, $t_{1.5}$ is a stage in the process of becoming a global intellectual monopoly where a leading corporation consolidates locally before trying to spread its power globally. In other words, even in the context of GVC and GIN, geographical and cultural proximity, together with the state's role fostering sectoral innovation systems at a local or national level (Malerba, 2002; Malerba & Orsenigo, 1997), remain relevant. The rest of this chapter will mobilize this framework for analysing the SGCC's experience.

3 The alignment of SGCC to China's innovation and energy policies

Chapter 4 described China's experience as a *great transformation* based on the accumulation of technological and organizational capabilities by imitating, gaining efficiency, and – since the 2000s – moving beyond an imitation-driven and towards an innovation-driven stage, catching-up in patents and trademarks. Nevertheless, this process has been limited to certain selected industries, and energy has been among them.

China's innovation policy aimed at becoming an innovation-driven country – as stated in its 13th Five-Year-Plan (2016–20) – intertwines with its energy policy. Policies for the latter are driven by China's goal to lead the clean energy transition, as observed by Barbara Finamore, Asia director for the Natural Resources Defense Council.[3] Ranking first in gas emissions together with the strategical geopolitical role of leading the ecological transition contributed to reverting China's initial position against global agreements. Since its 2005 Renewable Energy Law, the government and its SOEs are running efforts to reduce emissions by changing China's energy matrix, replacing coal's predominance with clean energy (Gu et al., 2016; Lin et al., 2013; Mah et al., 2017; Schuman & Lin, 2012). In terms of results, China is moving towards clean forms of energy with the commitment that, by 2040, electricity will be its primary source of final energy consumption. China is already the first producer of electricity in the world and has been considered the global leader in clean energy, the frontrunner in solar PV, wind, hydro and nuclear power (International Energy Agency, 2017).

Leading the energy transition by giving a central role to electricity contributes to explaining SGCC's evolution. China's major energy transmission and distribution company jumped in a few years to become the second corporation of the world in terms of revenues, according to the 2018 Fortune Global 500 ranking. In 2019, in part due to the decision of China's state to cut utility prices for industries,[4] the SGCC's revenues decreased, moving down the global industries ranking but remaining the world's largest utility with almost 1 million employees. SGCC has operations in the Philippines, Brazil, Portugal, Australia, Italy, Greece and Oman,[5] and it has plans to export wind and thermal power to Germany, India, Pakistan and Myanmar using China's Belt and Road Initiative.[6] SGCC could have just been a utility company growing due to China's industrialization and public promotion. However, we argue in this chapter that it is becoming a transnational intellectual monopoly.

SGCC is among China's top 100 innovators (China Clarivate Analytics, 2017). As declared on the company's web page, for the past seven years, it has been ranked the first among SOEs in patent ownership and invention. It also holds:

> 69 National Awards for Science and Technology, (...) 91 China Patent Awards, including 7 Chinese Patent Gold Awards and 25 China Standards Innovation and Contribution Awards, in which 7 are First Prizes. Besides, the company has also obtained 597 China Power Science and Technology Awards, including 59 First Prizes.[7]

These results are in line with its publications and patents' impressive evolution (Figure 9.1).

SGCC has set a goal to be the first company to develop a smart grid[8] based on artificial intelligence (AI) (Lin et al., 2013). While many countries were simultaneously trying to develop their smart grids, none had achieved a clear frontrunner advantage by the time when, in 2009, SGCC officially started its R&D venture to complete a smart grid by 2020, thus enlarging its intellectual monopoly. The SGCC's initiative included the creation of the Smart Grid Research Institute, which in addition to its facilities in China, has branches in California and Berlin.[9] In WIPO's (2019) report on AI's recent trends, SGCC appears as the only Chinese company in the top 20. In more concrete terms, SGCC has advantages in the data layer and

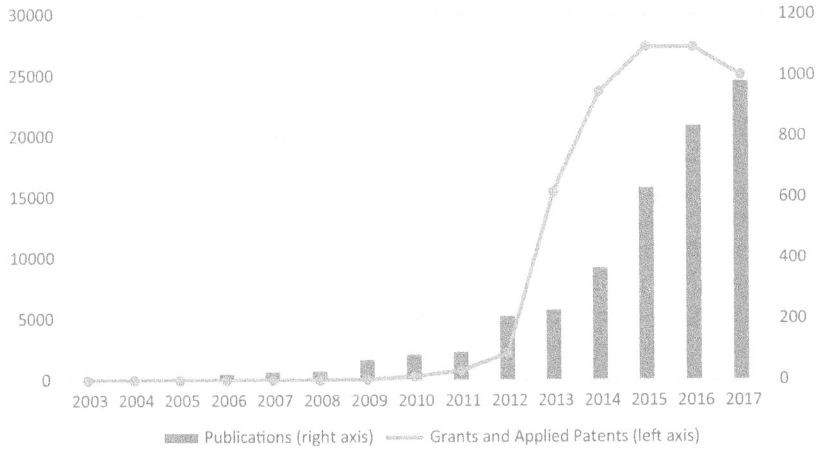

Figure 9.1 SGCC scientific publications and patents per year.
Source: Web of Science and Derwent Innovation.

application scenarios. It has applied AI technology to power grid control, power distribution networks, intelligent distribution transformers, renewable energy and inspection robots. All these AI applications are used for its smart grid, which is supposed to be a "ubiquitously powered internet of things" capable of reducing blackouts and automatically identify and handle breakdowns.[10] The development of a smart grid is aligned with the Chinese government's aims. Lin et al. (2013) identified 57 innovation policy tools for the development of such a grid, 26% of which were related to SGCC, followed by 23% of policies for scientific and technical development, which also frequently involved SGCC.

Overall, SGCC outperforms in scientific publications and patents. Our evidence, provided in Section 5, supports that these stylized facts correspond to an intellectual monopoly. Considering the model presented in Section 2, we also argue that SGCC is transitioning from a national to a transnational intellectual monopoly. Before presenting our results, the next section addressed our methodological approach.

4 Methodology

We used cluster analysis to build the SGCC's co-publications networks and compare these results with its patent portfolio co-ownership. The SGCC's publications[11] were retrieved from the Web of Science and applied and granted patents from the Derwent Innovation databases.

As in the previous chapters of this section, we proxied innovation networks by constructing co-publications' network maps. To that end, we performed a cluster analysis of SGCC's co-authors' affiliations to map the institutions that are more frequently publishing with SGCC. If SGCC is an intellectual monopoly, it should build innovation networks integrated by multiple organizations, and be capable of capturing most of their potential intellectual rents. Hence, it would not share most of the ownership of resulting patents neglecting the role of other participating organizations. This may be the case of universities because the SGCC's innovation strategy has heavily relied on them (Yi-chong, 2017, Chapter 7).

We retrieved every SGCC's publication until 2018 included (4,192 publications). This corpus was split into two periods (2003–10 and 2011–18) to have a sense of the evolution of SGCC's innovation networks. Data were processed with the CorText platform. We built co-occurrence maps[12] that associated SGCC and its co-authors according to their frequency of co-occurrence. To draw these maps, we followed the work of Tancoigne et al. (2014), including their proposed methodology for corpuses cleaning. Nodes sizes represented co-authorship frequency with SGCC. To focus on the SGCC's innovation networks – thus its systematically privileged partners –, we prioritized the top 101 research organizations for each period (SGCC plus its top 100 partnering organizations). In the first period, SGCC co-authored papers with only 79 institutions. The corresponding map depicts only the 76 institutions that surpassed a minimum proximity threshold (0.1). Overall, these network analyses provided information on: (i) the variety of stakeholders, (ii) their place in the SGCC's innovation networks, and (iii) the geographic scope of the SGCC's innovation networks.

In addition, to provide evidence on the topics being researched by the SGCC's different innovation networks, each one proxied as a cluster on its co-publications' network map, we also plotted for each cluster its most frequent research fields.

To determine to what extent SGCC shared potential intellectual rents with the organizations that participate in its innovation networks, we retrieved and analysed the SGCC's applied and granted patents from every patent office until and including 2017 (122,296 records). Our access to Derwent Innovation provided access to 25 different patent offices. However, in the SGCC corpus, 99% (120,937) of applied and granted patents corresponded to the China National Intellectual Property Administration, followed by WIPO (758, representing 0.62%) and USPTO (295, representing 0.24%). We will further discuss these figures later.

We compared results between both data sets in terms of the SGCC's partners and their countries of origin. Results are presented and discussed in the next section.

5 SGCC: on the way to becoming a transnational intellectual monopoly

5.1 SGCC's scientific publications

We analyse the SGCC's co-publications' network as a proxy of its corporate innovation system integrated by multiple innovation networks. It shows that while the SGCC's innovation networks initially relied mostly on local actors (Figure 9.2), in the more recent period, they are expanding beyond China (Figure 9.3) (foreign organizations are highlighted with a rectangle in both figures). By building diverse innovation networks, SGCC was also complying with Chinese government policies. In 2009, the central government launched the Technological Innovation Project, which fostered strategic

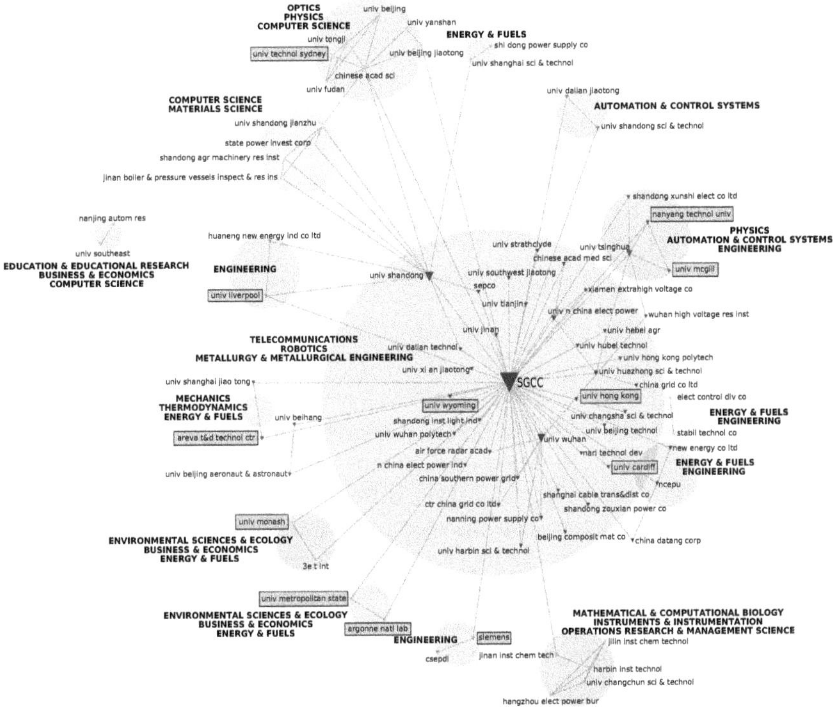

Figure 9.2 Network map. SGCC scientific publications' co-authorships (2003–10).
Source: Author's analysis based on Web of Science data extraction.

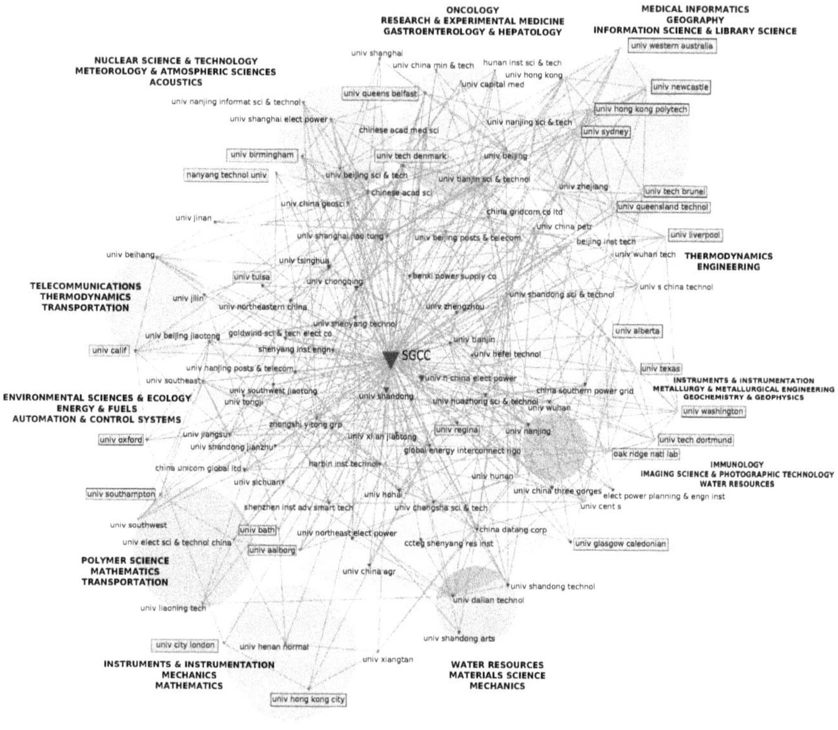

Figure 9.3 Network map. SGCC scientific publications' co-authorships (2011–18).
Source: Author's analysis based on Web of Science data extraction.

alliances and technological cooperation with universities and other research institutions (Yi-chong, 2017, Chapter 7).

In the first period (2003–10), SGCC was connected to 12 foreign institutions, including two multinationals (Siemens and Areva) and ten universities. These institutions came from seven different countries and represented 16% of the SGCC's partners. In the second period (2011–18), the number of foreign institutions among its top co-authors grew to 26 (117% increase), all of them are universities, from ten different countries. These results show that, over time, SGCC is broadening its innovation networks beyond China, not only to closer countries but also to core Western countries. Beyond the direct establishment of partnerships with foreign universities and those collaborations that initially took place connected by a Chinese university or PRO, another mechanism that has also contributed to expanding the SGCC's innovation network was its Foreign Direct Investment strategy. As it purchases other countries' local companies that have established collaboration with local universities, SGCC inherits those collaborations.

For instance, when SGCC bought a controlling stake in CPFL Energia, Brazil's largest power distributor, the latter already had R&D cooperation with the University of Campinas. SGCC inherited this link.[13]

Besides SGCC, in both periods, some institutions occupy bridging positions in the network. The Chinese Academy of Science connects its cluster with that of SGCC and with other Chinese institutions' clusters. Shandong University has also been a key partner for SGCC in a twofold way: as a co-author of 8.6% of SGCC's papers, and as a bridging institution, among others connecting SGCC with two clusters with foreign institutions in each period. As explained by Choi et al. (2011, p. 768), "(b)ridging organizations promote new connections to catalyse information flows and to create innovation opportunities". Even some foreign universities became bridging institutions in the second period, such as the Technical University of Dortmund connecting SGCC with Oak Ridge National Laboratory, the University of Texas and Washington University.

A difference between periods is that the total number of research institutions co-authoring with SGCC went from 79 to 864. This, in part, responded to the general increase of the SGCC's R&D reflected in its publications' growth (see Figure 9.1 in Section 3), but it also shows an expansion of its innovation networks. Additionally, between 2011 and 2018, there is no single institution co-authoring more than 8.5% of the SGCC's papers. In contrast, in the first period, its two main partners – Shandong University and Wuhan University – co-authored 14.8% and 13.9%, respectively. This happened even if total publications with these institutions increased around ten times. Hence, they are less important in relation to the whole set of the SGCC's co-authors but not in absolute terms. Being less dependent on single institutions is a sign of the larger scope of the SGCC's innovation networks within and beyond China. It also contributes to reduce the influence that a single organization can exercise over the content and distribution of profits from the research projects undertaken by SGCC, thus potentially strengthening its intellectual monopoly.

A final aspect to consider in the comparison between both periods is the place of Siemens and Areva. Their joint publications with SGCC refer to general power supply technologies, thus not related to the SGCC's main innovative aims. Considering also that they disappear from top partners and in line with Yi-chong (2012, Chapter 6) and Yi-chong (2017, Chapter 7), we consider these publications as the result of technical assistance provided by Siemens and Areva. Different multinationals were initially contacted by SGCC to develop new core technologies for UHV DC lines. However, these corporations wanted to keep the property of resulting patents. Hence, SGCC committed to innovating in UHV DC lines without them. It succeeded two years later (Yi-chong, 2017, Chapter 7). This experience is evidence of wannabe intellectual monopolies as still not prepared to establish technological cooperation with already incepted intellectual monopolies. By rejecting their offers, SGCC won the chance to become itself an intellectual monopoly.

The whole publications' corpus also evidences strong state support. Thirty percent of the SGCC's publications declared being funded by the National Natural Science Foundation of China, which was the SGCC's most frequently declared funding source, and 7% enjoyed funds from China's National Key Technology Research and Development Program. Other less frequent Chinese state funding sources declared in the SGCC's publications were the "National Program for Science and Technology 863" (5%) and the "National Basic Research Program of China 973" (4%).

Finally, the variety of fields covered by the SGCC's publications, especially in the second period where it even researched medical topics, is reflected in the diversity of clusters' most frequent topics. The SGCC's publications corroborate its continuous multi-technology and multi-product strategy, as it was observed for the cases of Amazon and Apple in the two previous chapters. Moreover, it is quite clear that the second period becomes more aligned to ecological transition matters with the SGCC's central cluster dealing with environmental and ecological research and other clusters focusing on water resources.

All in all, SGCC seems to be relying on its national innovation system to develop more transnational innovation networks on topics aligned to the ecological transition. Still, this transnationalization is not as developed as in recognized global intellectual monopolies; and considering China's specificities, it may never be. For instance, Roche and Novartis have less than 5% of its top 150 co-authors in Switzerland, whilst Pfizer (originally from the United States where this industry's innovations mostly take place) has around 50% of its top 150 co-authors in the United States (Rikap, 2019).

5.2 SGCC's patent portfolio

The SGCC's patent portfolio also sheds light on its condition as national intellectual monopoly on a (still uncertain) transition to become global or transnational. Regardless of its role setting international standards and the growth in foreign actors in its innovation networks, almost all its applied and granted patents (99%) correspond to the China National Intellectual Property Administration. Although the latter is becoming a central patent office worldwide, it can be expected that transnational intellectual monopolies will patent their results in various international patent offices as a sign of the greater quality of their innovations.

Anyway, a determinant feature of intellectual monopolies is their capacity to capture intellectual rents from innovation networks. To provide preliminary evidence on this behaviour for SGCC, we compare its publications' network with its patenting portfolio co-owners. SGCC monopolizes R&D results from its innovation networks, in particular from PRO, as it can be seen from the comparison between its vast and dense co-publications' network and the small share of patents that it co-owns with other organizations (Table 9.2).[14] Take, for instance, North China Electric Power University. It co-authored 8.5% of the SGCC's papers, but it only shared 1.5% of the SGCC's patents, and this is the SGCC's first patent co-owner, followed by companies and other universities sharing less than 0.5% of the total SGCC's portfolio. In fact, 78.5% of the SGCC's papers have at least one co-authoring organization, while only 21.4% of its applied and granted patents are shared with other organizations.

These results are in line with Yi-chong's (2017, Chapter 7) claim that SGCC imposes universities and other research institutions one-size fits all adhesion contracts where potential patents exclusively belong to SGCC. In

Table 9.2 Top SGCC's applied and granted patents' co-owners

Entity	*Distinct patents*	*Share in the SGCC's patents (%)*	*Share in the SGCC's publications (%)*	*Type of organization*
North China Electric Power University	1,792	1.5	8.5	University
Sanchuan Electric co ltd	442	0.4	–	Chinese corporation
Tsinghua University	417	0.3	6.84	University
Xi'an Jiaotong University	327	0.3	3.85	University
Southeast University	320	0.3	1.83	University
Shanghai Jiaotong University	288	0.2	1.83	University
China Electric Power Eng Consulting	280	0.2	–	Chinese corporation
Wuhan University	268	0.2	4.55	University
Zhengzhou Huali IT Co Ltd	255	0.2	–	Chinese corporation
Chongqing University	234	0.2	5.43	University
Hohai University	210	0.2	1.12	University
Beijing Guodiantong Network Tech Co Ltd	210	0.2	–	Chinese corporation
Huazhong Science Tech University	175	0.1	3.31	University
Lin Xiaoming	154	0.1	–	Individual
Lin Shuyan	154	0.1	–	Individual
Northeast Dianli University	152	0.1	1.02	University
Hon Hai Precision Industry Co Ltd	112	0.1	–	Foreign corporation

Source: Author's analysis based on Derwent Innovation data extraction.

relation to these adhesion contracts, the author stated that some university researchers complained that the SGCC was taking advantage of their budgetary needs to set unfair conditions, pretty much in line with the idea of subordinate research universities introduced in Chapter 5.

In terms of countries of origin, almost every applied or granted patent of SGCC belongs to Chinese actors since the second country of origin among patent assignees is Taiwan with a share of 0.11% (see Table 9.3). Taiwan's share is almost exclusively explained by patents co-owned with Hon Hai Precision Industry (Foxconn). This electronics' contract manufacturer is a Taiwanese firm based in China (see Table 9.2). It operates as a complier company in high-tech global intellectual monopolies' value chains (see Chapter 7).

Therefore, while SGCC is enlarging its innovation networks beyond China (see Figures 9.2 and 9.3), inventions are mainly owned by SGCC and, in relatively few cases, other Chinese organizations. Indeed, Arizona State University is the first foreign university to share patents with SGCC, and it only shares four applied or granted patents. Thus, foreign actors – even if they increasingly participate in SGCC's innovation networks – are mostly not participating in the distribution of intellectual rents. Besides the figures shown in Table 9.3, 27 other countries have co-authored publications with SGCC without sharing any applied or granted patent. These countries go from Australia, which shared 1.6% (67) of the SGCC's publications, to Greece (only one publication).

Table 9.3 Origin of patent assignees (either people or institutions)[a]

Country	*Number of distinct patents*	*Share in total SGCC's patents (%)*	*Share of the country in total SGCC's publications (%)*
China	122,169	100	100
Taiwan	136	0.1113	Not differentiated from China in the data base
United States	13	0.0106	4,5
Germany	8	0.0065	0,6
Hong Kong	5	0.0041	Not differentiated from China in the data base
Japan	3	0.0025	0,6
United Kingdom	2	0.0016	3,6
Singapore	1	0.0008	0,3
Bulgaria	1	0.0008	0

Source: Author's analysis based on Derwent Innovation and Web of Science.

a Four hundred and eighty-two patents included "undefined" among the countries of origin of the assignees.

Summing up, patent analysis shows that foreign co-owners are marginal and that the place of local co-owners is relatively less important in comparison with their appearance as scientific publications' co-authors. In fact, we do not present network maps for the SGCC's patents because they evidence the lack of regular partners, with only a dozen actors (including individuals working for SGCC) surpassing the minimum co-occurrence threshold to be plotted.

Overall, our results for SGCC are in contraction with the type of investments that loom large in US energy extraction and utility corporations. It was observed by Orhangazi (2018), in the United States, these companies privilege investment in tangible assets and keep intangibles lower. As we showed in this chapter, SGCC heavily invests both in tangible and intangible assets. Furthermore, our results are even more surprising considering that the number of cumulative granted and applied patents of the top eight world utility companies – besides SGCC – represents at most 4% of the SGCC's patent portfolio (see Appendix Table 9A.1.).

6 Final remarks

In this chapter, we argued that corporations aiming to become global intellectual monopolies rely on their national innovation system. We have illustrated this claim by analysing the experience of SGCC. SGCC can adequately be considered as an intellectual monopoly that profits from its innovation networks. This SOE barely co-owns patents with other organizations. Coupled with the vast diversity of partners in its co-publications' network, we provided evidence of its predatory behaviour. It appropriates R&D results from those networks, particularly from foreign actors, transforming this knowledge into intangible assets.

In terms of the scope of its monopoly, it is possible to consider SGCC as a national intellectual monopoly potentially on the way to globalize. The SGCC's case provides evidence of wannabe intellectual monopolies first and foremost relying on culturally and geographically close institutions. The expansion of their innovation networks to foreign organizations is a slower process where local research institutions, in particular PRO, are of utmost importance.

The SGCC's experience provides evidence of the global rise of intangible assets beyond intangible-intensive industries – like healthcare and the ICT, as we showed in Chapters 6–8. Knowledge is being also monopolized in industries that were not intensive in R&D. Additionally, as the SGCC's case shows, the inception of an intellectual monopoly demands enormous investments in R&D, which were at least in part covered directly by the Chinese state and that its inception does not necessarily lead to overall gains at its home country level. SGCC collects intellectual rents from its interactions with Chinese universities and smaller firms, but seldom shares the property of resulting patents. This empirical evidence needs to be further developed and complemented with other sources of information, such as qualitative analyses and empirical data on patent licensing and internal use of the SGCC's patented inventions. Nevertheless, results point to knowledge predation also from Chinese organizations. Although the overall effect in terms of development remains unclear, SGCC seems to be playing a key role in China's geopolitical and economic hegemony.

Beyond China and SGCC, we contributed to acknowledging that intellectual monopolies' inception is a process where companies are not necessarily born transnational. It seems that geographical, political and cultural proximity, as well as public policies encouraging national and sectoral innovation systems, contribute to establishing national intellectual monopolies.

The next chapter elaborates on intellectual rentiership and predation as common traits of all the selected cases studied so far in this book. Chapter 10 also reflects on the consequences for workers in the context of intellectual monopoly capitalism.

Notes

1 It is owned but not run by the state. It is ruled by the Enterprise Law, which "was designed to grant certain autonomy to enterprises and require enterprises to be responsible for their profits and losses, and it operates on the principle of a market system, without changing the old state ownership" (Yi-chong, 2012, p. 133).
2 https://www.iec.ch/globalvisions/SGCC/.
3 https://www.politico.eu/article/us-china-climate-renewable-energy-sustainability-leadership-investment/.
4 https://www.ft.com/content/0bb37c2e-3755-11ea-a6d3-9a26f8c3cba4?segmentId=b0d7e653-3467-12ab-c0f0-77e4424cdb4c.
5 SGCC bought 49% of Oman's Electricity Holding Company in late 2019, in what was called as the largest Chinese investment in the Middle East, https://www.ft.com/content/caeaed74-1fd7-11ea-b8a1-584213ee7b2b.
6 https://www.ft.com/content/68cdef50-f66a-11e5-803c-d27c7117d132.
7 http://www.sgcc.com.cn/html/sgcc_main_en/col2017112700/column_2017112700_1.shtml.
8 "By definition, a smart grid is a digitally enabled electrical grid that gathers, distributes, and acts on information about the behavior of all energy or power suppliers and consumers in order to improve the efficiency, importance, reliability, economics, and sustainability of electricity services" (Lin et al., 2013, p. 120).
9 https://www.geirina.net/ and http://www.geiri-eu.com/.
10 https://zhuanlan.zhihu.com/p/79702863.
11 The relevancy of scientific publications for industries, was already noticed by Godin (1996) more than two decades ago, and Grassano et al. (2019) recently reviewed the motives behind corporate publishing.
12 All the network maps in this paper follow a chi-square metric. See previous chapters in this section for an explanation on its advantages over other proximity measures.

13 http://www.saopaulo.sp.gov.br/ultimas-noticias/comitiva-chinesa-visita-unicamp-para-estreitar-parcerias-em-pesquisas/.
14 This feature is reinforced by the fact that SGCC refused to let go the property of innovative results of projects with multinationals. It may be stated that the same approach is being pursued for every collaboration; thus we should not expect other institutions exclusively owning patents that correspond to the SGCC's innovation networks.

References

Amsden, A. H. (1997). Editorial: Bringing production back in—Understanding Government's economic role in late industrialization. *World Development*, *25*(4), 469–80.
Antonelli, C. (1999). The evolution of the industrial organisation of the production of knowledge. *Cambridge Journal of Economics*, *23*(2), 243–60.
China Clarivate Analytics. (2017). *2017 Top 100 Chinese innovators*. Clarivate Analytics.
Choi, H., Park, S., & Lee, J. (2011). Government-driven knowledge networks as precursors to emerging sectors: A case of the hydrogen energy sector in Korea. *Industrial and Corporate Change*, *20*(3), 751–87.
Dosi, G. (1988). Sources, procedures, and microeconomic effects of innovation. *Journal of Economic Literature*, *26*(3), 1120–71.
Ernst, D. (2009). *A new geography of knowledge in the electronics industry? Asia's role in global innovation networks*. https://papers.ssrn.com/sol3/papers.cfm?abstract_id=2742923
Fan, P. (2006). Catching up through developing innovation capability: Evidence from China's telecom-equipment industry. *Technovation*, *26*(3), 359–68.
Freeman, C. (1987). *Technology policy and economic performance*. Pinter Publishers.
García-Herrero, A. (2019). Europe in the midst of China-US strategic competition: What are the European Union's options? *Bruegel Working Papers*, 3, 1–22.
Godin, B. (1996). Research and the practice of publication in industries. *Research Policy*, *25*(4), 587–606.
Grassano, N., Camerani, R., & Rotolo, D. (2019). Do firms publish? A multi-sectoral analysis. *DRUID Working Paper*, *21*.
Gu, S., Schwaag Serger, S., & Lundvall, B. A. (2016). China's innovation system: Ten years on. *Innovation*, *18*(4), 441–8.
International Energy Agency. (2017). *World energy outlook*. https://www.iea.org/weo/china/
Lee, K., Gao, X., & Li, X. (2016). Industrial catch-up in China: A sectoral systems of innovation perspective. *Cambridge Journal of Regions, Economy and Society*, *10*(1), 59–76.
Levín, P. (1977). Circuitos de innovación. *Revista Interamericana de Planificación*, *XX*(44). http://www.revistaespacios.com/a81v01n01/81010120.html
Li, D., Capone, G., & Malerba, F. (2019). The long march to catch-up: A history-friendly model of China's mobile communications industry. *Research Policy*, *48*(3), 649–64. doi:10.1016/j.respol.2018.10.019

Lin, C. C., Yang, C. H., & Shyua, J. Z. (2013). A comparison of innovation policy in the smart grid industry across the pacific: China and the USA. *Energy Policy, 57*, 119–32.

Liu, J., Chaminade, C., & Asheim, B. (2013). The geography and structure of global innovation networks: A knowledge base perspective. *European Planning Studies, 21*(9), 1456–73.

Lundvall, B. A. (1992). *National systems of innovation: Toward a theory of innovation and interactive learning* (Vol. 2). Pinter Publishers.

Lundvall, B. A. (2017). *The learning economy and the economics of hope*. Anthem Press.

Mah, D. N., Wu, Y. Y., & Hills, P. R. (2017). Explaining the role of incumbent utilities in sustainable energy transitions: A case study of the smart grid development in China. *Energy Policy, 109*, 794–806.

Malerba, F. (2002). Sectoral systems of innovation and production. *Research Policy, 31*(2), 247–64.

Malerba, F., & Orsenigo, L. (1997). Technological regimes and sectoral patterns of innovative activities. *Industrial and Corporate Change, 6*(1), 83–118.

Nelson, R. R. (1993). *National innovation systems: A comparative analysis*. Oxford University Press.

Noel, M., & Schankerman, M. (2013). Strategic patenting and software innovation. *The Journal of Industrial Economics, 61*(3), 481–520.

Orhangazi, Ö. (2018). The role of intangible assets in explaining the investment–profit puzzle. *Cambridge Journal of Economics, 43*(5), 1251–86.

Pagano, U. (2014). The crisis of intellectual monopoly capitalism. *Cambridge Journal of Economics, 38*(6), 1409–29.

Parrilli, M. D., Nadvi, K., & Yeung, H. W. (2013). Local and regional development in global value chains, production networks and innovation networks: A comparative review and the challenges for future research. *European Planning Studies, 21*(7), 967–88.

Rikap, C. (2019). Asymmetric power of the core: Technological cooperation and technological competition in the transnational innovation networks of big pharma. *Review of International Political Economy, 26*(5), 987–1021. doi:10.1080/09692290.2019.1620309

Schuman, S., & Lin, A. (2012). China's renewable energy law and its impact on renewable power in China: Progress, challenges and recommendations for improving implementation. *Energy Policy, 51*, 89–109.

State Grid Corporation of China. (2018). *Corporate social responsibility report*. State Grid Corporation of China.

Tancoigne, E., Barbier, M., Cointet, J. P., & Richard, G. (2014). The place of agricultural sciences in the literature on ecosystem services. *Ecosystem Services, 10*, 35–48.

World Intellectual Property Organization. (2019). *WIPO Technology Trends 2019. Artificial Intelligence*. WIPO.

Yi-chong, X. (2012). *The political economy of state-owned enterprises in China and India*. Palgrave Macmillan.

Yi-chong, X. (2017). *Sinews of power: The politics of the State Grid Corporation of China*. Oxford University Press.

Appendix

We also looked for these companies in the Web of Science standardized database of research institutions and could not find them. Therefore, in case they have scientific publications, they may be so few that the company name was not standardized. This reinforces their difference with SGCC.

Table 9A.1 Granted and applied patents. Major utility companies

Corporation	*Grated and applied patents*	*Granted patents*	*Industry ranking in market value (May 2019)*
SGCC	122,296	16,994	
Duke energy	27	12	1
Engie (ex GDF Suez)	944	355	2
National Grid (UK)	67	14	3
NextEra	48	21	4
EDF	1,932	756	5
Enel	1,179	536	6
Dominion resources	150	34	7
Iberdrola	192	77	8

Source: Derwent Innovation.

10

RENTIERSHIP, PREDATION AND THEIR IMPLICATIONS FOR WORKERS

1 Introduction

Conceiving innovation, and more broadly knowledge, as a power relation was the starting point of this book. Part 2 gave flesh and bones to this assertion by studying selected intellectual monopolies, analysing how they appropriate value and extract rents from the organizations participating in their production and innovation networks.[1] In this chapter, we build on these findings to further elaborate on the specificities of intellectual monopoly capitalism.

This chapter is structured around two discussions. The first one concerns the main sources of accumulation by dispossession used by intellectual monopolies, namely rentiership and predation. These are partially overlapping concepts. In a nutshell, while rentierism refers to the practice of capturing value produced elsewhere by assetizing (thus, privatizing) resources, predation is a direct relation of spoliation. Beyond internal capital accumulation (inside its legally owned capital), the intellectual monopoly captures value in the form of rents by transforming its knowledge results into assets. Furthermore, it predates knowledge (that it turns into intangible assets, increasing appropriated rents) and value from its innovation and production networks, respectively.

Assetized knowledge includes digital intelligence that springs from processing big data with machine learning algorithms and provides insights for orienting business and innovation. Data-driven intellectual monopolies retain exclusive access to data sources, thus to digital intelligence. This allows them to garner data-driven innovation rents. Chapters 7 and 8 referred to companies monopolizing access to continuous flows of data as data-driven intellectual monopolies. As leading firms become increasingly data-driven, regardless of their industry, data-driven rents become a core feature of intellectual monopoly capitalism.

The second discussion unfolded in this chapter refers to the implications for workers of intellectual monopoly capitalism. We provide a first distinction between different types of workers, from most precarious to those whose working conditions and salaries place them close to capitalists even if their reproduction still depends on selling their labour power.

While the first discussion, presented next, is, to some extent, a synthesis of this book's central argument, the second discussion developed in Section 3 was not systematically addressed until here. The complexities of the overall scenario we are trying to unpack led us to make the hard choice of leaving this paramount dimension of intellectual monopoly capitalism, until this chapter, undertheorized. An exception was Chapter 5, where we explored how participating in intellectual monopolies' innovation networks affects scholars and their working conditions. As universities and public research organizations participate in firms' innovation processes and even become themselves almost private firms, scholarship adopts characteristics of capitalist labour. Beyond scholars, the overall implications for workers will be outlined – even if only briefly – in this chapter. The chapter ends with reflections on the continuities and ruptures between intellectual monopoly capitalism and earlier stages in the development of capitalism concerning both analysed discussions.

2 The interplay between rentiership, predation and capital accumulation

In a nutshell, capital accumulation refers to the process by which value is created, whereas rentiership and predation do not create but redistribute value. Capitalism is thus explained by this two-fold process of value creation and distribution.

The market is capitalism's core distribution sphere. It was assumed that market relations are based on mutual wills. Commodity exchange is supposed to be a voluntary and symmetric relationship (Rikap, 2018a). Yet, since only money is directly exchangeable for any other commodity, every commodity exchange is, in fact, a power relation (Marx, 1867, Chapter 1). This is the power of the buyer. As explained by Orléan (2014), money gives its owner a tremendous strategic autonomy. The owner of the commodity surrenders to the money holder. The latter dominates because the former's reproduction depends on fulfilling the transaction, which exclusively depends on the will of the money holder (Rikap, 2018a).

Nevertheless, in the market, money provides a circumstantial, evanescent power. It lasts the second whereby commodities offer themselves. Once the transaction is completed, money (thus power) passes by. It now stands in the hands of the seller, which will now become a buyer.

Beyond and within market transactions, under intellectual monopoly capitalism, power relations are capable of overcoming the power of the buyer. Markets reflect these other power relations, as some commodities are no longer exchanged on the basis of independent and autonomous labour. Intellectual monopolies plan and organize production and innovation networks, which include setting the trading terms of exchange within those networks, with specific consequences at the level of value distribution. To address them, we build on the initial conceptualizations of rent and predation that were introduced in Chapter 2. We further develop them, considering common findings and conclusions of Chapters 6–9.

In Chapter 2, we argued that the privatization and assetization of intangibles generate, in Veblen's (1908b) words, a right to exclude. Intellectual monopolies are appropriating intangibles at the expense of the creative capacities of society. Following Veblen (1908a), knowledge is a historical common stock. New knowledge is an accretion to that stock. Hence, Veblen (1908a) considered trivial the creative contribution of any individual acting as inventor or discoverer in comparison with the past accumulated wisdom embedded in any productive breakthrough. Making a portion of this common stock excludable by transforming it into an intangible asset, therefore, disposes the community not only of access to the particular contribution of the inventor but greatly mutilates that common stock.

Once knowledge is privatized, it can be transformed into an intangible asset capable of trigging a sustained earning to its owner. This earning, as we discussed in Chapter 2, is the intellectual, technoscientific or knowledge rent (Birch, 2019; Durand & Milberg, 2020; Foley, 2013; Kaplinsky, 1998; Pagano, 2014; Teixeira & Rotta, 2012). Therefore, intangible assets provide a monopoly power.

2.1 The growing importance of data-driven innovation rents

Intellectual monopoly power has the potential to expand without limits in the digital economy. Chapters 7 and 8, on Apple and Amazon, respectively, elaborated on the traits of a specific intellectual monopoly that bases its continuous innovations and business diversification on monopolizing access to (big) data. These data are transformed into digital intelligence by processing and analysing them with machine learning algorithms. Machine learning is a general-purpose technology (Brynjolfsson et al., 2017; Dosi & Virgillito, 2019), and its most popular approach – deep neural networks – can even be considered as a general-purpose method of invention (Cockburn et al., 2018). This approach allows algorithms to keep learning by being continuously fed with new data. Resulting digital intelligence becomes an intangible asset that orients business and enables innovations. Tech giants' accumulation depends on the appropriation of data-driven intellectual rents.

Centralizing and analysing constant flows of data is not an entirely new phenomenon. However, it did not have the reach it achieved since the development of different technologies, usually bundled under the name Industry 4.0, that enable the collection, storage, processing and analysis of big data.

Digital intelligence's potential would not have been unleashed without ICT infrastructure, from supercomputers in datacentres to telecommunications, with 5G expected to take the data value chain to an unprecedented level.

Beyond digital economy paradigmatic corporations, data-driven intellectual monopolies are emerging in multiple industries. Chapter 9 explained that State Grid Corporation of China (SGCC) gathers and processes data with artificial intelligence for its smart grid. Although it comes from a traditional industry, far from ICT, SGCC is among top organizations in artificial intelligence patenting (World Intellectual Property Organization, 2019). Big pharma companies are also adapting to the digital economy, aiming to expand their legal intellectual monopoly (see Chapter 6) with data-driven rents. Even if they are still in an early-mature stage and far from fully acknowledging the potential of artificial intelligence for drug discovery, they are investing in R&D digitalization and artificial intelligence (Schuhmacher et al., 2020).

Other early examples of data-driven intellectual monopolies include genomics corporations like 23andMe and Myriad that make businesses with genes' databanks (Pistor, 2019; Rose & Rose, 2014). But probably the earliest example of the power and surveillance potential of monopolizing and centralizing access to data is given by the US government itself. Crypto AG was a company secretly owned by the CIA and, in its beginnings, West German intelligence. Since 1970, Crypto AG sold encryption devices to 120 countries, including Iran, India, Pakistan, the Vatican and Latin American (democratic and dictatorial) governments. The devices were produced in such a way that the US and German spy agencies could break the encryption codes and illegally harvest and analyse encrypted messages.[2]

To further elaborate on data-driven and other forms of intellectual rents, we extend Marx's ground-rent concept in dialogue with Veblen's notion of predation in the next sub-heading.

2.2 *Marx on rents and Veblen on predation*

Rent, for Marx (1894), means that the landowner appropriates a portion of total surplus value precisely because she holds the land, mine or oil well title. Veblen (1899) conceptualized predation as a direct manifestation of superior force. It is quite straightforward that landownership provides means to exercise such a direct manifestation of superior force as far as land is indispensable for farming.

Besides differential rents, Marx (1894) explains that even the worst quality land in use yields absolute rent, which is a monopoly rent. For the tenant to pay the landlord this rent, the former must sell agricultural commodities at a price higher than the production price or otherwise sacrifice its own profits, so absolute rent is a form of value appropriation (redistribution) in the same sense of intellectual and financial rentiership.[3] Furthermore, Marx's definition of landowners can be easily extended to rentiers in general:

> No other social class lives in so extravagant a manner; no other class claims such a right as this does to a traditional luxury in keeping with its 'estate', irrespective of where the money comes from; no other class piles debts upon debts in such a light-hearted way. And yet time and again they fall on their feet – thanks to the capital of other people that is put into the soil and yields them rent, completely out of all proportion to the profits the capitalist draws from this.
>
> (Marx, 1894, p. 859)

This quote resembles the idea of predators, as presented by Veblen (1899). According to Veblen, the basis of a predatory community is "the relation of superior and inferior, noble and base, dominant and subservient persons and classes, master and slave" (Veblen, 1899, p. 184). In all these cases, there is a direct or personal relationship between predator and prey, which was formally absent in the abstract idea of markets as voluntary encounters of buyers and sellers.

The resilience of a predatory relationship in contemporary capitalism differs from its archaic form because it now takes place globally and is extended beyond social reproduction to knowledge production. What both forms of predation share is, in line with Veblen (1899), a direct manifestation of superior force. Intellectual monopolies exercise their superior force against different types of subordinate organizations.

2.2.1 Why is it useful to distinguish between rentiership and predation?

While predation is a direct relation of spoliation, rentiership results from a distribution of total surplus value between capital enterprises generated by the assetization cum privatization of resources (land, knowledge, data, etc.). They are two forms of exercising superior force, but the nature of the relationship differs. Predation supposes a direct or personal relationship, an explicit or implicit sign-up contract between two parties where one party solely decides the contract terms. Rentiership, in turn, does not necessarily suppose such a contractual agreement. Table 10.1 summarizes all possible cases providing examples for each of them.

As it becomes self-evident from Table 10.1, there is no such process of pure standard capital accumulation because it assumes that knowledge remains a common stock and that there are neither financial assets nor private land ownership. In fact, capitalism unfolds as a combination of capital accumulation, rentiership and predation.

Table 10.1 The intersections and differences between rentiership and predation

		Rent: Yes	Rent: No
Predation	Yes	**Rentiership by means of predation (direct rentiership).** Example: Intellectual monopolies transform knowledge produced inside innovation networks (thus by different organizations that are directly subordinated to the intellectual monopoly, meaning it exercises a direct force over them) into intangible assets.	**Value predation.** Example: The leading company of a value chain, production network, or platform establishes sign-up contracts with subordinate firms (such as subcontractors and third parties). All the terms of the contract are defined by the former. The leader exercises a direct superior force that results in the predation of surplus value that corresponds to capital advanced by subordinate firms. Complier and laggard firms – the two types of subordinate firms identified in Chapter 2 – can solely accept or decline the agreement.
	No	**Rentiership at the system level (indirect rentiership).** Example: Intellectual rent extracted from privatizing the result of internal R&D. Other examples include financial rents and the different forms of ground-rent (including urban rent).	**Standard capital accumulation process.** It results from the general process of transformation of values into prices of production. The only power exercised here is the power of the buyer to decide if the transaction takes place or not, but it does not determine the conditions of the transaction. Commodities tend to be exchanged on their prices of production (a tendency because of supply and demand effects).

Table 10.1 also highlights that predation and rentiership sometimes coincide, but rents can be collected without an underlying predatory relationship, thus based on an *indirect* relation of spoliation only mediated by the (impersonal) market. Besides appropriating value from their production networks, intellectual monopolies collect rents from their in-house innovation

activity that is either protected with IPRs or kept secret. Here, intellectual monopolies garner rents from monopolizing access to knowledge, but without establishing a *direct* relation of (knowledge) spoliation with others. By curtailing access to an in-house invention, they *indirectly* deprive others from accessing to a portion of knowledge common stock but without exercising a direct relation of superior force with any other organization in particular. The intellectual rent is garnered when others access that portion of knowledge, either by licensing an IPR or consuming a commodity that required that knowledge to be produced.

Likewise, predation dose not always result in rents for the predator. Value predation takes place when there is a *direct appropriation of value* from a subordinate company. Intellectual monopolies define the terms of production and exchange, exercising *a direct manifestation of superior force*. They appropriate value by paying below commodities' production price when they buy and/or charging commodities' above it when they sell. Appropriated value is an appropriation of part of the surplus value produced elsewhere through a direct manifestation of superior force. The difference is not a rent but an unequal commodity exchange.

Finally, inside innovation networks, rentiership takes place by means of predation. Intellectual monopolies also assetize intangibles from knowledge produced in those innovation networks, thus directly manifesting its superior force with all the other participants. Since knowledge produced at the level of subordinate organizations is appropriated and turned into intangible assets by the intellectual monopoly, intellectual rents result from a predatory practice.

2.3 Intellectual monopolies as financial rentiers

Financial rentiership is another example of rentierism that is not based on predation. Financial rentiers do not directly subordinate others but indirectly appropriate part of total surplus value.

Intellectual monopolies pay the minimum possible taxes and enjoy exorbitant profits. These factors, together with their outsourcing dynamics analysed in previous chapters, explain their large cash holdings. Their financial strength opens the possibility to expand accumulation through M&As and act as venture capitals,[4] but also allows to increase rents, this time from financial assets (see Chapter 7). Intellectual monopolies keep their offshored savings in US treasury and corporate bonds, thus collecting financial rents (Bryan et al., 2017; Pozsar, 2018). In addition, they distribute colossal gains to shareholders as dividends and buybacks. Shareholders and asset managers also benefit from the mere inflation of the price of their stocks.

Overall, intellectual and financial rentiership intertwine. A particular way is reflected in changes in goodwill defined as the difference between a company's book and market value. While it is supposed to account for unmeasured intangibles, Serfati (2008) argues that goodwill also includes an overvalue because once a future M&A is made public, the market values of involved companies increase, thus artificially increasing goodwill (Eaglesham, 2020).

The intrinsic uncertainty of R&D opens the door to speculation. Since 1984, the US authorized companies to do IPOs with a deficit as long as they had sufficient intangible capital (Orsi & Coriat, 2006). Both "promising" biotechnology and tech start-ups have chosen this path as a way to fund their ongoing R&D. In some cases, the IPO arrived when the business was operational but not profitable (like Uber and WeWork). The typical market reaction has been a bet on innovation, speculating on the promising R&D results that those firms could achieve beyond their current operations. For instance, the current evolution of the Renaissance IPO exchange traded funds (ETF), which tracks recently listed US companies, has increased 60% between January and September 2020.

Intellectual monopoly capitalism develops hand in hand with a new type of shareholder: big asset managers that bet on healthy capitalism – thus, providing a stable (and eventually growing) stream of financial rents – in the long term. Vanguard, BlackRock and State Street Global Advisors hold together over 20% of the shares of the average S&P 500 company. As we mentioned in Chapter 4, the three together are the largest owners of 90% of S&P 500 firms and of between 20% and 60% of the biggest firms of major European and Japanese markets (Fichtner & Heemskerk, 2018). This gives them leverage to assume that in case of crises, the US government will back their assets.

These asset managers do not invest individually in each firm but in stock indexes, such as S&P 500 (Braun, 2020). ETP are a financial innovation. Vanguard even patented a mechanism to avoid taxes on mutual funds.[5] Furthermore, by joining the boards of many of the US biggest corporations, they became the only actors with access to inside information of most of the firms that rule global capitalism. No other organization has such diverse centralized data about capitalism, which positions them as potential data rentiers.

Asset managers bet on the health of a capitalist system led by big corporations. Betting on global capital accumulation allows them to bear the risk of investing in innovative but still not profitable corporations. Even if most of them will fail, they will still be investing in the few winners. Purchasing Amazon stocks (included in S&P 500 in 2005) has been a typical example of the latter.

2.4 The effects of predation and rentiership on capital accumulation

Predation, as well as rentiership, is a zero-sum game. What an intellectual monopoly gains from predation and rentiership is a portion of value that someone else is losing. Overall, predation and rentiership, as forms of accumulation by dispossession,[6] are not opposed to traditional forms of capital accumulation taking place within the boundaries of capital's legal ownership. In fact, they are complementary practices for the intellectual monopoly. Furthermore, intellectual monopolies rely on the ever-expanding scale of capital accumulation in their production networks to assure greater value creation, thus ever-expanding sources of predation. They also rely on the overall expansion of capitalism for rentiership.

Overall, intellectual monopoly capitalism results in expanding innovation networks favoured by knowledge's cumulativeness. However, at the system level, albeit witnessing impressive advances – in particular regarding digital technologies – the effects on growth have been curtailed. In other words, under intellectual monopoly capitalism, innovation-driven growth and accumulation are being highjacked.

As knowledge results are turned into intangible assets, intellectual monopolies fuel weak investment since the monopolization of knowledge by and beyond IPRs blocks potentially profitable opportunities (Durand and Gueuder, 2018). Hence, at the global level, intangible accumulation does not translate to overall growth of the economy, but it is associated with market power that increases prices per unit of investment (Rabinovich, 2020). As it was just mentioned, what intellectual monopolies gain from predation and rentiership, is a portion of value that someone else is losing. Those losing are surbordinate organizations that seek to at least partially compensate the profits that they would receive in a scenario where their products are sold at their prices of production. To (partially) cope with predation and rentiership, they super-exploit workers.

3 Implications for workers

As intellectual monopolies' rentiership and predation redistribute surplus value amongst capitalist firms, the hierarchy of power trickles further down and affects workers. Since the 1980s in the United States, the share of surplus value in total value-added increased (Rotta, 2018; Stockhammer, 2013). Within the workers' share, there have also been further redistributions due to workers' segmentation within and between intellectual monopolies and the different subordinate firms (innovative, complier and laggard, see Chapter 2). In this section, we briefly refer to the most salient traits.

Rotta (2018) and Moseley (1990) show a shift in the share of labour income in the US since the 1980s from productive to unproductive activities. The latter include supervisory positions and all the workers in knowledge and information, finance and insurance, real state, legal services, government services and non-profit organizations. Average worker's compensation in intellectual monopolies, whose activities are mostly under Rotta's (2018) unproductive label, are usually the highest. Employees enjoy the best benefits and working conditions and often receive bonuses and stock options, which contributes to explaining the decline in other workers' salaries.[7]

Innovating companies, defined as those that participate in innovation networks subordinating to intellectual monopolies, also offer their workers equity but often as a means to compensate for lower salaries compared to those of established big corporations, particularly those that became intellectual monopolies. Equity in innovating companies is a risky bet since the overwhelming majority of these companies fail. Innovating companies are generally struggling to either achieve an innovative breakthrough or settle their business. As a typical example of an innovating company, studies show that employees of start-ups generally argue that greater independence and responsibility compensate for their sometimes lower salaries and significant job insecurity (Kim, 2018; Sauermann, 2018).

Meanwhile, complier and laggard firms compensate a portion of intellectual monopolies' predation with the super-exploitation of their workers (Iñigo Carrera, 2016; Levín, 1997; Marini, 1977; Smith, 2016). These are firms that have lost their technical autonomy. The difference is that complier firms are early adopters (and adapters) of the techniques required by intellectual monopolies. Laggard firms survive by performing the simplest tasks within production networks offering low prices by worsening wages and working conditions, while casualization becomes the norm.

Wages and working conditions also deteriorate in complier firms. Foxconn exemplifies the extreme working conditions faced in complier firms to offer an appealing deal to intellectual monopolies and still assure its profit rate is above the interest rate (see Chapter 7). Overall, working conditions at subcontractor firms in Global Value Chains (GVC), the classical example of a complier company, have been widely described by the literature. Different authors have reconceived these chains as Global Poverty Chains and replaced upgrading as an aspiration or recommendation for downgrading as a fact (see Chapter 11).

Beyond GVC, data-driven intellectual monopolies outsource consultancy services, such as data analytics, to companies that pay relatively lower salaries than intellectual monopolies for qualified positions (see Chapter 8). These firms also act as complier companies that offload the burden of their sign-up contracts with intellectual monopolies onto their workers. A more brutal story, because it includes traumas due to overexposure to violent content, is that of tech giants' subcontracted content moderators. Regardless of the psychological consequences and stress related to this job, they earn US 28,800 USD a year while the average Facebook employee makes almost 8.5 times that amount as total compensation (salary, bonuses and stock options). Micromanaging their use of time and limiting room for mistakes, working conditions for content moderators are far from the relaxed environment of Facebook's facilities.[8]

At the bottom of the hierarchy, new forms of informality prevail in laggard firms. These are small firms creating low-quality and low-wage employment (Graña, 2018). In the limit, they include self-employed workers forced to become an "entrepreneur". It has long been analysed that entrepreneurship is pushed by unemployment in peripheral countries (Fields, 1990; Mead, 1994). The contemporary specific form of this obliged entrepreneurship has expanded worldwide and was dubbed the gig economy (crowd-work and work on demand). Workers bear all the risk of economic fluctuations, and employers save costs and dismissal lawsuits (Fleming, 2017; Friedman, 2014). Wannabe intellectual monopolies often profit from this new form of outsourcing, where workers become responsible for tangible capital commitment (their means of production). The labour contract is replaced by an extremely unstable and relatively cheap vendor's contract. They are paid when they work, thus even at the expense of their health and caring responsibilities. On the outside, they may appear to be micro-firms or pseudo-capitals, because they sell a commodity, which is a façade that relieves hiring companies from any working commitment. The social relation of work is hidden beneath the independent contractor or entrepreneur.

According to Friedman (2014), this new form of *on the spot* contract is the distinguishable feature of the gig economy, not the qualification of the workers or the technology or type of activity they perform. Although not exclusive of the digital industries, their expansion has contributed to multiply these extremely flexible working conditions. According to Deloitte, 42 million people will have this "alternative" work by 2020 in the United States, a three-fold increase from 2017.[9]

Under intellectual monopoly capitalism, as intangible assets concentrate in fewer hands and knowledge is increasingly monopolized, workers' segmentation not only concerns working conditions and salaries. As paradoxical as it may seem for an era where even *machines learn*, increasing numbers of workers are deprived of learning. Pagano (2014) recalls the Babbage principle of division of labour where tasks are split to minimize learning. Few people should learn how to conceive in a growingly complex world, while the majority becomes cheap executors of the former's decisions. When learning by doing becomes almost irrelevant, gig economy jobs can proliferate more easily.

So far, it seems as if working for an intellectual monopoly would grant a good salary, job stability and healthy and stimulating working conditions while working for any subordinate firm would downplay all or part of the former. However, what defines each worker's fate is a combination of the type of hiring firm and the qualification required for the job. Strategic activities for the enhancement of the intellectual monopoly, such as R&D and marketing, will typically be better remunerated whether workers are hired by the intellectual monopoly, or participate in other parts of its innovation networks, albeit the latter may probably earn less than the former. Flipping the coin, more routine tasks requiring fewer qualifications will be worse remunerated regardless of where they take place (Autor, 2015). Hence, when an intellectual monopoly does not outsource a routine task, its workers may also earn low wages and suffer casualization, even if they will be better than those performing similar tasks in a complier company. Amazon warehouse workers are a known example (see Chapter 8). Worse working conditions are accompanied by digital surveillance, a common practice way beyond Amazon. Amazon patented wristbands that track warehouse workers' hands at all times and inform when they are working efficiently.[10] Nonetheless, Amazon pays USD 15 an hour for this job, which is above the US minimum wage and above what other companies pay for similar jobs.

Finally, casualization and underpayment are not exclusive to less qualified jobs. Companies like Deloitte offer crowd-sourcing platforms for accounting, legal advice and other qualified tasks.[11] Intellectual monopolies also use precarious workers from around the world under the excuse of "finding talent". By 2018, Amazon, Google's parent Alphabet and Microsoft led the ranking of employers of "Optional Practical Training" in the United States. They use the program to offer precarious technical positions to students.[12]

Furthermore, Google has a team of subcontracted linguists that are responsible for producing data sets needed to make its intelligent assistant work.[13] A similar case is that of freelance app developers and content creators, examples of pseudo-capitals taking all the risks, without labour rights and forced to accept tech giants' fees (Bergvall-Kareborn & Howcroft, 2011, 2013; Brustein, 2016; Dolata, 2020; Forde, 2016; Rikap, 2018b). In relation to content creators but also concerning developers in open-source platforms (see Chapter 3), there is another complexity of our time. The distinction between leisure and productive work becomes fuzzy. This fuzziness contributes to (explicitly or implicitly) justify underpaid or even unpaid labour, expand casualization and, as a result, expand super-exploitation. Under the ideology of the entrepreneur, a whole system was put in place where creative workers are no longer directly hired. They live with the uncertainty of not knowing if their next creation will be appealing enough to provide them sufficient earnings to make ends meet.

4 Final remarks

Capitalism has always been, regardless of peaceful instances, a turbulent social formation. It has hitherto guaranteed the reproduction of human life, but by continually marginalizing a portion of humanity and risking the future of every living being. It has done so with the rhetoric of universalism while it systematically confronts humans. Intellectual monopoly capitalism is probably its harshest episode.

Total social knowledge no longer represents an integrated system, a social commons. Knowledge monopolization dissected parts of that totality. Therefore, its impact goes beyond limiting the public use of what was directly monopolized. It affects the whole functioning of the system. The economic literature has conceptualized under the form of economies of scope this property of knowledge. When ideas interconnect, their complementarity leads to results beyond the simple addition of their parts. While at the system level these economies of scope are curtailed, each intellectual monopoly manages to profit from a limited – though by no means negligible – economy of scope triggered by its systematic accumulation of intangible assets.

Intellectual monopolies are – simultaneously – capitalists, rentiers and predators. They maximize their appropriation of wealth ultimately at the expense of workers of all the subordinate firms but also including their own workers. Workers' further differentiation is a side effect of this process. Capitalism has always differentiated between simple and complex jobs. This historical distinction crystalizes in a structural differentiation of the working class between those conceiving and those executing commodity production processes. Intellectual monopoly capitalism has taken this distinction to an unprecedented level, while it also expands casualization to skilled workers. Workers' differentiation under intellectual monopoly capitalism results in a majority with earnings below what they need to reproduce themselves and their families. To tilt the scale, unions must regain the power they lost in Western countries and gain the power they never had in Asia. A global organization of labour is required. However, this is much easier said than done.

To conclude, intellectual monopoly capitalism reinforces global asymmetries and deepens income inequalities. There is a higher concentration of intellectual monopolies (and innovating companies) in core countries. Coupled with the higher concentration of complier companies in the peripheries, it reinforces underdevelopment and unequal exchange. In the next section, we delve into the specificities of intellectual monopoly capitalism for and in the peripheries.

Notes

1 We refer to production and innovation networks in a broad sense, including platforms.

2 https://www.washingtonpost.com/graphics/2020/world/national-security/cia-crypto-encryption-machines-espionage/.

3 The difference lays in the fact that the value appropriated as absolute rent was produced in the agricultural capital production process. It is still value appropriation because it is value that would have been redistributed to industrial capitals in the general process of transformation of value into prices of production. Marx (1894) observed that agricultural capital had a lower organic composition of capital than industrial capital. It is in this respect that Rotta and Teixeira (2018) explain that there is no such a thing as an absolute knowledge rent because in Marxist terms, there is no value creation in knowledge production. In Rikap (2013), I explained that knowledge is an activity essential to organize human experience. In generic terms, conceiving is a productive activity, but this activity is creative in nature. Since commodities represent value understood as a *re*production of labour time, it makes no sense to speak of the value of a creative product. Its reproduction time tends to be zero (the time it takes to explain a concept).

Thus inevitably, once a portion of knowledge is detached from the knowledge common stock and becomes an asset, the resulting monopoly rent is an appropriation of value produced elsewhere.

4 Amazon provides Amazon Web Services credit to promising start-ups as a form of venture capital that simultaneously induces those companies to remain customers once the credit is over (Amazon, 2020).

5 https://www.bloomberg.com/graphics/2019-vanguard-mutual-fund-tax-dodge/.

6 We build here on Harvey's (2000) concept understood as the survival of "primitive" forms of accumulation that include commodification and privatization of alternative forms of property such as commons, collective and state as well as colonial and imperial appropriation of assets.

7 See for instance https://www.bizjournals.com/sanjose/news/2019/06/12/median-pay-big-tech-aapl-fb-nflx-goog-intc-tsla.html.

8 http://www.businessinsider.com/a-day-in-the-life-of-an-online-content-moderator-2019-6 and https://www.theverge.com/2019/2/25/18229714/cognizant-facebook-content-moderator-interviews-trauma-working-conditions-arizona.

9 https://www.ft.com/content/856efc98-e578-11e9-9743-db5a370481bc.

10 https://gizmodo.com/amazonpatents-wristband-to-track-hand-movements-of-war-1822590549?IR¼T.

11 https://www2.deloitte.com/us/en/pages/operations/solutions/enterprise-crowdsourcing-solution-pixel.html.

12 https://www.bloomberg.com/news/newsletters/2020-06-17/laid-off-h1-b-visa-holders-have-only-bad-options.

13 https://www.theguardian.com/technology/2019/may/28/a-white-collar-sweatshop-google-assistant-contractors-allege-wage-theft.

References

Amazon. (2020). *Small business success in challenging times. 2020 Amazon SMB Impact Report*. Amazon.

Autor, D. H. (2015). Why are there still so many jobs? The history and future of workplace automation. *Journal of Economic Perspectives*, *29*(3), 3–30. doi:10.1257/jep.29.3.3

Bergvall-Kareborn, B., & Howcroft, D. (2011). Mobile applications development on Apple and Google platforms. *Communications of the Association for Information Systems*, *29*(1), 565–80. doi: doi.org/10.17705/1CAIS.02930

Bergvall-Kareborn, B., & Howcroft, D. (2013). The Apple business model: Crowdsourcing mobile applications. *Accounting Forum*, *37*, 280–89.

Birch, K. (2019). Technoscience rent: Toward a theory of rentiership for technoscientific capitalism. *Science, Technology, & Human Values*, *45*(1), 3–33.

Braun, B. (2020). *American asset manager capitalism*. doi:10.31235/osf.io/v6gue, SocArXiv, 18 June 2020. Web.

Brustein, J. (2016, April 19). The real story of how amazon built the echo. *Bloomberg Businessweek*. https://www.bloomberg.com/features/2016-amazon-echo/

Bryan, D., Rafferty, M., & Wigan, D. (2017). Capital unchained: Finance, intangible assets and the double life of capital in the offshore world. *Review of International Political Economy*, *24*(1), 56–86.

Brynjolfsson, E., Rock, D., & Syverson, C. (2017). *Artificial intelligence and the modern productivity paradox: A clash of expectations and statistics*. National Bureau of Economic Research.

Cockburn, I. M., Henderson, R., & Stern, S. (2018). *The impact of artificial intelligence on innovation.* National Bureau of Economic Research.

Dolata, U. (2020). *Platform-regulation. Coordination of markets and curation of sociality on the Internet* [SOI Discussion Paper]. Stuttgarter Beiträge zur Organisations- und Innovationsforschung.

Dosi, G., & Virgillito, M. E. (2019). Whither the evolution of the contemporary social fabric? New technologies and old socio-economic trends. *International Labour Review, 158*(4), 593–625.

Durand, C. (2019). *Predation in the age of algorithms: The role of intangibles assets.* CEPN.

Durand, C., & Gueuder, M. (2018). The Profit–Investment Nexus in an Era of Financialisation, Globalisation and Monopolisation: A Profit-Centred Perspective. *Review of Political Economy, 30*(2), 126–53.

Durand, C., & Milberg, W. (2020). Intellectual monopoly in global value chains. *Review of International Political Economy, 27*(2), 404–29. doi:10.1080/09692290.2019.1660703

Eaglesham, J. (2020). Goodwill sparks deep division, at least on balance sheets. *The Wall Street Journal.* https://www.wsj.com/articles/goodwill-sparks-deep-division-at-least-on-balance-sheets-11579613906?mod=hp_lead_pos3

Fichtner, J., & Heemskerk, E. M. (2018). The new permanent universal owners: Index funds, (Im) patient capital, and the claim of long-termism. *SSRN 3321597*

Fields, G. S. (1990). *Labour market modelling and the urban informal sector: Theory and evidence.* In D. Turnham, B. Salomé, & A. Schwarz (Eds.), The informal sector revisited (pp. 49–69). Organisation for Economic Co-operation and Development.

Fleming, P. (2017). The human capital hoax: Work, debt and insecurity in the era of Uberization. *Organization Studies, 38*(5), 691–709.

Foley, D. K. (2013). Rethinking financial capitalism and the "information" economy. *Review of Radical Political Economics, 45*(3), 257–68.

Forde, E. (2016). Is YouTube wrecking the music industry—Or putting new artists in the spotlight? *The Guardian. July, 18.*

Friedman, G. (2014). Workers without employers: Shadow corporations and the rise of the gig economy. *Review of Keynesian Economics, 2*(2), 171–88.

Graña, J. M. (2018). Labor market trends in a low and heterogeneous productivity country. Evidence from Argentina's manufacturing. *Brazilian Journal of Political Economy, 38*(2), 358–76.

Harvey, D. (2000). *Spaces of hope.* University of California Press.

Iñigo Carrera, J. (2016). The general rate of profit and its realisation in the differentiation of industrial capitals. In G. Charnock & G. Starosta (Eds.), *The new international division of labour* (pp. 25–53). Springer. http://link.springer.com/chapter/10.1057/978-1-137-53872-7_2

Kaplinsky, R. (1998). *Globalisation, industrialisation and sustainable growth: The pursuit of the nth rent.* Institute of Development Studies, University of Sussex.

Kim, J. D. (2018). Is there a startup wage premium? Evidence from MIT graduates. *Research Policy, 47*(3), 637–49.

Levín, P. (1997). *El capital tecnológico.* Catálogos. http://www.econ.uba.ar/www/institutos/economia/Ceplad/elcaptec.htm

Marini, R. M. (1977). *Dialéctica de la dependencia.* Era.

Marx, K. (1867). *El capital. Crítica de la economía política (Tomo I).* Fondo de Cultura Economica.

Marx, K. (1894). *El Capital. Crítica de la economía política (Tomo III).* Fondo de Cultura Economica.

Mead, D. C. (1994). The contribution of small enterprises to employment growth in Southern and Eastern Africa. *World Development, 22*(12), 1881–94.

Moseley, F. (1990). The decline of the rate of profit in the postwar U.S. economy: An alternative Marxian explanation. *Review of Radical Political Economics, 22*(2–3), 17–37. doi:10.1177/048661349002200202

Orléan, A. (2014). *The empire of value: A new foundation for economics.* MIT Press.

Orsi, F., & Coriat, B. (2006). The new role and status of intellectual property rights in contemporary capitalism. *Competition & Change, 10*(2), 162–79.

Pagano, U. (2014). The crisis of intellectual monopoly capitalism. *Cambridge Journal of Economics, 38*(6), 1409–29.

Pistor, K. (2019). *The code of capital: How the law creates wealth and inequality.* Princeton University Press.

Pozsar, Z. (2018). Repatriation, the echo-taper and the €/$ basis. *Global Money Notes, 11.* Credit Suisse.

Rabinovich, J. (2020). Financialisation and the 'supply-side' face of the investment-profit puzzle. *Journal of Post Keynesian Economics,* 1–29. doi:10.1080/01603477.2020.1734463

Rikap, C. (2013). Los productos de la Universidad actual: Concepto e innovación. *Realidad Económicano. 275.* http://www.sidalc.net/cgi-bin/wxis.exe/?IsisScript=UCC.xis&method=post&formato=2&cantidad=1&expresion=mfn=129422

Rikap, C. (2018a). El capitalismo como sistema de poder: Del dinero a la diferenciación del capital. *Filosofía de La Economía, 7*(2), 97–111.

Rikap, C. (2018b). Innovation as economic power in global value chains. *Revue d'Économie Industrielle, 163,* 35–75.

Rose, H., & Rose, S. P. R. (2014). *Genes, cells, and brains: The promethean promises of the new biology.* Verso Trade.

Rotta, T. N. (2018). Unproductive accumulation in the USA: A new analytical framework. *Cambridge Journal of Economics, 42*(5), 1367–92.

Rotta, T. N., & Teixeira, R. A. (2018). The commodification of knowledge and information. In M. Vidal, T. Smith, & T. Rotta (Ed.). The Oxford Handbook of Karl Marx.

Sauermann, H. (2018). Fire in the belly? Employee motives and innovative performance in start-ups versus established firms. *Strategic Entrepreneurship Journal, 12*(4), 423–54.

Schuhmacher, A., Gatto, A., Hinder, M., Kuss, M., & Gassmann, O. (2020). The upside of being a digital pharma player. *Drug Discovery Today.* doi:10.1016/j.drudis.2020.06.002

Serfati, C. (2008). Financial dimensions of transnational corporations, global value chain and technological innovation. *Journal of Innovation Economics & Management, 2,* 35–61.

Smith, J. (2016). *Imperialism in the twenty-first century: Globalization, super-exploitation, and capitalism's final crisis.* New York University Press.

Stockhammer, E. (2013). *Why have wage shares fallen? A panel analysis of the determinants of functional income distribution: for the International Labour Organisation (ILO) project "New Perspectives on Wages and Economic Growth."* International Labour Organization.

Teixeira, R. A., & Rotta, T. N. (2012). Valueless knowledge-commodities and financialization: Productive and financial dimensions of capital autonomization. *Review of Radical Political Economics*, *44*(4), 448–67.

Veblen, T. (1899). *The theory of the leisure class: An economic theory of institutions.* Macmillan.

Veblen, T. (1908a). On the nature of capital. *The Quarterly Journal of Economics*, *22*(4), 517–42.

Veblen, T. (1908b). On the nature of capital: Investment, intangible assets, and the pecuniary magnate. *The Quarterly Journal of Economics*, *23*(1), 104–36.

World Intellectual Property Organization. (2019). *WIPO technology trends 2019. Artificial Intelligence.* WIPO.

Part 3

EFFECTS OF INTELLECTUAL MONOPOLY CAPITALISM ON THE PERIPHERIES

11

WHY WE NEED NEW DEVELOPMENT POLICIES UNDER INTELLECTUAL MONOPOLY CAPITALISM

1 Introduction

Organizations from peripheral[1] countries do not occupy a significant place in the innovation networks of the intellectual monopolies analysed in previous chapters. Nevertheless, this does not mean that they are exempted from the effects of intellectual monopoly capitalism, which we have argued is a global phenomenon. These effects are the focus of this book's final part. In this and the following chapters, we elaborate on how intellectual monopoly capitalism expands the gap between the centre(s) and the periphery(ies) by further limiting development opportunities in the latter while favouring value appropriation by the former.

Following the Dependency Theory, underdevelopment is twofold. It refers both to the peripheries' specific features and to the interplay between developed and underdeveloped countries (see for instance, the seminal work of Dos Santos, 1970). Building on this tradition, we elaborate on specificities of the peripheries *vis-à-vis* transformations in the core under intellectual monopoly capitalism. We highlight two new forms of unequal exchange (Amin, 1974; Emmanuel, 1972): knowledge extractivism and data extractivism, which can be considered as particular cases of what we call intangibles extractivism. These forms of extractivism may or may not take place as predatory practices defined as direct manifestations of superior force since, frequently, intangibles extractivism is a practice that goes unnoticed, as in the case of what will be called blind knowledge transfer in Chapter 13.

Knowledge extractivism refers to science and technology from the peripheries that are monetized in core countries, usually by corporate intellectual monopolies and eventually by academic intellectual monopolies. This form of extractivism mainly affects leading universities and public research organizations from so-called emerging or middle-income countries. Chapters 12 and 13 further elaborate on this form of extractivism for selected case studies.

Concerning data, we argue that a new layer in the international division of labour is emerging. It splits the world between raw data providers and a handful of data-driven intellectual monopolies (see Chapters 7 and 8). These corporations extract, process and analyse raw data, producing digital intelligence that is afterwards monetized (UNCTAD, 2019). Unprocessed data is valueless, but as continuous streams of data are centralized and processed with deep learning and neural networks, algorithms improve by themselves and learn faster. Peripheral countries (and even Europe) are net providers of raw data and pay for digital intelligence. Some authors conceive this unequal exchange as a new form of colonialism, dubbed data or digital colonialism since data is grabbed from around the world but monetized in a few companies from the United States with China in a (distant) second place (Couldry & Mejias, 2019a, 2019b; Kwet, 2019).

Intangibles extractivism result in a higher concentration of intangible assets in the hands of a few corporations from the core, which expands their rents at the expense of knowledge and data produced in the peripheries. A vicious cycle is established between intangibles extractivism and the lack of technological autonomy in the peripheries.

Hence, reviewing ways to overcome technological dependency becomes all the more critical under intellectual monopoly capitalism. To that end, this chapter assesses policy advice given by the National Innovation Systems' (NIS) approach, including Mazzucato's (2015) Entrepreneurial State. Additionally, the chapter analyses Global Value Chains (GVC) upgrading recommendation (Gereffi, 2014). We will do so in connection with catching-up as a strategy to develop technological capabilities (Pérez & Soete, 1988). All these frameworks are interconnected. As explained by Arocena (2018), both NIS and catching-up literature grew inspired by the experience of some East Asian countries. Furthermore, scholars working within all these frameworks have recognized that even if their communities have remained detached, they share a concern for development and the certainty that developing autonomous technological capabilities is indispensable for economic development. Attempts to combine innovation systems with GVC were driven by these objectives (Jurowetzki et al., 2018; Lema et al., 2019; Pietrobelli & Rabellotti, 2009, 2011).

The rest of this chapter is organized as follows. Section 2 overviews innovation studies as well as GVC upgrading policy recommendations for development. Next, Section 3 explores the conceptual limits of the overviewed policies under intellectual monopoly capitalism considering the historical traits of the peripheries. Section 4 concludes.

2 Policy recommendations for technological autonomy at the national and firm levels

2.1 *Innovation studies: the state as the architect of the system*

After the seminal work of Freeman (1982), the innovation systems' framework has conceptualized innovation as an interactive, uncertain and cumulative process (Johnson & Lundvall, 1994). Knowledge is at the basis of innovation systems, conceived as interactive learning environments (Lundvall, 2017), and takes different forms: know-what, why, how and who (Johnson & Lundvall, 1994). Another vital element of the innovation systems' concept is that it combines two modes of learning and innovation: the Science, Technology, and Innovation (STI) mode, with an experience-based mode of learning by Doing, Using, and Interacting (DUI-mode). The former is a science-based mode that connects science with technology, whereas the latter involves tacit-knowledge (Jensen et al., 2007).

Firms were conceived as the core of each innovation system. Nevertheless, the focus on innovation systems restricted to national borders, the National Innovation System (NIS), highlights the active role assigned to the state in the promotion of innovation (Lundvall, 1992; Nelson, 1993). The state participates in the definition of norms and standards that steer innovation, provides technological infrastructure and acts as the glue that brings the system together (Freeman, 1987; Lundvall, 1992). It was also observed that public policy – such as R&D investment, innovation incentives and investment in higher education including technical training – contributes to shaping national innovation capacity defined as a country's ability to produce and commercialize innovations that are *new-to-the-world* (Furman et al., 2002).

As synthesized by Chaminade et al. (2009), this literature distinguishes between mature and emerging NIS and suggests specific policy recommendations to deal with their respective systemic problems. The emerging system corresponds to developing or underdeveloped countries and is characterized by missing or weak links and components. According to Chaminade et al. (2009, p. 366), "only some of their building blocks are in place and (...) the interactions among the elements are still in formation and thus the system appears to be fragmented". In these cases, the NIS approach considers that states should create the necessary conditions for capability-building for innovation (Lundvall et al., 2009). It is assumed that once the links and components are in place, the NIS will mature, which is a condition for development.

Summing up, the state is the architect of the NIS. Its policies should contribute to building bridges and constructing missing components, thus solving systemic failures (Chaminade et al., 2009; Lee et al., 2014; World Bank, 2010). Lundvall (2017) explains that, in order to be at the frontier of global society's transformations, policies must ensure the creation, reshaping and demolition of industrial complexes. In a way, he is saying that the state should motorize or be the engine behind Schumpeter's (1934) creative destruction. The state is not supposed to be in charge of producing the innovations itself, even if it had done so, but to encourage both formal and informal interactions between different innovative actors and to build bridge institutions for articulating the links of the system (Di Meglio & López Bidone, 2010; Lundvall, 2002; Piqué, 2016; Wade, 2012).

Within innovation studies literature, keeping a systemic view that recognizes the central role assigned to the state, the entrepreneurial state approach has won momentum.

2.1.1 The entrepreneurial state

Mazzucato (2015) observes that the US state was an entrepreneur behind revolutionary innovations since the Cold War, from the internet to different prescription drugs. However, the returns of those major endeavours have been gathered by powerful corporations (such as Apple, Google and Big Pharmaceuticals), examples of what this book has conceived as intellectual monopolies.

According to Mazzucato (2015), the US tax system is not providing the expected returns for those investments due to tax avoidance, tax evasion and the global trait of contemporary capitalism. Therefore, she argues that when the state takes the risks that firms are not willing to take, the potential returns should not be exclusively appropriated by private firms. As a risk-taker, the state should receive part of those returns. To that end, she suggests creating different institutions that could provide a "risk-reward dynamic" with a more collective distribution of the rewards. Furthermore, she argues that this could contribute to equitable and stable growth as well as to trigger even more significant innovations. These arguments are picked up by the author in a later work where she insists on the government's responsibility to tilt the playing field setting the direction of change that will prompt bottom-up exploration, discovery and learning. In this later contribution, Mazzucato (2016) also points out that states must develop mechanisms to increase the risks taken by large companies in innovation processes.

***

Both approaches share a systemic view of innovation and the implicit conception of a state with at least some capacity to organize and govern the NIS. Besides, the innovation systems' literature has reconsidered NIS and policy recommendations under globalization. Resulting contributions include analyses of the intersections between NIS – with different degrees of completeness – and the place of local firms in GVC (Fagerberg et al., 2018; Jurowetzki et al., 2018; Pietrobelli & Rabellotti, 2009, 2011). The main policy recommendations for development given from a GVC perspective are overviewed next.

2.2 Global value chains and catching-up

Driven by Gereffi, GVC literature analyses governance within supply chains considering outsourcing and offshoring. Power relations are identified in the governance of the chain, particularly but not exclusively exercised by GVC leaders (Dallas et al., 2019; Gereffi, 2014; Gereffi et al., 1994, 2005; Ponte & Sturgeon, 2014; Sturgeon, 2009).

Its initial version as Global Commodity Chains conceived the role of the state as centrally focused on industrial and, especially, trade policies and international trade regulations (Bair, 2005). Policies ought to prevent value created inside a country from squeezing through international trade. However, this focus was somehow lost and upgrading in the chain became their main policy recommendation for emerging and underdeveloped countries. Upgrading in the GVC meant that local companies should move up the ladder in terms of value creation and capture within the chain (Gereffi, 2014; Giuliani et al., 2005; Humphrey & Schmitz, 2002; Lee & Gereffi, 2015). It requires local companies to absorb technology (Dedrick & Kraemer, 2015). Humphrey and Schmitz (2002) distinguished between process upgrading, product upgrading (manufacture a product with higher unit value), functional upgrading (increasing skills) and inter-chain upgrading (apply learned competencies from one chain to another one). Later, Bolwig et al. (2010) argued that assessments on GVC upgrading should also consider the effects on poverty, labour, gender and the environment.

Technological catching-up and leapfrogging could contribute to upgrading since they are conceived as strategies to reduce productivity gaps (Abramovitz, 1986; Fagerberg & Godinho, 2004; Lee & Lim, 2001; Lee & Malerba, 2017; Pérez & Soete, 1988). To this end, the role of the state has proven to be paramount in the experience of East Asian countries (Amsden, 1992; Lee & Lim, 2001).

In simple terms, when latecomers catch-up, they "follow the path of technological development of the advanced countries" (Lee & Lim, 2001, p. 460). Leapfrogging, on the contrary, involves skipping stages or creating new paths. According to Pérez and Soete (1988), leapfrogging results from windows of opportunity due to shifts in generations of technology. Latecomers can quickly adopt the new technology, while forerunners could be locked in existing technologies falling into the "incumbent trap". Lee (2013) reinforced this argument by stating that short cycle technologies (that change at high speed) offer greater catching-up opportunities if latecomers have at least some absorption capabilities. From this thesis, Lee and Malerba (2017, p. 346) state that windows of opportunity for latecomers spring from the reluctance of forerunners to adopt new technologies due to their higher costs.

Next, we reflect on the limitations of all the overviewed policy recommendations in the context of intellectual monopoly capitalism.

3 Shortfalls of innovation systems and GVC policy recommendations

We find two main shortfalls of the above-overviewed approaches, which are particularly relevant in the context of intellectual monopoly capitalism.

(i) They assume that peripheral countries' states have the enforcement capacity to regulate foreign corporations and (ii) do not sufficiently explore underdevelopment structural causes, in particular why firms operating in the peripheries have insufficient innovation and upgrading incentives.

(i) Intellectual monopoly capitalism renews the question on the bargaining power of states within and outside their frontiers. Overviewed frameworks recognize that multinational corporations accumulate technology and capture most of the chain's value. Hence, at least to some extent, developing a country's NIS and local firms upgrading in GVC will depend on the interplay with these foreign leaders. The state is supposed to regulate foreign companies and make them deploy their technology internally, favouring local companies' learning and adoption of new technologies. However, there are conceptual limitations and empirical evidence against the feasibility of this assumption (see Chapters 12 and 13). Since the spread of intellectual monopoly capitalism, the sole exception has been China. However, as we explained in Chapter 4, it was precisely China's exceptionality that gave its state the required power to protect its local firms from intellectual monopolies and, over time, leverage their success to expand its aspiring global hegemony further.

Peripheral countries also experience the direct pressures of core countries, depend on external financial support and face pressures to deregulate working conditions and lessen taxes to attract GVC leaders' offshoring and outsourcing. Crouch (2010) has argued that peripheral states lack the enforcement capacity to divert big corporations' aims when they operate inside their frontiers.

> When large corporations from the advanced countries invest in very poor countries, there is usually a major imbalance between the institutions of the corporations and those of the local state (Dixon et al., 1986; Ite, 2004; Rondinelli 2002). The former will be well equipped and staffed, with a high level of resources, and with clear hierarchies and internal procedures. The local state is likely to have very low levels of resources and poor means of internal communications and enforcement. In such circumstances it is very difficult for the local state to live up to the legal fiction that it constitutes an "authority" and the investing firm a private entity subject to its authority. The firm is likely to be able to pick and choose which local laws it obeys and which ignores, as enforcement and inspection are likely to be poor (Crouch, 2010, p. 163).

This critique mainly concerns the idea of creating an entrepreneurial state for development (Mazzucato, 2015; Mazzucato & Penna, 2016). As intellectual monopolies organize and plan global innovation networks exercising knowledge predation (see in particular Chapter 2 and Book's Section 2), the feasibility of an entrepreneurial state for the peripheries is seriously put into question. These are states without sufficient bargaining power to confront global corporations monopolizing access to knowledge. In fact, peripheral states end up subordinated due to local firms' lack of technological autonomy, while intellectual monopolies extract knowledge and data. Furthermore, given global tax avoidance and IPRs offshoring (Bryan et al., 2017; Pozsar, 2018), what are the odds of less powerful states when they attempt to regulate global intellectual monopolies?

(ii) Concerning local firms, innovation studies, GVC and catching-up frameworks recognize them – in general – as neither demanding nor actively performing in-house R&D (Albornoz et al., 2017; Arocena & Sutz, 2010; Rodrik, 2004, 2008). In the case of less developed countries, Pietrobelli and Rabelloti (2009, p. 214) added that most knowledge is imported.[2] Most of the firms operating in the peripheries are laggard companies in terms of productivity and value creation (Altenburg, 2009). However, these frameworks tend to assume that insufficient R&D investment could be counterbalanced by putting in place the right policies, such as those discussed earlier. We argue that their shortfall here comes from an incomplete analysis of the causes of local firms' lack of innovation or upgrading incentives.

In Latin America, experience shows that public R&D will not be complemented with private investments because local companies enjoy alternative sources of profits (ground rent, international debt and cheap labour) (Graña & Kennedy, 2017; Iñigo Carrera, 2007; Starosta, 2018). Moreover, in Africa and Latin America, entrepreneurship has been considered as supply-push, not led by the need to deploy a creative idea but pushed by unemployment (Fields, 1990; Mead, 1994). This lack of innovation capacity and the existence of alternative sources of profits raise even more doubts about the feasibility of policies aimed at connecting the NIS.

Firms that continuously enjoy alternative sources of profits will not be compelled to invest in R&D. As this practice extends in time, it will be reinforced by the absence of innovation skills. As global intellectual monopolies continuously innovate on the basis of their innovation networks, the technological gap will further widen. In fact, publicly funded R&D from non-core countries may end up contributing to expanding global intellectual monopolies' garnered rents (see Chapters 12 and 13).

Similar concerns had already been raised on the effects of transnational corporations' subsidiaries and the links with local firms. Where indigenous firms are not sufficiently competitive, transnational corporations tend to use non-core countries to locate routine activities or knowledge exploiting activities with few spillovers, or they leech off of local R&D efforts (Chaminade et al., 2009, p. 370). Hauge (2019) scrutinizes the experience of Ethiopia, dubbed the "African lion". He concludes that the world economy has changed since South Korea and Taiwan emerged as tigers. It is now more complicated to deploy industrial policy aimed at pushing or forcing foreign investors to transfer technology locally because transnational corporations have multiple suitable outsourcing locations. The author states that policies in Ethiopia have created carrots to attract multinationals (such as financial incentives) but did not create the stick (technology local spillovers and local content requirements, which are forbidden by the WTO). As a result, local firms are technologically dependent and laggards. Still, even with the right policies, Hauge (2019) recognizes that political and socio-economic dimensions will also be determinant factors in a country's potential for industrialization.

Hence, the conditions for GVC's value appropriation, as well as for the extraction of knowledge and data assetized by intellectual monopolies from the core, are not only explained by intellectual monopolies' planning capacities (as conceptualized in the first two parts of this book). They are also found in the specificities of the peripheries, in particular in the production structure of these countries.

In the rest of this section, we address specific limitations of each of the overviewed policy recommendations.

3.1 Not an emerging but a structurally incomplete innovation system

The NIS concept was introduced for explaining the experience of Japan (Freeman, 1987) and looking at Denmark's case for inspiration (Lundvall, 2017, Chapter 14). In the peripheries, the concept was applied ex-ante, extrapolated from the experiences of industrialized and some newly industrialized countries. Only a few behavioural patterns regarding innovation could have been considered as working in a system-like manner when the concept gained space in public speeches, policies and academic literature (Arocena & Sutz, 2000; Dutrénit & Puchet, 2017; Intrakumnerdi & Chaminade, 2007). Dutrénit and Puchet (2017) recognize that various STI indicators improved in many developing countries due to the policies promoted by the OECD to build NIS. However, the authors emphasize that success has been limited, and high levels of inequality, poverty and exclusion remain.

The innovation systems' literature accurately assesses these countries' innovation capabilities. They identify missing links and components and recognize difficulties for overcoming these constraints. However, they tend to jump too quickly to the policies that should be implemented in order to build mature NIS such as those of core countries, without sufficiently analysing why links and components are missing (the disease/s). This leads to overestimating the chances to evolve from an emerging to a mature innovation system.[3]

The NIS literature identifies that private firms do not have incentives to innovate in developing countries. However, before sufficiently delving into the reasons of the latter, prevailing policy recommendations promote private firms' R&D investment (through tax exemptions, public procurement, funding public-private partnerships, among others). A related and unanswered question is why do firms from these countries survive given that

– overall – they systematically lag in terms of production techniques? Given that innovation and production are organized beyond national borders, to what extent and how is global capitalism limiting non-core countries' development of indigenous innovation capabilities?

A preliminary answer was provided above: local firms survive through alternative sources of profit. Those firms that do not exclusively rely on these forms of valorization, have shortened their productivity gap but still typically occupy subordinate places in GVC. Hence, innovation policies should be complemented with policies that curtail alternative sources of profits and that limit value appropriation from global leaders acting as intellectual monopolies.

In the best-case scenario, as Arocena (2018, p. 7) argues for the peripheries, relatively few companies participate in the NIS, which are those that can take profit from existing innovation policies. Most firms (either complier or laggard companies, see Chapter 2) use public innovation incentives for DUI-learning. Policies become an opportunity to expand profits in the short-term without achieving structural changes. It is unclear how these firms could move from DUI-learning towards STI-learning. Viotti (2002) had argued that, in the peripheries, there is no genuine innovation but only incremental innovation, diffusion and learning. Under intellectual monopoly capitalism, this seems to be all the more true because the speed of technological change driven by these corporations may further restrain indigenous innovation regardless of R&D incentives provided by the state.

3.2 Further limitations to the entrepreneurial state

The entrepreneurial state proposal, and to some extent the NIS literature, tends to downplay that conflicts and political interests are at stake in every innovation process. In non-core countries, power relationships not only include the actors of the NIS but also pressures from core countries' states and international organizations.

In more concrete terms, among specific policy recommendations, Mazzucato (2015) suggested that states should receive a golden share of IPRs of innovations that they contributed to achieving. This policy does not seem effective to reap intellectual rents for several reasons. Intellectual monopolies cross-licence their patents. Therefore, they neither collect nor pay significant royalties, which could then be shared with the state. Moreover, they get most of their intellectual rents from sales associated with their innovations and not from royalties (see Chapter 12). On the contrary, innovating firms (such as start-ups) significantly profit from royalties but they are mostly concentrated in core countries. It is there, as shown by Balland et al. (2020), where IPRs are concentrated. Besides, intellectual monopolies declare intellectual property where they are not taxed and even create shell corporations that own IPRs (see Chapter 7, on Apple). Solving tax avoidance requires a global effort that is way beyond a single (non-core) state capacity.

A second suggestion, income-contingent loans, does not consider that leader corporations are characterized by financial strength; they actually accumulate idle funds in tax havens (see Chapter 10). This is particularly the case of high-tech and pharmaceutical corporations (Dolata, 2017, 2019; Montalban & Sakinç, 2013). Financial strength reinforces intellectual monopoly power and acts as another barrier for newcomers. Furthermore, core-countries' intellectual monopolies operating abroad do not need state financial support albeit they sometimes profit from state benefits when settling in different territories.

Income-contingent loans could benefit small companies but will not reap intellectual monopolies' garnered rents. So far, promising start-ups, conceptualized as subordinate innovating companies in this book (Chapter 2), mostly rely on venture capital. These funds, more often than not, come from intellectual monopolies that may eventually acquire them. Fintech, in particular by big corporations, is becoming another funding alternative (Frost et al., 2019; Stulz, 2019). In this respect, Jacobs and Mazzucato's (2016) proposal of State Investment Banks (SIB) could play a role in replacing these sources of funding. However, it will not reap intellectual rents from established intellectual monopolies extracting knowledge from the peripheries.

Funding constraints primarily affect laggard companies in the peripheries; SIB could contribute to overcome the effects of macroeconomic instability on these firms and also foster the adoption of existing technology by facilitating tangible capital expenditures. However, given that these companies lack innovation incentives and capabilities, it is far from straightforward that funding will be used to effectively catch-up. Moreover, Gallagher and Yuan (2017) show that in Latin America, more than 40% of SIB funds between 2007 and 2014 were restricted to energy and infrastructure projects that were fossil-fuel intensive and accelerate climate change and pollution. In line with the first critique we made to the entrepreneurial state approach in this sub-heading, this experience shows why political power relationships driven by economic interests cannot be left outside innovation analysis and policy recommendations. Innovation is not always synonymous with progress.

3.3 Downgrading and global poverty chains

GVC leaders are intellectual monopolies. As further developed in Chapters 2 and 7, they exclusively *know-who* can do what and *know-how* to plan and organize the chain. Following Durand and Milberg (2020), this intangible asset triggers vertical natural monopoly rents from network externalities. Leaders also exclusively know-how (Johnson & Lundvall, 1994) to handle inventories and data along the supply chain. Additionally, they often have legal monopolies over the technologies and trademarks of the whole chain, such as in garment and high-tech industries. In this context, upgrading has slim chances of success, as found by several recent studies (Carballa et al., 2020; Selwyn, 2019; Selwyn et al., 2019; Smith, 2016; Suwandi, 2019).

According to Selwyn (2019), GVC analysis recommends upgrading because it assumes that poor countries' low wages reflect low productivity levels. He explains that these arguments do not distinguish between national average productivity (which are often relatively low) and the productivity of the firms participating in GVC. Moreover, they depart from a wrong assumption, which is that workers are paid according to the value they produce. Thus, lower wages are supposed to signal lower productivity and lower value creation. On the contrary, following a Marxian tradition, he continues arguing that the productivity-wage relation is primarily determined "by labour's social reproduction costs and by the balance of power between capital and labour" (Selwyn, 2019, p. 82). Among the provided examples, Mexican maquilas and Foxconn's Chinese operations stand out. The latter case is also explored by Smith (2016), who raises a similar point for the case of Bangladeshi workers and the garment industry. He states that low wages are what render high mark-ups possible. The same argument is explored by Suwandi (2019) for the experience of Indonesia. All these authors emphasize the prevalence of imperialist relations of exchange to explain how companies from the core appropriate a portion of the value produced in the peripheries.

In line with these findings, recent work under the Global Production Network (GPN) framework has emphasized that, in terms of economic development, tracking value capturing trajectories within GPN is more important than the locations of value production (Yeung & Coe, 2015). We thus argue that understanding the distinction between value creation and capturing, given predatory relations established by intellectual monopolies, is of utmost importance (see Chapters 2 and 10).

The pressures exercised by GVC leaders on suppliers also undermine workplace health and safety (Smith, 2016). A particular discussion in this respect concerns the promotion of industries with adverse effects on development, such as the mining GVC. Mining techniques used in the peripheries have harmful effects on health and the environment (Eisler, 2003; Machado et al., 2011). Still, some authors suggest upgrading in this GVC as a strategy for opening windows of opportunity for innovative local suppliers (Iizuka et al., 2019; Pietrobelli et al., 2018). Even if upgrading is accomplished and eventually local companies become leaders of mining GVCs, this leading role will expand the megamining industry, together with its adverse effects on development, including the generation of disease like cancer and pollution.

At the macroeconomic level, Carballa et al. (2020) studied the relationship between participating in GVC and three dimensions of upgrading: value capture, investment and social upgrading. Their findings point to three types of countries: the social upgrading mirage, the reproduction of the core and immiserizing growth. Countries from the first group are relatively isolated from the GVC dynamics, and their success during the authors' analysed period is mostly explained by the commodity boom (Latin America and Africa) and financial inflows (Europe's periphery). The second group shows how GVCs have contributed to the reproduction of the core, where the value captured is high and disconnected from tangible capital expenditure. Finally, the third group comprises countries that rapidly joined the GVC, with higher tangible capital accumulation (most of the Asian and Eastern European countries). In these countries, social outcomes are weak and the appropriation of value is lower than in the core. The authors conclude that GVCs have contributed to deepening the gaps between countries.

Beyond studied cases, upgrading presents additional limitations under intellectual monopoly capitalism due to the limits imposed on the circulation of knowledge. Finally, the last decade has shown a slowdown in GVC trade (Shin, 2019; World Bank, 2020) that accelerated with the US-China trade war (Ernst, 2020) and the CoVid-19 pandemic. Simultaneously, there has been an acceleration of the globalization of intangibles, led by the digital economy. This scenario highlights that other dynamics than GVC should be considered at the global level.

3.4 Intellectual monopolies narrow windows of opportunity

A solution for the overviewed shortfalls of GVC upgrading could be to remain outside GVC during a period within the catching-up process. Lee (2019) summarizes this strategy as *in-out-in*. However, not only GVCs undermine catching-up opportunities but the extended and expanding knowledge monopoly of contemporary leading corporations.

Global intellectual monopolies systematically innovate at a too-fast a pace to be reached. Moreover, they use patents to limit competition and when choosing suppliers, they may share their technology but then capture most of the resulting value (Coe & Yeung, 2015; Foley, 2013; Rikap, 2019; Yeung & Coe, 2015). Outsourcing (of manufacturing and innovation) may further limit latecomers' opportunities because the extra costs associated with the adoption of a new production technique (and the uncertainty of developing new technology) can be diverted to other links of the network (as shown in the previous sections of this book). Therefore, windows of opportunity for catching-up or leapfrogging shrink even more. As Lee and Lim (2001) and Li et al. (2019) had concluded, in industries with higher innovation rhythm, catching-up opportunities are limited.

A further limitation concerns the idea of windows of opportunity. It is implicitly assumed that the new technology was produced outside of the forerunner, who will decide whether to adopt it or not.[4] What is not considered in this argument is that intellectual monopolies plan and organize production and innovation networks, blurring the frontier between producer and user of the new technology. It is not the intellectual monopoly, but the complier and laggard companies participating in its production networks that will have to decide whether to adopt new technological requirements to remain as suppliers. Hence, when the segment of the production process where innovation is taking place is outsourced, it is not the forerunner who is challenged by the new technology but often a latecomer without technological autonomy that operates as the former's supplier.

If, regardless of global intellectual monopolies, a peripheral country succeeds in promoting national champions, an additional shortfall should be considered. The promotion of national champions does not automatically lead to develop innovation capabilities at the level of the whole country. Barnard et al. (2009) observed that Korean champions played a limited role in the development of the country's NIS, mainly because the technological gap with the rest of the firms was too broad. Besides, Korea's experience should be contextualized. Japan was interested in its industrialization in order to integrate both economies and become stronger in its dispute against China (Kvangraven, 2020).

The same could be said about Huawei and other *national champions* from China. So far, catching-up in China is mostly concentrated in some enterprises from a few industries (Godinho & Ferreira, 2012; Gu et al., 2016; Guo et al., 2019; Hawes & Chew, 2011; Humphrey et al., 2018; Li et al., 2019; Li & Cheong, 2017; Wen, 2017; Wu & Gereffi, 2018). Furthermore, as explained in Chapters 4 and 9, China is a unique case due to the size of its internal market and its place in what used to be the new international division of labour (Fröbel et al., 1980; Milberg & Winkler, 2013). Moreover, since GVC-trade has been shrinking for more than a decade, it is highly unlikely even for India, with similar conditions as those that led to the emergence of Chinese intellectual monopolies, to undergo a similar experience.

All in all, successful catching-up experiences in some industries from selected countries should always be contextualized. As Kvangraven (2020) points out, it is a mistake to directly assume that enough policy space to copy dubbed successful experiences would suffice for GVC upgrading or catching-up. The politics, institutions, internal history and place of each country in global capitalism push countries that directly apply these policies to a dead end.

4 Final remarks

In this chapter, we started to delve into the implications of intellectual monopoly capitalism on the peripheries. We pointed out that two new forms of extractivism emerge: knowledge and data extractivism as specific cases of intangibles extractivism.

On this basis, and considering the results of previous sections, we analysed the limitations of innovation, GVC and catching-up studies to fully acknowledge the global and local context faced by the peripheries.

We argued that policy recommendations focus on treating symptoms. The NIS focuses on incomplete NIS and the entrepreneurial state approach argues that the problem is that states do not garner rewards from their investment in R&D. This book is an attempt to move beyond these symptoms. Understanding the specificities of the peripheries *vis-à-vis* core countries as well as introducing conflict and political tensions in the organization of innovation systems are indispensable for understanding the interplay between a peripheral state and global intellectual monopolies.

At the firm level, upgrading in a GVC and catching-up or leapfrogging were also evaluated. We argued that intellectual monopoly capitalism has further limited knowledge circulation deepening the subordination of peripheral countries' firms participating in the GVC.

Policies are elements of the social process, which thus depend on a country's *context and production relations*, something Schumpeter (1942, p. 108) identified as a point of agreement with Marx. In this vein, policy recommendations should evolve with the context, acknowledging the limitations of existing states as well as the fact that states are contested territories. More often than not, they will be representing the interests of dominant classes, favouring the spread of intellectual monopoly capitalism. Grassroots movements and other forms of social organizations are of utmost importance, not only in the peripheries, to push for counterbalancing trends (see Chapter 14).

In the following chapters, we delve into intangibles extractivism in order to conceptualize further the peripheries' *context and production relations.*

Notes

1 In Chapter 1 we explained that we refer to core and peripheral countries because we include China in the core, which is not a developed country. Moreover, the persistence of divergence brought into question the idea of "developing countries" which implicitly refers to a progression towards development. In addition, given the heterogeneities within the core and the periphery, we use these concepts in plural.

2 For instance, Africa's pharmaceutical imports represent between 70% and 90% of its consumption (Campbell, 2020).

3 An innovation system could be emerging towards a mature system but could also be evolving towards a more dependent and incomplete system, or even remain static for extremely long periods. Even mature NIS could become weaker. For instance, when global intellectual monopolies offshore links of their innovation networks, they may leave behind or weaken links with institutions from their home country.

4 "The incumbent who commands the highest productivity from existing technologies finds no reason to adopt new technologies" (Lee & Malerba, 2017, p. 346).

References

Abramovitz, M. (1986). Catching up, forging ahead, and falling behind. *The Journal of Economic History*, *46*(2), 385–406.

Albornoz, M., Barrere, R., & Sokil, J. (2017). Las Universidades Lideran la I+D en América Latina. In Albornoz, M. (Ed.) *El Estado de la Ciencia 2017* (pp. 31–44). RICyT.

Altenburg, T. (2009). Building inclusive innovation systems in developing countries: Challenges for IS research. In B. A. Lundvall, K. Joseph, C. Chaminade, & J. Vang (Eds.), *Handbook of innovation systems and developing countries: Building domestic capabilities in a global setting* (pp. 33–56). Edward Elgar.

Amin, S. (1974). *Accumulation on a world scale: A critique of the theory of underdevelopment.* Monthly Review Press.

Amsden, A. H. (1992). *Asia's next giant: South Korea and late industrialization.* Oxford University Press on Demand.

Arocena, R. (2018). Power, innovation systems and development. *Innovation and Development*, *8*(2), 271–85.

Arocena, R., & Sutz, J. (2000). Looking at national systems of innovation from the South. *Industry and Innovation*, *7*(1), 55–75.

Arocena, R., & Sutz, J. (2010). Weak knowledge demand in the South: Learning divides and innovation policies. *Science and Public Policy*, *37*(8), 571–82.

Balland, P.-A., Jara-Figueroa, C., Petralia, S. G., Steijn, M. P., Rigby, D. L., & Hidalgo, C. A. (2020). Complex economic activities concentrate in large cities. *Nature Human Behaviour*, *4*(3), 248–254.

Bair, J. (2005). Global capitalism and commodity chains: Looking back, going forward. *Competition & Change*, *9*(2), 153–80.

Barnard, H., Bromfield, T., & Cantwell, J. (2009). The role of indigenous firms in innovation systems in developing countries: The developmental implications of national champion Firms' response to underdeveloped National Innovation Systems. In Bengt-Åke Lundvall & K. J. Joseph & Cristina Chaminade & Jan Vang (Eds.) *Handbook of Innovation Systems and Developing Countries: Building domestic capabilities in a global setting* (pp. 391–440). Edward Elgar Publishing.

Bolwig, S., Ponte, S., Du Toit, A., Riisgaard, L., & Halberg, N. (2010). Integrating poverty and environmental concerns into value-chain analysis: A conceptual framework. *Development Policy Review*, *28*(2), 173–94.

Bryan, D., Rafferty, M., & Wigan, D. (2017). Capital unchained: Finance, intangible assets and the double life of capital in the offshore world. *Review of International Political Economy*, *24*(1), 56–86.

Campbell, J. (2020, May 22). *Scaling up African pharmaceutical manufacturing in a time of COVID-19.* https://www.cfr.org/blog/scaling-african-pharmaceutical-manufacturing-time-covid-19

Carballa Smichowski, B., Durand, C., & Knauss, S. (2020). Participation in global value chains and varieties of development patterns. Cambridge Journal of Economics. https://doi.org/10.1093/cje/beaa046

Chaminade, C., Lundvall, B. A., Vang, J., & Joseph, K. J. (2009). Designing innovation policies for development: Towards a systemic experimentation-based approach. In Bengt-Åke Lundvall & K. J. Joseph & Cristina Chaminade & Jan Vang (Eds.) *Handbook on innovation systems and developing countries: Building domestic capabilities in a global setting* (pp. 360–79). Edward Elgar Publishing.

Coe, N. M., & Yeung, H. W. C. (2015). *Global production networks: Theorizing economic development in an interconnected world.* Oxford University Press.

Couldry, N., & Mejias, U. A. (2019a). Data colonialism: Rethinking big data's relation to the contemporary subject. *Television & New Media*, *20*(4), 336–49.

Couldry, N., & Mejias, U. A. (2019b). *The costs of connection: How data is colonizing human life and appropriating it for capitalism*. Stanford University Press.

Crouch, C. (2010). The global firm: The problem of the giant firm in democratic capitalism. In Coen, D., Grant, W. and Wilson, G. *The Oxford handbook of business and government* (pp. 148–72). Oxford University Press.

Dallas, M. P., Ponte, S., & Sturgeon, T. J. (2019). Power in global value chains. *Review of International Political Economy*, *26*(4), 666–94.

Dedrick, J., & Kraemer, K. L. (2015). Who captures value from science-based innovation? The distribution of benefits from GMR in the hard disk drive industry. *Research Policy*, *44*(8), 1615–28.

Di Meglio, F., & López Bidone, E. (2010). Contribuciones al proceso innovativo regional a partir de la vinculación Universidad-Empresa. Caso de estudio: Polo informático UNICEN. In G. Campos, F. Piñero, & S. Figueroa (Eds.), *Transformaciones Recientes de las Universidades Latinoamericanas. Agendas y Actores en la producción de Conocimiento* (pp. 217–46). BUAP-UNCPBA-UAZ.

Dolata, U. (2017). *Apple, Amazon, Google, Facebook, Microsoft: Market concentration-competition-innovation strategies*. Stuttgarter Beiträge zur Organisations-und Innovationsforschung, SOI ....

Dolata, U. (2019). Privatization, curation, commodification. *Österreichische Zeitschrift Für Soziologie*, *44*(1), 181–97.

Dos Santos, T. (1970). The structure of dependence. *The American Economic Review*, *60*(2), 231–6.

Durand, C., & Milberg, W. (2020). Intellectual monopoly in global value chains. *Review of International Political Economy*, *27*(2), 404–429. doi:10.1080/09692290.2019.1660703

Dutrénit, G., & Puchet, M. (2017). Tensions of science, technology and innovation policy in Mexico: Analytical models, institutional evolution, national capabilities and governance. In Kuhlmann, S. and Ordóñez-Matamoros, G. *Research handbook on innovation governance for emerging economies*. Edward Elgar Publishing 205–231.

Eisler, R. (2003). Health risks of gold miners: A synoptic review. *Environmental Geochemistry and Health*, *25*(3), 325–45.

Emmanuel, A. (1972). *Unequal exchange* (Vol. 1). Monthly Review Press.

Ernst, D. (2020). *Competing in artificial intelligence chips: China's challenge amid technology war*. Centre for International Governance Innovation.

Fagerberg, J., & Godinho, M. M. (2004). *Innovation and catching-up*. Georgia Institute of Technology.

Fagerberg, J., Lundvall, B., & Srholec, M. (2018). Global value chains, national innovation systems and economic development. *The European Journal of Development Research*, *30*(3), 533–56.

Fields, G. S. (1990). *Labour market modelling and the urban informal sector: Theory and evidence*. In D. Turnham, B. Salomé, & A. Schwarz (Eds.) The informal sector revisited (pp. 49–69). Organisation for Economic Co-operation and Development.

Foley, D. K. (2013). Rethinking financial capitalism and the "information" economy. *Review of Radical Political Economics*, *45*(3), 257–68.

Freeman, C. (1987). *Technology policy and economic performance*. Pinter Publishers. http://tocs.ulb.tu-darmstadt.de/122470664.pdf

Fröbel, F., Heinrichs, J., & Kreye, O. (1980). *The new international division of labour: Structural unemployment in industrialised countries and industrialisation in developing countries.* Cambridge University Press.

Frost, J., Gambacorta, L., Huang, Y., Shin, H. S., & Zbinden, P. (2019). *BigTech and the changing structure of financial intermediation.* Bank of International Settlements.

Furman, J. L., Porter, M. E., & Stern, S. (2002). The determinants of national innovative capacity. *Research Policy, 31*(6), 899–933.

Gallagher, K. P., & Yuan, F. (2017). Standardizing sustainable development: A comparison of development banks in the Americas. *The Journal of Environment & Development, 26*(3), 243–71.

Gereffi, G. (2014). Global value chains in a post-Washington Consensus world. *Review of International Political Economy, 21*(1), 9–37.

Gereffi, G., Humphrey, J., & Sturgeon, T. (2005). The governance of global value chains. *Review of International Political Economy, 12*(1), 78–104.

Gereffi, G., Korzeniewicz, M., & Korzeniewicz, R. P. (1994). Global commodity chains. In Gereffi, G., Korzeniewicz, M (Eds.) *Commodity chains and global capitalism* (pp. 1–14). Praeger.

Giuliani, E., Pietrobelli, C., & Rabellotti, R. (2005). Upgrading in global value chains: Lessons from Latin American clusters. *World Development, 33*(4), 549–73.

Godinho, M. M., & Ferreira, V. (2012). Analyzing the evidence of an IPR take-off in China and India. *Research Policy, 41*(3), 499–511.

Graña, J. M., & Kennedy, D. (2017). Rezago productivo y sus fuentes de compensación. La vigencia de los limitantes estructurales del ciclo económico argentino al comienzo del siglo XXI. *Cuadernos Del CENDES, 34*(95), 91–116.

Gu, S., Schwaag Serger, S., & Lundvall, B. A. (2016). China's innovation system: Ten years on. *Innovation, 18*(4), 441–8.

Guo, L., Zhang, M. Y., Dodgson, M., & Gann, D. (2019). Huawei's catch-up in the global telecommunication industry: Innovation capability and transition to leadership. *Technology Analysis & Strategic Management, 31*(12), 1395–1411.

Hauge, J. (2019). Should the African lion learn from the Asian tigers? A comparative-historical study of FDI-oriented industrial policy in Ethiopia, South Korea and Taiwan. *Third World Quarterly, 40*(11), 2071–91.

Hawes, C., & Chew, E. (2011). The cultural transformation of large Chinese enterprises into internationally competitive corporations: Case studies of Haier and Huawei. *Journal of Chinese Economic and Business Studies, 9*(1), 67–83.

Humphrey, J., Ding, K., Fujita, M., Hioki, S., & Kimura, K. (2018). Platforms, innovation and capability development in the Chinese domestic market. *The European Journal of Development Research, 30*(3), 408–23.

Humphrey, J., & Schmitz, H. (2002). How does insertion in global value chains affect upgrading in industrial clusters? *Regional Studies, 36*(9), 1017–27.

Iizuka, M., Pietrobelli, C., & Vargas, F. (2019). *The potential for innovation in mining value chains. Evidence from Latin America.* United Nations University-Maastricht Economic and Social Research Institute.

Iñigo Carrera, J. (2007). *La formación económica de la sociedad argentina. Volumen I, Renta agraria, ganancia industrial y deuda externa. 1882–2004.* Imago Mundi.

Intrakumnerdi, P., & Chaminade, C. (2007/09). *Innovation system policies in less successful developing countries: The case of Thailand.* Centre for Innovation, Research and Competence in the Learning Economy (CIRCLE), Lund University.

Jacobs, M., & Mazzucato, M. (2016). *Rethinking capitalism: Economics and policy for sustainable and inclusive growth*. John Wiley & Sons.

Jensen, M. B., Johnson, B., Lorenz, E., & Lundvall, B. A. (2007). Forms of knowledge and modes of innovation. In Lundvall, B. A. (Ed.) *The Learning Economy and the Economics of Hope* (pp. 155–82). Anthem.

Johnson, B., & Lundvall, B. A. (1994). The learning economy. *Journal of Industry Studies, 1*(2), 23–42.

Jurowetzki, R., Lema, R., & Lundvall, B. (2018). Combining innovation systems and global value chains for development: Towards a research agenda. *The European Journal of Development Research, 30*(3), 364–88.

Kvangraven, I. H. (2020). Beyond the stereotype: Restating the relevance of the dependency research programme. *Development and Change*, 1–37. doi:10.1111/dech.12593

Kwet, M. (2019). Digital colonialism: US empire and the new imperialism in the Global South. *Race & Class, 60*(4), 3–26.

Lee, J., & Gereffi, G. (2015). Global value chains, rising power firms and economic and social upgrading. *Critical Perspectives on International Business, 11*(3/4), 319–39.

Lee, K. (2013). *Schumpeterian analysis of economic catch-up: Knowledge, path-creation, and the middle-income trap*. Cambridge University Press.

Lee, K. (2019). *The art of economic catch-up: Barriers, detours and leapfrogging in innovation systems*. Cambridge University Press.

Lee, K., Juma, C., & Mathews, J. (2014). Innovation capabilities for sustainable development in Africa. In Monga, C. and Lin, J (Eds.), *The Oxford handbook of Africa and economics. Volume 2.* (pp. 272–86). Oxford University Press.

Lee, K., & Lim, C. (2001). Technological regimes, catching-up and leapfrogging: Findings from the Korean industries. *Research Policy, 30*(3), 459–83.

Lee, K., & Malerba, F. (2017). Catch-up cycles and changes in industrial leadership: Windows of opportunity and responses of firms and countries in the evolution of sectoral systems. *Research Policy, 46*(2), 338–51.

Lema, R., Pietrobelli, C., & Rabellotti, R. (2019). Innovation in global value chains. In Ponte, S., Gereffi, G., and Raj-Reichert, G (Eds.) *Handbook on global value chains* (pp. 370–384). Edward Elgar Publishing.

Li, D., Capone, G., & Malerba, F. (2019). The long march to catch-up: A history-friendly model of China's mobile communications industry. *Research Policy, 48*(3), 649–64. doi:10.1016/j.respol.2018.10.019

Li, R., & Cheong, K.-C. (2017). Huawei and ZTE in Malaysia: The localisation of Chinese transnational enterprises. *Journal of Contemporary Asia, 47*(5), 752–73.

Lundvall, B. A. (1992). *National systems of innovation: Toward a theory of innovation and interactive learning* (Vol. 2). Pinter Publishers.

Lundvall, B. A. (2002). The university in the learning economy. *Presentation on the Future Role of Universities, Strasbourg, 26*, 1–31.

Lundvall, B. A. (2017). *The learning economy and the economics of hope*. Anthem Press.

Lundvall, B. A., Vang, J., Joseph, K. J., & Chaminade, C. (2009). Innovation system research and developing countries. In Bengt-Åke Lundvall & K. J. Joseph & Cristina Chaminade & Jan Vang (Eds.) *Handbook on innovation systems and developing countries: Building domestic capabilities in a global setting* (pp. 1–31). Edward Elgar Publishing.

Machado, H., Svampa, M., Viale, E., Giraud, M., Wagner, L., Antonelli, M., Giarracca, N., & Teubal, M. (2011). *15 mitos y realidades de la minería transnacional en la Argentina*. Editorial El Colectivo-Ediciones Herramienta.

Mazzucato, M. (2015). *The entrepreneurial state: Debunking public vs. private sector myths* (Vol. 1). Anthem Press.

Mazzucato, M. (2016). From market fixing to market-creating: A new framework for innovation policy. *Industry and Innovation*, *23*(2), 140–56.

Mazzucato, M., & Penna, C. (2016). *The Brazilian innovation system: A mission-oriented policy proposal*. Centro de Gestão e Estudos Estratégicos.

Mead, D. C. (1994). The contribution of small enterprises to employment growth in Southern and Eastern Africa. *World Development*, *22*(12), 1881–94.

Milberg, W., & Winkler, D. (2013). *Outsourcing economics: Global value chains in capitalist development*. Cambridge University Press.

Montalban, M., & Sakinç, M. E. (2013). Financialization and productive models in the pharmaceutical industry. *Industrial and Corporate Change*, *22*(4), 981–1030.

Nelson, R. R. (1993). *National innovation systems: A comparative analysis*. Oxford university press.

Pérez, C., & Soete, L. (1988). Catching up in technology: Entry barriers and windows of opportunity. In G. Dosi, C. Freeman, R. R. Nelson, G. Silverberg, & L. Soete (Eds.), *Technical change and economic theory* (pp. 458–79). Francis Pinter.

Pietrobelli, C., Marin, A., & Olivari, J. (2018). Innovation in mining value chains: New evidence from Latin America. *Resources Policy*, *58*, 1–10.

Pietrobelli, C., & Rabellotti, R. (2009). The global dimension of innovation systems: Linking innovation systems and global value chains. In Bengt-Åke Lundvall & K. J. Joseph & Cristina Chaminade & Jan Vang (Eds.) *Handbook of innovation systems and developing countries: Building domestic capabilities in a global setting* (pp. 214–40). Edward Elgar Publishing.

Pietrobelli, C., & Rabellotti, R. (2011). Global value chains meet innovation systems: Are there learning opportunities for developing countries? *World Development*, *39*(7), 1261–69.

Piqué, M. P. (2016). Sistema Nacional de Innovación y la planificación de los subsistemas de capital. La política tecnológica como capítulo de una estrategia de desarrollo en el presente latinoamericano. *Enfoques*, *27*(1), 143–62.

Ponte, S., & Sturgeon, T. (2014). Explaining governance in global value chains: A modular theory-building effort. *Review of International Political Economy*, *21*(1), 195–223.

Pozsar, Z. (2018). Repatriation, the echo-taper and the €/$ basis. *Global Money Notes*, *11*. Credit Suisse.

Rikap, C. (2019). Asymmetric power of the core: Technological cooperation and technological competition in the transnational innovation networks of big pharma. *Review of International Political Economy*, *26*(5), 987–1021. doi:10.1080/09692290.2019.1620309

Rodrik, D. (2004). *Industrial policy for the twenty-first century*. Available at SSRN: https://ssrn.com/abstract=666808

Rodrik, D. (2008). *One economics, many recipes: Globalization, institutions, and economic growth*. Princeton University Press.

Schumpeter, J. A. (1934). *The theory of economic development: An inquiry into profits, capital, credit, interest, and the business cycle* (Vol. 55). Transaction Publishers.

Schumpeter, J. A. (1942). *Capitalism, socialism and democracy*. Routledge.

Selwyn, B. (2019). Poverty chains and global capitalism. *Competition & Change, 23*(1), 71–97.

Selwyn, B., Musiolek, B., & Ijarja, A. (2019). Making a global poverty chain: Export footwear production and gendered labor exploitation in Eastern and Central Europe. *Review of International Political Economy, 27*(2), 377–403.

Shin, H. S. (2019). *What is behind the recent slowdown?* Bank of International Settlements.

Smith, J. (2016). *Imperialism in the twenty-first century: Globalization, super-exploitation, and capitalism's final crisis*. New York University Press.

Starosta, G. (2018). Global capital accumulation and the specificity of Latin America. In M. Vidal, T. Smith, T. Rotta, & P. Prew (Eds.), *The Oxford handbook of Karl Marx* (pp. 710–29). Oxford University Press.

Stulz, R. M. (2019). *FinTech, BigTech, and the future of banks*. National Bureau of Economic Research.

Sturgeon, T. J. (2009). From commodity chains to value chains: Interdisciplinary theory building in an age of globalization. In J. Bair (Ed.), *Frontiers of commodity chain research* (pp. 110–35). Stanford University Press. http://isapapers.pitt.edu/84/

Suwandi, I. (2019). *Value chains: The new economic imperialism*. Monthly Review Press.

UNCTAD. (2019). *Digital Economy Report 2019: Value creation and capture–Implications for developing countries*. United Nations.

Viotti, E. B. (2002). National learning systems: A new approach on technological change in late industrializing economies and evidences from the cases of Brazil and South Korea. *Technological Forecasting and Social Change, 69*(7), 653–80.

Wade, R. H. (2012). Return of industrial policy? *International Review of Applied Economics, 26*(2), 223–39.

Wen, Y. (2017). *The rise of Chinese transnational ICT corporations: The Case of Huawei* [PhD Thesis]. Communication, Art & Technology: School of Communication.

World Bank. (2010). *Innovation policy: A guide for developing countries*. World Bank Publications.

World Bank. (2020). *World Development Report 2020: Trading for development in the age of global value chains*. World Bank Publications.

Wu, X., & Gereffi, G. (2018). Amazon and Alibaba: Internet governance, business models, and internationalization strategies. In van Tulder, R., Verbeke, A. and Piscitello, L. (Eds.) *International business in the information and digital age* (pp. 327–56). Emerald Publishing Limited.

Yeung, H. W., & Coe, N. M. (2015). Toward a dynamic theory of global production networks. *Economic Geography, 91*(1), 29–58.

12

SINGAPORE'S INNOVATION HUB. A SOURCE OF RENTS FOR INTELLECTUAL MONOPOLIES*

1 Introduction

Different cities around the world (such as London, New York, Shenzhen, Qatar and Singapore) are emerging as innovation hubs (Belderbos et al., 2014; Chen & Ogan, 2017; Knight, 2014). These hubs can be defined as geographically limited spaces where synergies between firms, public research institutions and the state reinforce innovation. In the case of Singapore, since the 2000s, its government has sharply increased its Research & Development (R&D) investment and introduced different sets of policies, including science and technology plans aimed at creating an innovation hub. Policies included tax credit to companies investing in R&D, multiple instruments to promote start-ups' creation, and assigned a key role to the National University of Singapore (NUS) and the Nanyang Technological University (NTU). Both universities should deliver the needed talent and be innovative organizations collaborating with established firms and creating spin-offs.

In globalized capitalism, there is an open question on who will capture the intellectual rents from such hubs. To answer this question, this chapter analyses Singapore's innovation hub from the intellectual monopoly capitalism framework. Previous chapters have argued that contemporary capitalism is led by intellectual monopolies that plan and dominate innovation networks collecting intellectual rents from their successful results. Intellectual monopolies may outsource or offshore innovation modules in those hubs, garnering innovation rents, therefore potentially profiting from hubs as enclaves of science and technology. This can be particularly the case with developing or emerging countries pursuing knowledge and/or innovation hub strategies. In this context, our study of Singapore's hub contributes to understanding the distribution of rents in innovation hubs in non-core countries.

Our methodology combines exploratory interviews conducted at the beginning and the end of our investigation, with grey literature and statistics on Singapore start-ups, patent co-ownership and innovation rents (thus not every form of intellectual rent but only those related to innovations, see Chapter 7).

* This chapter is co-authored with Prof. David Flacher (COSTECH, Université de Technologies de Compiègne).

Overall findings show that the Singapore state is subsidizing (directly but also indirectly) intellectual monopolies while the NUS, the NTU and start-ups' innovation subordinates to those monopolies. University research is mostly dependent on public research grants, and the state is start-ups' most frequent funding source. Simultaneously, research lines are set according to business needs and seeking for research commercialization. Furthermore, while the state funds the riskiest innovations, if successful, intellectual monopolies acquire the start-ups, turn them into regular subordinate suppliers or simply patent and profit from university research outcomes. Both the NUS and the NTU participate in transnational innovation networks, as evidenced by the multiple agreements and patents co-owned with leading multinational corporations. Generally, these research collaborations allow intellectual monopolies to save money, reduce their risk and garner the intellectual rents from successful results. Intellectual monopolies are thus profiting not only from their corporate R&D settled in Singapore but also predating knowledge from Singapore's research universities and start-ups (all of which rely on public funds). Hence, the chapter invites us to question the possibilities for a non-core state to effectively capture part of the intellectual rents triggered by R&D that it significantly funded, passing over powerful transnational intellectual monopolies from core countries.

The rest of this chapter is organized as follows: Section 2 elaborates on knowledge hub policies in the context of intellectual monopoly capitalism with a focus on Singapore's experience. Section 3 introduces our approach and methodology. Section 4 presents our findings, and results and conclusions are discussed in Section 5.

2 Knowledge hubs: the case of Singapore

In a recent review paper on cluster studies and Global Value Chains (GVC), Gereffi and Lee (2016) argue that despite the ongoing dialogue between the GVC and cluster literature, there is a lack of understanding of the interplay between GVC and industrial clusters in the global south. Clusters and hubs are close concepts. While the notion of clusters is more focused on a critical mass of firms concentrated in local geographic spaces (see seminal work of Porter, 1998), the idea of hubs has been developed to speak of the geographic concentration of a particular production process: that of knowledge and innovation. The innovation hub notion was coined in policy documents for Singapore and South Africa and referred to the aim of concentrating in the same location innovative companies with education and research institutions, such as universities and public research organizations (PROs), and venture capital (Aggarwal, 1995 cited in Wan et al., 2005; Kahn & Reddy, 2001; Moodley, 2003). Research institutions do not play a relevant role in clusters' framework, whereas they have been placed at the centre stage of innovation hubs. Anyway, hubs can be conceived as a cluster where the critical mass of firms corresponds to start-ups and other innovating companies and is complemented by other key organizations such as universities and PROs.

Therefore, drawing on Gereffi and Lee's (2016) argument, this chapter contributes to bridging the gap between GVC and clusters by analysing an innovation hub and the role of GVC leaders. As we explained in Chapters 2 and 7, following Durand and Milberg's (2020) taxonomy of rents from intangibles, GVC leaders can be considered as intellectual monopolies because each has the exclusive knowledge of who can do what within its chain. This form of knowledge, defined by Johnson and Lundvall (1994) as *know-who*, is an advantage that enables to set the chain in motion, hence to organize it and put it together. Having the exclusive knowledge of GVCs structure and participants is an intangible asset that triggers vertical natural monopoly rents from network externalities (Durand & Milberg, 2020). In a global context of intellectual monopoly capitalism, hubs may end up favouring intellectual monopolies' rent-seeking activity, further subordinating public science to private interests. If this is the case, unequal distribution of intellectual rents will reinforce centre-periphery dynamics.

By focusing on the case of Singapore, we expand the dependency theory on the unequal exchange of value between the centre and the periphery (Emmanuel, 1972). We include the unequal distribution of intellectual rents that results from innovations achieved in non-core countries, a form of knowledge extractivism (see Chapter 11).

Singapore has historically depended on foreign multinationals' activity and technology (Wong & Goh, 2013). Since the late 1990s, the state has put in place policies to transform the country into a knowledge and innovation hub aimed at developing local capabilities. These policies were synthesized in 'Science and Technology' (S&T) Plans, renamed 'Research, Innovation, Enterprise' Plans since 2011. Colossal public investments in R&D have supported these policies (Mok, 2015; Sidhu et al., 2014).

In these plans, the Singapore government assigned to the NUS and the NTU a role that resembles that of Georgia Tech in the transformation of Atlanta into an innovation-driven economy (Youtie & Shapira, 2008). As our interviewees pointed out and as confirmed by the NUS, NTU and government's official websites, the government (i) prioritized public investment in R&D for strategic fields (Sidhu et al., 2014) and promoted a scheme of competitive grants that privileges applied research[1] and partnerships with private firms, (ii) stimulated talent imports, (iii) promoted university spin-offs and entrepreneurship, and (iv) attracted foreign direct investment in higher education and research. This meant attracting foreign world-class universities both to settle branch campuses and to partner with the NUS and the NTU. In this context, patenting and creating start-ups became as encouraged and rewarded as publishing in high-impact factor journals.

Among many other policies within the mentioned lines, the S&T 2010 plan launched the Visiting Investigatorship Programme aiming "to bring top scientists to Singapore to help develop new capabilities in key areas" (Ministry of Trade and Industry, 2006, p. 18). In 2008, the Singaporean government also created the National Framework of Innovation and Enterprise aimed at commercializing "leading-edge technologies developed by the public research institutes (PRI) and institutes of higher learning (IHL) of Singapore through the creation of new high-technology ventures." Next, in 2012, the Campus for Research Excellence And Technological Enterprise (CREATE) was established. It is an international research and innovation centre inside the NUS campus that also includes the NTU. It hosts joint research labs with foreign universities (such as the MIT, Berkeley and Peking University) and industrial partners. CREATE focuses on research with commercial potential (Ministry of Trade and Industry, 2009). Regarding competitive grants, interviewees explained that, in some cases, it is not required to find private matching funds but only letters of support from private companies. Proving a private interest in the project was enough to increase a project's chances to be granted the funds.

Concerning stimulating spin-offs and entrepreneurship, start-up incubators were created as well as specialized programs like the NUS's Graduate Research Innovation Programme. Moreover, besides horizontal policies to stimulate overall business expenditure in R&D,[2] the Singaporean government deployed a bundle of policies to encourage technology start-ups' creation (Cheah et al., 2016a; Intarakumnerd & Goto, 2016). The first R&D incentive for start-up enterprises dates from the late 1990s. Considering that start-ups need cash for investing in R&D, this first incentive – still available – allowed them to apply for cash grants. Since 2010, start-ups can also deduct up to 400% (maximum of S$800,000) of their expenditures from their income before paying taxes. Expenditures that can be deducted include R&D investment, intellectual property rights (IPRs)-related expenses and acquisition of automation equipment (Intarakumnerd & Goto, 2016).

The government also introduced more venture-friendly regulations. It made the bankruptcy process faster (from 29 to 10 months) and less costly. It put in place a scheme of partial tax exemption for new start-up companies[3] in a country with one of the lowest corporate tax rates (17%).[4] On top of these measures, the government provided a series of funds and policies to attract venture capital as well as a specific grant to promote start-up creation managed by A*Star (Singapore's Agency for Science, Technology and Research) (Cheah et al., 2016a). In a Global Entrepreneurship Monitor report from 2014, among the 27 countries considered, Singapore ranked first on government policies that facilitate entrepreneurship (Chernyshenko et al., 2015).

Summing up, Singapore's innovation hub relies on the planning capacity of its state, including both financial and political decisions aimed at making the NUS and the NTU the engines of the hub as well as to develop a cluster of start-ups that should become the hub's bedrock. Yet, Singapore became an innovation hub as intellectual monopoly capitalism was spreading. In the following sections, we aim to evaluate the success of this strategy by considering results in terms of university research commercialization, spin-offs and overall start-up creation coupled with an assessment of the distribution of intellectual rents among the actors participating in the hub.

3 Approach and methodology

We conducted a mixed-methods case study relying on two types of data: qualitative data from in-depth interviews and quantitative data from Singapore's official surveys and Derwent Innovation database. From the latter, we retrieved NUS and NTU international patent portfolios until 2017 included. We complemented our analysis with grey literature from the NUS, the NTU, and the Singaporean government (including reports where the hub strategy was presented).

Regarding qualitative data, we performed in-depth semi-structured interviews to 15 stakeholders in November 2016 and 8 in April 2019 including: (i) managers of the NUS and the NTU; (ii) researchers from the NUS and NTU chosen following a snowball sampling; (iii) managers of overseas higher education institutions settled in Singapore[5]; and (iv) those responsible for the scientific cooperation from a core country (France) embassy in Singapore. Interviews lasted between 30 and 90 minutes. By way of respecting our commitment to the interviewees, we have not disclosed their identities.

We conducted interviews at the beginning of our investigation because we wanted to understand better Singapore's higher education and research system, the state policy, the strategies of its leading institutions and researchers' perceptions, logic and practices. We conducted a second round of interviews two years and a half later to validate our findings.

The initial interviews contributed to developing further hypotheses that were later confirmed in our quantitative analysis. They provided evidence on the strong influence of the Singaporean government on the NUS and NTU, as well as on Singapore's overall science, technology and innovation system. All our interviewees agreed that the government priorities became their institutions' priorities and that researchers looked at the national plans when applying for funds for orientation on topics and projects with higher chances to be accepted.

The second round of interviews provided concrete examples that validated our quantitative findings, improving our understanding of the reasons that explain those results. These interviews allowed us to confirm the nature of university relations with the state, foreign and local firms as well as to understand the specificities of university-industry collaborations and start-up creation in Singapore. In more concrete terms, these interviews provided additional information on alternative forms of research commercialization, in particular on start-ups and the difficulties to assure venture capital and compete with global leaders.

For our quantitative analysis, we retrieved NUS and NTU international patent portfolios from the Derwent Innovation database. We analysed these universities' most frequent patent co-owners, paying particular attention to the proportion of patents shared with local and foreign corporations. We considered whether global leaders performing research with the NUS or the NTU, as mentioned by our interviewees (and checked at the NUS and NTU official websites and documents), are also patenting innovative results with these universities.

Finally, we analysed the distribution of intellectual rents from innovations conducted in Singapore extracted from its National Survey of Research and Development for the year 2018. This survey provides two indicators that considered together are a proxy of intellectual rents from innovation activities: licensing revenues and sales revenues from products resulting from R&D activities. We compared patent ownership and innovation rents among different types of actors: universities, public research organizations and the private sector, distinguishing between local and foreign companies. We also analysed these data from 2013 onwards from the corresponding surveys, and only marginal changes are recorded. Since this information comes from a survey responded by each organization, we note that these data may be, to some extent, inaccurate because private actors may have incentives to lie. This shortfall was somehow compensated by our second round of interviews. They validated overall achieved results, in particular, that the NUS and the NTU are barely profiting from their patents. Our findings are presented in the next section.

4 Empirical findings

Government reports and various scholars highlight that Singapore's knowledge and innovation hub strategy was successful (Olds, 2007; Sidhu et al., 2011, 2014). Moreover, both the NUS and the NTU claim that they are not only leading institutions in teaching and research but also in what interviewed managers and researchers – following S&T plans – call their "Enterprise" mission. Enterprise includes patenting, university-industry partnerships and the creation of start-ups. In this section we: (1) assess the NUS and NTU international patent portfolio together with their most promoted university-industry research partnerships, (2) build on secondary sources to consider growth, success and challenges of start-ups in Singapore and (3) analyse the distribution of intellectual rents from licences and sales revenues from commercialized products and processes attributed to R&D performed in Singapore. Our results will question the positive assessment of Singapore's innovation hub. In particular, we will show that the success in terms of innovation results is mostly economically benefiting foreign multinational companies that can be considered intellectual monopolies.

4.1 NUS and NTU patents and collaborations with industry

In a decade, the NUS has almost fivefold increased granted patents per year, from 25 in 2009 to 119 in 2018 (National University of Singapore, 2019). Moreover, Derwent Innovation data show that nine international patents were granted to the NTU in 2011 (in line with previous years' data). By 2017, that figure had jumped to 62, and in fiscal year 2018–19, the NTU was granted with 126 local and international patents (Nanyang Technological University, 2019).

To evaluate the results of their research collaborations with industry, we focus next on both universities' private co-owners for the 2000–17 period. The NUS co-owns applied or granted international patents with 43 corporations, 26 of which are foreign companies including Huawei, BASF and General Electric. BASF is the NUS's 6th patent co-owner (with 24 co-owned granted or applied patents). Globalfoundries, a large Singaporean corporation, is the next corporation in importance, sharing 14 patents. However, only nine firms are among its top 100 patent co-owners, four of which are local companies (see Table 12A.1 in Appendix). The NUS shared 40 applied or granted international patents (2% of total NUS patents in the chosen period) with local companies and 80 (4%) with foreign companies. These percentages seem relatively low since the NUS promotes its industrial partnerships as a huge success. In the case of the NTU, it has 43 applied or granted patents co-owned with local firms (3.4% of total NTU patents in this period) and 55 with foreign ones (4.3%). In terms of partnering companies, the NTU co-owns patents with 14 foreign corporations – including Huawei, BMW and Siemens – and 12 local companies (see Table 12A.2 in Appendix).

The institutional setting developed in Singapore contributed to expanding university-industry collaborations that, as we could verify in our interviews, greatly exceed partnerships that led to co-owned patents. The NUS has 57 ongoing research collaborations with industrial partners, including four corporate laboratories with big local corporations and one with Grab, a local unicorn company (Grab-NUS Artificial Intelligence Lab). Partnerships with global corporations from the United States and China include a corporate laboratory with Applied Materials Inc., the Institute of Data Science with Microsoft, and research partnerships with Alibaba, Cisco, and ExxonMobil.[6]

Total partnership figures are not available for the NTU, but it currently hosts six corporate laboratories. In its last annual report, the NTU announced that it created two new corporate laboratories. One is "in digital manufacturing with HP, with S$84 million (almost USD 60 million) over four years, with strong support from the government", and the other one with Surbana Jurong, a Singaporean government-owned consultancy for projects on urban technologies (Nanyang Technological University, 2019). The other four corporate laboratories are the Rolls-Royce@NTU,[7] ST Engineering-NTU, SMRT-NTU Smart Urban Rail Corporate Laboratory and Delta-NTU Corporate Laboratory for Cyber-Physical Systems. Other highlighted collaborations involve Volvo Buses and WeBank (Tencent).

Until 2017 included, neither the NTU nor the NUS co-owned any granted or applied patent in international patent offices with any of the respective corporations of their corporate laboratories.

According to our interviews, CREATE research centres have led to other research collaborations besides those presented above. CREATE's partners include big pharmaceuticals like Roche, Merck, AstraZeneca, Novartis and GlaxoSmithKline as well as other multinational corporations such as Fujitsu, IBM, Danone, Boeing, Shell, Toyota, ExxonMobil, Alstom, Vestas, BMW and Siemens. From all these companies, only IBM shares granted or applied patents with the NUS (two patents until 2017 included). Only BMW and Siemens are NTU's patent co-owners. An interviewee explained that his partnerships with big pharmaceuticals under CREATE corresponded to Singapore's National Research Foundation grants where the companies only need to write letters of support when the researchers are applying for the grant, but do not commit their own funding. Without sponsoring academic research, in these cases, big pharmaceuticals still manage to steer public R&D according to their interests.

Interviewees also explained that in some partnerships the Singaporean government matches the sponsorship of the private company, which increases the interest of foreign firms. As one of the interviewees said:

> Why would they choose Singapore instead of other universities like MIT or Harvard or Stanford? Why would they travel far? Unless, Singapore offers some kind of incentive...
>
> (Interviewee 1, university scholar)

Matching grants seem to be successful since the share of R&D invested in Singapore's higher education sector by private companies increased in this period, from 2.9% in 1994 to 13.1% in 2016. This highlights the attractiveness of the sector for corporations. Lower costs and the quality of the research performed by the NUS, the NTU and the leading global universities participating in CREATE may drive companies (in particular multinationals, as was pointed out by interviewees) to partner with universities in Singapore.

However, interviewed researchers pointed out that the NUS and the NTU faced difficulties when negotiating intellectual property with enterprises. When there is private funding, interviewees explained that both universities frequently prefer to receive a one-time payment fee from the private company when signing the collaboration agreement. IPRs of eventually achieved results become an exclusive right of the firm because patenting is expensive, and then the university is not paid back in royalties. So even in projects with multinationals, ownership may end up exclusively in the hands of the firm. Concerning the types of private partners, most of the examples provided by interviewed researchers and managers corresponded to foreign multinationals. One of our interviewees, who works managing IPRs in one of Singapore's leading universities, argued that:

> Local companies are very weak in giving research money, but the government is helping them.
>
> (Interviewee 2, university manager)

Summing up, although the NUS and the NTU have institutionalized university-industry partnerships, most of them have not led to co-owned patents. When they did, foreign multinational corporations stood out as the NUS and NTU's most frequent private co-owners. Altogether, co-patenting and research collaboration results raise the question of the real benefits left to the NUS and the NTU and, more broadly, to the Singaporean government in the terms analysed by Mazzucato (2015) and discussed in Chapter 11 because both universities remain highly dependent on state funds for research. In fiscal year 2018/19, public funds represented around 90% of the NUS research funds, and 74% of the NTU research grants came from the government ministries (Nanyang Technological University, 2019; National University of Singapore, 2019).

4.2 Start-ups and university spin-offs in Singapore

Singapore currently has over 3,000 start-ups.[8] Until 2019 included, the NUS incubated more than 300 (National University of Singapore, 2019). The NTU's last annual report states that 12 spin-offs and 30 start-ups were created in the fiscal year 2018–19 (Nanyang Technological University, 2019). Kam et al. (2017) surveyed high-tech start-ups in 2016. In this survey, they included a group of tracer firms that had been interviewed in 2010 and survived. Their overall results show that Singapore has been a thriving hub in terms of start-ups' creation and that the lifespan of these companies is in line with the US figures (half are still alive after five years). However, start-ups in Singapore remain dependent on public money, in particular for R&D. Kam et al. (2017) found that, besides own funding, the second most important funding source for high-tech start-ups is public support. It was received by 64.2% of surveyed start-ups, while only around 30% had received venture capital money.

Concerning R&D investments, business expenditure in R&D (BERD) has not achieved the government targets, leading to a higher share of public investment in total R&D in Singapore. The share of the local plus foreign BERD decreased between 1994 (62%) and 2013 (58.2%) (OECD data). Furthermore, within the private sector, foreign companies remain mainly responsible for the R&D performed in Singapore, accounting for 74% of total BERD in 2018 (see Table 12.1). Start-ups, which are included in the share of Small and Medium Enterprises (SMEs), have the smallest BERD share. In fact, their actual BERD is even smaller because a significant proportion comes from the incentives given by the Singaporean government.[9]

Moreover, start-ups in Singapore are generally small regarding employment and revenues, with a quarter of them without recording revenues at all (Kam et al., 2017). According to the 2015 SMEs development survey, 47% of SMEs operating in Singapore showed no turnover growth, and 6% had a declining turnover; similar figures were observed in the previous years (DP Information Group, 2015). The fact that most start-ups fail is a global phenomenon. However, they are promoted not only because they create jobs but also because it is expected that some of them, even if not just a few, will become stronger and bigger businesses. So far, only two local companies can be classified as unicorns[10]: Grab and Trax. By looking at both companies' websites, we found that Grab was originated in Malaysia and later moved to Singapore due to the benefits provided by the state. Trax was created in Singapore but due to a business opportunity brought by a foreigner. It was not an idea that was born in the hub.

Therefore, why aren't there more start-ups becoming successful businesses in Singapore? When assessing young start-ups' main challenges, Kam et al. (2017) found that they are mostly related to starting the business (recruiting personnel and obtaining financing). However, mature start-ups

Table 12.1 Sources of R&D expenditure in 2018

Source	*R&D expenditure (S$ billions)*	*Proportion inside enterprise sector (%)*	*Proportion of total R&D expenditure (%)*
1) Local small and medium enterprises	0.72	12.83	7.79
2) Local large enterprises	0.74	13.04	7.92
3) Foreign companies	4.18	74.13	45.03
Total private sector (1+2+3)	5.64	100	60.75
Government sector	1.07	–	11.52
Higher education sector	1.65	–	17.79
Public research institutes	0.92	–	9.94
Total	9.28	–	100.00

Source: Authors' compilation based on National Survey of Research and Development in Singapore.

ranked dependence on major customers among their top concerns. In particular, those mature start-ups that had been interviewed as young start-ups in 2010 and were interviewed again in 2016 ranked dependence on major customers as their top concern, whereas in 2010 their top concern was high investment costs to expand their business. It seems that as time passes and the company becomes operational, at some point, a glass ceiling curtails its development that eventually turns the start-up into a subordinate company. This result is in line with the argument put forward in Chapter 2. Start-ups were classified as typical examples of subordinate innovating companies: they are characterized by a short lifespan and assume the riskiest R&D steps or modules within intellectual monopolies' innovation networks from which the latter garners most of the intellectual rents. While most start-ups end in bankruptcy or remain as subordinate companies, some are acquired by big corporations acting as intellectual monopolies. Remarkably, the latter is the main goal of Singapore's university spin-offs and incubated start-ups.

> Of course, a success story for a start-up is that, at a certain stage, they get acquired by big boys and girls, like Google.
>
> (Interviewee 2, university manager)

> The aim is not to sell the product. It is to develop the product up to a point when a major manufacturer says: "it is interesting, we like to introduce that into our portfolio". Selling takes too much, (...) another level of investment, including marketing and putting things out there. I don't think we are doing this, unless the government says: "hey look this is proven, and you should do a made in Singapore thing".
>
> (Interviewee 3, university scholar)

> Most successful will be bought, and many have as their objective to be bought. Very few want to become a billion-dollar company like Pfizer. Most companies rather be bought by the big ones. The big get bigger. The rich get richer.
>
> (Interviewee 4, university scholar)

This is another sign of their otherwise weaker positions and reflects that university entrepreneurs are not attempting to turn their business into a standalone enterprise. Brown (2016) explains that successful university spin-offs are often acquired by big corporations due to their inability to grow and upscale and/or because of insufficient financial resources, even if they have novel intellectual property. The author continues explaining that, in the case of Scotland, many start-ups are created by postgraduate students to assure funding to carry on their academic research rather than effectively creating a start-up. Our interviewees – as well as Kam et al. (2017) – point in the same direction for the case of Singapore start-ups.

The aim to be acquired by a big player was also stated by venture capitalists. Birch (2017, p. 476) quotes a venture capital investor explaining that his focus is not to fund companies with potential for an initial public offering (a sign of actual or potential profitability of the company itself). He aims "to find companies which are developing a disruptive technology where the disruption is sufficiently apparent that it will trigger a strategic acquisition by an incumbent in the market."

Summing up, Singapore is becoming a start-up nation, but the Singaporean state is its main venture-capitalist. Moreover, those creating these innovative companies tend to accept beforehand that their best possible scenario is to be acquired, typically by a big corporation. Furthermore, those that succeed with their business, once established, become dependent on major customers, which – given the business landscape of Singapore – also points to subordination to intellectual monopoly.

Overall, our findings signal strong innovation-oriented R&D outcomes from the NUS and the NTU, as well as a dense start-up landscape. Yet, they also suggest unequal relations in terms of R&D economic benefits between the NUS, the NTU and start-ups on the one side, and foreign corporations on the other. Since all the former rely on the Singaporean government as a primary funding source, these results also point to an indirect appropriation of public resources by foreign multinationals. Next, we investigate further this dimension by analysing the distribution of innovation rents in Singapore's hub.

4.3 Distribution of innovation rents in Singapore

Concerning the distribution of Singapore's innovation hub rents, our main finding is that even though universities and public research institutions own 14% of total patents in Singapore, almost 100% of the innovation rents are appropriated by private enterprises (see Table 12.2). The public sector, including universities, is not capturing rents from its research results (less than 1% as a whole, and 0.02% if we only look at the higher education sector).[11] In terms of dollars that each sector extracts per owned patent, universities receive 758 times fewer dollars per patent than the private sector. Although competitive research grants in Singapore prioritize applied research, it is possible to partly justify this result by the nature of university patenting, probably closer to basic research, thus harder to garner intellectual rents. Anyway, since universities' rents are almost zero, and considering their collaborations with industry, there is a clear sign of private assetization of public knowledge.

This result is consistent with the outcomes of our interviews. Researchers claimed that their universities were barely garnering intellectual rents from *ble 12.2* Intellectual rents' indicators in 2018 (S$ million unless stated otherwise)

evenue indicators	*Private sector*	*Government sector*	*Higher education sector*	*Public research institutes*	*Total*
censing revenue from patents and new technologies developed in Singapore	268.16	0.94	6.00	5.66	280.76
oportion from total	95.51%	0.33%	2.14%	2.02%	100.00%
les revenue from commercialized products/processes attributed to R&D performed in Singapore	31,769.97	0.18	0.24	35.81	31,806.20
oportion from total	99.89%	0.0006%	0.001%	0.11%	100%
otal R&D-related revenues (licensing + sales)	32038.13	1.12	6.24	41.47	32086.96
oportion from total	99.85%	0.00%	0.02%	0.13%	100.00%
atents owned (cumulative until December 31, 2019)	8,579	107	771	657	10,114
hare of total patents	84.8%	1.1%	7.6%	6.5%	100%
ollars per patent: (Licensing revenues + Sales revenues)/ Patents owned	3,734,483.04	10,467.29	8,093.39	63,120.24	3,172,529.17

ource: Authors' compilation based on National Survey of Research and Development in Singapore.

their R&D activities. Moreover, NUS and NTU managers evidenced the difficulties of research commercialization, both by patenting and creating successful university spin-offs. In the case of patents, those shared with enterprises are not appealing for other private companies because the firm co-owning the patent enjoys it for free, without sharing the profits neither paying royalties to the other owners. Thus, innovation rents are created but not enjoyed by public research institutions. For instance, in a big project on water management and security, a consortium was formed with university researchers from the NUS, a multinational company from the Netherlands, and government funding. Some of the achievements were patented, but the NUS could not licence them, while the multinational uses co-owned patents' results for its consultancies.

Results are also in line with the NUS, NTU and A*Star recent changed in strategy: fewer and more selective patenting. An interviewee also pointed out that its university patenting office is asking researchers to show that a company is interested in licensing the technology before starting the patenting process.

The innovation rents that the NUS and NTU are not garnering from their inventions are probably higher because we can neither measure professors' privilege nor the lack of resources to patent every single invention at the university level. There may be inventions made at these institutions but not owned by them, as discussed in Schoen and Buenstorf (2013) for German universities.

Additionally, the distribution of innovation rents within private corporations appears to be very favourable to foreign firms. Foreign companies hold 86.1% of private companies' innovation rents (Table 12.3). Two indicators are used to measure these rents: licensing revenues and sales revenues from products resulting from R&D activities. What we observe is that foreign companies usually do not license their patents; they instead use innovations to increase revenues by commercializing resulting products. On the contrary, Singaporean enterprises – regardless of their size – have higher shares of innovation rents from royalties than from sales associated with R&D results. Hence, compared to foreign companies, they are weaker in creating value from commodities produced embedding R&D results

Table 12.3 Licensing and sales revenues per type of enterprise in 2018 (S$ million unless stated otherwise)

	Local small and medium enterprises	*Local large enterprises*	*Foreign companies*	*Total*
A) Licensing revenue from patents and new technologies developed in Singapore	21.84	221.54	30.28	273.66
Share of licensing revenues (A) per type of enterprise	8.0%	81.0%	11.1%	100.0%
Licensing revenues per patent (A / C * 100)	10,892.77	221,983.97	5,430.42	31,898.82
B) Sales revenue from commercialized products/ processes attributed to R&D performed in Singapore	645.25	3,569.88	27,554.84	31,769.97
Share of sales revenues (B) per type of enterprise	2.0%	11.2%	86.7%	100.0%
Sales revenue's per patent (B / C * 100)	321,820.45	3,577,034.07	4,941,685.80	3,703,225.32
C) Patents owned (Cumulative until December 31, 2019)	2,005	998	5,576	8,579
D) Total dollars due to patenting activity (A+B)	667.09	3791.42	27585.12	32043.63
Proportion of total income due to patenting (A / D * 100)	2.1%	11.8%	86.1%	100.0%

Source: Authors' compilation based on National Survey of Research and Development in Singapore.

than selling access to their innovations. Overall, data show that mostly foreign companies are profiting from all the R&D done in Singapore (see Tables 12.2 and 12.3). This is true, regardless of total public investment in R&D. In 2018, the government invested 35% of total R&D expended in Singapore, a percentage that was 37% in 2013 and has remained relatively stable around the two figures since then.

All in all, our results show that the NUS and the NTU, and more broadly public research organizations, are almost not garnering innovation rents regardless of their R&D capabilities. Even when they patent successful results with the potential to be commercialized, they still do not gather significant rents. Also, by distinguishing according to the type of company (foreign vs. local), we found that foreign companies appropriate most of the innovation rents of the Singaporean hub. Local companies (including start-ups) appear weaker in terms of developing new products based on their R&D results than in selling access to their innovations. This further limits their development opportunities.

5 Discussion and concluding remarks

While policies in Singapore were successful in creating an innovation hub, we provided empirical evidence on how private companies hold almost 100% of resulting intellectual rents. Among companies, foreign ones loom large, appropriating 83.3% of total private companies' innovation rents.

As confirmed by our interviews, the NUS and the NTU are actively attempting to commercialize R&D outcomes (by increasingly patenting results and creating start-ups). However, they barely collect intellectual rents from that activity. Legal monopoly innovation rents resulting from IPRs have been the most visible (and studied) phenomenon of intellectual monopoly capitalism (Boldrin & Levine, 2008; Durand & Milberg, 2020; Lambert, 2019; Pagano, 2014; Rikap, 2019). However, not every patent will yield a stream of revenues for its owner, and co-owned patents can result in the benefit of only one or some co-owners. Furthermore, as our interviewees agreed, in some industries patents can be easily circumvented, and infringement accusations are expensive and can take many years. All the latter reduces private companies' interest in licensing university patents.

Moreover, Singapore-based start-ups are not becoming standalone actors fuelling Singapore's economy. In previous chapters, we have argued that start-ups – even from the Silicon Valley – are mostly risk-takers and, when successful, they generally end up subordinating to intellectual monopolies or acquired by them. Singapore start-ups seem to qualify as innovating companies that, if successful, are compelled to share rents with intellectual monopolies. Since the state is the main funder of start-ups in Singapore, it may be said that it is indirectly subsidizing foreign intellectual monopolies. As long as the Singaporean government assures these companies a higher rate of profit than other countries (with similar institutional, political and economic stability) in the region, Singapore likely remains as a hub.

In this respect, this chapter's findings broaden the scope of the intellectual monopoly framework, by empirically showing how foreign corporations' profit from the innovation hub of an emerging country. It may be argued that intellectual monopolies not only profit from public R&D from their home countries, as shown by Mazzucato (2015), but also from the research capacity and public funds of emerging economies, thus deepening global asymmetries by monopolizing knowledge funded and produced by peripheral countries' organizations.

This chapter's results are thus in line with Cooke's (2006) concluding remark on global bioscientific knowledge networks. According to the author, the formation of knowledge clusters in certain regions has "begun to exert spatial knowledge monopoly effects that are already bringing 'increasing returns' as multinationals establish R&D facilities to capture 'knowledge spillover' advantages from cluster conventions of both 'open science' and 'open innovation.'" (Cooke, 2006, p. 457). The same can be said for Singapore's hub.

Hence, our findings question the real nature of Singapore's hub success, as highlighted by different authors (Cheah et al., 2016b; Mok, 2015; Sidhu et al., 2014). Unlike these studies, we not only studied Singapore's hub results in terms of science and technology indicators but also included an analysis of innovation rents' distribution. This is what allowed us to distinguish between Singapore's success in terms of science and technology achievements, and its relative failure when it comes to garnering rents. Innovation rents' distribution is of utmost importance because neither IPRs, nor the creation of start-ups by themselves, guarantee the economic valorization of the achieved results.

As we have explained in this book, innovation is produced by transnational innovation networks organized through power relationships. These networks are increasingly dominated by intellectual monopolies. While innovation is produced collectively by multiple organizations, the capacity to turn results into intangible assets, and thus to extract (intellectual) rents, lays mostly in the hands of intellectual monopolies. Eventually, they may share the rents with innovating companies that played a paramount role in achieving the results but, overall, there is an unequal distribution of the profits extracted from innovation. As stated by Yeung and Coe (2015), what is at stake is who captures the value created from R&D. In Foley's (2013) words, in Singapore, foreign corporations are appropriating surplus value, thanks to innovations produced by Singaporean universities and start-ups, which were mostly funded by the state. Summing up, since intellectual monopolies predate knowledge from a non-core country, our results provide evidence of knowledge extractivism (see Chapter 11).

To conclude, Singapore's hub strategy, widely opened to foreign multinational companies, poses limits to development and increases inequalities and firms' heterogeneity. Nevertheless, results should not lead us to conclusions against public investment in R&D. On the contrary, there is a need for a complete rethinking of public policy. Policy recommendations should consider both the allocation of public funding for R&D and the state's potential to tilt the scale against global intellectual monopolies. Chapter 14 is an attempt to further elaborate on these remarks.

Funding

This work was supported by the Institut Francilien Recherche Innovation Société under their Postdoctoral Fellowship programme and the exploratory project "ACIDES-Sud".

Notes

1 Basic research share in total public R&D expenditure between 2015 and 2020 was reduced to 15%. It was 34% in 2014 (11.8% in pure basic and 22.2% in strategic basic) (Ministry of Trade and Industry, 2009, 2016).
2 Currently, the Singapore government gives up to 100% of tax deduction for "qualifying expenditure for eligible R&D activities in Singapore." https://www.edb.gov.sg/en/why-singapore/business-friendly-environment.html.
3 https://www.iras.gov.sg/irashome/Businesses/Companies/Learning-the-basics-of-Corporate-Income-Tax/Corporate-Tax-Rates--Corporate-Income-Tax-Rebates-and-Tax-Exemption-Schemes/.
4 Singapore ranks 129 in the list of country's corporate tax rate https://tradingeconomics.com/country-list/corporate-tax-rate.
5 Chicago Business Scholl, ESSEC, INSEAD Singapore, Sorbonne-Assas International Law School Singapore, and the representation of Université Sorbonne Paris Cité in Singapore.
6 https://www.nrf.gov.sg/programmes/corporate-laboratory@university-scheme and http://nus.edu.sg/research/research-capabilities.
7 Rolls-Royce@NTU was established in July 2013 with a total funding of S$75 million for manpower with a target of 30 patents and 260 publications over a five-year period. The corporate laboratory was recently renewed with additional S$88 million and the NTU states that this is Rolls Royce's largest collaboration with a university (Nanyang Technological University, 2019).
8 https://www.edb.gov.sg/en/why-singapore/business-friendly-environment.html.
9 There are no detailed figures on the proportion of public R&D monies that are received by type of enterprise. Thus, we cannot calculate the share of SMEs' R&D expenditure that is actually funded by the Singaporean government.
10 Privately owned start-up companies with a value of over USD 1 billion.
11 Not every patent resulting from common research is co-owned by universities and companies. As previously mentioned, universities may receive one-time lump-sums when they resign property of research funded by private companies. Even though the information on the concerned amounts are not available, nothing in our interviews supports the idea that these lump-sums might be significantly important. Given also that universities receive matching grants from the public sector when private firms fund their research, we can reasonably assume that these lump-sum only partially compensate for the public investment in each public-private R&D project and that their existence does not change our main findings.

References

Belderbos, R., Du, S., & Somers, D. (2014). Global cities as innovation hubs: The location of R&D investments by multinational firms. *DRUID Academy. Aalborg, Denmark.* http://Druid8. Sit. Aau. Dk/Druid/Acc_papers/Rdv4by82h7nbyph96iuix18cu71s. Pdf

Birch, K. (2017). Rethinking value in the bio-economy: Finance, assetization, and the management of value. *Science, Technology, & Human Values*, *42*(3), 460–90.

Boldrin, M., & Levine, D. K. (2008). *Against intellectual monopoly.* Cambridge University Press.

Brown, R. (2016). Mission impossible? Entrepreneurial universities and peripheral regional innovation systems. *Industry and Innovation*, *23*(2), 189–205.

Cheah, S., Ho, Y. P., & Lim, P. (2016a). Role of public science in fostering the innovation and startup ecosystem in Singapore. *Asian Research Policy*, *7*(1), 78–93.

Cheah, S., Ho, Y. P., & Lim, P. (2016b). Role of public science in fostering the innovation and startup ecosystem in Singapore. *Asian Research Policy*, *7*(1), 78–93.

Chen, X., & Ogan, T. L. (2017). China's emerging Silicon Valley: How and why has Shenzhen become a global innovation centre. *European Financial Review*, 55–62. https://www.europeanfinancialreview.com/chinas-emerging-silicon-valley-how-and-why-has-shenzhen-become-a-global-innovation-centre/

Chernyshenko, O. S., Uy, M. A., Jiang, W., Ho, M. R., Lee, S. P., Chan, K. Y., & Yu, T. (2015). *Global entrepreneurship monitor 2014 Singapore report.* Nanyang Technological University.

Coe, N. M., & Yeung, H. W. C. (2015). *Global production networks: Theorizing economic development in an interconnected world.* Oxford University Press.

Cooke, P. (2006). Global bioregions: Knowledge domains, capabilities and innovation system networks. *Industry and Innovation*, *13*(4), 437–58.

DP Information Group. (2015). *SME Development (SMED) Survey. Service and productivity improvements top SME priorities for the next 12 months.* DP Information Group.

Durand, C., & Milberg, W. (2020). Intellectual monopoly in global value chains. *Review of International Political Economy*, *27*(2), 404–29. doi:10.1080/09692290.2019.1660703

Emmanuel, A. (1972). *Unequal exchange* (Vol. 1). Monthly Review Press.

Foley, D. K. (2013). Rethinking financial capitalism and the "information" economy. *Review of Radical Political Economics*, *45*(3), 257–68.

Gereffi, G., & Lee, J. (2016). Economic and social upgrading in global value chains and industrial clusters: Why governance matters. *Journal of Business Ethics*, *133*(1), 25–38.

Intarakumnerd, P., & Goto, A. (2016). *Technology and innovation policies for small and medium-sized enterprises in East Asia.* Asian Development Bank Institute. https://papers.ssrn.com/sol3/papers.cfm?abstract_id=2812432

Johnson, B., & Lundvall, B. A. (1994). The learning economy. *Journal of Industry Studies*, *1*(2), 23–42.

Kahn, M. J., & Reddy, B. D. (2001). Science and technology in South Africa: Regional innovation hub or passive consumer? *Daedalus*, *130*(1), 205–34.

Kam, W. P., Ping, H. Y., & Crystal, N. S. J. (2017). *Growth dynamics of high-tech start-ups in Singapore a longitudinal study.* NUS Entrepreneurship Centre.

Knight, J. (2014). *International education hubs.* Springer. http://link.springer.com/content/pdf/10.1007/978-94-007-7025-6.pdf
Lambert, T. E. (2019). Monopoly capital and innovation: An exploratory assessment of R&D effectiveness. *International Review of Applied Economics*, 1–14.
Mazzucato, M. (2015). *The entrepreneurial state: Debunking public vs. private sector myths* (Vol. 1). Anthem Press.
Ministry of Trade and Industry. (2006). *Science & technology plan 2010. Sustaining innovation-driven growth.* Singapore Prime Minister's Office.
Ministry of Trade and Industry. (2009). *Research innovation enterprise 2015. Singapore's future.* Singapore Prime Minister's Office
Ministry of Trade and Industry. (2016). *Research innovation enterprise 2020 plan. Winning the future for science and technology.* Singapore Prime Minister's Office.
Mok, K. H. (2015). The quest for global competitiveness: Promotion of innovation and entrepreneurial universities in Singapore. *Higher Education Policy*, *28*(1), 91–106.
Moodley, S. (2003). Cluster formation in the ICT sector: The case of South Africa. *Journal of Information Technology Impact*, *3*(3), 111–20.
Nanyang Technological University. (2019). *Illuminating possibilities. Annual Report 2019.* Nanyang Technological University.
National University of Singapore. (2019). *National Univeristy of Singapore. Annual Report 2019.* National University of Singapore.
Olds, K. (2007). Global assemblage: Singapore, foreign universities, and the construction of a "global education hub". *World Development*, *35*(6), 959–75.
Pagano, U. (2014). The crisis of intellectual monopoly capitalism. *Cambridge Journal of Economics*, *38*(6), 1409–29.
Porter, M. E. (1998). Clusters and the new economics of competition. *Harvard Business Review*, *76*(6), 77–90.
Rikap, C. (2019). Asymmetric power of the core: Technological cooperation and technological competition in the transnational innovation networks of big pharma. *Review of International Political Economy*, *26*(5), 987–1021. doi:10.1080/09692290.2019.1620309
Schoen, A., & Buenstorf, G. (2013). When do universities own their patents? An explorative study of patent characteristics and organizational determinants in Germany. *Industry and Innovation*, *20*(5), 422–37.
Sidhu, R., Ho, K.-C., & Yeoh, B. S. (2011). Emerging education hubs: The case of Singapore. *Higher Education*, *61*(1), 23–40.
Sidhu, R., Ho, K.-C., & Yeoh, B. S. (2014). Singapore: Building a knowledge and education hub. In Knight, J (Ed.) *International Education Hubs* (pp. 121–43). Springer. http://link.springer.com/chapter/10.1007/978-94-007-7025-6_8
Wan, D., Ong, C. H., & Lee, F. (2005). Determinants of firm innovation in Singapore. *Technovation*, *25*(3), 261–8.
Wong, K. N., & Goh, S. K. (2013). Outward FDI, merchandise and services trade: Evidence from Singapore. *Journal of Business Economics and Management*, *14*(2), 276–91.
Youtie, J., & Shapira, P. (2008). Building an innovation hub: A case study of the transformation of university roles in regional technological and economic development. *Research Policy*, *37*(8), 1188–204.

Appendix

Table 12A.1 NTU patents' corporate co-owners (2000–17)

Corporation	*Type*	*Ranking*	*Number of distinc documents*
SINGAPORE TECH DYNAM PTE LTD	Local corporation	11	10
INSIGHTRA MEDICAL INC	Foreign corporation	11	10
YISSUM RES DEV CO	Foreign corporation	12	8
GLOBALFOUNDRIES SG PTE LTD	Local corporation	13	8
MENICON CO LTD	Foreign corporation	13	8
LOCKHEED CORP	Foreign corporation	15	6
ROBERT BOSCH SEA PTE LTD	Local corporation	16	5
HUAWEI	Foreign corporation	16	5
THALES SOLUTIONS ASIA PTE LTD	Local corporation	17	4
SUT SERAYA PTE LTD	Local corporation	17	4
BMW	Foreign corporation	17	4
SIEMENS PTE LTD	Foreign corporation	17	4
ACOUSTICAL TECH SG PTE LTD	Local corporation	18	3
LIGHTLAB SWEDEN AB	Foreign corporation	18	3
PURECHEM ONYX PTE LTD	Local corporation	19	2
GASHUB TECHNOLOGY PTE LTD	Local corporation	19	2
TECHNOLITE (SINGAPORE) PTE LTD	Local corporation	19	2
ST MICROELECTRONICS ASIA	Foreign corporation	19	2
DAIOH SHINYO CO LTD	Foreign corporation	19	1
PROGEN PTE LTD	Local corporation	20	1
INTERNAT SEMICONDUCTOR PRODUCT	Local corporation	20	1
ADVANCED ELECTROACOUSTIC PTE LTD	Local corporation	20	1
DYESOL LTD	Foreign corporation	20	1
NINGBO SUNNY OPOTECH CO LTD	Foreign corporation	20	1
PEC LTD	Foreign corporation	20	1
SANTEN PHARMA CO LTD	Foreign corporation	20	1

Source: Authors' compilation from Derwent Innovation.

Table 12A.2 NUS patents' corporate co-owners (2000–17)

Corporation	*Type*	*Ranking*	*Number of distinct documents*
CHARTERED SEMICONDUCTOR MFG CO	Local corporation	5	28
BASF SE	Foreign corporation	7	24
STMICROELECTRONICS ASIA	Foreign corporation	19	8
GLOBALFOUNDRIES SG PTE LTD	Local corporation	20	7
HADASIT MED RES SERVICE	Foreign corporation	21	6
TEMASEK LIFE SCIENCES LAB LTD	Local corporation	21	6
IMEC CORP	Foreign corporation	22	5
ISIS PHARMACEUTICALS INC	Foreign corporation	22	5
KINERGY PTE LTD	Local corporation	22	5
HUAWEI	Foreign corporation	23	4
MULTICLONAL THERAPEUTICS INC	Foreign corporation	23	4
OSTEOPORE KOREA CO LTD	Foreign corporation	25	3
TEXAS INSTRUMENTS INC	Foreign corporation	24	3
AUCKLAND UNISERVICES LTD	Foreign corporation	24	3
IRIDEX CORP	Foreign corporation	24	3
Apple	Foreign corporation	24	3
HONEYWELL PTE LTD	Local corporation	24	3
OKI TECHNO CT PTE LTD	Foreign corporation	25	2
60 DEGREES PHARMACEUTICALS LLC	Foreign corporation	25	2
OSTEOPORE INTERNAT PTE LTD	Foreign corporation	25	2
ILLUMINA INC	Foreign corporation	25	2
IBM	Foreign corporation	25	2
MPORT PTE LTD	Foreign corporation	25	2
TOSHIBA CORP	Foreign corporation	25	2
HOPE TECHNIK PTE LTD	Local corporation	25	2
JURONG CONSULTANTS PTE LTD	Local corporation	25	2
CET TECHNOLOGIES PTE LTD	Local corporation	25	2
ABB LUMMUS GLOBAL INC	Foreign corporation	26	1

(*Continued*)

Corporation	*Type*	*Ranking*	*Number of distinct documents*
GEN ELECTRIC	Foreign corporation	26	1
PGS GEOPHYSICAL AS	Foreign corporation	26	1
SEAGATE TECHNOLOGY LLC	Foreign corporation	26	1
ALLIUM MEDICAL LTD	Foreign corporation	26	1
AMERICAN PRESIDENT LINES CO PTE LTD	Foreign corporation	26	1
KRATON POLYMERS US LLC	Foreign corporation	26	1
DAVOS LIFE SCIENCE PTE LTD	Local corporation	26	1
MUSTARD TECHNOLOGY PTE LTD	Local corporation	26	1
TEO WAY YONG & SONS PTE LTD	Local corporation	26	1
MUVEE TECHNOLOGIES PTE LTD	Local corporation	26	1
WONG FONG ENGINEERING WORKS 1988 PTE LTD	Local corporation	26	1
ST ELECTRONICS INFO SOFTWARE S	Local corporation	26	1
CELLONICS INC PTE LTD	Local corporation	26	1
OFFSHORE TECHNOLOGY DEV PTE LTD	Local corporation	26	1
YONGNAM HOLDINGS LTD	Local corporation	26	1

Source: Authors' compilation from Derwent Innovation.

13

PHARMACEUTICAL KNOWLEDGE EXTRACTIVISM FROM A SEMI-PERIPHERAL UNIVERSITY

1 Introduction

Innovations are increasingly produced in transnational networks where modules take place in multiple locations and involving diverse actors, including start-ups and research institutions, particularly universities (Cooke, 2006; Ernst, 2008, 2009, 2016; Linden et al., 2009; Liu et al., 2013; Rikap, 2018, 2019). In this book, we have shown that intellectual monopolies organize and plan innovation networks appropriating knowledge in a predatory behaviour with other participants. Innovations' benefits (spill-overs, labour productivity, consumer welfare and profits) may not be enjoyed where the innovation took place. This particularly affects non-core countries that participate in international knowledge flows, occupying a dependent or subordinated position (Arocena & Sutz, 2000; Beigel, 2010). Therefore, given the structural features of underdevelopment, it is relevant to analyse the peripheries' specific consequences of the growing concentration of intellectual rents by corporations (and eventually research bodies) from core countries.

In this chapter, we elaborate on semi-peripheral research institutions' participation in global innovation networks. We define a semi-peripheral research institution as a leader in its region that nonetheless occupies a peripheral position globally. Public universities are the principal producers of knowledge and the main working place for researchers in developing countries (OECD, Programme on Innovation, Higher Education and Research for Development, 2012). In Latin America, this central place is explained by public universities' capabilities but also by the little research and development (R&D) performed and funded by private enterprises. Local firms are usually demanders of technical assistance (Albornoz et al., 2017; Arocena & Sutz, 2010; Rodrik, 2008). Therefore, a weak or insufficient public knowledge demand has been pointed out as the primary constraint for the development of public-private research collaborations in the region (Albornoz et al., 2017; Arocena et al., 2015; Arocena & Sutz, 2010). What has been less studied is how this context propels universities to engage in transnational innovation networks or how they end up contributing to them without even noticing it as their R&D results become constitutive parts of foreign intangible assets.

As shown by recent bibliometric studies (Noh & Lee, 2019; Skute et al., 2019), the academic literature has mostly used the following indicators to account for research institutions' contribution to innovations: (1) number and types of agreements with industry, (2) level of university patenting and (3) diversification of budgetary sources, particularly the weight of private sponsorship of research and royalties from patents.

Our central argument is that this group of most used indicators accounts for research institutions' economic gains from collaborating with private actors and from knowledge assetization. Therefore, they should be complemented with an analysis of the institution's actual contribution to private R&D, regardless of the associated economic return. We propose two complementary dimensions of analysis to account for their contribution in terms of R&D results. (1) Bind knowledge transfer, defined as university papers cited in international patents and (2) university-firm co-authorship of scientific publications. This quantitative analysis is supplemented with in-depth interviews with researchers with a proven contribution to global research networks.

This more complete and complex analysis allows us to account for a possible scenario that has been overlooked by the literature that focuses on most used indicators. Subordinate research universities were defined in Chapter 5 as those that do not garner significant intellectual rents from their participation in intellectual monopolies' global innovation networks. Their R&D outcomes integrate innovation processes, but most intellectual rents are garnered by intellectual monopolies. In the case of these universities, contributions in terms of R&D results do not correlate with the level of economic benefits they garner. We thus propose to speak of knowledge extractivism because knowledge is extracted from where it was produced, and assetized by another organization, typically from a core country. This scenario reproduces the unequal conditions prevailing in the world that result in cores and peripheries.

To acknowledge the existence of knowledge extractivism in the context of intellectual monopoly capitalism, we analyse the contribution of a semi-peripheral university to pharmaceutical innovation networks. This field is paradigmatic for studying innovation dynamics between public and private actors. In Chapter 6, we showed that big pharmaceuticals are intellectual monopolies that outsource innovation modules developing, steering, controlling and appropriating rents from transnational innovation networks where universities and other academic research organizations participate. Here we delve into the place of semi-peripheral research institutions in these networks.

We have selected the University of Buenos Aires (UBA), Argentina's biggest and best-ranked university and a leader in Latin America, an exemplary case of a semi-peripheral university (Beigel, 2017; García de Fanelli, 2007). Our quantitative analysis, which was based on a corpus of publications extracted from Web of Science and a corpus of patents obtained from Derwent Innovation, is complemented by semi-structured in-depth interviews with UBA researchers.

Anticipating our results, we show that the UBA participates in pharmaceutical transnational innovation networks but without collecting intellectual rents. We thus argue that knowledge is extracted from the UBA and assetized by academic institutions and private corporations from core countries.

The rest of this chapter is organized as follows. Section 2 briefly overviews the main traits of intellectual monopoly capitalism in connection with the literature on academic dependency to further develop the proposed knowledge extractivism concept. Next, Section 3 elaborates on what is being measured by different indicators used for studying university-industry links and explain our methodology. Our findings are presented in Section 4 and discussed in Section 5, where we also conclude.

2 Knowledge extractivism from the peripheries under intellectual monopoly capitalism

When analysing non-core countries, the academic literature agrees that there is a lack of demand for technology transfer from public research organizations (including public universities) to the private sector (see Chapter 11, in particular the discussion on alternative sources of profits for laggard firms). Latin America is characterized by a lack of new innovative firms (Amorós et al., 2019) and most local companies do not invest in R&D, being mostly demanders of technical assistance (Albornoz et al., 2017; Arocena et al., 2015; Arocena & Sutz, 2010). Indeed, in Argentina, the most frequent contracts are those providing services, in particular technical assistance (Arza & Carattoli, 2012; Dávila, 2006; Juarros, 2006; Rikap, 2017; Riquelme & Langer, 2013).

However, local firms and even multinational firms operating in the peripheries may not be the only ones that can profit from semi-peripheral universities' research capabilities. These institutions' R&D could also be part of global innovation networks that, as we showed in this book, are led by corporate (and sometimes also academic) intellectual monopolies from core countries. Intellectual monopolies have monopolized access to knowledge garnering intellectual rents from their own and others' R&D results. They organize and plan global innovation networks subordinating other participants. Some universities and public research organizations from core countries, in particular from the United States, partner with intellectual monopolies in less unequal terms, collecting part of the resulting intellectual rents (see Chapter 5).

From data to science and technology results, intellectual monopolies use intangibles to fuel innovation. Building on Levín (1997) and Pagano (2014), innovations – with their corresponding increase in intellectual rents – reinforce intellectual monopolies' power.

Concerning the pharmaceutical industry, in Chapter 6, we showed that big pharmaceuticals are intellectual monopolies appropriating intellectual rents from their innovation networks. These networks are mostly integrated by US institutions, followed by academic research institutions from other core countries. Overall, this book's empirical results have shown that subordinate organizations that participate in innovation networks – including subordinate research universities – are mostly concentrated in core countries, with a few cases from the so-called emerging economies like Israel or Korea. These results point to the endurance of a historical trend acknowledged by Prebisch (1950) by the mid-20th century. The broad technological gap between the core and the peripheries is a structural explanation of underdevelopment. The core may have widened since Prebisch's contributions – for instance, including China – but it is still highly concentrated. Innovation flows are not limited by national boundaries since actors from multiple countries work together. Still, they are subjected to a particular geographical distribution with uneven technological capabilities worldwide.

It could have thus been concluded that intellectual monopoly capitalism, even if it involves firms from the peripheries that participate in intellectual monopolies' production networks as subordinated firms, does not affect R&D institutions from the peripheries. Nonetheless, the absence of institutions from the peripheries among the most frequent participants of intellectual monopolies' innovation networks does not mean that they do not contribute to those networks. Contributions may be hidden because partnerships are not as frequent as those with core countries' research institutions and innovating firms. Given their condition as institutions from peripheral countries, they may be occupying extremely subordinated positions.

To provide evidence of how intellectual monopoly capitalism impacts the peripheries, we study a semi-peripheral research institution. We are interested in identifying if and how our chosen university participates in structures dominated by intellectual monopolies from core countries.

Beyond intellectual monopolies, the question of how institutions from peripheral countries participate in global knowledge networks has been addressed by the academic dependency approach. In a nutshell, this framework identifies that research questions, methodologies and general guidelines of the research performed in non-hegemonic countries are influenced by the patterns and requirements of hegemonic countries (Alatas, 2003; Beigel, 2010; Kreimer, 2006). Subordinate positions result from unequal access to funding. Most research funds come from core countries, thus researchers from the peripheries adapt and accept rules imposed by financing institutions and core countries' research organizations that lead the groups that apply for competitive grants. Concerning these international collaborations, it was claimed that researchers from non-hegemonic countries occupy subordinate positions in science's global division of labour, typically specializing in activities with a high technical content (Alatas, 2003; Kreimer, 2014).

Other authors suggest a more nuanced perspective of the meanings of academic dependency, highlighting that the peripheries are not mere passive importers of knowledge (Beigel, 2014; Beigel et al., 2018). They argue that the concept of academic dependency should also acknowledge fields' internal asymmetries and heterogeneities, considering circuits of recognition at different levels (international, regional and local) (Beigel et al., 2018). The latter and other studies on the production and circulation of knowledge – like Medina (2013) – argue that there are spheres of relative autonomy in the peripheries. In any case, all this literature recognizes that core countries influence the peripheries' research agendas and methodologies.

We build on the dependency theory to identify the concrete ways in which global leader corporations and research institutions that have become intellectual monopolies subordinate academic institutions with recognized R&D capabilities from the peripheries. In the next section, we present our proposed methodology.

3 Complementing existing indicators for studying university's technology transfer

Comprehensive bibliometric analyses show that university patenting and quantifying and sorting links between research institutions and firms stand out as the most used indicators for accounting for universities' technology transfer (Noh & Lee, 2019; Skute et al., 2019). Studies on university patenting grew since the Bayh Dole Act and, in general, due to the tightening of intellectual property rights (Baldini, 2008; Berman, 2011; Mowery, 2005; Noh & Lee, 2019; Owen-Smith & Powell, 2003; Skute et al., 2019; Stephan et al., 2007). Also, since the 2000s, special attention was paid to the number and type of university agreements with third parties (Curi et al., 2012; Noh & Lee, 2019; Siegel et al., 2007; Skute et al., 2019). These two indicators are typically built using data from Technology Transfer Offices (TTOs) (Curi et al., 2012; Siegel et al., 2007).

Another standard indicator for measuring university engagement in innovation processes is the consequent diversification of its funding sources (Castro-Martínez & Sutz, 2011; Clark, 2004; Michael, 2005; Vincent-Lancrin, 2006). Particular attention is given to private sponsorship of research and the commercialization of results, including royalties (Johnstone, 2009). In this context, Muscio et al. (2013) examine whether public and private research funding compete or complement each other. From a critical standpoint, Slaughter and Leslie (1997) had already explained that researchers from English-speaking countries compete for private funding tied to targeted, applied research, strategic to big corporations. In the case of Argentina, studies focus on public budget shortfalls and typically look at the emergence of alternative resources as compensation for block-grants' insufficiency (Brotto, 1999; García de Fanelli, 2012; Rikap, 2017).

These indicators have in common that they measure universities' technology transfer by analysing economic returns and institutionalized results (such as legal contracts and patents). For the specific case of the peripheries, new indicators were proposed aiming to measure universities' contributions to development (Arocena et al., 2017, Chapter 9). They were also included in the RICyT (2017) manual for measuring university links in Ibero-America. Despite capturing a portion of the local specificities of semi-peripheral universities, such as their contribution to promote generalized access to higher education, they tell an incomplete story. By focusing on universities' closest environment (from local to national levels), they overlook that leading research universities from non-core countries may also be participating in transnational innovation networks. From a dependency theory perspective, it is expected that this participation will be in a subordinate position. Hence, to complement the most used indicators, we propose to analyse the contribution of a semi-peripheral university to innovation by considering its research outcomes.

Semi-peripheral universities tend to be surrounded by low private investment in R&D. They usually enjoy significant public block-grants – mainly oriented to teaching, given their size – but still face structural budget shortfalls, which partially explain the lack of skilled or sufficient professionals at their TTOs. At the same time, unlike peripheral institutions, selected groups of researchers from semi-peripheral institutions, often trained in core countries, produce at the knowledge frontier, making their university a regional leader. The UBA has highly cited, world-renowned researchers leading teams of brilliant younger scholars (that potentially did or will do part of their training abroad) (Beigel, 2017). Considering these features, we propose to study (1) blind knowledge transfer and (2) scientific publications' co-authorship with private firms, in connection with most used indicators. This overall assessment will be more accurate, in particular, by distinguishing between the UBA's contribution to (global) innovation networks and related economic benefits.

Citing scientific publications in patent applications is a way to look at the contribution of science to technology, Codner et al. (2012) called it blind technology transfer. We rename it blind knowledge transfer since cited publications may be far from technological contributions but still represent a knowledge transfer. Although this is a less frequent indicator, it has been recognized as valuable for measuring the contribution of public science to private innovations (Ahmadpoor & Jones, 2017; Codner et al., 2012; Codner & Perrota, 2018; Hicks et al., 2001; Jaffe & Trajtenberg, 2002; Meyer, 2000; Wang & Li, 2019).

To find the UBA's blind knowledge transfer in the pharmaceutical field, we used the Web of Science (WoS) and Derwent Innovation databases. We retrieved all the UBA papers from WoS Pharmacy and Pharmacology field published between 1998 and 2017. From a total of 1,398 papers, we only considered the 1,232 that had a DOI. Next, we looked for the DOI of those papers in the cited references of Derwent Innovation patents and analysed the resulting corpus.

We also studied university-industry co-authorship (Confraria & Vargas, 2019; Zhou et al., 2016). Publications were considered as one of the most important channels of university-industry knowledge transfer in Latin America (Dutrénit & Arza, 2010). We considered the total number of publications by type of co-author.

Our quantitative research is coupled with in-depth interviews with UBA researchers that have proven participation in pharmaceutical transnational knowledge networks. Interviewees were chosen from the list of corresponding authors of cited papers in international patents.[1] Our sample contains a total of 57 papers with 49 different corresponding authors, 32 of which were UBA scholars. From this group, we interviewed 21 researchers associated with 27 different papers of our sample.[2] Interviews were conducted in November-December 2018 and April 2019 at the UBA and ranged between 40 and 90 minutes in length. Interviews validated quantitative results and provided further proof of blind knowledge transfer as well as concrete examples of knowledge extractivism beyond those found in our quantitative analysis.

Researchers were asked about: (i) their cited paper (whether they had worked with or had been contacted by the patent owner, how that paper was funded, etc.), (ii) their funding sources, including in-depth questions concerning private sponsorship of research and technical assistance, (iii) patents (if they tried to patent, and, in that case, the obstacles they could have had and if they licensed the patent), (iv) science, technology and innovation (STI) policy since 2005 in Argentina – particularly concerning university-industry collaborations and (v) evaluation criteria (how important it was to collaborate with industry or own a patent in comparison with publishing papers that have been highly cited).

The next section presents and discusses our findings.

4 Knowledge extractivism from the UBA's pharmacy research

We first apply the most commonly used indicators for studying university-industry collaborations to the UBA case. As we have explained, these indicators infer participation from associated economic returns and by assessing institutionalized links at the university level. The latter refers to signed contracts with the UBA's TTOs. Next, we complement these results with an analysis of the UBA's research contribution to transnational innovation networks considering universities' main research outputs (scientific publications). The whole presentation combines quantitative analysis with results from our interviews, thus providing a more acute depiction of the case under study.

4.1 Indicators based on measuring universities' economic return from university-industry collaborations

We start by looking at the UBA's budget. The UBA receives colossal public block-grants because undergraduate education is tuition-free, and there are no access restrictions. Thus, its own resources[3] – which include private funds and other public funds besides block grants – represent around 20% of its total annual budget (USD 16.7 million in 2012). Within UBA's own resources, training agreements of the School of Economic Sciences stand out as the UBA's most significant source of private revenues (37% of total own resources in 2012). Postgraduate education tuition and fees follow, representing 25.7%. Research faculties' own resources were just 3.9% of the UBA's total own resources in 2012, thus around 0.65% of UBA's total budget (Rikap, 2017).

Considering agreements with industry, in the UBA, they represented less than 8% of its budget in 2012, including a majority of technical assistance. That year, the UBA signed only four (new) research agreements with private sponsors. In comparison, for instance, Harvard signed 73.[4] At the faculty level, TTOs data shows that, between 1997 and 2011, 89% of total third-party agreements signed by the UBA's Pharmacy School were technical assistance or other mainly routine activities.

Since formal technology transfers registered at TTOs are not the only possible knowledge transfer from universities to industry (Codner & Perrota, 2018; Grimpe & Hussinger, 2013; Link et al., 2007), this data should not be automatically taken as conclusive. However, all our interviewees confirmed this result. Some interviewees add that when local companies occasionally reach the UBA for an R&D agreement, they expect quick results that can never be granted in advance. Hence, agreements with local companies frequently end up not been signed, or the project is dropped soon after it starts. Interviewees also agreed that foreign companies occasionally contact them but claim that signing agreements is a long process, so they prefer to collaborate by other means. Beneath this explanation underlies the limitation of the used indicator; it misses links that bypass TTOs.

The UBA has even weaker results in terms of international patenting: six granted patents.[5] Three of them are dead because owners failed to pay annual fees, which highlights that they were not generating enough revenues. The remaining three correspond to the same invention and are co-owned with Columbia University. They are still alive because, as the interviewed UBA inventors explained, Columbia pays the annual fees. It was also Columbia that drafted and filed the patents. Since Columbia covered all the patenting expenses, the agreement was that the UBA will not receive royalties.

Patenting at the local level, especially in the pharmaceutical field, does not seem a good alternative. If the achievement is path-breaking, it can easily be stolen and patented in international offices. If it is not pathbreaking, the chances of licensing the patent are slim because a firm would have to agree to pay royalties for an invention that may not result in an innovation. Meanwhile, application and maintenance costs remain high. Interviewed researchers that own or owned national patents have never licensed them. The only exception is a product that treats baldness called EcoHair, currently sold by Garré Guevara. The patent is owned by Argentina's Research Council (CONICET), but royalties are partly distributed to the UBA because the invention was achieved in a UBA-CONICET research institute.

Interviewed researchers explained these poor results by the lack of infrastructure and funding for patenting at a global level. As we explained in Chapter 2, patenting also demands skills to face claims in courts and a deterrence capacity that set a high entry barrier (Pagano, 2014). In addition to budget constraints, patenting demands an active behaviour towards property rights, not only in terms of the management of private assets but also to enforce and reinforce property rights themselves (Birch, 2017). All this is out of the reach for Argentinean universities and the CONICET. Among the consequences we found the following example of a predatory practice between universities with different bargaining power:

> We applied for a European patent with a university in Scotland. (...) This university did not do any research but only the paperwork to get the patent that nobody funded here
>
> (Interviewee 1, own translation).

Furthermore, patenting and licensing is not seen as a unanimous concern by interviewed researchers. They are all deeply committed to improving people's life by their findings, but not all of them care about the commercialization of successful results. Interviewed researchers think of commercialization as a corporate matter. For this reason, some of them (unsuccessfully) seek to draw firms' attention. How the patent will be filled and who will own it is not generally perceived as researchers' areas of concern. Unlike Vallas and Kleinman's (2008) results, it seems that in the UBA the discovery-oriented logic is not intertwined with entrepreneurial market practices. Needless to say that the secrecy problem – delaying publications until the patent is granted – could also contribute to explain these results. Summing up, there are many reasons why university patenting is not a good indicator for measuring the contribution of a semi-peripheral university to innovation networks.

All indicators considered, it appears that the UBA is not contributing to innovation networks but only providing technical assistance to laggard local companies without patenting achievements or significantly performing new research for third parties. Still, this conclusion could be biased by the indicators used. If we distinguish between creating knowledge and capturing intellectual rents from its assetization, it may be the case that the UBA contributes to transnational innovation networks as a subordinate research university, thus without capturing associated rents. Private funds related to research commercialization will be slim, and patents and budget-related indicators might be inaccurate.

4.2 The UBA's contribution to global innovation networks assessed from an analysis of its scientific publications

4.2.1 Blind knowledge transfer

Fifty-seven out of 1,232 (4.6%) UBA papers were cited in international patents from three patent offices: USPTO, European Patent Office and Korean Intellectual Property Office. Tijssen (2019) recently showed blind knowledge transfer figures for leader institutions focused on applied or technological research, such as Hannover Medical School (3.1%), MIT (4.6%) or ETH Zurich (1.9%). These figures are in line with the UBA's results for pharmacy and pharmacology.

In our sample, there were 146 total citations in international patents, since some publications were cited more than once (most cited paper appeared in 13 patents), and they belonged to 141 patent families. The average lapse between the publication and the patent application citing the paper was 5.6 years. Hence, more blind knowledge transfer can be expected from papers published from 2013 onwards. Interviews reconfirmed the absence of a link with the patent owners. Some interviewees acknowledged that the patented invention was an idea that they had when they published the paper.

> In the paper, we show that a milk component is a type of sugar that is in higher proportion in the cow's colostrum. And we were able to isolate it. By isolating these compounds, they could be incorporated into baby food formulas because of their importance for brain development. This is what they patented. I was telling young researchers at the time to start a project on this... it wasn't done. Isolating those compounds from colostrum is cheap, but nobody did it. Well, yes, now I know this company did it
>
> (Interviewee 2, own translation).

Figure 13.1 shows the distribution of the type of institutions owning patents that cite UBA's pharmacy papers for the chosen period. There is an absolute majority of corporations, none of which is a local company. Many are global leaders that can be considered as intellectual monopolies, such as BASF, Elli Lilly, Merck, Monsanto and Siemens. Within universities, there are no Argentinean institutions but mainly US top research-universities, such as Columbia, California, Stanford, Wisconsin Madison, Texas Austin and Michigan. Among public research organizations, almost every institution is from the United States.

The prevalence of the United States is further explored in Figure 13.2, which depicts the nationality of our sample of patent owners. The United

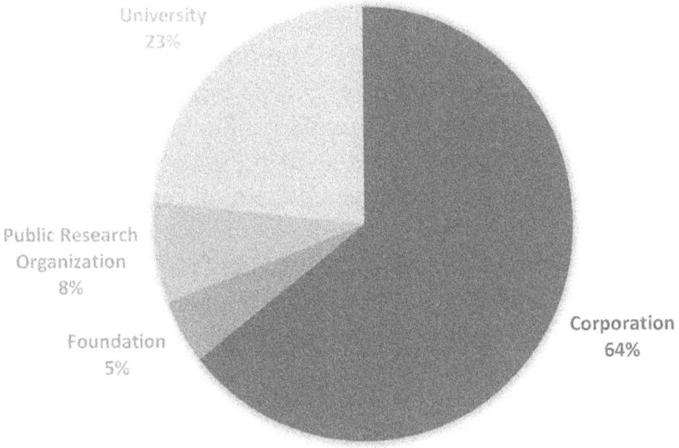

Figure 13.1 Type of institutions owning patents that cite UBA pharmacy and pharmacology publications.

Source: Author's analysis based on Derwent Innovation and Web of Science.

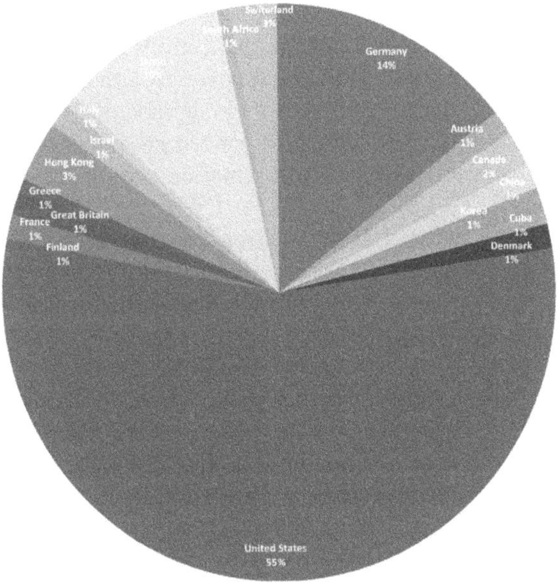

Figure 13.2 Country of origin of the owners of patents citing UBA pharmacy and pharmacology publications.

Source: Author's analysis based on Derwent Innovation.

States is followed, from afar, by Germany and Japan. This result is not surprising considering the place of those countries in the pharmaceutical industry (Baranes, 2016; Khanna, 2012; Montalban & Sakinç, 2013). Moreover, owners come from core countries except for a Cuban public research organization and a South African company. Therefore, results show that knowledge is being extracted from a semi-peripheral research institution and redirected to core countries where intellectual rents are potentially being collected.

All in all, the level of blind knowledge transfer from the UBA's pharmacy research is aligned to that of leading universities, and the principal benefactors of these promising results are core countries' global corporations and top research institutions.

4.2.2 University-industry co-authorship

We consider university-industry co-authorship by analysing the types of UBA co-authors and their relative importance between periods (1998–2007 and 2008–17) (Table 13.1).

The comparison between periods shows that both local and international corporate co-authors grew more than total co-authors. In particular, international corporations have one of the highest growth rates. In the second period (2008–17), the UBA co-authored 7.1% of its pharma publications with corporations. Co-publishing with corporations is, of course, less frequent than co-authoring with academic institutions due to the core activity of each type of organization; thus, the relative growth of their importance between periods is even more telling of their significance.

The UBA-industry co-authorship in pharmaceutical research is way above Argentina as well as other Latin American countries' co-authorship with industry (0.9% and 1.6%, respectively) (Confraria & Vargas, 2019). This gap not only speaks of the UBA's research capabilities but also points to the internal heterogeneities of national innovation systems. These heterogeneities justify institutional-level analyses, especially for the case of semi-peripheral universities that differ from their national science and innovation general environment. Further research should be done on the citations received by the UBA's co-published papers with firms in comparison to total citations, among other possible indicators of the quality of published investigations. In any case, results indicate that the UBA's contribution is more significant than what would result from just looking at the most used indicators (Section 4.1).

At the firm level, the UBA's most frequent corporate co-authors between 1998 and 2017 include big pharmaceuticals like AstraZeneca, Boehringer Ingelheim GmbH, Bristol Myers Squibb and Eli Lilly. Excepting for Biousidus, a local firm, international corporations have published more or the same number of articles with the UBA than local corporations.

Table 13.1 UBA's pharmacy publications by type of co-author

Institution	*1998–2007*			*2008–17*			*Growth total frequency (%)*	*Growth frequency in distinct papers (%)*
	Total frequency	*Frequency in distinct papers*	*Proportion total publications*	*Total frequency*	*Frequency in distinct papers*	*Proportion total publications*		
UBA	817	593	94.7	1101	703	91.1		
International University	247	150	24.0	553	250	32.4	124	67
Argentinean University	106	81	12.9	212	163	21.1	100	101
CONICET	81	78	12.5	145	132	17.1	79	69
Argentinean Hospital	76	51	8.1	220	135	17.5	189	165
International Public Research Organization	32	30	4.8	74	53	6.9	131	77
International Hospital	24	17	2.7	81	47	6.1	238	176
Argentinean Public Research Organization (excluding CONICET)	20	18	2.9	66	47	6.1	230	161
Foundation	19	19	3.0	54	39	5.1	184	105
UBA CONICET	18	16	2.6	34	32	4.1	89	100
International Firm	13	13	2.1	42	32	4.1	223	146
Argentinean Firm	10	9	1.4	26	24	3.1	160	167

Source: Author's analysis based on Web of Science.

Finally, concerning scientific publications, our interviews show that sometimes big pharmaceuticals appropriate UBA's research and try to publish (and patent) it first.

> I had a terrible experience with a big pharma. They have a drug for bone cancer. Suddenly we found that it inhibited a receptor from a nervous system cell that has importance in multiple sclerosis. (...) We went to a congress in Edinburgh to present this result. When we returned, someone from the organizing committee told us that in the neuroscience division of this big pharma they started the same investigation. She told us to patent right away. I went to my faculty but did not get support. I think they don't have the know-how to patent; neither the CONICET nor the UBA
>
> (Interviewee 3, own translation).

5 Discussion and final remarks

Although in this book we have studied intellectual monopoly capitalism as a global phenomenon, in this chapter, we gave an account of regional and institutional specificities that demand researchers to adapt how the same phenomenon is studied in different contexts. We argued that the sole use of the most widespread indicators to analyse the contribution of research institutions to innovation (research agreements with corporations, university patenting and diversification of budgetary sources) lead to misleading results. By using these indicators, the academic literature has concluded that semi-peripheral institutions do not significantly contribute to innovation networks. The problem is that this conclusion emerges from indicators that do not measure the actual contribution but the institution's associated economic returns.

Acknowledging that global intellectual monopolies appropriate knowledge by exercising a predatory relation with the participants of their innovation networks (Chapter 2), and that this particularly affects subordinate research universities (Chapter 5), we argued for an additional analysis capable of accounting for research contributions to innovation. Therefore, we complemented the most used indicators by studying the UBA's actual R&D contribution to transnational innovation networks regardless of its economic returns. We proxied the latter by studying universities' primary research outcome: scientific publications. We considered: (1) blind knowledge transfer and (2) university-industry co-authorship. Our findings were combined with the results of in-depth interviews with researchers participating in pharmaceutical transnational knowledge networks.

Altogether, our analysis has allowed us to distinguish between research institutions' participation in innovation networks and their capacity to collect revenues from that activity. Those universities that do not collect these economic benefits can be considered subordinate research-universities (see Chapter 5) even if they are not among intellectual monopolies' privileged research collaborators. This chapter's results also contribute to understanding the specificities of geopolitical asymmetries within transnational innovation networks under intellectual monopoly capitalism. In concrete terms, our two-fold analysis allows us to account for knowledge extractivism as a specific form of academic dependency where knowledge is extracted from a semi-peripheral research institution and assetized by corporations or leading academic institutions from core countries.

In terms of results, the most widely used indicators show that the UBA obtains very little economic return from its research activities. There are only three active international patents, all from the same project, and interviews confirmed that the UBA does not obtain any benefit from them. Narrowing down our analysis to the pharmacy field, only 10% of the contracts with third parties signed by the UBA's Pharmacy School between 1997 and 2011 requested new research. In terms of the university budget, at the total level of the UBA, 80% of the funds are public block-grants mainly used to pay salaries; the remaining 20% comes mostly from internship fees, postgraduate education and extracurricular courses tuitions. Funding obtained through agreements with third parties (including technical assistance) at the total level of the UBA represents less than 2% of its overall budget.

At the same time, research outcomes and our interviews point to a significant contribution of the UBA to pharmaceutical global innovation networks. In line with the figures of leading global institutions in different disciplines (Tijssen, 2019), 4.6% of the UBA's pharmacy publications between 1998 and 2017 are cited by international patents exclusively owned by foreign organizations with a predominance of companies (64% of patents) and the United States as patent owners' country of origin (55%). In the interviews, we confirmed the absence of links with companies and other organizations that own patents that cite UBA pharmacy publications. Moreover, corporate co-authorship is growing more than proportionally to the increase in the total number of co-authorships, and global intellectual monopolies are privileged among corporate co-authors. Our interviews provided additional information about UBA researchers suffering extortive practices and theft of ideas by big pharmaceuticals.

All in all, if we consider that the UBA does not generally capture rents from its R&D results (as shown by most used indicators), we conclude that its contribution to transnational pharmaceutical innovation networks is a case of *knowledge extractivism* from the periphery to the centre. It directly favours global intellectual monopolies as well as academic intellectual monopolies and even other companies from core countries. This chapter also showed that knowledge extractivism takes place both as a predatory relationship, thus a direct manifestation of superior force, such as the drug for bone cancer example, but that it is also orchestrated without any direct relationship, as in blind knowledge transfer cases.

Moreover, knowledge extractivism is not only a result of the spread power of global intellectual monopolies but also a consequence of a subordinate political context. On the one hand, peripheral states promote public-private collaborations – influenced by a dominant global discourse imposed by the centre – as an alternative to public budget shortfalls and without the capacities to prevent global intellectual monopolies from profiting from that policy. On the other hand, local firms lack incentives to invest and engage in R&D (see Chapter 11), which leads states to further insist on those policies without acknowledging the restrictive effects of knowledge assetization in the core to catching up in the peripheries. The consequence for the UBA in terms of the orientation of its research agenda is an open question that integrates our future research programme.

Although our conclusions correspond to our specific case study, the general methodological framework presented can be applied to other institutions to determine the existence of knowledge extractivism. Altogether, the different indicators considered in this chapter allow distinguishing universities' contributions to innovation networks from whether they capture or not associated intellectual rents.

To conclude, further research could complement our results by considering the distinction between university-owned and university-invented patents, which to our knowledge has always been applied to study core-countries' universities (Crespi et al., 2006; Schoen & Buenstorf, 2013). In line with our results, it can be expected to find significant differences between owned and invented patents in the case of semi-peripheral research institutions. Likewise, further research could also consider the case of global corporate publishers. On the one hand, the global oligopolistic market of multinational publishers controls high impact factor journals and charge for accessing knowledge results. On the other hand, a complementary market charges researchers for publishing their articles in less recognized journals (Truth, 2012). The former sometimes also charge researchers to publish their research. These markets reproduce global inequalities because research institutions from the peripheries more often than not will lack the means to access, and especially the means to publish in international journals (Naidorf & Perrotta, 2017). These publishers end up regulating how knowledge is produced and act as validation agencies that are uncritically assumed as valid parameters of original knowledge (Rikap & Naidorf, 2020).

In the next chapter, beyond general policy discussions, we will consider these and previous chapters' findings to elaborate on specific recommendations to counterbalance intellectual monopoly capitalism.

Notes

1 From that list, we considered only those whose main author was affiliated to the UBA. When the main author was not reachable, we interviewed the head of the corresponding laboratory.

2 To preserve interviewees' anonymity, we will refer to them by consecutive numbers instead of using their names.

3 In Argentina, all resources other than public block-grants are classified as *own resources*.
4 Data retrieved from Harvard Office of Technology Development and the UBA's Superior Council public data.
5 Information retrieved from Derwent Innovation database by mid-2018. Our access included all the information from USPTO, WIPO, European, Japan, Australian, British, Canadian, French, German, Russian and Korean patent offices.

References

Ahmadpoor, M., & Jones, B. F. (2017). The dual frontier: Patented inventions and prior scientific advance. *Science, 357*(6351), 583–7.

Alatas, S. F. (2003). Academic dependency and the global division of labour in the social sciences. *Current Sociology, 51*(6), 599–613.

Albornoz, M., Barrere, R., & Sokil, J. (2017). Las Universidades Lideran la I+D en América Latina. In Albornoz, M (Ed.) *El Estado de la Ciencia 2017* (pp. 31–44). RICyT.

Amorós, J. E., Poblete, C., & Mandakovic, V. (2019). R&D transfer, policy and innovative ambitious entrepreneurship: Evidence from Latin American countries. *The Journal of Technology Transfer, 44*, 1396–1415.

Arocena, R., Göransson, B., & Sutz, J. (2015). Knowledge policies and universities in developing countries: Inclusive development and the "developmental university." *Technology in Society, 41*, 10–20.

Arocena, R., Göransson, B., & Sutz, J. (2017). *Developmental universities in inclusive innovation systems: Alternatives for knowledge democratization in the global South*. Springer.

Arocena, R., & Sutz, J. (2000). Looking at national systems of innovation from the South. *Industry and Innovation, 7*(1), 55–75.

Arocena, R., & Sutz, J. (2010). Weak knowledge demand in the South: Learning divides and innovation policies. *Science and Public Policy, 37*(8), 571–82.

Arza, V., & Carattoli, M. (2012). El desarrollo de la biotecnología y las vinculaciones público-privadas, una discusión de la literatura orientada al caso argentino. *Realidad Económica, 266*, 49–71.

Baldini, N. (2008). Negative effects of university patenting: Myths and grounded evidence. *Scientometrics, 75*(2), 289–311.

Baranes, A. I. (2016). *An original institutionalist approach to the structure, conduct, and performance of the pharmaceutical industry: The importance of intangible assets* [PhD Thesis]. University of Missouri-Kansas City.

Beigel, F. (2010). *Autonomía y dependencia académica: Universidad e investigación científica en un circuito periférico: Chile y Argentina, 1950–1980*. Editorial Biblos.

Beigel, F. (2014). *Introduction: Current tensions and trends in the world scientific system*. Sage Publications Sage.

Beigel, F. (2017). Científicos Periféricos, entre Ariel y Calibán. Saberes Institucionales y Circuitos de Consagración en Argentina. Las publicaciones de los Investigadores del CONICET. *Dados, 60*(3), 825–65.

Beigel, F., Gallardo, O., & Bekerman, F. (2018). Institutional expansion and scientific development in the periphery: The structural heterogeneity of Argentina's academic field. *Minerva, 56*(3), 305–31.

Berman, E. P. (2011). *Creating the market university: How academic science became an economic engine*. Princeton University Press.

Birch, K. (2017). Rethinking value in the bio-economy: Finance, assetization, and the management of value. *Science, Technology, & Human Values*, *42*(3), 460–90.

Brotto, A. (1999). Los 'Recursos Propios' en el Presupuesto Universitario. In Sánchez Martínez, E. (Ed.) *La Educación Superior En La Argentina, Transformaciones, Debates y Desafíos*. (pp. 293–294) Ministerio de Cultura y Educación, Secretaría de Políticas Universitarias.

Castro-Martínez, E., & Sutz, J. (2011). Universidad, conocimiento e innovación. In M. Albornoz & A. Arellano Hernández (Eds.), *Ciencia, tecnología y universidad en Iberoamérica* (pp. 101–17). EUDEBA. http://www.conicit.go.cr/servicios/listadocs/informes/ciencia_universidades.pdf#page=103

Clark, B. (2004). *Sustaining change in universities*. Open University Press.

Codner, D. G., Becerra, P., & Díaz, A. (2012). Blind technology transfer or technological knowledge leakage: A case study from the South. *Journal of Technology Management & Innovation*, *7*(2), 184–95.

Codner, D. G., & Perrota, R. M. (2018). Blind technology transfer process from Argentina. *Journal of Technology Management & Innovation*, *13*(3), 47–53.

Confraria, H., & Vargas, F. (2019). Scientific systems in Latin America: Performance, networks, and collaborations with industry. *The Journal of Technology Transfer*, *44*(3), 874–915.

Cooke, P. (2006). Global bioregions: Knowledge domains, capabilities and innovation system networks. *Industry and Innovation*, *13*(4), 437–58.

Crespi, G. A., Geuna, A., & Verspagen, B. (2006). University IPRs and knowledge transfer. Is the IPR ownership model more efficient. *6th Annual Roundtable of Engineering Research, Georgia Tech College of Management*, 1–3.

Curi, C., Daraio, C., & Llerena, P. (2012). University technology transfer: How (in) efficient are French universities? *Cambridge Journal of Economics*, *36*(3), 629–54.

Dávila, M. (2006). Vinculación Universidad-Sector Productivo-Estado En La Facultad De Agronomía De La Universidad De Buenos Aires: La Apertura Al Medio Como Eje De Transformación Institucional'. *La Vinculación Universidad-Empresa: Miradas Críticas Desde La Universidad Pública, Buenos Aires: Miño y Dávila Editores*.

Dutrénit, G., & Arza, V. (2010). Channels and benefits of interactions between public research organisations and industry: Comparing four Latin American countries. *Science and Public Policy*, *37*(7), 541–53.

Ernst, D. (2008). *Can Chinese IT firms develop innovative capabilities within global knowledge networks?* https://papers.ssrn.com/sol3/papers.cfm?abstract_id=2742950

Ernst, D. (2009). *A new geography of knowledge in the electronics industry? Asia's role in global innovation networks*. https://papers.ssrn.com/sol3/papers.cfm?abstract_id=2742923

Ernst, D. (2016). *Global strategic patenting and innovation–Policy and research implications*. East-West Center Working Papers.

García de Fanelli, A. M. (2007). The challenge of building research Universities in middle-income countries: The case of the University of Buenos Aires. In P. G. Altbach & J. Balán (Eds.), *World class worldwide transforming research Universities in Asia and Latin America* (pp. 260–85). Johns Hopkins University Press.

García de Fanelli, A. M. (2012). Financiación de la Educación Superior Argentina: Cambios y continuidades entre los años 90 y la primera década del 2000. *Educación Superior y Sociedad*, *16*(1), 16–36.

Grimpe, C., & Hussinger, K. (2013). Formal and informal knowledge and technology transfer from academia to industry: Complementarity effects and innovation performance. *Industry and Innovation*, *20*(8), 683–700.

Hicks, D., Breitzman, T., Olivastro, D., & Hamilton, K. (2001). The changing composition of innovative activity in the US—A portrait based on patent analysis. *Research Policy*, *30*(4), 681–703.

Jaffe, A. B., & Trajtenberg, M. (2002). *Patents, citations, and innovations: A window on the knowledge economy*. MIT Press.

Johnstone, D. B. (2009). Worldwide trends in financing higher education: A conceptual framework. *Financing Access and Equity in Higher Education*. http://gse.buffalo.edu/org/IntHigherEdFinance/files/Publications/foundation_papers/(2009)_Worldwide_Trends_in_Financing_Higher_Education.pdf

Juarros, M. F. (2006). La Vinculación Universidad-Empresa-Sector de la producción de bienes y servicios, vista por los docentes investigadores. El caso de la Facultad de Farmacia y Bioquímica de la Universidad de Buenos Aires. In S. Llomovatte, F. Juarros, J. Naidorf, & A. Guelman (Eds.), *La vinculación universidad-empresa: Miradas críticas desde la Universidad pública* (pp. 171–212). Miño y Davila.

Khanna, I. (2012). Drug discovery in pharmaceutical industry: Productivity challenges and trends. *Drug Discovery Today*, *17*(19), 1088–102.

Kreimer, P. (2006). Dependientes o integrados?: La ciencia latinoamericana y la nueva división internacional del trabajo. *Nómadas*, *24*, 199–212.

Kreimer, P. (2014). "Citizen of the world" or a local producer of useful knowledge? That's the question. In H. Sabea & F. Beigel (Eds.), *Academic dependency and professionalization in the south: Perspectives from the periphery* (pp. 151–66). *EDIUNC- Sephis.*

Levín, P. (1997). *El Capital Tecnológico*. Catálogos.

Linden, G., Kraemer, K. L., & Dedrick, J. (2009). Who captures value in a global innovation network?: The case of Apple's iPod. *Communications of the ACM*, *52*(3), 140–44.

Link, A. N., Siegel, D. S., & Bozeman, B. (2007). An empirical analysis of the propensity of academics to engage in informal university technology transfer. *Industrial and Corporate Change*, *16*(4), 641–55.

Liu, J., Chaminade, C., & Asheim, B. (2013). The geography and structure of global innovation networks: A knowledge base perspective. *European Planning Studies*, *21*(9), 1456–73.

Medina, L. R. (2013). *Centers and peripheries in knowledge production*. Routledge.

Meyer, M. (2000). Does science push technology? Patents citing scientific literature. *Research Policy*, *29*(3), 409–34.

Michael, S. (2005). Financing higher education in a global market: A contextual background. In S. Michael & M. Kretovics (Eds.), *Financing higher education in a global market* (pp. 3–32). Algora Publishing.

Montalban, M., & Sakinç, M. E. (2013). Financialization and productive models in the pharmaceutical industry. *Industrial and Corporate Change*, *22*(4), 981–1030.

Mowery, D. (2005). The Bayh-Dole Act and high-technology entrepreneurship in US universities: Chicken, egg, or something else? In G. Libecap (Ed.), *University entrepreneurship and technology transfer: Process, design, and intellectual property* (pp. 39–68). Elsevier. http://s1.downloadmienphi.net/file/downloadfile4/206/1391153.pdf#page=62

Muscio, A., Quaglione, D., & Vallanti, G. (2013). Does government funding complement or substitute private research funding to universities? *Research Policy, 42*(1), 63–75.

Naidorf, J., & Perrotta, D. (2017). La privatización del acceso abierto. Nuevas formas de colonización académica en América Latina y su impacto en la evaluación de la investigación. *Universidades, 73*, 41–50.

Noh, H., & Lee, S. (2019). Where technology transfer research originated and where it is going: A quantitative analysis of literature published between 1980 and 2015. *The Journal of Technology Transfer, 44*(3), 700–40.

OECD, Programme on Innovation, Higher Education and Research for Development. (2012). *Research universities: Networking the knowledge economy*. OECD.

Owen-Smith, J., & Powell, W. W. (2003). The expanding role of university patenting in the life sciences: Assessing the importance of experience and connectivity. *Research Policy, 32*(9), 1695–711.

Pagano, U. (2014). The crisis of intellectual monopoly capitalism. *Cambridge Journal of Economics, 38*(6), 1409–29.

Prebisch, R. (1950). Crecimiento, desequilibrio y disparidades: Interpretación del proceso de desarrollo económico. In CEPAL (Ed.) *Estudio Económico de América Latina y el Caribe* (pp. 3–89). CEPAL, United Nations.

Red Iberoamericana de Indicadores de Ciencia y Tecnología (RICYT). (2017). *Manual Iberoamericano de Indicadores de Vinculación de la Universidad con el Entorno Socioeconómico*. RICYT.

Rikap, C. (2017). The corporization of a public university with free undergraduate education: Endangering autonomy at the University of Buenos Aires. *World Social and Economic Review of Contemporary Policy Issues, 8*, 44–59.

Rikap, C. (2018). Innovation as economic power in global value chains. *Revue d'Économie Industrielle, 163*, 35–75.

Rikap, C. (2019). Asymmetric power of the core: Technological cooperation and technological competition in the transnational innovation networks of big pharma. *Review of International Political Economy, 26*(5), 987–1021. doi:10.1080/09692290.2019.1620309

Rikap, C., & Naidorf, J. (2020). Ciencia privatizada en América Latina. *Con-Ciencia Social, 3*, 57–76.

Riquelme, G. C., & Langer, A. (2013). Los docentes universitarios y la producción y circulación del conocimiento: Un estudio sobre universidades argentinas. *CIAN-Revista de Historia de Las Universidades, 16*(1), 81–114.

Rodrik, D. (2008). *One economics, many recipes: Globalization, institutions, and economic growth*. Princeton University Press.

Schoen, A., & Buenstorf, G. (2013). When do universities own their patents? An explorative study of patent characteristics and organizational determinants in Germany. *Industry and Innovation, 20*(5), 422–37.

Siegel, D. S., Veugelers, R., & Wright, M. (2007). Technology transfer offices and commercialization of university intellectual property: Performance and policy implications. *Oxford Review of Economic Policy, 23*(4), 640–60.

Skute, I., Zalewska-Kurek, K., Hatak, I., & de Weerd-Nederhof, P. (2019). Mapping the field: A bibliometric analysis of the literature on university–industry collaborations. *The Journal of Technology Transfer, 44*(3), 916–47.

Slaughter, S., & Leslie, L. L. (1997). *Academic capitalism: Politics, policies, and the entrepreneurial university.* ERIC. http://eric.ed.gov/?id=ED409816

Stephan, P. E., Gurmu, S., Sumell, A. J., & Black, G. (2007). Who's patenting in the university? Evidence from the survey of doctorate recipients. *Economics Innovation and New Technology, 16*(2), 71–99.

Tijssen, R. (2019). *On science industry linkages worldwide.* The 13th Workshop on The Organisation, Economics and Policy of Scientific Research.

Truth, F. (2012). Pay big to publish fast: Academic journal rackets. *Journal for Critical Education Policy Studies, 10*(2), 54–105.

Vallas, S. P., & Kleinman, D. L. (2008). Contradiction, convergence and the knowledge economy: The confluence of academic and commercial biotechnology. *Socio-Economic Review, 6*(2), 283–311.

Vincent-Lancrin, S. (2006). What is changing in academic research? Trends and futures scenarios. *European Journal of Education, 41*(2), 169–202.

Wang, L., & Li, Z. (2019). Knowledge flows from public science to industrial technologies. *The Journal of Technology Transfer*, 1–24. doi.org/10.1007/s10961-019-09738-9

Zhou, P., Tijssen, R., & Leydesdorff, L. (2016). University-industry collaboration in China and the USA: A bibliometric comparison. *PloS One, 11*(11), e0165277.

14

TILTING THE SCALE AGAINST INTELLECTUAL MONOPOLY CAPITALISM

1 Introduction

More than ever knowledge (hence, innovation) is power and this book has analysed how contemporary capitalism is driven by those monopolizing it. In a nutshell, we conceived intellectual monopolies as knowledge monopolies that rely both on concentrating intellectual property rights (IPRs), secrecy and other mechanisms (Chapter 2) to extract rents from the assetization of intangibles. They even profit from open access and knowledge commons initiatives (Chapter 3). Intellectual monopolies organize production and innovation networks extracting value from the former and knowledge from the latter. Knowledge is monetized, thus increasing intellectual monopolies' rents at the expense of other organizations participating in the innovation process, including innovating firms but also, as conceptualized in Chapter 5, different types of research universities and public research organizations. Building on Veblen (1899), we have defined these practices as modern forms of predation (see Chapters 2 and 10). A consequence has been the lessening of the link between innovation and growth (Chapters 1 and 10), thus affecting global capitalism at large, with particular consequences for the peripheries (Chapters 11–13).

Chapters 6–9 have provided evidence of different intellectual monopolies, including their engagement in technological cooperation with each other while also competing for technology, predating from other organizations (see in particular Chapter 6). Albeit their global reach, intellectual monopolies rely on their home countries' national innovation systems, especially during their emergence (Chapter 9). Moreover, we have distinguished among types of rents collected by these monopolies, drawing on Durand and Milberg's (2020) taxonomy (see in particular Chapter 7). Chapters 7 and 8 paid special attention to data-driven intellectual rents, defined as rents that emerge from privatizing access to continuously expanding data sources that are processed and analysed with machine learning algorithms. Once data are processed with artificial intelligence, digital intelligence is produced as privatized and assetized knowledge, thus power. As the digital economy expands, more data are created, expanding the power of those controlling access to them.

This final chapter shares reflections on the paths and ways to overcome this general context. It seeks to open questions and engage others to tilt the scale against intellectual monopolies. We elaborate policy recommendations for the public sector in more abstract terms, but also focus on specific policies for the peripheries. Overall, these reflections are inspired by Pfotenhauer and Juhl's (2017, p. 70) claim to "take into account broader social, political, and moral conceptualizations of statehood in discussing the benefits and challenges associated with the relationship between innovation and society".

Intellectual monopolies challenge but also underpin their corresponding (core) states' power. Moreover, their emergence is partially attributable to core states' policies, in particular from the United States and China (Chapter 4). States are not a separate, neutral institution detached from social (class, gender, race) struggles characterizing capitalism. Rulers represent fractions, often in line with those that mostly contributed to funding their campaigns. Furthermore, as had been synthesized by Strange (1996, p. 6) concerning the differences between existing states, "(m)any, perhaps most, societies have to be content with the mere appearance of autonomy, with a facade of statehood." In the hierarchy of power, peripheral states are below core states and their intellectual monopolies.[1]

This book has also shown that the peripheries are being severely hampered under intellectual monopoly capitalism, as chances for structural change further shrink. Intellectual monopolies deepen underdevelopment by profiting from knowledge and data extractivism (see Chapters 11–13). Knowledge produced in the peripheries is assetized in the centres further limiting the former's development opportunities. Moreover, data extractivism opened a new colonizing arm, data colonialism.

Besides limiting every form of extractivism, peripheral states should heavily invest in planning transformative innovations capable of building new sustainable industries. Peripheral countries should cease competing to attract outsourcing and offshoring and cooperate to establish minimum labour market regulations, forbidding new and old forms of informality and granting minimum working conditions.

When it comes to transforming reality, states should neither be the only, nor the main political actor. Our reflections seek to inspire and contribute to the fights of social movements, unions and the public in general. We end reflecting on scientists' responsibilities to counterbalance intellectual monopoly capitalism.

Next, we elaborate on the challenges of building a new (common) knowledge regime. In Sections 3 and 4, we appoint preliminary thoughts on alternative policies. Section 3 focuses on data-driven intellectual monopolies and Section 4 suggests policies to limit knowledge and data extractivisms in the peripheries. Section 4 also recommends investing heavily in science and technology to create new industries from scratch, attempting to generate structural changes. Section 5 moves beyond policy recommendations and highlights the role of social disrupts, political movements and workers' unions to counterbalance intellectual monopoly capitalism and build long-term alternatives. The book ends with an introspective reflection on the role of (social) scientists, in Section 6.

2 A new (common) knowledge regime

This book has contributed to the literature that highlights that IPRs favour knowledge owners but seldom benefit actual inventors (Dreyfuss & Frankel, 2014; Pistor, 2019). Furthermore, if we conceive knowledge as common stock in the light of Veblen's (2012) ideas, IPRs not only limit the use of final knowledge steps leading to innovation but mutilate knowledge as a whole, limiting economies of scope (see Chapters 3 and 10).

Counterbalancing trends include different forms of knowledge commons as well as open access initiatives. However, Chapter 3 has shown how intellectual monopolies also profit from them. An immediate reaction could be to curtail intellectual monopolies' participation in these environments. However, it would be hard to accomplish and probably contested since it will go precisely against the idea of open access. An alternative could be to regulate their participation. In the case of open source, unlike the extended Apache Licence 2.0, Copyleft limits the privatization of code based on open-source code.

Beyond these counterbalancing trends, to significantly tilt the scale, the current private knowledge regime needs to be overcome. IPRs are not doing the job they were supposed to do (encourage and protect the inventor). An apparent example concerns academic research copyrights. In order to publish, scholars must refuse copyrights or pay to publish in open access. In this respect, the few global publishers owning international journals are examples of intellectual monopolies (Rikap & Naidorf, 2020).

There is a difference between access to knowledge and the permission to use it. Knowledge protected with IPRs is public in terms of access, but private when it comes to using it. On the contrary, published papers, unless in open access, are privatized knowledge in terms of access but once access is granted, they are free to use. A new commons knowledge regime should simultaneously consider knowledge access and use. In this respect, sci-hub – a website that grants access to academic publications – works as a democratizing development policy. Remarkably, its creator is considered a terrorist by the US state. Moreover, a global public or commons knowledge regime is compatible with rewarding the inventor, for instance, as a onetime payment funded with a portion of the corporate taxes that are now avoided by intellectual monopolies.

This reform is all the more important in moments like the Covid-19 pandemic. Big pharmaceuticals are imposing exorbitant prices for treatments that were majorly funded with public funds (Cleary et al., 2020), and that result from previous research done mostly by research universities and public research organizations. As this book is being finished, serious concerns are being raised on prices and the distribution of potential vaccines. Some big pharmaceuticals are already anticipating high prices, and core countries' states are running to assure national supply without global coordination that is the only effective way to terminate the pandemic.

A commons knowledge regime could actually start from health and biomedical sciences (HBMS). They should become the first global public good. A global institution (potentially emerging from comprehensive reform of the World Health Organization) should take care of organizing and planning the production and distribution of essential drugs and treatments. This would be a transformative and democratizing policy for development. Albeit living in a capitalist society, solidarity could prevail over monopoly and also over competition when it comes to health issues. Making the pharmaceutical industry a publicly owned industry will not lead to fewer drugs and treatments because overall R&D – including pharmaceutical companies R&D – on HBMS is already primarily funded by states (see Chapter 6).

Overall, since it is mostly a small group of corporations that concentrates IPRs (Clarivate Analytics, 2020; Pistor, 2019), why aren't states and, more importantly, people in general not sufficiently battling against them? Part of the answer is that capitalism has built a culture that celebrates private property and individual gains. This culture is implicit in the promotion of "entrepreneurship" as a form of individual freedom that is frequently highly unstable and risky and hides unemployment or informal working conditions. Driven by neoliberal policies such as the New Public Management discourse, this culture has penetrated otherwise public realms like science, education and health.

Therefore, to understand the nature and potential of knowledge as common stock, a cultural change is required. It needs to be sufficiently strong to pressure governments to withdraw from international IPRs agreements and to build knowledge commons in the meantime. This cultural change should embrace knowledge beyond its productive use. Knowledge contributes to developing human capabilities. Democratizing its access through public (free) education requires to guarantee that local populations can critically understand knowledge's state of the art and further elaborate on it. Overall, greater public funding for science, technology and learning in all its forms is indispensable.

3 Containment measures against data-driven intellectual monopolies

Once raw data are centralized and processed, they become knowledge that is being privatized and assetized by a special type of intellectual monopoly against which particular containment measures should be put in place while more general transformations are on their way.

Data privacy acts were aimed at limiting these companies' power, but they further contribute to knowledge privatization by fostering individual property over data. Moreover, even after the establishment of those acts, data-driven intellectual monopolies keep profiting from harvesting data. Aho and Duffield (2020) analyse Europe's general data protection regulation (GDPR) and conceptualize it as a policy aimed at protecting individual freedoms. The legislation does limit cases like the Cambridge Analytica scandal but does not impede tech giants' data harvesting. Furthermore, loopholes in the regulation have been outlined. Most US tech giants have their European base in Ireland, whose Data Protection Commission is not complying with Europe's GDPR.[2] Therefore, data privacy laws will not by themselves eliminate these corporations' data-driven intellectual rents.

An alternative could be to reform antitrust policies, which, as we explained in Chapter 4, are based on a consumers' welfare logic installed in the United States in the 1970s by the Chicago Boys. Data-driven intellectual monopolies can offer free products or cheap prices to consumers because their real business is digital intelligence, and the products are the excuse to make people create required data. Given their market dominance, breaking data-driven intellectual monopolies, particularly GAFAM companies, remains an option. Still, it would require a clear stand of the US state against ambassadors of its hegemony. As this book is being written, what to do with these companies is being debated at the US Congress.

Given the tight technological cooperation among data-driven intellectual monopolies, even if they are forced to break up, they may still work altogether, sharing databases to maximize extracted rents and predation. Unlike the US tech giants, their Chinese counterparts were compelled to have separate businesses. For instance, Alibaba is formally separated from Ant Group and Alibaba Health. However, since they are all controlled by the same holding company, it remains easy to share data sets to boost each business.

A step towards an effective regulation could be to charge these companies a revenue tax, as France intended to do but so far failed. A revenue tax could contribute to compensate for the misalignment between the place where profits are taxed and where these companies operate. Moreover, a decisive measure could be to charge them data withholding taxes. Data-driven intellectual monopolies act as landowners. The owners of digital databases created from centralizing third-party – individuals or organizations – data should thus be progressively taxed. They should pay according to the size of their databases. A relatively simple way to proxy size (if required information is not provided) is to consider datacentres' square metres. Unlike land, data withholding taxes should not be charged according to where the datacentres are located. This would benefit core countries, in particular the United States, home of 40% of the world's hyperscale datacentres (Synergy

Research Group, 2019). The tax collection could take place at the global level considering the global scale of these corporations, but also to assure that no country sets a zero tax on data centres, therefore favouring their relocation at the expense of the rest of the world. Tax revenues could be shared according to countries' share of Internet penetration, or – even better for development – through a progressive scheme favouring less developed countries. Additional policies for development are introduced in the next section.

4 Beyond taking containment measures, an offensive step for the peripheries

As theorized by the dependency school, underdevelopment and development are two sides of the same coin (Dos Santos, 1970). Underdevelopment has multiple faces, from greater inequality, poverty levels and fewer opportunities, to dependent and subordinated productive structures, with incomplete technical capacities and lack of technological autonomy. *New to the world* innovations have historically been concentrated in core countries, and this has worsened under intellectual monopoly capitalism.

Science and Technology (S&T) supremacy has been paramount to explain geopolitical differences and conflicts between countries and regions, at least since the post-war period. However, under intellectual monopoly capitalism, S&T supremacy lies in the hands of intellectual monopolies. The Covid-19 crisis has not only re-signified states' capabilities but turned apparent the power of global intellectual monopolies, in particular from digital and pharmaceutical industries. The geopolitical map of the world is in dispute, and dependency is being expressed in new – complementary – ways (knowledge and data extractivism). Furthermore, digitalization is even transforming private relationships and shaping our behaviours (Zuboff, 2015). Overall, innovations are transforming social relations.

Hence, policy recommendations must be anchored in a deep awareness of global and local dynamics. However, Chapter 11 has shown that the literature has fostered a narrow role for the public sector as S&T funding source and promoter, overlooking public organizion and performance of S&T.

4.1 Limiting all forms of extractivism[3]

4.1.1 Knowledge extractivism

Over 70 years ago, Prebisch (1950) referred to technological dependency as a major cause of underdevelopment. Besides some exceptions of catching-up countries in certain technologies (with China as the paramount 21st century example), by the end of the 20th century, Niosi and Bellon (1996 in Arocena & Sutz, 2000) pointed out that international flows of technology remained concentrated in developed countries. This was a sign of both the slim technical gap between them and the prevailing wide gap with underdeveloped nations. The analyses in Chapters 6–9 reinforced this conclusion, a quarter of a century later. The emergence of global innovation networks led by intellectual monopolies from the core has not been an opportunity for development.

Some peripheral countries (like India, Brazil, South Africa and Argentina) have state-of-the-art academic research capabilities but occupy a subordinate place in the international division of academic labour. Academic dependency, where core countries' institutions define research programmes and questions and leave more routine tasks to researchers from the peripheries, prevails in international academic collaborations (Arvanitis, 2011; Beigel et al., 2018; Kreimer, 2014). This contributes to partially displace paramount research questions for development, from diseases associated with poverty pockets to permanent macroeconomic instability, to multiple research problems that emerge from considering the specificities of capitalism in these regions.

Knowledge extractivism adds to these previous features. We defined it as the multiple ways in which science and technology elaborated in the peripheries are assetized in core countries, usually by corporate intellectual monopolies and eventually by academic intellectual monopolies (see Chapters 11–13). Ideally, states should protect promising results from assetization, while allowing local research communities to access and further develop them. Such a policy would require higher public S&T budgets in peripheral countries and has limited feasibility, given that the global knowledge regime favours privatization.

An alternative, while pushing for a radical transformation of the international knowledge regime, could be to regulate university-industry collaborations with multinational corporations. These companies do not spill over their technology, thus generally do not contribute to local firms' catching up. On the contrary, they appropriate and turn into intangible assets promising R&D results from locally leading universities and public research organizations. These institutions lack the enforcement skills and resources to litigate against knowledge extractivism. Public research should privilege other links that can contribute to development, such as collaborations between universities and public research organizations, collaborations with local actors, social movements, workers' unions and state dependencies. Therefore, states could also promote these links while discouraging those with multinationals.

A change in scientific evaluation criteria, now mostly focused on publications in peer-review journals from core countries, could also contribute to limiting knowledge extractivism. While peripheral countries' evaluation criteria foster fast publication, thus global disclosure, core countries' corporate and academic intellectual monopolies assetize knowledge.

4.1.2 Data extractivism

Peripheral countries are net providers of raw data that is freely harvested and monetized by a handful of data-driven intellectual monopolies mostly from the United States and China (see Chapters 7, 8 and 11). This form of data or digital colonialism reinforces underdevelopment (Couldry & Mejias, 2019a, 2019b; Kwet, 2019). Data privacy laws, inspired by the law passed in Europe, are being implemented in countries like Brazil, Thailand, South Korea, South Africa and India.[4] As we argued above, these regulations are tricky because as much as they try to limit tech giants' access to data, they still fall short and further promote a culture that celebrates private property of intangibles.

An alternative could be to force data-driven intellectual monopolies to transfer data using state-owned infrastructure in every country. The price of this service could include withholding taxes on data exports. A step further could be to still charge them for privately appropriating data and also force them to store them in local datacentres. Some peripheral regions host local data-driven intellectual monopolies, like MercadoLibre in Latin America. Given the importance of some digital services, like e-commerce and e-payments, states should regulate these giants too, for instance, with the same regulations applied to banks because, besides e-payments, e-commerce is intertwined with new forms of private credit and asset management (Frost et al., 2019).

In countries where tech giants' operations are underdeveloped, there is a chance for national and even local authorities to develop state-owned platforms. Tech giants are now expanding cloud servicing to the peripheries. This is the case of cloud computing in South East Asia.[5] There is, therefore, a small window of opportunity for states to coordinate and offer state-owned public clouds before data-driven intellectual monopolies capture this market.

The pandemic has been an opportunity for developing state-owned digital initiatives. In Indonesia, a state-owned enterprise already manages the digital payment service LinkAja. Brazil has seen the emergence of several public platforms since the pandemic, like the delivery platform FiqueNoLar that operates in the northern part of the country. In Argentina, the state launched a public and free to download e-payment application and Correo Compras, an e-commerce platform. In Bahía Blanca, a medium-sized city also from Argentina, the local government has put in place an e-commerce platform for local producers called "Desde casa Bahia" ("From home Bahía"), that can be accessed from this link https://desdecasa.bahia.gob.ar/. Another alternative has been the cooperative organization of producers, such as the e-commerce platform http://www.reddecomercializacion.com/. Beyond local initiatives, a regional initiative to build a public e-commerce and e-payments system could play a paramount role in a regional development plan, which is our subject matter in the next sub-section.

4.2 Planning public production and innovation networks

Mission-oriented policies are defined as S&T policies aimed at developing radical innovations in strategic sectors, creating new industries by steering technological trajectories (Chiang, 1991; Ruttan, 2006). In the case of non-core countries, Mazzucato and Penna (2016) argue that more mission-oriented national innovation systems could contribute to development. To that end, as indicated by Freeman (1996), they should be complemented with other policies and regulations to have ubiquitous effects on the whole economy, such as policies to assure wide dissemination and access to achieved results (Mowery et al., 2010).

However, when these policies are suggested for the peripheries, they do not take into account that most firms are complier and laggard companies that we defined in Chapter 2 as two types of subordinate companies participating in intellectual monopolies' production networks and platforms. As we argued in Chapter 11, innovation imperatives are absent because these firms find alternative sources of profits. Furthermore, when integrated into global production networks, they may prefer to remain subordinated to intellectual monopolies, thus technologically dependent on the latter, as far as they can keep unloading the weight of subordination on their super-exploited workers (see Chapter 10). Therefore, even if a mission-oriented policy is implemented for a strategic sector, it is highly likely that it will not engage significant private investment. Moreover, it is far more complicated to assure the dissemination of achieved results in the peripheries than in core countries, precisely because of most firms' laggard characteristics.

Hence, a still challenging but relatively more feasible option for peripheral states could be to take full care of radical innovation processes. Peripheral states should occupy the central planning role, leading major revolutionary projects in promising fields that are not already dominated by global intellectual monopolies. Peripheral states should complete innovation projects and develop necessary productive capacities. For instance, considering the importance of health for development and the neglected place given by big pharmaceuticals to poor regions' endemic diseases, healthcare could be publicly planned. Public planning healthcare should consider from the scientific research at public universities and research organizations to public drug production for promising new drugs or treatments. Productive capacities in this industry are usually absent in the peripheries, albeit cases where indigenous innovation takes place.[6]

In case of successful results, it should be considered that positive effects will not spill over unless S&T and innovation policies are integrated into a broader development plan at the regional or, if this is not feasible, at the country level. Innovations by themselves are not magical solutions for underdevelopment. In fact, some of the most innovative countries are also extremely unequal (think of the United States, China and the United

Kingdom). Considering global growing inequalities and marginalization, life in the peripheries will not be as unequal, working conditions will be better and healthier and the environment will be less damaged if states pursue development plans that go beyond planning S&T.

Some further caveats include recognizing that science, technology and innovation do not escape from capitalism's power structures. An independent and progressive research agenda for the peripheries is a great challenge in itself. A further consideration is that states should protect promising knowledge results from private assetization in the sense of the discussion introduced above in Section 2.

Planning such innovation projects from scratch is a hazardous and expensive endeavour, especially for a single (peripheral) state. Collaboration between states from the same region could build upon each other's sovereignty and capacities. Regional cooperation could also facilitate decoupling from global networks where local organizations occupy subordinate places, by complementing their productive matrices. Cooperation could begin among those governments sharing concerns and political orientation. State representatives should work together with social movements, unions and local communities to determine and systematically revise regional S&T priorities. In this way, a *to-be-created* supra-national institution focused on finding and funding challenging S&T projects could remain anchored in local needs. Likewise, since states are battlefields, social organizations and unions should participate in the decision-making processes of this new potential institution to assure that a long-term development goal is pursued. The next section further discusses the role of these actors.

5 Counterbalancing intellectual monopoly capitalism

Capitalism is a system based on asymmetries and inequalities (of income, wealth, between classes, genders, races, countries and more). Quite striking for a system born from the motto "*Liberté, égalité, fraternité*". As time passes by, this broken promise of modernity becomes all the more apparent. Inequalities deepen as knowledge is monopolized, digital surveillance reinforces firms and states control capacities over workers and citizens, and political conflicts never cease – with the US-China tech cold war at the current epicentre.

Social disrupts are an expected recurring outcome, and we have seen them everywhere in the 21st century. The specific motives differed, but there is a common root: people are fed up with capitalism's growing inequalities, with a stagnant or even declining "middle class" in developed countries for several decades already and the highest gains accumulating at the global level for those in the richest 5% (Milanovic, 2016).

There is another shared feature; demonstrations are increasingly being organized online. The same technology that is used for surveillance, for broadcasting extreme right and even fascist ideas, and that drives the US-China world hegemony conflict, is also being used as a counterbalancing weapon. Internet, particularly social networks, is a powerful tool for the organization of grassroots movements. Workers' unions can also learn from each other's experiences online.

The absence or weakness of unions and social movements in some parts of the world has benefited intellectual monopolies rentiership and predation. For instance, hiring workers with a vendor contract not only hides the working relation (see Chapter 10) but also impedes unionization as it currently stands. Still, unions are adapting and workers organizing. In 2018, Google employees managed to stop the company from renewing an artificial intelligence contract with the Pentagon and to cancel its plans for a censored search engine for China. And, in 2020, 2,000 employees urged the company to cease selling technology to the US police after George Floyd's killing. These initiatives should be taken by workers in other companies and contribute to unionization. Unions should be reconceived as a political actor capable of exercising their influence beyond wage claims. Workers' organization is indispensable to counterbalance the power of intellectual monopolies, given both their global reach and states' internal contradictions and limitations.

Peripheral countries should cease competing to attract outsourcing and offshoring by allowing worse wages and working conditions. As mentioned above in this chapter, world cooperation agreements to establish minimum labour regulations, forbidding new and old forms of informality and granting minimum working conditions are urgent. However, these agreements require great social pressures to take place. When it comes to transforming capitalism, social disrupts, grassroots social movements and unions play a crucial role.

To illustrate their paramount importance, let us briefly consider taxes. It is crystal clear that the global taxing system has failed. As pointed out in Chapters 7 and 10, global intellectual monopolies declare profits and IPRs in tax havens and use tax loopholes to minimize paid taxes. Global tax reform should consider the separation between ownership and control. Intellectual monopolies control production and innovation networks beyond their legal ownership and have the capacity to trickle down the burden of taxes. However, the intertwined relationship between global intellectual monopolies and their home (core) states renders highly unlikely to accomplish such global tax reform without intense social pressure. Even the recent US corporate tax reform was not – at least so far – successful in this respect (Clausing, 2020). Then, as far as tax havens are not eliminated, there will still be room for tax avoidance and evasion (Zucman, 2015). Countries acting as tax havens will not comply with a global reform unless huge social disrupt forces them to do so.

Additionally, workers' protests must be coordinated at the level of the global production network because the production unit is no longer the factory but the network. The same applies to global innovation networks. Intellectual monopolies' recognized employees have greater bargaining power than workers in subordinate firms, which are precisely those that generally need a more urgent improvement in their salaries and working conditions. "*Workers of the world unite, you have nothing to lose but your chains*" (Marx & Engels, 1848) can and must become an everyday reality for the French Revolution motto to be more than aspirational.

6 Final remarks on the role of social scientists and science in general

I decided to dedicate my final reflections to myself and my colleagues. As social scientists, we are responsible for uncovering intellectual monopoly capitalism, its multiple dimensions, and dynamics. However, we are often forced to narrow down, to shrink ideas to fit them in a 10,000-word paper that is not up to the task of our epoch. We need to be bold and ask challenging questions, to bridge the gap between general trends and specific, in-depth analyses. I hope this book has opened more reflections than offering answers. It was meant to be an exercise of unity, a way to start integrating my ideas about contemporary capitalism that so far have been split in different papers.

Beyond social sciences, this book speaks to scientists in general. It speaks to those that still conceive science as a universal (and neutral) truth. "Pure" scientists are also political actors and actresses. Research is never neutral, and this book has given illustrative examples, including how scientists contribute to knowledge assetization and corporate profits even without intending to do it when their research becomes a blind knowledge transfer (see Chapter 13).

Too many examples are out there to neglect our social and political responsibilities. The sugar industry tried to promote dental research aimed at finding "effective means of controlling tooth decay by methods other than restricting carbohydrate intake" (Fabbri et al., 2018, p. 13). Similar examples refer to the tobacco industry's attempt to link genetics and addiction to explain that genetic influences caused nicotine addiction. A more recent example is research stating that Monsanto's (now Bayer) glyphosate is not cancerogenic. And what should be said about those transforming poor populations into laboratories? Astronomic research budgets are spent to *prove* the obvious (proper nutrition contributes to people's health; more teachers at school improve learning outcomes) by quantifying social outcomes that can never be properly isolated. Even worse, Coville et al.'s (2020) randomized controlled trial threatened with and eventually cut water supply to low-income families to increase their likelihood of paying the bills in Nairobi. Why are these efforts not addressing the underlying causes of poverty, inequality and underdevelopment that explain, among others, why those families cannot pay water bills?

Our research priorities should consider social and environmental impacts, which requires integrating other social actors in the definition of S&T agendas. As argued by Arocena (2018, p. 6), innovation (and we add knowledge as a whole) "as a social process includes both cooperation and conflict, so its actual outcomes are highly dependent on the 'internal' distribution of power among the actors that get involved in the process." It is up to us how we deal with this and where we stand.

I do know where I stand. I want to contribute to building a world without any form of social inequality, where our differences result from real choices and not from external impositions. To that end, I cannot afford to lose a generalist perspective, aiming to connect what may look like unrelated problems and try to build a complete and coherent conceptualization of capitalism. I hope this book has contributed to show why seemingly disconnected topics are interrelated, therefore why such a comprehensive understanding is urgent.

Notes

1 As an illustrative example beyond those presented in this book, after Bolivia's coup in 2019, Elon Musk publicly claimed on Twitter "We will coup whoever we want!", speaking of the US and after a critique related to how Tesla was favoured by the coup in relation to Bolivia's lithium extraction.
2 https://www.politico.com/story/2019/04/24/ireland-data-privacy-1270123.
3 We do not provide here recommendations to limit natural resources extractivism because it has not been the focus of this book.
4 https://www.endpointprotector.com/blog/data-protection-legislation-around-the-world-in-2020/.
5 https://www.ft.com/content/1e2b9cd9-f82e-4d3b-a2d8-f20c08bdc3aa?segmentId=b0d7e653-3467-12ab-c0f0-77e4424cdb4c.
6 This is even the case of India, generally considered as an example of a leading country in generics production, which still depends on China for almost 70% of active pharmaceutical ingredients' procurement (Chatterjee, 2020).

References

Aho, B., & Duffield, R. (2020). Beyond surveillance capitalism: Privacy, regulation and big data in Europe and China. *Economy and Society*, *49*(2), 187–212.

Arocena, R. (2018). Power, innovation systems and development. *Innovation and Development*, *8*(2), 271–85.

Arocena, R., & Sutz, J. (2000). Looking at national systems of innovation from the South. *Industry and Innovation*, *7*(1), 55–75.

Arvanitis, R. (2011). La division internationale du travail scientifique Dossier édité par Terry Shinn, Dominique Vellard et Roland Waast, Cahiers de la recherche sur l'éducation et les savoirs. N° 9, 2010. *Revue d'anthropologie Des Connaissances*, *5*, 635–37.

Beigel, F., Gallardo, O., & Bekerman, F. (2018). Institutional expansion and scientific development in the periphery: The structural heterogeneity of Argentina's academic field. *Minerva, 56*(3), 305–31.

Chatterjee, P. (2020). Indian pharma threatened by COVID-19 shutdowns in China. *The Lancet, 395*(10225), 675.

Chiang, J. T. (1991). From 'mission-oriented'to 'diffusion-oriented'paradigm: The new trend of US industrial technology policy. *Technovation, 11*(6), 339–56.

Clarivate Analytics. (2020). *Derwent top 100 global innovators 2020.* Clarivate Analytics.

Clausing, K. A. (2020). Profit shifting before and after the tax cuts and jobs act. *SSRN 3274827*

Cleary, E. G., Jackson, M. J., Folchman-Wagner, Z., & Ledley, F. D. (2020). Foundational research and NIH funding enabling emergency use authorization of remdesivir for COVID-19. *MedRxiv.* https://www.medrxiv.org/content/10.1101/2020.07.01.20144576v1

Couldry, N., & Mejias, U. A. (2019a). Data colonialism: Rethinking big data's relation to the contemporary subject. *Television & New Media, 20*(4), 336–49.

Couldry, N., & Mejias, U. A. (2019b). *The costs of connection: How data is colonizing human life and appropriating it for capitalism.* Stanford University Press.

Coville, A., Galiani, S., Gertler, P., & Yoshida, S. (2020). *Enforcing payment for water and sanitation services in Nairobi's slums.* National Bureau of Economic Research.

Dos Santos, T. (1970). The structure of dependence. *The American Economic Review, 60*(2), 231–36.

Dreyfuss, R., & Frankel, S. (2014). From incentive to commodity to asset: How international law is reconceptualizing intellectual property. *Michigan Journal of International Law, 36*(4), 557–602.

Durand, C., & Milberg, W. (2020). Intellectual monopoly in global value chains. *Review of International Political Economy, 27*(2), 404–429. doi:10.1080/09692290.2019.1660703

Fabbri, A., Lai, A., Grundy, Q., & Bero, L. A. (2018). The influence of industry sponsorship on the research agenda: A scoping review. *American Journal of Public Health, 108*(11), e9–e16.

Freeman, C. (1996). The greening of technology and models of innovation. *Technological Forecasting and Social Change, 53*(1), 27–39.

Frost, J., Gambacorta, L., Huang, Y., Shin, H. S., & Zbinden, P. (2019). *BigTech and the changing structure of financial intermediation.* Bank of International Settlements.

Kreimer, P. (2014). "Citizen of the world" or a local producer of useful knowledge? That's the Question. In H. Sabea & F. Beigel (Eds.), *Academic dependency and professionalization in the south: Perspectives from the periphery* (pp. 151–66). EDIUNC- Sephis.

Kwet, M. (2019). Digital colonialism: US empire and the new imperialism in the Global South. *Race & Class, 60*(4), 3–26.

Marx, C. & Engels, F. (1848/1967). The Communist Manifesto. Penguin.

Mazzucato, M., & Penna, C. (2016). *The Brazilian innovation system: A mission-oriented policy proposal.* Centro de Gestão e Estudos Estratégicos.

Milanovic, B. (2016). *Global inequality: A new approach for the age of globalization*. Harvard University Press.

Mowery, D. C., Nelson, R. R., & Martin, B. R. (2010). Technology policy and global warming: Why new policy models are needed (or why putting new wine in old bottles won't work). *Research Policy*, *39*(8), 1011–23.

Pfotenhauer, S. M., & Juhl, J. (2017). Innovation and the political state: Beyond the myth of technologies and markets. In Godin, B. and Vinck, D. (Eds.) *Critical Studies of Innovation* (pp. 68–93). Edward Elgar Publishing.

Pistor, K. (2019). *The code of capital: How the law creates wealth and inequality*. Princeton University Press.

Prebisch, R. (1950). Crecimiento, desequilibrio y disparidades: Interpretación del proceso de desarrollo económico. In CEPAL (Ed.) *Estudio Económico de América Latina y el Caribe* (pp. 3–89). CEPAL, United Nations.

Rikap, C., & Naidorf, J. (2020). Ciencia privatizada en América Latina. *Con-Ciencia Social*, *3*, 57–76.

Ruttan, V. W. (2006). *Is war necessary for economic growth?: Military procurement and technology development*. Oxford University Press.

Strange, S. (1996). *The retreat of the state: The diffusion of power in the world economy*. Cambridge University Press.

Synergy Research Group. (2019). *Hyperscale data center count jumps to 430; Another 132 in the Pipeline*. https://www.srgresearch.com/articles/hyperscale-data-center-count-jumps-430-mark-us-still-accounts-40

Veblen, T. (1899). *The theory of the leisure class: An economic theory of institutions*. Macmillan.

Veblen, T. (2012). On the nature of capital. In Veblen, T. *The place of science in modern civilization and other essays* (pp. 247–66). Project Gutenberg.

Zuboff, S. (2015). Big other: Surveillance capitalism and the prospects of an information civilization. *Journal of Information Technology*, *30*(1), 75–89.

Zucman, G. (2015). *The hidden wealth of nations: The scourge of tax havens*. University of Chicago Press.

INDEX

Milton Keynes UK
Ingram Content Group UK Ltd.
UKHW052008170624
444208UK00016B/242

9 780367 750299